Rebels and Conservatives

DOROTHY AND WILLIAM WORDSWORTH AND THEIR CIRCLE

112399

Rebels and Conservatives

DOROTHY AND WILLIAM WORDSWORTH
AND THEIR CIRCLE

by *AMANDA M. ELLIS*

Indiana University Press

BLOOMINGTON & LONDON

88

To
Louis T. Benezet

Contents

Illustrations

Preface

Dorothy and William Wordsworth, their friends, and associates lived most of their lives through the periods of the French Revolution and the Napoleonic wars. These times were in many ways like our own. Idealism followed by disillusionment, the young rebelling against authority, the struggle between liberals and conservatives, the Negro question, the enfranchisement of all of voting age, wars and the threat of wars, the campaign against poverty, the Santo Domingo question, and attempts to encourage the arts—all were highlights of Wordsworth's day, as they are of ours. Ethical and religious concepts were changing, as they are today. Yet, we must not deal with the Wordsworths and their circle in terms of the twentieth century, but in the light of their own times.

A fresh look at the group as individuals is, I think, necessary. The innumerable books that found Wordsworth narrow in his views especially need re-examination. One proof often used to bolster this point of view is his objection to a railroad's being built to Grasmere and Keswick. Wordsworth's critics would have done well to have studied carefully why Wordsworth objected to the railroad. They would have found that he anticipated by a hundred and fifty years the thinking of his countrymen when he stated he wished the Lake Country preserved for its natural beauty and pointed out that there was already adequate transportation, and that a railroad would have ruined the countryside. When manufacturers backed up those capitalists desiring the railroad and said they would send hundreds of their employees by car loads to Grasmere for their vacations, Wordsworth's reply that these employers would do well to pay their workers a living wage and give them a decent working day so that they could pay to go on a vacation where they chose, not where their employers dictated, is, I believe, hardly the thinking of a man of narrow views, but one with ideas far ahead of his day.

The very term Lake Poets is a misnomer. The Wordsworths did not convert their friends into believing for any length of time that the lake country was an ideal location. Coleridge did not live there long; Southey used Keswick as a base from which at times to write on subjects far from that region and as a convenient anchor for his family. Among prose writers, Charles Lamb, after a visit to Grasmere, found himself a more passionate lover of his city, London; De Quincey made his home at Dove Cottage a comparatively short time.

It has been pointed out that men of the eighteenth century had inherited a medieval dislike and fear of mountains; Wordsworth's poetry helped dispel this fear and instilled in many the love for them he and Dorothy felt. Wordsworth was not an innovator when he wrote of men and women of the soil. Cowper, Gray, and Crabbe had written of them earlier; yet Wordsworth made his country people more acceptable until eventually Hardy and Synge could write of them without an explanation.

This book, designed for the general reader as well as for the scholar, aims primarily to give the reader personalities, people as real as I can make them, relying always on authentic, reliable information. I have not attempted to make this a book of literary criticism. I have realized, however, that a writer's work is part of his life and, therefore, I have given as much about each author's writing as I felt was essential to define his personality. I have tried to show, however, more than has any other writer to date, how much of Wordsworth's and Coleridge's poetry grew out of Dorothy Wordsworth's observations; at times, the very wording of their poems being hers as recorded in her diaries. Yet even here, I took care lest the reader lose the fact that I was using this material only to show the mental stature of Dorothy Wordsworth and her effect on the two poets. Her value has too long been overlooked by many critics. I contend that she loved Coleridge and he loved her for a time. The fact that she suppressed her love accounts, in part, I believe, for her premature senility.

I have leaned far more heavily on the prose writings of the poets than most authorities have, as their ideas on political, economic, and social issues are important.

Books about an author usually deal with him in detail and then merely mention the names of those who were his friends. I have chosen the writers and others who associated most with the Wordsworths and have given biographical accounts of each, depending on the extent of their acquaintanceship with the Wordsworths. In presenting the biographies I have used, in modified form, a device which I greatly admired in John dos Passos' *U.S.A.*, that of including many biographical characters in a work in which there are a few main characters. These short sketches follow a device used in much twentieth century writing, of violating the time sequence. For example, in writing of Wordsworth's meeting William Godwin, I have given an account of Godwin's life, of his wife Mary Wollstonecraft, and, to show how his teachings backfired, accounts of the liaison between his daughter Mary Wollstonecraft Godwin and Percy Bysshe Shelley, as well as that between his stepdaughter Claire Clairmont and Byron. Chronologically, the account of the Godwins, Byron, and Shelley ends in 1851. My narrative then goes back to Godwin's meeting with Wordsworth in 1793.

I believe I have examined all extant material on or about the Wordsworths and their circle in this country and in England, where I did research for seven summers. I have now spent seventeen years on this book. I began using footnotes, but the vast number of them caused me to discard them in favor of what I hope is a more informal and readable text for the general reader and the scholar. The extensive bibliography (five hundred books and manuscripts and a hundred articles), I believe, is sufficient to give authority to the text. Because of the length of the bibliography, I have used the short form, now found in many books.

I am deeply indebted to the British Museum, the Victoria and Albert Museum, the museum at Grasmere, to the Bodleian Library, the Fitz Park Museum in Keswick, the Cambridge University Library, to the trustees of Dove Cottage and to some of Wordsworth's descendants who spoke to me of the Wordsworths and De Quincey as though they were still alive. I am especially indebted to Mrs. Dorothy Dickson of The Stepping Stones, Ambleside, and to the Rev. Christopher Wordsworth of Hythe, Kent. The National Library of Scotland, the New York City Public Library, the Widener Library at Harvard, the Manchester Reference Library, the Morgan Library, New York, the Houghton Library at Harvard, the Keats Memorial House, Hampstead, the Library of Congress, the Charles Leaming Tutt Library at Colorado College, the Free Library of Philadelphia, the Public Library of Cleveland, the University of Colorado Library, and the Air Force Academy Library, have been most helpful. I am indebted, also, to the Director of the National Portrait Gallery in London and to Miss Willa Taylor of the Gallery, who have been helpful on many occasions; I am indebted to the Gallery itself, not only for permission to use photographs of pictures in their collection, but also for photographing some portraits not hitherto photgraphed. I wish to express my appreciation also to the National Library of Scotland, the Library of Congress, the Huntington Library, the good folk at Keswick and Llangollen, and *Time* magazine for the photographs and illustrations used. As many eighteenth century photographs were dull because of the limitations of photography of the day, I had all the illustrations of people rephotographed and highlighted by Robert McIntyre. I am appreciative of Louis T. Benezet's encouragement while I worked on the latter section of this book. I am indebted to Miss Louise Kampf, Librarian Emerita at Colorado College, and to Miss Reta W. Ridings, Head Reference Librarian, for helping me procure rare books and photostats of needed material, to Mrs. Dorothy Wikelund, Professor Russell Noyes, and Professor Newton Stallknecht for their comments, and to Mrs. Elizabeth Taylor and Mrs. Virginia Labonté for typing this book.

As Colorado College's Professor of English and Writer in Residence, I have had some additional time to spend on this volume. I am grateful to President Louis T. Benezet and his successor, President Lloyd Worner, for this honor and consideration.

AMANDA M. ELLIS

Colorado College,
October, 1965

Rebels and Conservatives

DOROTHY AND WILLIAM WORDSWORTH AND THEIR CIRCLE

CHAPTER I

Years "Fostered Alike by Beauty and by Fear"

DRIVING BY KESWICK ROAD TO THE MARKET TOWN OF COCKERMOUTH AT THE ENTRANCE OF THE LAKE COUNTRY in England, travelers in the mid-eighteenth century admired Mount Skiddaw in the distance, and, in the foreground, the large fields filled with haycocks, the dense woods with their fine old trees that seemed to tower to the clouds. In the town itself, trim gardens, luxurious hedges, immense rose bushes, and white elder trees surrounded the houses, many built of wood, looking as if they had been "planked by the makers of ships."

John Wordsworth and his family, however, lived in a more attractive residence, a manorial red-brick building close to the bridge over the Derwent River. Its cellar was well stocked with rum, gin, brandy, and wines, red and white; its beautiful walls were panelled and its fireplaces were marble. Behind the house, a garden, with rose and privet hedges and huge elder trees, led to the Derwent River with its rock falls, shallows, and "ceaseless music." There, the young Wordsworth children, carefully shielded from passers-by, bathed sometimes through a whole summer's day, or ran naked in the garden. Sometimes in the summer, they roamed through woods and over hills until they were bronzed, looking occasionally at distant Mount Skiddaw's lofty height.

To the east, rose the ancient towers of Cockermouth Castle, in ruins, where in spring and summer birds nested. There, the children often picked wild flowers, and once little William bravely entered the dungeon beneath the castle . . . where, a prey "to the soul appalling darkness," he made his first acquaintance "with the grave."

In 1765, the house had been painted and renovated for twenty-

3

four-year-old John Wordsworth, an attorney, before his marriage to eighteen-year-old Anne Cookson, the daughter of William Cookson of Penrith. The name, variously spelled, often Wadsworth, was usually spelled Wordsworth by the eighteenth century. Anne, also of Yorkshire stock, was the heiress of the last Crackenthorpe, an old Westmorland family. To the young Wordsworths, were born five children: Richard, in 1768; William, in 1770; Dorothy, on Christmas day, 1771; John, in 1772; and Christopher, in 1774.

John Wordsworth was a busy man whom his children did not see much. Their mother, however, bestowed on them a peaceful and tranquil love, never bothering them with schemes she had had for them. She was not "puffed up by false, unnatural hopes" for them, nor did she burden them with unnecessary tasks. Free, unoppressed, they enjoyed life. Fond of nature, she passed on this love to her children. Hence, they loved the music of the river or the silence of the nearby lake as they rowed upon it; they were certain there were not "vales more beautiful than ours." They loved to watch the moon rise and its reflection on the lake. William loved

> a little rill
> Of water sparkling down a rocky slope
> By the wayside.

He was fascinated by

> the rainbow or the cuckoo's shout,
> An echo, or the glow-worm's faery lamp,

by the river that, he believed,

> flows on
> Perpetually, whence comes it, whither tends,
> Going and never gone;

by a skylark

> native to the heavens
> There, planted like a star,

as well as by the

> lightning and the thunder's roar,
> Snow, rain and hail, and storm implacable.

In the summer, the boys flew kites; in the winter, they skated on river and on lake. While the boys hunted birds' nests and plundered them,

Dorothy, tender and sensitive, lover of all wild things, watched the birds' nests; once, day by day observing a "sparrow's bright blue eggs together laid" in a nest, seeming to fear it though wishing to be near it. When the boys chased butterflies, she, unwilling to have any harm come to the fragile beauties, feared lest the dust be brushed off their wings. When she first saw the sea and heard its voice, she wept.

William and Dorothy, twenty months his junior, were special companions. Indeed, he said later, she was his "eyes and ears"; more sensitive than he, she always understood his moods. Yet, she was unlike her brother who was far from gentle; in his walks, often alone, he sought

> Deep pools, tall trees, black chasms, and dizzy crags,
> And towering towers; he loved to stand and read
> Their looks forbidding, read and disobey
> Sometimes in the act, and evermore in thought.

Once, he hung

> Above the raven's nest, by knots of grass
> And half-inch fissures in the slippery rock
> But ill sustained and almost (so it seemed)
> Suspended by the blast that blew amain.

Whereas Dorothy, too, loved the out-of-doors, she was never daring; she liked nature's gentler moods.

William, more than all the other Wordsworth children, was often stubborn, wayward, and difficult to manage. High tempered, once when punished over-harshly by his grandparents, he contemplated killing himself with one of the foils he found in the attic. Another time, when he and Richard were spinning tops in his grandfather's drawing-room, he dared his brother to strike his whip through the portrait of one of his ancestors on the wall. "Dare you to strike your whip through the old lady's petticoat," he urged. Richard was horrified. "Then here goes," William shouted gleefully as he struck his whip right through the venerable lady's looped petticoat. Nor did the severe punishment he received daunt him in the least. His mother told a friend he was the only one of the five children whose future caused her concern. "He will be remarkable," she said, "either for good or for evil." Richard, she knew, was cautious, never in trouble; John, shy and quiet; Christopher, competent and dependable; Dorothy, a little lady.

At times, the boys made gruesome discoveries in their wanderings in the forest and on the nearby mountains. Once, riding with a groom on the eastern side at Penrith, when he was visiting his grandparents, William becoming separated from the groom, found himself on the moors near a hollow, where he found an old mouldering wooden post driven into the ground. Near it, on the turf, were carved the letters "T. P. M." Shivering with horror and terror, he knew the letters stood for "Thomas Parker Murdered," and that here, as was the custom of the time, the murderer had been gibbeted, right where he committed the crime. Leaving hurriedly, William looked in vain for his guide. Suddenly, the whole landscape frightened him as it seemed changed into something "rich and strange."

The children were awed, too, by the many vagabonds, peddlers, discharged soldiers, beggar-women and their children, leech-gatherers, and sometimes the wild, bright-eyed insane that were allowed to wander about the countryside. Although at times afraid of some of them, the children were never terrified by them. They learned early that some beggars told true stories of their need and were to be fed, while others were mere charlatans.

Mrs. Wordsworth did not care for the new-fangled educational ideas of Rousseau and his followers. Scorning the tales with pronounced morals that were popular at the time, she taught her children the classic tales of Robin Hood, Jack the Giant Killer, tales from *The Arabian Nights*, and stories of love and adventure like the Arthurian legends and those found in the Scotch ballads.

Busy though he was, John Wordsworth taught William, and presumably his other sons, large portions of Milton, Shakespeare, and Spenser; he introduced them to Fielding's novels, *Gil Blas*, *Don Quixote*, and *Gulliver's Travels*. The Wordsworth children had been taught to scorn the fashionable Sandford and Merton books before they were nine. Their mother taught them the catechism and attended church with them.

Though Mrs. Wordsworth and her husband taught the children for a time, later the two older boys, Richard and William, were sent briefly to the grammar school at Cockermouth. Finding the school not very good, their parents transferred them to the Dame School for younger children of the upper classes at Penrith. An elderly lady, Mrs. Ann Brickett, who believed in the mores of a vanishing England, ran the school; she was "no bad teacher, but indifferent to methods." She had the children memorize large portions of the Bible and read *The Spectator*, copies of which the Hutchinson children brought to school. They observed the country festivals at Shrove Tide, Easter, and May Day. At Easter time, the little boys rolled their Easter eggs down from Penrith Beacon; on May Day, the little girls brought their dolls to school, garlanded with flowers, and during school hours, hung them from the school windows. The Wordsworth boys liked the Dame School; even more, they loved their serene home presided over by a mother, modest, benign, and good, "the heart and hinge" of the five children.

Dorothy, at home with her younger brothers, often visited her grandparents at Penrith. In March, 1778, while they were there, their mother, visiting a friend in the south, slept between damp sheets and became seriously ill as a result. Pneumonia developed and she soon died. The children "trooping together" were desolate and lonely, bewildered, unable to comprehend death. Their mother, as she lay dying, asked that six-year-old Dorothy be entrusted to the care of her cousin, Elizabeth Threlkeld. Thus, the close-knit family group was separated. John Wordsworth, devoted to his wife, never regained his usual cheerfulness.

Unable to attend both to his business and to the education of all his children, he kept the younger boys at home and sent Richard and William to Hawkshead Grammar School, founded in 1585 by Edwin Sandys, Archbishop of York. An excellent school, attended by sons of farmers, local gentry, clergy, and professional men, it charged an entrance fee of a guinea a year.

The school excelled in teaching mathematics; classical studies filled the rest of the curriculum; in addition, a Mr. Mingay taught the boys dancing, which the Wordsworth boys liked. Since Hawkshead school could not house all of the hundred boy pupils, some dwelt in the homes of various residents of the town. William and Richard were assigned to the cottage of Anne Tyson. A motherly woman, she saw to it that her charges attended the Friends Church, where William thought the minister spent much time telling God of "his attributes rather than seeking spiritual communion with Him" for his parishioners. A congenial woman, Anne Tyson made her boys feel at home. Alone in his little room at night, William felt secure as he listened to the roaring wind or looked out through the ash tree nearby at the moon "in splendour crouched among the leaves." When school closed for the day, he and the other boys set snares for woodcocks, plundered birds' nests, scaled high crags to search for the raven's nest, gathered hazelnuts in the fall, fished in spring and early summer, skated and boated on Lake Windermere with his companions, or bowled at a nearby inn. Occasionally, the boys hired ponies and rode until moon-

light. William, though usually with his schoolmates, at times climbed
Penrith Beacon's perilous ridge alone and there hung while

> With what strange utterance did the loud, dry wind
> Blow through my ears; the sky seemed not a sky
> Of earth, and with what motion moved the clouds.

He sometimes imitated the hooting of owls and waited with anticipation until the owls replied.

Though, like the other boys, he could be destructive, William at
times remembered Dorothy's tenderness toward plants and birds.
Once, when he kicked a tuft of meadow lilies, he suddenly stopped
and wondered why he had done that. Seeing a lamb reflected in a pool,
he started to throw a rock at the reflection and then stopped. Soon he
loved more and more "the spacious firmament on high," the "blue
etherial sky," the sun, the moon, the clouds, the mountains, and the
plains. He grew interested in the tramps, peddlers, and discharged
soldiers who roamed the countryside. Some of them told him tales of
their youth, old Scottish ballads, or the hardships they had encountered
without becoming bitter or depressed. Sometimes he wandered over
the countryside with a peddler who lived part of the year at Hawkshead. From these wanderers, the thirteen-year-old later said he gathered a store of "home-felt wisdom." When he was fifteen, the best
students were asked to write verses celebrating the bicentenary of
Hawkshead School. William wrote a hundred lines of heroic couplets
in which The Spirit of Education, personified as a goddess, spoke to
the boys about modern education. The poem was reminiscent of
Alexander Pope. That summer when given a brown note-book, in it
he began composing ten other poems.

Meanwhile, Dorothy was with her grandparents at Penrith from
Christmas until June, when Miss Elizabeth Threlkeld and her
brother William came to take her to her new home in Halifax. The
cousin of Dorothy's mother, Miss Threlkeld, was a serene, happy
person who had shown her fondness for children in bringing up her
sister Anna's five orphan children, Martha, Edward, Anne, Samuel
and Elizabeth Ferguson. Soon Dorothy said, "the loss of a mother
can only be made up by such a friend as my dear aunt"; and years
later, she called her "the very best-tempered woman and the most
thoroughly intent on doing right I ever knew." The fair-haired, wild-
eyed, brown-skinned little girl won her aunt's heart at once, as she
showed her excitement during the journey by stagecoach when they
traveled by lakes, through valleys where sheep grazed, past inns before

which were beautiful horses and coaches, past other stagecoaches whose drivers lifted their whips in greeting to their driver, finally over long, tiresome moors, and then down the steep hill to arrive at Halifax.

She soon felt at home, part of the large family there; Martha Ferguson was almost sixteen; Edward, fourteen; Anne, twelve; Samuel and Elizabeth, about her own age. Her Uncle William's twins were younger. She became friends, too, with the Pollard children, Jane becoming her intimate and closest friend throughout her life. From Aunt Threlkeld, she learned sewing, reading, and writing; with the other children, she went to dancing school. She loved to go into the town, where her aunt had a milliner's and draper's shop, and where her Uncle William and Mr. Pollard, both merchants, met the weavers and manufacturers. On Saturdays, the streets were crowded with people eager to patronize the dealers in fruits, vegetables, pottery, and crockery, whose stalls lined the streets; on cloth-market days, the weavers brought great bundles of their wool and silk for merchants to see. Fair Days, when cattle crowded the streets, were even more exciting and confusing. Crowds came, too, when white-haired, frail Mr. John Wesley came to preach.

One sermon of his especially caused much discussion, though Dorothy did not understand what it was about. It seemed the people in Halifax had difficulty in having their money accepted because of "the coiners" who tampered somehow with money. Her cousin Martha told her how the "king of the coiners" had been captured and hanged in chains and his body left hanging as a warning. She showed Dorothy the bones of two other coiners still hanging in their rusty chains, while the right hand of one pointed toward the scene of his crime. Whenever Dorothy passed it, she closed her eyes to shut out the terrifying sight. When she was eleven, corn rioters passed Aunt Threlkeld's house, crying for food to be given them. She shuddered later when she remembered the leaders finally had been hanged on Beacon Hill.

When she was ten, she went to the best school in the neighborhood, the Boys' Grammar School at Hipperholme. Each day, she walked two miles along the wooded slopes, past a brook, until she reached the school at the top of a high hill. When she was thirteen, she went to a day school. Unlike the fashionable schools of the day, those Dorothy attended did not teach "elegant accomplishments" like making samplers, learning music and drawing. She did, however, learn French and cultivated a taste for "the wholesome pasturage" of good, old English reading. At fourteen, she read *Clarissa Harlowe*, and before she was sixteen had, in her own library, copies of the works of Shakespeare, Milton, Fielding, Homer, Goldsmith, *Gil Blas*, and *The Spectator*. Both her uncle and Mr. Pollard were interested in the circulating library founded in 1768, largely through their efforts. A zealous committee passed on the books considered proper, once burning *The Trial of Lady Ann Foley*, which someone had imprudently persuaded the committee to buy. The committee had purchased the poems of the new Scottish poet, Robert Burns. In addition to this library and one at her aunt's home, there was a bookstore kept by Mr. Edwards in the Old Market, where Dorothy and Jane often went to examine books by authors old and new, often in fine vellum bindings.

Although Dorothy liked books, they did not come first with her. In Halifax, she led a gay social life as did most young people. She loved parties, dances, and the long walks she and Jane Pollard took together. They talked about the most fashionable way to wear their hair, how soon they could wear high-heeled shoes, or the dream house each hoped for. Years later, Dorothy told Jane's daughter, she had yearned for

> A cottage in a verdant dell
> A pure unsullied household well
> A garden stored with fruits and flowers
> And sunny seats and shady bowers
> A file of hives for humming bees
> Under a row of stately trees
> And, sheltering all this faery ground,
> A belt of hills must wrap it round
> Not stern, or mountainous, or bare
> Nor lacking herbs to scent the air;
> Besprinkled o'er with trees and rocks,
> And pastured by the blameless flocks
> That leave their green trees to invite
> Our wanderings to the top-most height.
> Such was the dream I fondly framed
> When life was new and hope untamed—
> There with my one dear friend to dwell
> Nor wish for ought beyond the dell.

The death of John Wordsworth on December 30, 1783, deeply affected all the Wordsworth children. Among his many duties, Mr. Wordsworth had had those of the Bailiff and Recorder of the Borough of Cockermouth and of Coroner of the Seignory of Millom. Returning from conducting two inquests in that remote district, just before Christmas, he lost his way one cold, stormy evening, and was forced to spend the night in a shelterless spot. He arrived home very ill and died a few days later. Richard, John, and William were at home at the time, having come to spend Christmas with their father. On "a snowy, windy day," January 5, he was buried beside his wife. He had died with his financial affairs most involved, leaving less than £3,000 in cash to his children, barely enough to see them through school. Sir James Lowther, later Earl of Lonsdale, owed him £4,700 for legal and other business; others owed him money, too. The Wordsworth children were left to the guardianship of two uncles, their father's elder brother, Richard, and their mother's brother, Christopher Crackenthorpe Cookson, who lived with his parents at Penrith.

Christopher assumed the task of settling his brother-in-law's estate, taking "to some private place of safety" all the papers concerning Sir James Lowther's debt. Though Sir James owed John Wordsworth not only money for services, but also for sums paid out for him, he was long successful in withholding payment of this debt. An unscrupulous politician, married to the daughter of George III's prime minister, Lowther, though it was well known that he oppressed his dependents and made a fortune by graft, was so powerful that he easily avoided his obligations. In fact, he rose in influence until he became Earl of Lonsdale. To the elder son, Richard, was assigned the task of attempting to collect the Lowther debt. Richard also sold the Wordsworth furniture, except the bookcases, filled with good books.

The month-long Christmas holidays the boys were to spend with their Uncle Richard or his eldest son; the summer vacations, with Uncle Kit and his parents. Dorothy was to remain with Aunt Threlkeld. The death of the father united again the Wordsworth children in a spiritual bond that only death broke. The boys were happy with their father's relatives; with Uncle Kit and his parents, life was otherwise, Dorothy learned, when, at sixteen, she was summoned to Penrith "to make herself useful."

Grandfather Cookson and his wife, who considered themselves deeply religious, saw in lively, high-spirited Dorothy an "untractable and wild spirit," a good example of "original sin," and decided to tame her. Pouring out her loneliness to Jane Pollard, Dorothy found some relief as she wrote, "One would imagine a Grandmother would feel for her grandchild all the tenderness of a mother when that Grandchild had no other parent, but there is no such tenderness in her manner, nor anything affectionate. While I am in her house, I cannot consider myself as at home—I feel like a stranger. You cannot think how gravely and silently I sit with her and my Grandfather, you would hardly know me. You are well acquainted that I was never remarkable for taciturnity, but now I sit for whole hours without saying anything excepting that I have a shirt to mend, then, my Grandmother and I have to set our heads together and contrive the most notable way of doing it, which I daresay in the end we always hit upon, but really the contrivance takes up more time than the shirt is worth. Our only conversation is about *work, work,* or what kind of a servant such a one's is, who her parents are, what places she lived in, why she left them, etc. etc. What, my dear Jane, can be more uninteresting than such conversation as this? Yet, I am obliged to set upon the occasion as *notable* a face as if I was delighted with it, and that nothing would be more agreeable to me; notability is preached to me every day, such a one is a very *sedate, clever,* notable girl, says my Grandmother. My Grandmother's taste and mine so ill agree, that there is not one person who is a favorite with her that I do not dislike."

Indeed, Dorothy found her Grandmother's friends, like Miss Custs, whom Uncle Kit was courting, "a mixture of ignorance, pride, affectation, self-conceit, and affected nobility"; she could endure their ignorance, she said, "if they did not think so well of themselves." In fact, she soon had a positive aversion to "useful people." Yet, she told herself she could not expect as much of people without education as of those with it. As her grandparents considered reading a waste of time, she snatched time to read only when her grandmother was away; writing letters was considered only time-consuming; hence, for a long time, Dorothy wrote her long letters to Jane late at night in her room. There was little gaiety. Even the assemblies proved dull, for there were more women present than men "so two ladies were obliged to dance together." Walking was considered unladylike and hence Dorothy could no longer often enjoy the out-of-doors as she always had.

Her sole companions at Penrith, not "notable," were Mary and Peggy Hutchinson, of whom she became very fond. The parents of the ten Hutchinson children had died when the children were young, leaving their care to various relatives. Six of the children, including Peggy and Mary, remained in Penrith with their mother's sister, Elizabeth Monkhouse. Mary, who had been in school at Penrith with William, told Dorothy how she remembered her own mother's weeping when Dorothy's mother died, for the two women long had been friends. Mary and Dorothy at times managed to take walks together; frequently, they contrived to steal "out to each other's houses, and when we had our talk over the kitchen fire, to delay the moment of parting" by pacing "up one street and down another by moon or starlight." Occasionally the girls met at the vicar's home, for Dorothy's Uncle William was courting the vicar's daughter.

Dorothy looked forward to summer, when her brothers would come for the long holiday. Truly, their arrival was a reunion, for she had not seen all of the boys for a long time. She wrote Jane that "William and Christopher are very clever boys, at least so they appear in the partial eyes of a sister. No doubt I am partial and see in them virtues that by everyone else will pass unnoticed. John (who is to be the sailor), has a most excellent heart, he is not so bright as either William or Christopher, but he has very good common sense and is very well calculated for the profession he has chosen. Richard (the oldest) I have seen. He is equally affectionate and good, but is far from being as clever as William, but I have no doubts of his succeeding in his business for he is very diligent and far from being dull, he only spent a night with us. Many a time have Wm., Jn, C, and myself shed tears together, tears of the bitterest sorrow, we all of us, each day, feel more sensibly the loss we sustained when we were deprived of our parents, and each day we do receive new insults. You will wonder what sort; believe me, the most mortifying, the insults of servants." The young Wordsworths' grandparents, it seems, had scolded the young people before the servants; at tea time, they had discussed before the servants the fact that the Wordsworths were left little money and had "nothing to be proud of." The servants, as a result, were so insolent to the young people as to make "the kitchen as well as the parlour quite unsupportable." James, the groom from whom William was once lost, "has gone so far," Dorothy said, "as to tell us we had nobody to depend upon but my Grandfather," and he bemoaned the fact the five unwelcome guests "took as much waiting upon as any *gentleman*"; Dorothy had to entreat as favors the services to which she was entitled. She was even more dismayed by Uncle Kit's obvious dislike of William. Yet, there was close companionship among the young people. The boys planned with her a rosy future, lent her their books, reminisced with her of their home. William, she cherished most, partly because he suffered the most abuse, partly because the two were equally moved by the beauty of sunlight on the water, the greenness of meadows after a rain, the majesty of the peaks at sunset. She made him even more aware of the beauty in woods, field, and stream. When the boys left for school, they sent her books which she stealthily read.

Uncle William finally became aware of Dorothy's plight and had her come to his house from nine to eleven every morning for lessons in French, Arithmetic, and Geography. Unlike her grandmother, who believed letters were written only to say "that one is well and such stuff as that," Uncle William allowed Dorothy to release her pent-up feelings in letters to her friends during lesson-hours. Dorothy wrote of reading *The Iliad*, of the gift from William of Burns' poetry, which her grandmother disapproved of—all about a lousy field mouse—of her decision not to wear high heels yet, even though Jane Pollard was wearing them; Dorothy had decided that since she was so very little she'd "appear as girlish as possible"; she told of wearing her hair curled about her face "in light curls frizzed at the bottom and turned at the ends." She sent Jane a lock of her hair and a thimble "to remind you of my affection for you." She thanked her for the handkerchief Jane had made and worked for her. "Oh Jane, it is a valuable handkerchief." She wrote Jane that her Uncle William was showing signs of affection for her. Her first Christmas at Penrith was thoroughly unpleasant. She had been invited to visit her Uncle Richard, with whom her brothers were to spend their Christmas vacations, but her grandparents refused to allow her to accept the invitation. Shortly before Christmas her grandfather died.

The next summer Dorothy found was more pleasant, though not all the Wordsworth boys were at Penrith. Fifteen-year-old John, now a sailor with the East India Company, through the influence of Sir John Robinson, a family friend and member of Parliament, was on his first trip to Barbados; nineteen-year-old Richard, who had left school at fifteen rather than be under his grandparents' domination, had gone to London to become a solicitor; at times, however, he visited at Penrith and always kept in close touch with Dorothy and his brothers. Thirteen-year-old Christopher spent the vacation at Penrith and seventeen-year-old William divided his time between Hawkshead, the Lake Country, and Penrith. To William, his sister seemed "a gift there first bestowed." That summer, as when they were children, they roamed the woods, climbed high among the ruins of Brougham Castle and sat many an hour looking through a window's open space, or lay on the grass among the wild flowers, reading Burns' poems, talking of William's plans to be a poet and of his decision to have his sister always with him, helping his dream become a reality. At times, Mary Hutchinson walked with them.

That summer, William hoped to remain at Penrith longer than the younger boys since he was to attend Cambridge in the fall, but his uncles insisted he go to Hawkshead with Christopher. There he was to remain for the nine weeks until college began. Dorothy busied herself at Penrith sewing and getting William's clothing ready for college. William finally managed affairs so that he spent three weeks at Penrith before going to St. John's College, Cambridge.

_____

CHAPTER II

From "Unprofitable Talk" to "Fervent Discourse" about "Abolishing Poverty" and of "Equality for All Men"

ALTHOUGH JOHN HAD DECIDED TO STUDY FOR THE LAW AT STAPLE INN AND FOREGO A COLLEGE EDUCATION, WILLIAM convinced his guardians that it was necessary for him to go to the University.

Dorothy hoped he would find Cambridge all he anticipated. She realized it was not easy for people to become attracted to him; as she told Jane later, "You must be with him more than once before he will be perfectly free in conversation"; she added that his "appearance is not in his favor"; in fact, "he is rather plain . . . he has an extremely thoughtful face, but when he speaks it is often lighted up with a smile which I think very pleasing."

One of his tutors, Edward Frewen, a friend of his Uncle William, procured for him a scholarship after he had been at St. John's College, Cambridge University, only a week. Trying to live frugally, he took cheap rooms high up on the south side of the court. As his bedroom had no windows, he usually pulled his bed up to the door of his study so that he could see the top of the chapel window at Trinity College, under which stood the statue of Sir Isaac Newton. His college career began auspiciously; after the college examination in June, he and four others were placed in the second class. After that, his career was far from distinguished. He was so well prepared in mathematics that he believed he did not need to study it. Euclid, being the science of measuring the earth, interested him; he found a definite relationship between the symbols of geometry and the forms of nature. Hence, to these "lonesome sciences," he now gave considerable serious thought,

16

as he also did in later years, deriving from them "pleasure calm and deep." He read unassigned books, not only in English, but also in Latin and Greek; he studied Italian with a scholar residing in town, Agostino Isola; he taught himself some French and Spanish. Thus, neglecting his assigned college work, he occupied himself with subjects more to his taste.

Enjoying a freedom he had never known before, he busied himself more often as, "with loose and careless mind," he wandered about the streets, at times stopping to shop or to go to the tailor's. As a freshman, he soon decided he was

> . . . not for that hour
> Nor for that place . . .

In lordly condescension, he felt his teachers were not wise or profound, only "twittering popinjays"; the curriculum, he found "timid"; the compulsory chapel and prescribed classes "revolting"; the examination system that weighed men "as in the balance," despicable.

He welcomed the companionship of some of the students, though the fellows of his own college did not interest him, nor did he establish relationships with most of them; they were, for the most part, studying for the clergy. With other students, especially with a group who had been his classmates at Hawkshead, he

> sauntered, played, or rioted; we talked
> Unprofitable talk at morning hours,
> Drifted about along the streets and walks,
> Read lazily in trivial books, went forth
> To gallop through the country in blind zeal
> Of senseless horsmanship, or on the breast
> Of Cam sailed boisterously, and let the stars
> Come forth, perhaps without one quiet thought.

Though the "manners of the young men were very frantic and dissolute" at Cambridge, only once was Wordsworth the worse for liquor. On that occasion, at a wine party in Milton's former rooms at Cambridge, occupied by a Hawkshead friend, Birkett, he toasted Milton until he was dizzy. He was sober enough, however, to run back to St. John's in time for evening chapel.

He found himself before long again enjoying his long walks in the country, though missing the mountains and lakes he loved, learning to appreciate "the level fields," the willow-bordered Cam River, and the chalk hills to the east and south. Yet, he continued to enjoy the more formal life at Cambridge where velvet and silk stockings were worn in the evenings and where wine parties were the accepted mode of social intercourse.

He thought only one of his college professors interesting or worth knowing, whereas at Hawkshead, he had been tremendously impressed with William Taylor, a teacher he admired and revered. There was no one like Mr. Taylor at Cambridge. In fact, when the Master of St. John's died in 1788, William refused to pin a Latin or English epitaph on his coffin pall, as the other boys did. "I felt no interest in the deceased person, with whom I had had no intercourse and whom I had never seen but during his walks on the college grounds," he said.

During his second year at Cambridge, he caused grave concern to his guardians, who complained he had spent £300 in two years and was undecided regarding what he wished to do when he completed college. His third year, even Dorothy was concerned about his failure to take some of his examinations. "I am very anxious about him just now," she wrote in the spring of 1790, "as he will shortly have to provide for himself; next year he takes his degree; when he will go into orders I do not know, nor how he will employ himself; he must when he is three and twenty either go into orders or take pupils; he will be twenty in April." His indecisiveness contrasted with the attitudes of John and Richard, who were settled in life; John, a sailor with the East India Company, was doing well; Kit, studying at Cambridge, seemed destined to become master of Trinity College there.

At the end of his third year, William was still not interested in college. Instead of applying for a fellowship, he went for a walking trip through France and the Alps with a college friend, Robert Jones. Back in England, he visited Dorothy briefly and then returned to Cambridge, where in January, 1791, he finally received his A.B. degree. His dilatory habits for the next year caused concern to all his relatives. After leaving Cambridge, he spent three or four months in London ranging "free as a colt at pasture on the hills"; he did not seek frequent intercourse with men of "literature or rank"; though "undetermined to what course of life I should adhere," he announced he was preparing himself to take religious orders in the Church of England.

Before taking these vows, however, he wanted to see more of life, he explained. In London, therefore, he enjoyed seeing Mrs. Siddons at the theatre, admired thoroughly the clowns, conjurers, and harlequins at Sadler's Wells, applauded Burke, whom he heard speak in the House of Commons. As in the country, at times he took solitary walks about the city streets even in bad weather

... when unwholesome rains
Are falling hard, with people yet astire,
The feeble salutation from the voice
Of some unhappy woman ...

greeting him as he passed. Once, passing the refreshment bar of a theatre, he sighed as he saw a harlot's little boy, almost a baby, sitting on the bar while the riff-raff of the place played with "oaths, and laughter, and indecent speech." Still marking time, he spent the summer in Wales with a friend. His negligence cost him a possible fellowship at Cambridge.

Yet idle in September, he was summoned by a family friend who believed he could secure for him a position as curate in the church at Harwich. As the position was a good one, Wordsworth thought it best not to seem to refuse it; instead, he lied to his would-be benefactor and said he could not accept the position as he was not of age. He had turned twenty-one in April. In October, he returned to Cambridge and stated that on the advice of Uncle Cookson, he was going to study oriental languages. In late November, he wrote from Brighton that he had decided to leave Cambridge and go to France to study French, concerned, however, because "I have no resolution and ... have not prepared myself for the enterprise by any discipline among the Western languages ... know little of Latin and scarce anything of Greek." Dorothy wrote her friend, Jane, that William expected to study French to qualify "for the office of travelling companion to some young gentleman." Obviously, William realized that with most of his inheritance spent, he had to find some type of position and did not wish to be a clergyman.

William Wordsworth arrived in Paris on November 30, 1791. Not politically minded at first, he had read with little interest only the "major political pamphlets of the day." Though he saw the city torn by the Revolution, tossed "like a ship at anchor, rocked by storms," he sauntered about Paris as a tourist visiting the suburbs of St. Anthony, "Mont Marte, southward to the Dome of St. Genevieve"; loitered about

Tavern, Brothel, Gaming-house, and Shop,
Great rendevouz of worst and best, the walk
Of all who had a purpose or had not.
I stared and listened with a stranger's ears,
To Hawkers and Haranguers, hubub wild.

Near the ruins of the Bastille, where recently so many had been beheaded, he sat in the sun rejoicing "at the destruction of such a symbol of tyranny," yet feeling little emotion, and like a souvenir hunter, picking up a stone from the rubbish. By no means a discerning art collector or critic, he visited the Carmelite convent to see the Magdalene of Le Brun, before which music was played. This picture, one of the favorites of the day, Wordsworth considered "exquisitely wrought."

Having an introduction to one of the members of the Legislative Assembly, he visited the chambers, where the debates centered on the revolt of the Negroes in St. Domingo and the government's attempts to secure order. The French settlers were Royalists and at that time were using the revolt, the opposition said, to undermine the position of the mulattos to whom the Assembly had granted civil rights. The Assembly refused to send troops to aid the white settlers unless there was a guarantee they would not be used against the black race. Brissot, one of the deputies, a champion of the colored people and an opponent of slavery, led the debates. Later, Brissot advocated war against kings as proof that the country was worthy of liberty. Undoubtedly, Wordsworth met some Girondists, the idealists among the Revolutionary group. The debates and those he heard in the Jacobin Club, a Revolutionary organization, fascinated twenty-one year old William.

At that time, it seemed the French Revolution really would succeed. Parliament, demanding a centralized government of unlimited power, had planned a state with a hereditary monarch, Louis XVI, a constitution, and legal safeguards of freedom. Many saw the dawn of a new era with feudal privileges abolished, with the representatives of the people making laws, imposing taxes, declaring war and peace, opening all civil and military careers to all citizens. National finances had been reformed; laws made more just; civil offices opened not only to Catholics but also to Jews and Protestants for the first time. The majority of the clergy and twenty-seven of the nobles had taken their places in the Assembly. King Louis XVI and Queen Marie Antoinette, outwardly accepting the situation, had made plans ranging from that of escaping from France to that of fostering rebellion to regain their former power.

The clergy, now for the first time subservient to the state, were supported by it as were the charities formerly maintained by the church. Yet some of the religious men and women resented the fact that no longer would France permit them to take orders from the Pope. They resented the fact that marriage, one of the functions previously performed by the Church and treated as a sacrament, was now regarded as a civil function, performed by the state. Some clergy forbade priests to pronounce even mystical blessing over persons who had not had their marriages "proclaimed in the church," contending a civil marriage was null and void and a marriage by a constitutional priest "an insult to religion." There was a wide rift between the clergy who went along with the government and those who refused to do so. Fanatical and radical groups were growing in number and in strength. In July, 1791, there had been serious riots and bloodshed. Catholic prelates refusing to swear allegiance to the Constitution, and some embittered by confiscation of the property of emigrant nobles, despised the Girondists in control of the Assembly. Moreover, Prussia and Austria, fearful lest democracy spread within their borders, were eager to wage war against France. Wordsworth, however, saw the good accomplished by the Revolution and was thrilled by it.

After five days in Paris, the twenty-one-year-old Englishman traveled down the Valley of the Loire to Orleans, whose fertile plains, lush orchards, wheat fields, and low, white, lime-slate cliffs were an ideal setting for the magnificent old castles, châteaux, and cathedrals. The soft, gentle climate seemed mirrored in the friendly inhabitants. They had long been proud of their universities and medical school, the many fine libraries in the universities, and in their monasteries and hospitals.

Orleans usually had been a popular resort for Englishmen. Now, however, when William reached Orleans on Tuesday, December 6, 1791, he found no other Englishmen there. They, along with many of the nobility, had left for cities where they found fewer privations. Monasteries and nunneries the Revolutionists were rapidly turning into public institutions; the government was renaming streets that bore stigma of royalty; political prisoners were being brought to Orleans for trial; young patriots were departing to serve the cause of the Revolution.

In the house in Rue Royal where he had chosen to live, lodged three young cavalry officers and a young gentleman. Wordsworth easily became their friend and with them attended meetings of their "literary club." These young men did not favor the Revolution. In fact, polished "in arts and punctilio versed," they scrupulously avoided talking of "the good and evil of the times," for all societies, regardless of how unpolitical their purpose, were suspect by the government. These young gentlemen were all aristocrats, for before the Revolution no one could hold an office in the army unless he was of noble birth. Resenting being deprived of some of their privileges, they hated the new order. Soon, Wordsworth found their conversations and debates dull. Equally boring, in time, became their card parties and "routs." At first, then, he was content merely to be a spectator of the Revolution; he was

Tranquil, almost, and careless as a flower
Glassed in a greenhouse, or a parlour
While every bush and shrub, the country through
Is shaking to the roots.

His early detachment was the result, he later said, of lack of understanding and of being inadequately informed of the events. "All things," he said seemed to him "loose and disjointed."

Through the group of young officers in Orleans, Wordsworth met Paul Vallon, a lawyer's clerk, and his sister, Annette Vallon, the daughter of the late surgeon of the Hôtel Dieu at Blois, an ancient institution where nuns nursed the poor who were ill. Annette's father had been the fourth in his family to serve in this capacity; he had trained two sons to succeed him. After Annette's father's death, her mother had married another surgeon. Ardent Catholics, the Vallons sent Annette to be educated in one of the convents; two of Annette's cousins were priests, who took the oaths required by the Civil Constitution of the Clergy. At first, the Vallons had supported the Revolution, believing it was based on justice, but when nunneries and monasteries were dissolved, when pressure was put on the priests to give up their positions, when the Sisterhood of the Hôtel Dieu dissolved, when Annette's brother Paul was almost guillotined for his views, the family became strong Royalists. They shuddered when the government forbade priests to keep records of marriages, baptisms, and deaths, ordered the clergy to give up publishing marriage banns, and insisted that marriage be treated as a mere formality. The Vallons considered a mere civil marriage "null and void and a marriage by a constitutional priest an insult to religion." When priests refusing to sanction the latest decrees of the government were deprived of their churches, they and their congregations often managed to meet in secret in barns.

Others, approving of the Revolution, managed to attend the meetings of a Revolutionary group, the Friends of the Constitution, which kept in touch with the Jacobin Club in Paris where "people played with the lives of private citizens." William Wordsworth, unlike the Vallons, soon shared the ideas of the Jacobins and the Friends of the Constitution.

Pretty twenty-five-year-old Annette, unsophisticated, warmly sympathetic, exuberant, gay, impulsive, an extreme extrovert, agreed to teach William French—and in a short time became more than teacher. Wordsworth, though he had strong sexual desires, said he had had "slight shocks of young love-liking" at Hawkshead. Yet, in England he certainly had been no philanderer. He had enjoyed the companionship of Dorothy's friend Mary Hutchinson, a quiet, serene girl, and of Robert Jones' sisters; but there had been no passion in these relationships.

Fascinated by Annette, on the other hand, he believed her to be his first love. When she left Orleans in the spring to be with her mother and stepfather in Blois, he followed her. She was passionately in love with him. He was not long content away from her. Conscious that they were "hovering within the eddy of a cavernous blast," they secretly met night after night. Enjoying their "uneasy bliss," seeing innumerable obstacles to marriage, "one delirious hour" they turned aside from "law and custom" and entrusted "To Nature a happy end to all." In that "unguarded moment," was dissolved "virtuous restraint."

Later, Annette wrote, "I cannot be happy without him, I desire him every day . . . he will never picture accurately the need I feel for him to make me happy; mastered by a feeling which causes all my unhappiness, I cherish always his domination over me, and the influence of his dear love on my heart which is always concerned with him. His image follows me everywhere; often when I am alone in my room with his letters I think he has entered." William was happy also with his mistress.

In Blois, in addition to Annette, his associates were a varied group. Again, he lodged in a house where some military officers of the Bassigny Regiment lived. Most of them, Royalists at heart, were determined to undo what the Revolution had accomplished. Hostile to new ideas, they tried to convert Wordsworth to their way of thinking. Wordsworth admired them as men;

> Some of these wore swords
> That had been seasoned in the wars, and all
> Were men well born; the chivalry of France.

Yet, unlike them, he was at heart a democrat, believing

> . . . that we were brothers all
> In honor, as in one community,
> Scholars and gentlemen; where, furthermore

Distinction open lay to all that came
And wealth and title were in less esteem
Than talents, worth, and prosperous industry.

While the young officers were excited and thrilled over the defeat
of 2,000 French by the Austrians and were hoping the defeat would
aid the Royalist cause, when in panic the defeated troops murdered
their general, Wordsworth remained as horrified at his friends' satisfaction as at the ignominious defeat; "the massacre of their general, a
dance performed with savage joy round his burning body, the murder
of six prisoners, are events which would have arrested the attention of
the reader of the annals of Morocco."

Why, he queried again and again in letters to his brother and
friends, could not the Royalists see that one cannot go back to things
as they were? Yet, the Royalists actually believed that if an army, say
that of Germany, were at the gates of Paris this miracle could be
accomplished. In fact, Wordsworth said, "there are in France some
millions—I speak without exaggeration, who believed it would be
possible to make material changes in their constitution, reinstate the
clergy in its ancient splendour," restore to the nobility the position it
had enjoyed and to the king the authority he had had.

Wordsworth began to be thrilled as he saw the youths who believed
in the Revolution crowding the roads, on their way to war, though he
wept at the farewell, "domestic severings, female fortitude," the
patriot's devotion, encouraged "with a martyr's confidence." The martial music, parades, banners spread, moved him immeasurably. He
was no longer merely a spectator. He sympathized thoroughly with
the Revolution. Part of this devotion to the French cause came from
Michel Beaupuy and from others he had met in a Revolutionary club,
the Friends of the Constitution.

Thirteen years Wordsworth's senior, Beaupuy, a descendent of
Montaigne, was one of six brothers, the oldest of whom had served
in the Legislative Assembly, one of whom had become a priest, three
of whom had been killed fighting for France. Traveling as a soldier
throughout France, Beaupuy had studied conditions there. Hence,
when he took part in the election of the States-General, he stated that
conditions in France made it imperative that the nobels sacrifice some
of their privileges for the good of the country. Steeped in philosophy
and politics, Captain Beaupuy knew whereof he spoke. Yet, he aroused
the displeasure of his fellow officers, who thought his ideas bordered
on treason. In twenty-one-year-old Wordsworth, however, he found
a willing listener and soon an admirer. In fact, Beaupuy was one of

the most benign, gracious, and generous men Wordsworth had ever known, raised, as were many, by the Revolution, to "heroic levels of unselfishness and self-sacrifice." Beaupuy had great compassion on the poor, who suffered in France even more bitterly than the half-starved, long-depressed peasantry in England. Like other idealists of the day, Beaupuy looked forward to a time when cruel power and poverty would be abolished and a responsible democracy, healthy and alert, would bring "better days to all mankind." Wordsworth wrote of him

> Man he loved
> As man; and, to the mean and the obscure,
> And all the homely in their homely works
> Transferred a courtesy which had no air
> Of condescension . . .
>
> . . . Oft in solitude
> With him did I discourse about the end
> Of civil government, and its wisest forms;
> Of ancient royalty, and chartered rights,
> Custom and habit, novelty and change;
> Of self respect, and virtue in the few
> For patrimonial honour set apart,
> And ignorance in the laboring multitude.

Agreeing with Rousseau that man's nature was essentially noble, they decided that man's instinctive desires would impel him to build liberty on firm foundations. Wordsworth lamented the senseless actions taken against the church when he thought of the closing of the Hôtel Dieu or looked at a ruined monastery and at a matin bell that "would sound no more." Yet, he agreed with Beaupuy that though the Revolutionists made costly errors, "by patient exercise of reason," by refusing to mistrust and to lack hope, true liberty could be obtained and "men made worthy of liberty."

Beaupuy moved his English friend by recounting tales of human misery. He told of a nobleman's son separated from the girl of lowly station whom he loved, of their being parted by sealed order of the king because of their difference in rank, of the girl's being sent to a nunnery after the birth of their child, and of the lover's grief. He pointed out a starving peasant girl and commented, " 'T is against *that* that we are fighting." Wordsworth

> . . . with him believed
> That a benignant spirit was abroad

Which might not be withstood, that poverty
Abject as this would in a little time
Be found no more, that we should see the earth
Unthwarted in her wish to recompense
The meek, the lowly, patient child of toil,
All institutes for ever blotted out
That legalised exclusion, empty pomp
Abolished, sensual state and cruel power
Whether by edict of the one or few;
And finally, as sum and crown of all,
Should see the people having a strong hand
In framing their own laws; whence better days
To all mankind. . . . .

Believing in devotion and sacrifice, Beaupuy enlisted Wordsworth as an ardent revolutionist. Always, Wordsworth had felt concern for the wretched and believed their condition should and could be bettered.

In July, the fruitful companionship of Wordsworth and Beaupuy came to an end, as the latter's regiment left the Loire for active service on the Rhine. The two never saw one another again. Beaupuy was wounded in La Vendée, recovered, was made a general, and was killed in 1796 fighting against the Austrians in the battle of the Elz on the Rhine.

Writing poetry, talking and walking with Beaupuy and other officers, intensely in love with Annette, William, in 1792, was contented. Despite the fact that she was pregnant, Annette was happy, too.

Once her family discovered she was bearing William's child, the Vallons became hostile to the young man. It was bad enough for their daughter to be unwed and pregnant, but for the father of the child to be a man with Revolutionary sympathies, to the Royalist Vallons seemed abominable. The parents forbade the young people to see one another. They did manage to meet, however. Yet, despite William's love, even when Annette was bearing his child, he seems to have made no effort to marry her. True, he was not a Catholic and the difficulties of a church marriage such as the Vallons would have insisted upon were great; true, he had no money or prospects of a profession unless he became a clergyman as his guardians urged. How would a French Roman Catholic girl fit into that plan? Both families, Annette and William knew, would oppose the marriage. He left Annette alone to make some explanation to her family of why there was no marriage, and to plan her confinement. In Wordsworth's poems, there is ample evidence that the two planned to marry sometime and that he wished to be "In honourable wedlock with his love." Yet, he evidently had not the stamina to do more than wish.

As Annette's condition became apparent and her family's hostility continued, she left Blois for Orleans in September, 1792, to be with her friends, the Dufours, to stay until the birth of her child. William went too, and remained until near the end of October.

Probably at the very time he was there, fifty-three political prisoners who had been removed for Orleans to Versailles were slaughtered by the same bands who had ruthlessly massacred others in Paris prisons. As disturbances increased in Orleans, the city was put under martial law. Tension continued when the Revolutionary forces pushed back the Prussians and when the Convention declared France a Republic.

Finally, without funds, Wordsworth had no course left but that of returning to England. He, therefore, signed a document authorizing M. Dufour to represent him as father when his and Annette's child was baptized; still, there was no marriage.

Wordsworth arrived in Paris on October 29. The following morning he found crowds thronging the streets; the guillotine, again set up in the Place du Carrousel, had already lopped off the heads of victims who were friends of or sympathizers with Robespierre and of nine émigrés bearing arms. Crowds were demanding the execution of the king and his family, who were prisoners in the Temple. As William crossed the square where so recently had lain the "dead upon the dying heaped," passed the Palace lately stormed "by a furious host," accompanied by the cannon's roar, he felt bewildered. He had had such confidence in the Revolution. And now came these tragedies. Yet, his judgment told him "the earthquake is not satisfied at once." He did agree with those who believed the king should be brought to trial, for he had long had little confidence in monarchs. He, like Beaupuy, had believed more could be accomplished by reason than by strife. Yet, in Paris, again he saw tyranny and mob rule. As he saw many of the Jacobins and Girondists whom he admired murdered, he even longed for a dictator who could clear the way for good, democratic government. He turned to the political writing of Algernon Sidney, John Harrington, and John Milton for guidance.

On December 15, 1792, still in Paris, he learned of the birth of his daughter. In the Communal Archives of Orleans, in the Parish of Sainte-Croix, is recorded the baptism of "a girl born the same day in this parish to William Wordsworth, Anglois, and Marie-Anne Vallon, her father and mother; named Anne-Caroline by Paul Vallon and Marie-Victorie Adelaide Peigné, wife of André Augustin Dufour, William Wordsworth being absent. . . ." Shortly after the birth of his daughter, William returned to London without seeing either the baby or Annette, expecting to return soon. Had not lack of money forced him to return to London, he believed he would soon have become associated with a Girondist group, many of whom were eventually victims of the guillotine. He later wrote

> Doubtless, I should then have made common cause
> With some who perished; happy perished, too,
> A poor mistaken and bewildered offering.

When Annette returned home to Orleans with her baby, she was not allowed to keep it with her; it was "put out to nurse," but she visited her little daughter daily, resenting being deprived of the baby because she and William had not been married. She looked forward to the day when she would be William's wife and could "rejoice in having Caroline always with me. I will then myself give her the care I am jealous of her receiving from other hands."

CHAPTER III

Agitators against "Things as They Are"

BACK IN LONDON, IN DECEMBER, 1792, WILLIAM, FULL OF THEORIES FOR REFORM, AND STILL AN ARDENT SUPPORTER OF the Revolution, stayed for seven months with his brother Richard, now a successful attorney, with whom, however, he had little in common. Richard, in fact, had little patience with his brother's political ideas, which were at white heat. Quickly, William prepared for publication the poems he had written; Joseph Johnson, a distinguished editor, for whom Mary Wollstonecraft was a reader, published both *Descriptive Sketches*, dedicated to William's friend Robert Jones, and *An Evening Walk*, dedicated to Dorothy Wordsworth. The verses, which William had hoped would show his family he could do something well, were not favorably received. Even Dorothy thought they showed evidence of being hastily written. "The poems," she pointed out, "contain many passages exquisitely beautiful, but they also contain many faults, the chief of which are obscurity, and a too frequent use of some particular expressions and uncommon words." A beautiful expression, she reiterated, "ought to have been cautiously used," for, when used three or four times, has lost its effectiveness.

Reviews of the poems were mixed: some sharply criticizing "harsh and prosaic lines" and "ill-chosen images," one reviewer finding "some passages . . . which display imagination," only one critic finding a few verses having "new and picturesque imagery." Discouraged, William looked in vain for a position.

London, at that time, was the center of a campaign conducted by Thomas Clarkson and William Wilberforce against the slave trade. Their first effort to have a bill passed outlawing slavery had failed in Parliament. The bill passed the House of Commons, but was defeated in the House of Lords. Considering slavery as merely one of the evils of the old order, William was more concerned, when, following the execution of Louis XVI, France declared war against England on February 1, 1793. Distressed at the complacency of many of his kinsmen, favoring France rather than England, young William resented seeing English youth sent to war by the thousands, and many "Left without glory on the battlefield." He resented the actions of a minister like Pitt, who, Wordsworth felt, was interested in pressing the war against France to protect the commercial interests of England abroad and to champion the rights of the rich, meanwhile treating the poor with scorn.

When there were prayers in churches for English victory, young Wordsworth was unable to join in the prayers. Feeling that his elders were sacrificing youth to keep existing social conditions as they had been, he railed against those who, he felt, had much to account for,

> . . . who could tear,
> By violence, at one decisive rent,
> From the best in England their dear pride,
> Their joy in England . . . .

When a revised edition of a speech by Richard Watson, the Bishop of Llandaff, appeared, Wordsworth was enraged. The article praised, as unexcelled, the British Constitution and British laws, especially those regulating the treatment of the poor. Contrasting England with France, the Bishop said that Parliamentary reform was unnecessary; British courts of law were always just; the British had all the equality desirable, for peasants and mechanics should have nothing to do with legislation. See what happened in France when they did! The poor in England were well off, possessing, said the Bishop, a ninth of the rented land of the country.

Wordsworth's spirited reply left nothing unsaid. Showing his contempt for royalty and aristocracy, he announced that monarchy should die, as from it sprang most social ills. He pointed out how hereditary titles often breed insolence and flattery; how in the "thorny labyrinth of litigation" the "verbosity of unintelligible statutes" and the "consuming expense" of long-drawn-out trials, justice often miscarried. Poverty in England, he insisted, was ugly and crippling. War, he concluded, was wicked, being waged by so many of the poor and leaving so many more in want.

Telling his brother Richard of the letter he had written, William was finally prevailed upon not to publish it. His reasons? First, Dorothy seconded Richard's advice and urged him not to, reminding him that the lawsuit to gain for the Wordsworths the property that was rightly theirs had long dragged through the courts. Why damage their case now? Moreover, Richard reminded him that since "the suspension of the Habeas Corpus Act the Ministers have great powers." He recalled the arrest of the shoemaker, Thomas Hardy, and of Thomas Paine who had been brought to trial and indicted for having denied the title of William III and Mary to the throne, for having stated that Parliament was corrupt and that "Monarchy is tyranny." Not until many years later was the letter published. Wordsworth was content to express his sentiments in his poems.

Continuing to write, trying in vain to secure a job, he was torn by remorse as letters came from Annette. "Come, my love, my husband," she wrote, "and receive the embraces of your wife and daughter. She is so pretty, poor little thing, so pretty that the affection I have for her will drive me mad if I do not have her continually in my arms. She grows more like you every day. I seem to be holding you in my arms. Her tiny heart often beats against my own; I seem to feel her father's; but why, Caroline, are you so insensible? Why does not your heart stir when your mother's is beating so? Oh, my beloved, soon it will be stirred when I shall say to her, 'Caroline, in a month, a fortnight, a week, you are going to see the most beloved of men, the most tender of men.' Caroline's heart will be moved, she will feel her first real emotion and that will be love for her father." Much as he wished to see Annette and their child, the war with France made this seem an impossibility.

Meanwhile, undoubtedly the young poet enjoyed the coterie of young Revolutionists whom his publisher, a progressive in politics, frequently entertained. Among them was William Woodfall, a publisher and the author of *The Letters of Junius;* he was imprisoned for his too frank views when the government for a time curtailed freedom of speech. Here, too, was William Godwin, already known as an "agitator against things as they are," whose *Political Justice*, published later, in 1793, stated that revolutions "suspend the wholesome advancement of science and confound the process of nature and of reason." Political, social, and religious reforms, Godwin contended, can come only "with the illumination of our understanding." Believing firmly in "the perfectibility of man," Godwin stated man could make a more perfect world; government, law, property, and marriage, he saw as "restraints upon liberty and obstacles to progress." Abolition of these, he affirmed, would make a better and eventually an ideal society.

That Wordsworth found these ideas stimulating may be proved

by his nine meetings with the older man, between February and August, 1795. Among those Wordsworth met at Godwin's parties were Thomas Holcroft, a dramatist who had been confined to Newgate Prison on the charge of high treason; young Frend who had been expelled from Cambridge for advocating peace with France; "Mr. Higgins," a social reformer who founded an asylum for pauper lunatics; and William Dyer, who, like Wordsworth, had known and cherished William Taylor, the schoolmaster at Hawkshead. The acknowledged leader of the radical group was William Godwin.

Born on March 3, 1756, William Godwin was from childhood a precocious child. "I remember, when I was a very little boy, saying to myself, 'What shall I do when I have read through all the books in the world?' " he once wrote. An unusual child, he could not remember ever playing games, but he recalled vividly being concerned with religious and intellectual matters. His body was always "weak and puny"; his posture, bad; except with a few friends, his social presence, awkward. Yet, in a few select spirits, he aroused admiration and wonder, for his intellect was always keen. His parents, middle class nonconformists, gave him an excellent education, first at Mr. Akers' school at Hindolveston, next, at age eleven, as the sole pupil of Mr. Samuel Newton; then again, for a short time, at Mr. Akers' school and, finally, at Hoxton, where he read about sixteen hours a day. Completing the courses there, he began preaching, stressing the denial of the divinity of Christ. Wearying of preaching, he planned to teach, and wrote a pamphlet stating his views on education. Hoping to limit his school to twelve students, he planned to teach them foreign languages when they were ten, to introduce them to history, then have them read *Plutarch's Lives*, and a French volume on the Revolution; he proposed, also, to lead them into a desire to aid the poor. His proposed school did not appeal to parents.

Hence, he turned to writing at twenty-seven. Here, his talents were recognized and he received employment, though at a meager salary, on the staff of *The English Review*, a historical monthly. This led to his writing also for *The Political Herald*, a Whig magazine. Then, in 1793, appeared his book, *Enquiry Concerning Political Justice*. Godwin's writings had appealed essentially to the intellectuals and some other youths. Now, many enthusiastic young men and women called themselves "Godwinites" or "Godwinians," wrote verses honoring him, called him "Great Master." In London, he "was gazed at in wonder"; when he visited Western England, in 1794, he found "not a person in hardly any town or village, who had any acquaintance with modern publications, who had not heard of the *Enquiry Concerning Political Justice*, or that was not acquainted in great or small degree with the contents of that work . . . I was nowhere a stranger." In Europe, too, he was admired. One youth said he so believed Godwin's ideas he was willing to die a martyr for them. Young William Wordsworth, however, later disagreed with one of Godwin's theories, really the essence of that philosopher's ideas, for Godwin contended that the more humble man was less capable of contributing to the public good than the educated man.

"No," said Wordsworth, "mental power and genuine virtue often lie in the humblest shepherd or cottager." Yet he agreed with Godwin that "days of greater virtue and more ample justice will descend upon the earth."

Godwin was quite as attractive to women as he was to young men. A coterie of beautiful and intellectual women sought him out. Beautiful Mrs. Reveley, wife of Gilbert (better known as Willy) Reveley, animated, fascinating, and charming, vied with auburn-haired, lively, gay Amelia Alderson, "the Belle of Norwich," for the philosopher's attentions. Many a swain, including the Prince Regent, had succumbed to the attractions of Amelia's well-formed figure, her fine carriage, her gaiety and polished manners. One admirer said she always reminded him of "a lovely Bacchante . . . so voluptuous, yet so delicate and feminine, especially when she sang, which she did sweetly." The actress, Elizabeth Inchbald, "a piquante mixture between a lady and a milkmaid," whose slight stammer kept her from playing major roles, was courted by the highest ranks of nobility, who were proud of her visits and whose "coronets were seen waiting at the door of her lodgings to bear her, from household toil, to take the airing of luxury and pride," for her life was spent in alternation between poverty and riches. William Godwin admired some of the narratives she wrote and was glad to criticize them as soon as they were written. Her tragedy, it was said, was that "the men who loved and admired her were too worldly to take an actress and a poor author, however lovely and charming, for a wife." Yet, Godwin, had he been able, at least at one time, would have done so. Mrs. Mary Robinson, whom the great actor Garrick had befriended and trained for the stage, had so bewitched the Prince of Wales as she played in "The Winter's Tale," that she, flattered by his telling her that her manners were irresistible, her smile "victory," had deserted her husband and become the Prince's mistress. He gave her a bond for £20,000 payable when he came of age, as proof of his affections. But shortly he tired of her and, when he met her driving in the park, "affected not to recognize her." She was then twenty-three. Though an arrangement was made for an annuity of £500 a year in exchange for the bond, often the annuity was in arrears. Later, she became the mistress of Colonel Tarleton, who had returned from America. That affair terminated when the lady became partly paralyzed. Then, still witty and beautiful—she was painted by Romney, Gainsborough, and Reynolds—although confined to a chair the remainder of her life, she turned to writing. Admiring her beauty and pluck, Godwin became a great friend of hers.

The philosopher learned to his sorrow that women could at times assume men's rights, when he met Mary Hays, "young, unlearned, acquainted with not any language but her own; possessing no other merit than a love of truth and of virtue, an ardent desire of knowledge." When she was filled "with republican ardour, her sentiments elevated by a high-toned philosophy, her bosom glowed with the virtues of patriotism." A zealous political and moral reformer, she had begun to champion the cause of woman's freedom. Her novels, not of the first order, brought her to the attention of Godwin, some of whose friends thought her a strange, wild creature. One young man said, in fact, "To hear a thing, ugly and petticoated, ex-syllogize a God with cold blooded precision and attempt to run religion through the body with an icicle, an icicle from a Scotch hog-trough, I do not endure it!" When she proposed marriage to William Godwin, he declined her offer. Instead, refusing also the advances of Mrs. Reveley, now a widow, he proposed to Miss Alderson, addressing his proposal to her father. Her father declined the offer; whether his refusal was based on his own judgment or that of his daughter, who had just met John Opie, whom she married two years later, no one knows.

Later, Godwin became seriously interested in Mrs. Mary Imlay, better known as Mrs. Wollstonecraft. William Wordsworth had first met her when he brought his poems to Joseph Johnson in the hope of publication. Godwin had met the serene, calm, beautiful, copper-haired, dark expressive-eyed young woman three years earlier, at Johnson's home, along with Tom Paine. They had talked of religion, of Voltaire, and of monarchy. Godwin had read only a little of Mary's writing, and had been displeased with it, criticizing its composition in "not very respectful tones." They parted equally displeased with each other. They later met a few times, before she went to France in

1792, but "made a very small degree of progress toward a cordial acquaintance." Now, after an exhausting experience in France, Mary had returned, deserted by her lover, brokenhearted, with her two-year-old daughter Fanny, and Godwin found her fascinating.

Mary Wollstonecraft had been born into a family of opposites. Her mother had "an indolence of character" which prevented her paying much attention to her children's education. "But," her daughter Mary said, "the healthy breezes of a neighboring heath on which we bounded at pleasure, volatilized the humors that improper food might have generated. And to enjoy open air and freedom was paradise after the unnatural restraint of our fireside, where we were often obliged to sit four or five hours together, without daring to utter a word, when my father was out of humor." And Edward Wollstonecraft was often out of humor. A despotic father, he regarded his whims as law regardless of reason or of consistency. His elder son was, like his father, a tyrant to his brothers and sisters. The father had inherited a substantial fortune, which he lost through mismanagement. Having no profession, he turned to farming in which he encountered failure after failure. With six children, three boys and three girls to provide for, Mr. Wollstonecraft had his problems. As the fortune dwindled, the family moved frequently; between 1764 when Mary was five and 1780 when her mother died, the family home had changed seven times. These changes were especially difficult for the older children, Edward and Mary. The other children, Eliza and Everina, and the little boys, James and Charles, stood the moves better.

The older brother was spoiled, the "idol of his parents and the torment of the rest of the family. Such indeed is the force of prejudice," Mary says, "that what was called spirit and wit in him was cruelly represented as forwardness in me. . . . Extreme indulgence had rendered him so selfish that he only thought of himself, and from tormenting insects and animals, he became the despot of his brothers and still more of his sisters. He seemed to take a peculiar pleasure in tormenting and humbling me, and if I ever ventured to complain of his treatment to either my father or mother, I was rudely rebuffed for presuming to judge of the conduct of my eldest brother."

Easily angered, Mr. Wollstonecraft, when aroused, let out a stream of furious words and struck hastily at his dogs, his children, and his wife. More than once, Mary came between her parents, covering her mother with her body which took the blows. Yet her mother seemed unable to feel any warmth or sympathy toward her daughter. Once or twice, Mary had confided secrets to her mother and they had been told and laughed at. The girl suffered, too, when beggars were driven unfed from her parents' door. Often she tried to give the beggars her breakfast, unperceived. Though her religion was not of the orthodox variety, many a night she "sat up conversing with the Author of Nature," making verses and singing hymns of her own composing. She thought that only "an Infinite Being could fill the human soul."

When Mary was sixteen, she met Fanny Blood, a meeting that marked a turning point in her life. The Wollstonecrafts had gone in 1775 to live in Hoxton, next door to a clergyman named Clare. The clergyman and his wife noting Mary's intelligence, introduced her to a young friend of theirs, Fanny Blood, who "sang and played with taste" and who "drew with uncommon fidelity and neatness." A friendship soon developed between the girls, and Mary "now conscious of her rusticity and ignorance" strove to be like her friend. The first result of this friendship was Mary's succeeding in having a room of her own, as did Fanny, where she could study and improve herself. As the Wollstonecraft finances became worse, in 1778 Mary left home to be a companion to a Mrs. Dawson, the wealthy widow of a retired tradesman at Bath. For two years, she remained there; then, as her mother's health was failing rapidly, she returned home and cared for her until her death.

When Mary discovered that her father was living with one of the servants and that he had carried on a liaison with her before his wife's death, she left home to live with the Bloods, while her sister Everina went to keep house for her brother, now a lawyer. Another sister, Eliza, was married to a man of violent temper and changeable moods. The marriage finally became so volatile that Mary was concerned that her sister would go insane unless she was separated from the tempestuous husband. With the law upholding a husband's marital rights, it was daring for Mary to plan to take her sister away. Yet this she did, and kept her in hiding until an agreement was reached for Eliza to live her life unmolested.

Mary settled the question of supporting herself, Eliza, and Fanny Blood whose family was as usual in need, by having the three of them start a school at Islington. Mary Wollstonecraft was mistress of the school; the others, her assistants. Mary had original ideas on education, favoring coeducation, physical training for girls, playgrounds, limited lesson periods for young children; moreover, she insisted that "only that education deserves emphatically to be termed cultivating the mind which teaches young people how to begin to think." Soon after the school was started, it was moved to Newington Green. There, she met Dr. Joseph Johnson, a publisher, who "treated her with particular kindness and attention, and had a long conversation with her and desired her to repeat her visit often."

The school went well, until the absence for a time of Mary, who had gone to Portugal to be with her friend Fanny Blood, now wed to Hugh Skeys, a merchant in Lisbon. Ill with consumption, expecting a baby, Fanny had called for her friend. Mary arrived only to see Fanny die in childbirth, on November 29, 1785. Back at work in her school that had suffered badly during her absence, Mary finally gave it up. "Life," she wrote, "seems a burden almost too heavy to be endured."

Though she was ill and discouraged about her own life, the financial insecurity of Fanny's father and mother troubled her more. Rev. John Hewlett, a clergyman friend, told her she could earn money by writing. Hence, she wrote her first book, *Thoughts on the Education of Daughters*. With the £10 Joseph Johnson, the publisher, gave her for the copyright, she succeeded in getting Fanny's parents to Ireland where they soon were in comfortable circumstances. An offer of £40 to work as a governess solved her own financial problems.

Being governess to Lady Kingsborough's three daughters, the eldest aged fourteen, offered Mary a totally new experience. "Lady K.," she confided, "is a clever woman and a well-meaning one, but not of the order of being I could love." She was distressed "to see a woman without any softness in her manners caressing animals and using infantine expressions"—behavior she regarded as ludicrous; but added, "a fine lady is a new specimen to me of animals." Mary, moreover, was distressed that the eldest girl, who had a wonderful capacity but "such a multiplicity of employments it has not room to expand itself and in all probability will be lost in a heap of rubbish called accomplishments." Though she was in a social circle quite unlike that in which she had moved, Mary was admired. Yet, after a year, the position terminated, for Lady Kingsborough found her children more devoted to Mary than to herself. The children wrote affectionately to Mary long after she had left them; her one comment was, "Thank heaven that I was not so unfortunate as to be born a lady of quality." Such ladies, she had found, had neither brains nor intellectual curiosity.

Back in London, she soon became a contributor to, and a literary advisor for Joseph Johnson's *Analytical Review*. At his home, she met stimulating conversationalists like William Godwin, William Hazlitt, and Tom Paine. For Johnson, she translated several books on education and religion, *The Elements of Morality for Children*, with an *Introductory Address to Parents* from the German of Salzmann and *On the Importance of Religious Opinions* by Necker. These publications proving successful, Mary set up housekeeping and looked after her brothers, sisters, and father. Everina was sent to Paris to improve her French; Eliza, to a school as a day-pupil and later as a teacher; James, to Woolwich for training that enabled him to enter the navy. Her father, until his death, looked to her for support, and received it.

In 1789 when the National Assembly was set up in France, when the Bastille fell, when the women of France marched on Versailles, when the king, queen, and their children were taken to Paris, all London was excited. Some felt distrust and aversion; others solidly upheld the French in their newly found freedom. Among the latter, was a group called the Society for Commemorating the Revolution in Great Britain. Addressing the group, Dr. Richard Price, a nonconformist minister, said he had "lived to see thirty millions of people, indignant and resolute, spurning at slavery and demanding liberty with an irresistible voice." Then he expressed his hope for the enlargement of political freedom in Europe, stemming from the example France had set. Disagreeing thoroughly with Dr. Price, Edmund Burke, who had espoused the American Revolution, severely reprimanded his adversary in an article entitled, "Reflections on the Revolution in France."

Deeply stirred by events in France, and at that time sympathetic with them, Mary Wollstonecraft replied to Burke, in a 150-page pamphlet entitled, "A Vindication of the Rights of Man, in a Letter to the Rt. Honorable Edmund Burke, Occasioned by His Reflections on the Revolution in France." Suddenly Mary Wollstonecraft had a wide reading public. She emerged from being the protégé of the publisher and a hack writer and became overnight a young woman of literary merit. Twice published, her work was said to contain "the most dashing polemics in our language"; others praised Mary's "sheer virility" and her sentences that "have the quality of a sword-edge" as they "flash with the rapidity of a practised duelist."

Encouraged by the praise given her reply to Burke, Mary wrote in six weeks, a work on which she had been meditating many years. Considering herself as one who was defending "one-half of the human species, labouring under a yoke which through all the records of time has degraded them from the station of human beings and almost sunk them to the level of brutes," she wrote her "Vindication of the Rights of Woman," stating first her desire "to persuade women to endeavor to acquire strength, both of mind and body," and appealed to men to emancipate women by snapping their chains so that they would have "helpmeets," by being content with a "rational fellowship instead of slavish obedience." Given their freedom, women, she affirmed, would be "more observant daughters, more affectionate sisters, more faithful wives, more reasonable mothers—in a word, better citizens." To achieve these ends, Mary advocated reforms in the education of women, including physical education training in "the act of healing" so that they could be physicians as well as nurses; training that would enable them to manage a farm or a shop; training in government so that instead of being "arbitrarily governed without having any direct share allowed them in the deliberations of government," they might have their representatives in the government.

"The Vindication" met criticism, as Mary knew it would. Many were shocked at the idea of the profession of medicine being especially well suited to women. Even bolder seemed her ideas on coeducation and equal moral standards for men and women.

Believing that the French Revolution would lead the way to a betterment of social conditions in all countries of the world, hoping it would do away with injustice and bring true liberty, Mary welcomed it. After living two years in France, in which she saw clearly many of the evils that the Revolution brought, she wrote, "Anarchy is a dreadful state and all men of sense and benevolence have been anxiously attentive to observe what use Frenchmen would make of their liberty, when the confusion incident to the acquistion should subside; yet while the heart sickens over a detail of crimes and follies, and the understanding is appalled . . . it is perhaps difficult to believe that out of this chaotic mass a fairer government is rising than has ever shed the sweets of social life on the world. But things must have time to find their level."

While in France, she met and fell in love with Gilbert Imlay, five years older than she, a land speculator who owned some twelve thousand acres in America. Loving him wholly and unreservedly, she soon lived with him as his wife. Though they were not married, according to her code she was as truly married to him as if every legal and religious ceremony had been observed. For a time, the two were extremely happy, despite the fact that Imlay's business frequently took him out of France. When their child was born, Mary named her Fanny for the friend who had meant so much to her. The Imlays were happy in the birth of the baby and seemed increasingly devoted. Gradually, though, Imlay's absences increased in length. When Mary went to

Sweden, he did not join her; unhappy, rarely hearing from him, Mary
went to England. When she found he was in love with a new friend,
she tried to drown herself, but was rescued and brought back to
health by friends, who felt only pity for the man, "who, being in possession of such a friendship and attachment as those of Mary, could
hold them at a trivial price, and like the base Indian, throw a pearl
away, richer than all his tribe."

In 1796, her *Letters Written During a Short Residence in Sweden,
Norway, and Denmark*, were published. Here, she wrote on a variety
of subjects, ranging from her love of the country, fresh air and exercise, her hatred of injustice and oppression, her deep appreciation of
family happiness and tranquility, to her profound conviction that
neutrals are, in the end, losers, not gainers by war, her disgust with
war profiteers, pious frauds, and public executions. When William
Godwin read the book he remarked, "If there was a book calculated to
make a man in love with the author, this appears to me to be the book."

In fact, Godwin did fall in love with Mary Wollstonecraft, courted
her, and married her. Having long contended that "Marriage is a law
and one of the worst laws," they first lived together without benefit
of clergy. Both having reverence for the higher, the inward law, not
the external bond, they decided not to have a marriage ceremony.
Then, when Mary was pregnant, Godwin decided they should have
the wedding ceremony; accordingly, they were wed at Old St. Pancras
Church, March 29, 1797, in the presence of a single witness, Godwin's life-long friend, James Marshal.

Writing to his friend Thomas Wedgwood, Godwin, attempting to
reconcile his theories and his practice, wrote, "Some persons have
found an inconsistency between my practice in this instance and my
doctrines. But I cannot see it. The doctrine of my *Political Justice* is
that an attachment in some degree permanent between two persons of
the opposite sex is right, but that marriage, as practiced in European
countries, is wrong. I still adhere to that opinion. Nothing but a
regard for the happiness of the individual, which I had no right to
injure, could have induced me to submit to an institution which I
wish to see abolished, and which I would recommend to my fellow-
men never to practice, but with the greatest caution."

As a matter of fact, the married life of the Godwins was far from
conventional. They had taken a house at 29, The Polygon, but Godwin had also taken quarters in the Evesham Building, twenty doors
away. Each morning he went to his office after breakfast, and stayed
there until noon, often until dinner time in late afternoon. He and

Mary seldom went out in company together. "I still mean to be independent," Mary wrote a friend.

Godwin's pious mother, who had never been able to understand her son, wrote following his marriage, "Your broken resolution in regard to matrimony encourages me to hope you will ere long embrace the Gospel, that sure word of promise to all believers." She hoped he would be a good husband and father, "filling your place with propriety in both relations," and as he was "transformed in a moral sense," she hoped he might be in a spiritual one, "which last will make you shine with the radiance of the sun forever." Wishing the bride and groom joy, she sent them a box of eggs, and offered them a small featherbed.

The world looked on these arrangements with skepticism or amusement. Mrs. Barbauld told Mrs. Beecroft, "In order to give the connection as little as possible the appearance of such a vulgar and debasing tie as matrimony, the parties have established separate establishments, and the husband only visits his mistress like a lover when each is dressed, rooms in order, etc. And this will possibly last til they have a family, then they will probably live quietly in one ménage, like other folks."

Trying to be amusing, Godwin's friend, Amelia Alderson, wrote to a companion, "Heigho! What charming things would sublime theories be if one could make one's practice keep up with them; but I am convinced it is impossible, and am resolved to make the best of everyday nature." Less charitable was Mrs. Inchbald, on whom Godwin had showered attentions, for she withdrew her invitation to the philosopher to share her box at a theatre party, saying "When you next marry, I may act differently!" She, Mrs. Siddons, Godwin's actress friend, and Mrs. Siddons' sister, Mrs. Twiss, said they could not compromise themselves by being seen with Mary, now that she admitted she and Imlay had not been married.

Others, however, entertained the Godwins frequently and were entertained by them. John Opie, the artist, was painting Mary's portrait.

Husband and wife were truly in love with one another. "I love you," Mary wrote him, "better than I supposed I did when I promised to love you forever—and I will add what will gratify your benevolence if not your heart, that on the whole I may be termed happy. You are a tender, affectionate creature and I feel it thrilling through my frame giving and promising pleasure. . . . A husband is a convenient part of the furniture of a house, unless he be a clumsy fixture. I wish you, from my soul, to be riveted in my heart, but I do not desire to have you always at my elbow . . . though at the moment I should not care if you were." Godwin confessed reading this letter four times, and told Mary how happy she made him.

As her pregnancy continued, Mary spent less time in public. She was busy writing a novel and a set of books for children. She was pleased at the attentions her husband gave her daughter Fanny, and happy in the thought that she was carrying a child, whom they had decided to call William. She had no fear of the ordeal of giving birth to "William"; Fanny's birth had caused her no trouble; this next birth she believed would not prove difficult. In fact, she assured Godwin she would be downstairs to dine with him the day following birth; she was scornful of women who indulged themselves in a month's confinement. She had engaged a Mrs. Blenkinsop, matron and midwife of the Westminster Lying-in Hospital, to attend her, and had been examined by Dr. George Fordyce and Dr. Anthony Carlisle. On Wednesday, August 30, at five o'clock in the morning, her labor pains began. The baby, a girl, was born at 11:20 that night after the mother's continuous pain. After the birth, Mary suffered greatly, and still in acute pain at two o'clock in the morning, she told the midwife to tell Godwin she had not yet discharged the placenta. Rushing to Westminster Hospital, Godwin brought Dr. Poignand, physician and "male midwife," who set to work at once to remove the placenta. He reported to Godwin that it had broken as he removed it, but he had removed all the pieces. He was wrong. Losing a great deal of blood, fainting again and again, Mary continued to suffer. On Thursday afternoon, Mary said she wished to call Dr. Fordyce for consultation. Despite the fact that Dr. Poignand saw no necessity for summoning him, Godwin went for him. At three o'clock he came, and said Mary was out of danger.

On Saturday, despite Godwin's concern and the visits of three doctors, Mary seemed weaker. That night, she had fever and chills. By Tuesday, as she was yet weaker, another physician, Dr. Clarke, was summoned. He wished to operate, but Mary was too weak to withstand the operation to remove the pieces of placenta that were poisoning her. With the group of doctors and another nurse in attendance, everything known excepting surgery was done to relieve her pain. Still suffering, on Sunday evening, September 10, at 2:40 A.M., she died, happy that Godwin wished her baby to be named Mary, and saying of her husband: "He is the kindest, best man in the world."

She was buried in Old St. Pancras Churchyard, near where she had been married. On her headstone, Godwin placed a simple inscription:

Mary Wollstonecraft Godwin
Author of
A Vindication
Of the Rights of Woman:
Born 27 April, 1759:
Died 10 September, 1797.

Too grief stricken to attend her funeral services, Godwin wrote a friend, "There does not exist her equal in the world. I know from experience we were formed to make each other happy."

With two children, Fanny and Mary, to rear, Godwin turned busily to writing, but not until years later did he again emerge as a notable figure. Then, when Malthus attempted to prove the futility of Utopian speculation in a world of excessive population, Godwin arose to answer him. Godwin had married five years after Mary's death, buxom, clever Mrs. Mary Jane Clairmont, a widow with two children and no fortune. To them was born a son, William. Mary Jane's quick temper and obvious dislike of some of Godwin's cronies made her seem "so damn'd disagreeable," said one of Godwin's friends, that they came infrequently to see the philosopher. Aaron Burr, one of Godwin's friends, found her on the contrary "a sensible, amiable woman," who admired her husband tremendously. Accustomed to more luxuries than Godwin could provide, noting always Mary's portrait still hanging in the study, and that many of her husband's friends were admirers of his first wife, her role was not an easy one. Wordsworth was among those who continued to visit Godwin.

Godwin lived to see some of his ideas boomerang. The first explosion came when twenty-year-old, tall, slender, blue-eyed, fairskinned, dark curly-haired Percy Bysshe Shelley, and his childlike young wife, diminutive, brown-eyed Harriet came to visit with the philosopher. Idealistic, passionately fond of beauty, Shelley had early felt the spirit of revolt. When only a young boy at Eton, he had rebelled against the fag system which made the younger boys almost servants to those older; fighting those whom he resisted, he gained the name "Mad Shelley." Then, too, he was noted for his love of reading, and his keen appreciation of natural beauty. Many a day, escaping from uncongenial comrades, he tooks his books and, lying on the bank of a stream, read the afternoon away. Other hours he wrote verses, and read them to his delighted sisters, who shuddered at some of his wildly romantic tales. At Oxford, too, he rebelled, this time against religion, astonishing the school authorities by sending them a copy of a pamphlet, *The Necessity of Atheism*, which he circulated throughout the University. Expelled, he eloped with sixteen-year-old Harriet Westbrook, an Oxford schoolgirl, and with her went to Ireland to help that country in its struggle for freedom. Writing pamphlets and circulating them, the two young people tried to arouse the Irish, who seemed reluctant to be saved. Though the eighteen-year-old's ideas were scoffed at, so wise were his statements, today considered eloquently expressed, that some of the very measures he advocated have since become laws.

Wearying of Ireland, the young couple went to Lynmouth, England, a beautiful place where mountain and sea merge and where streets with picturesque thatch-roofed cottages climb up steep hills. Back in London, writing poetry, and comparatively happy with Harriet, he discovered that William Godwin, whose books he admired, was still living. So wise were Godwin's books that Shelley had surmised the philosopher must surely have been dead a long time!

Harriet wrote how she and her husband loved the philosopher and his whole family. "His manners are so soft and pleasing that I defy even an enemy to be displeased with him. There is one of the daughters of that dear Mary Wollstonecraft living with him. She (Fanny) is nineteen years of age, very plain, but very sensible. The beauty of her mind fully over-balances her countenance. There is another daughter (Mary) who is very like her mother, whose picture hangs in the study. She must have been a most lovely woman. Her countenance bespeaks her a woman who would dare to think and act for herself. I wish you could share the pleasure we enjoy in his company. He is quite a family man. He has one son by his present wife, a little boy of nine years old. He is extremely clever, and no doubt will follow the same enlightened path that Godwin has, before him."

Christine Baxter, a friend of the Godwins, told of the third girl in the household, Claire Clairmont, who was "lively, and quick-witted, and probably unmanageable. Fanny was more reflective, less sanguine, more alive to the prosaic obligations of life, and possessed of a keen sense of domestic duty, early developed in her by necessity and by her position as the eldest of this somewhat anomalous family. Godwin, by nature as undemonstrative as possible, showed more affection to Fanny than to anyone else. He always turned to her for any little service. . . . It seemed as though he would fain have guarded against the possibility of her feeling that she, an orphan, was less to him than the others. To Godwin, she had always seemed like his eldest child, the first he had cared for or who had been fond of him. His dependence on her was not surprising, for no daughter would have tended him with more solicitous care; besides which, she was one of those people willing to do anything for anybody, who are always at the beck and call of others, and was always in request."

Others wrote more penetratingly of Fanny's shyness, sensitivity, and melancholy. Her half sister, Claire Clairmont, once wrote her, "Now do not be melancholy, for heaven's sake, be cheerful; so young in life and so melancholy!" Fanny replied that she could not change her disposition, however much she might wish to. "I cannot help envying you your calm, contented disposition, and the calm philosophical habits of life which pursue you, or rather which you pursue everywhere."

Aaron Burr recalled how, at that time, nine-year-old William, having heard how some important men lectured, decided "he would also lecture; and one of his sisters (Mary, I think) writes a lecture which he reads from a little pulpit which they have erected for him. He went through it with great gravity and decorum. The subject was, 'The influence of governments on the character of a people.' After the lecture, we had tea, and the girls danced and sang for an hour, and at nine (I) came home."

Little Mary with her piercing gray eyes and auburn hair, though equally sensitive, had a more cheerful disposition than Fanny. Even as a child, her favorite pastime was writing stories. She appealed especially to the Shelleys.

Two years after they met, while Mary and Shelley were visiting her mother's grave, Shelley told the seventeen-year-old girl that he loved her, and persuaded her, accompanied by Claire Clairmont, to elope with him. True, he had a wife and two children, but had not Godwin written how stupid the marriage ceremony was? Once out of England, they would invite Harriet to join them. When, on July 28, 1814, they went to Calais, France, Mrs. Godwin pursued them, trying in vain to persuade the girls to return home. Instead, they and Shelley traveled through France and Switzerland, where Shelley actually asked Harriet to join them.

Shaken by her sister's actions, Fanny brooded. "I am not well; my mind always keeps my body in a fever." Deciding she would like to leave home and keep occupied, she was encouraged by a friend who attempted to have her mother's sisters take her to Dublin, where she hoped to teach. She had never seen those aunts for whom her mother had done so much, but she agreed to meet Aunt Everina in London, "when my future will be decided." Convinced that with her mother's notoriety, as well as that of her sister Mary and Claire, Fanny would be considered too great a risk, and hence would never be suited to teach young ladies, her aunt so advised Fanny.

Feeling unwanted, Fanny decided that suicide was the only escape. After she left home in October, 1816, apparently to visit her aunts in Dublin, she wrote Godwin, Mary, and Shelley, "I depart immediately to the spot from which I hope never to remove." Both Godwin and Shelley immediately set out separately to seek her; they were stunned by an item in a Bristol newspaper telling of the suicide by laudanum of an unknown young woman, on October 9, at an inn in Swansea. She had left a note: "I have long determined that the best thing I could do was to put an end to the existence of a being whose birth was unfortunate, and whose life has been a series of pain to those persons who have hurt their health in endeavoring to promote her welfare. Perhaps to hear of my death will give you pain, but you will soon have the blessing of forgetting that such a creature ever existed as . . ."

The name had been torn from the page, and the scrap of paper containing it burned. The newspaper said her stockings were marked with the letter "G"; her stays, with the initials "M.W."

Godwin was convinced the girl was Fanny. Desirous, however, of avoiding further scandal, he did not claim the body, but told her friends she had died suddenly of a pulmonary ailment while visiting her aunts. Shelley wrote a poem, her only epitaph, concluding with the words:

"This world is all too wide for thee."

A month later, Harriet Shelley drowned herself; her body was recovered; and on December 29, Mary and Shelley were married. Friends of Godwin were amazed when the old man boasted his daughter had married a baronet. Even Mary smiled in disgust as she remarked, *"Oh, philosophy!"*

Mary's troubles did not end with her marriage. Shelley's debts mounted; their children did not live long; Shelley found one "Soul's sister" after another, always attracted by someone new. He brooded over the Lord Chancellor's statement that followed Harriet's suicide: Shelley's ideas on marriage were so "immoral and vicious," the Lord

Chancellor said, that he could not entrust the poet with the guardianship of his children. They had been placed in the care of an Army doctor, named Hume, who would place the boy, when he was seven, in a good private school under the care of an orthodox clergyman; the little girl, to be reared by Mrs. Hume, would be taught to say morning and evening prayers, to ask a blessing on her food, and to read improving books, and some poetry, including Shakespeare, carefully, and to avoid licentious lines. Shelley could visit his children twelve times a year in the presence of Doctor and Mrs. Hume.

Mary busied herself in writing and in 1817 dedicated her most famous work, *Frankenstein*, a novel about a horrible monster, to her father. A hundred and fifty years later, it is still widely read and frequently dramatized. As Shelley became more unconventional in morals and even in dress, Mary became increasingly conventional, desiring approval.

She delighted in her husband's humanitarianism. He kept a list of those in need, and, a ministering angel, relieved them from his own purse. He encountered a sick woman on Hampstead Heath, going from door to door to seek shelter, and brought her to Leigh Hunt's home where she was cared for. He enjoyed playing or sailing boats with Leigh Hunt's children. The deaths of his and Mary's two children saddened him until he felt at times he

> Could lie down like a tired child
> And weep away the life of care
> Which I have borne and yet must bear.

Believing he could never forget the sight of a feverish dying child, he shunned crowds, depending on a few friends for companionship. Writing poem after poem, he reflected himself in many of them; in none better, perhaps, than in the poem where he compared himself to the moon, writing:

> Art thou pale for weariness
> Of climbing heaven, and gazing on the earth
> Wandering companionless
> Among the stars that have a different birth,
> And ever-changing, like a joyous eye
> That finds no object worth its constancy?

Indeed, Shelley was weary of trying to convince his countrymen that he was sincere as he said that he was dissatisfied with England as it was, because he knew there should be and could be a better England. At twenty, expelled from Oxford, he had set out to reform mankind, beginning with Ireland. In his "Address to the Irish People," he had tried to show them that "Catholic Emancipation, Universal Suffrage, and the Repeal of the Union" were essential for Ireland's salvation. The Irish heeded him not and considered him mad. They could not comprehend this man who wanted to be free and happy, but could not be unless everyone around him was free and happy too. He warred against convention, because he believed it imposed on men unreasonable disciplines; self alone, he contended, can control self. He dreamed of a golden age when man would be

> Equal, unclassed, tribeless, and nationless,
> Exempt from awe, worship, degree, the king
> Over himself . . . .

Realizing there would be a long and hard struggle to improve the physical surroundings, education, and working conditions of the masses, he gave concrete suggestions for bringing about these better conditions. Annual parliaments would help educate the electorate by keeping politics constantly before them. Both in his youth and in his later years, he said he advocated not universal suffrage but gradual extension of the suffrage until the ignorant were prepared for it. To this end, he wished "abolition of rotten boroughs, enfranchisement of large unrepresented towns, with perhaps a property qualification." He wished all England to vote on whether Parliament should reform itself. Wider suffrage, he believed, necessitated universal education at public expense. Other changes he pled for included disbanding the standing army, complete religious toleration, abolition of sinecures and tithes, and disestablishment of the Church of England. "There is no real wealth but the labor of man," he contended, as he attacked the large landowners whom he considered a menace. The ideal government was a Republic, he reminded his readers. Women when bound by even stronger conventions than men, he considered a hindrance to true liberty; but once emancipated, women, he knew, would be a strong constructive force. His ideal society required also extensive prison reforms. Last, he advocated vegetarianism, contending that the consumption of animal food makes us cruel, if not depraved. In "A Philosophical View of Reform," he said he hoped the reforms he envisioned could come about through Parliament; if they could not, then they had to come through violence. Liberty must be preserved. And what is Liberty? Shelley had an answer:

For the labourer thou art bread,
And a comely table spread
For his daily labour come
To a neat and happy home.
Thou art clothes, and fire, and food
For the trampled multitude
No—in countries that are free
Such starvation cannot be
As in England now we see.

Many of his countrymen believed, despite these words, that Shelley was the demon of change; few saw him as the angel of revolt. In Germany and Italy, however, he was revered as were his beliefs.

One July day, Shelley and his friend, Edward Williams, set sail for Lerici, before a gathering storm. They never reached shore, though their wives watched for them anxiously for eleven days. Then, the badly mutilated bodies were washed ashore, Shelley's having in a pocket two books, a Sophocles and a Keats, the latter turned back as though it had just been read.

Mary wished the body to be buried near that of their little boy in the Roman cemetery her husband had thought so beautiful; but the sanitary laws forbade bodies once interred in quicklime being so buried. On discovering the mutilated bodies, Trelawny, a friend of Shelley's, had buried the bodies in quicklime temporarily, to preserve them from the sea, and then had notified Mary of the deaths. He now suggested that the bodies be burned and the ashes buried. The bodies were burned on the shore, but as Shelley's heart withstood the flames, Trelawny snatched it from the fire. It and Shelley's ashes were buried in the Protestant Cemetery in Rome, near the grave of John Keats. To his epitaph, Trelawny added Shakespeare's words:

Nothing of him doth fade,
But doth suffer a sea change
Into something rich and strange.

After Shelley's death, Mary sought to prove her affection for him and to clear his name from criticism. She wrote voluminously to gain money to give her son a conventional education, hoping he would think "like other people," never unmindful that one day he would be a baronet. Not until he had inherited his title and fortune and until she had chosen the proper wife for him did she relax. Told in 1823 that she resembled her mother, Mary told Leigh Hunt, "This is the most flattering thing anyone could say of me."

Godwin, concerned about Mary's conduct, was proud when his son William after several attempts at commercial enterprises, toward which his education had been directed, turned from engineering and architecture to literature. His essays and a novel, his father considered "strong"; he was a reporter on the *Morning Chronicle* and founded a literary society, "The Mulberries." His bad manners and his too frequent visits annoyed some of his father's friends, including Charles Lamb. He died in 1832 during a cholera epidemic.

Godwin's teachings boomeranged again when his stepdaughter Claire pursued George Gordon, Lord Byron, twenty-eight, sought after by many women. Byron had been bombarded by love letters from an unknown lady who also sought, in vain, admission to his home. Finally, she signed her name Claire Clairmont, and asked that Byron recommend her to the director of Drury Lane Theatre. When this favor was granted, Godwin's stepdaughter grew bolder, saying that she had loved Byron for a year. "I do not expect you to love me; I am not worthy of your love . . . Have you any objection to the following plan? On Thursday evening, we may go out of town together by some stage or mail; about the distance of ten or twelve miles. There we shall be free and unknown; we can return early the following morning . . ."

Not hearing from him, a few days later, she again asked when, how, and where Byron would meet her. Bored, surfeited by women who pursued him, Byron was intrigued by the thought of a pretty girl with a lovely voice. Feeling jaded, he decided that a new "sensation" might prove stimulating and so agreed to spend the night with her.

Lord Byron, a dashingly handsome young man, was the son of "Mad Jack Byron," who died when the boy was three, and of a silly mother possessing a violent temper, who alternately spoiled and punished him. Distressed, as he suffered from a brace on his club foot, he was yet more deeply hurt by hearing his mother call him "a lame brat," a taunt for which he never forgave her. At ten, he inherited the title "Lord Byron" and the family estates. His education at Harrow and Cambridge was marked with distinction, though at the University he posed as a gentleman of leisure who studied little. As a matter of fact, he studied hard and spent much time writing. Always dramatic, he used as his favorite drinking cup a human skull. Excelling in some athletic feats, he swam the Hellespont. When the *Edinburgh Review* criticized his first poems, he retaliated by attacking a group of poets, including Wordsworth, whose verses he called "simply inane prose"; Dryden and Pope, he said, were real poets. After two years of conti-

Wordsworth's "Daffodils" by the Lake,
From a photograph by G. P. Abrahamson,
Keswick

"The Trees at Grasmere," from a photograph
by G. P. Abrahamson, Keswick

The Mountains and Valley at Grasmere,
photographed by G. P. Abrahamson, Keswick

William Wordsworth, by Robert Hancock
(1798), National Portrait Gallery, London

Mary Wollstonecraft, from the portrait by John Opie, National Portrait
Gallery

nental travel, coming home with a "collection of marbles, skulls, and hemlocks, tortoises and servants," he wrote two cantos of *Childe Harold's Pilgrimage*, "awoke and found himself famous." Fascinating did Englishmen find these highly colored romantic accounts of Spain, Portugal, Albania, Greece, and Turkey. Eagerly sought out and fawned upon, Byron basked in his popularity, asking, indolently, why women found him so attractive. His marriage, at twenty-seven, to Anne Isabella Milbanke, who like others had pursued him, was followed within a year by a separation and a divorce; she charged him with committing adultery with his half-sister. And now, here was Claire Clairmont asking him to spend a night with her.

Journeying in a superb carriage, modeled after that of Emperor Napoleon, Byron set out to meet Godwin's stepdaughter. The night proved interesting; but Byron soon forgot the lady until in May, in Italy, he met her traveling with her sister Mary and Shelley. For Claire, he had neither respect nor love; yet, every evening she came up to Byron's home to join her lover, leaving at daybreak. She worked tirelessly copying for him his verses for his poems, *The Prisoner of Chillon* and the new stanzas for *Childe Harold*. Melancholy, when she discovered she was bearing his child, she found him merely bored. He would bring up the child, but he didn't care if he never saw Claire again. Shelley, dazzled by Byron's brilliance, was yet infuriated at his treatment of Claire.

When, on January 12, 1817, the baby was born, Mary Shelley wrote her father of the new child, announcing at the same time her marriage to Shelley. The latter wrote to Byron, saying that the baby "is very beautiful and although her frame is of somewhat a delicate texture, enjoys excellent health. Her eyes are the most intelligent I ever saw in so young an infant. Her hair is black, her eyes deeply blue, and her mouth exquisitely shaped. She passes here for the child of a friend in London, sent into the country for her health . . ." Byron wrote a friend quite casually that "Shelley has written to me about my daughter (the last bastard one), who it seems is a great beauty; and wants to know what he is to do about sending her . . . will you think of some place for remitting her here, or placing her in England? I shall acknowledge and breed her myself, giving her the name of Biron (to distinguish her from little Legitimacy), and mean to christen her Allegra, which is a Venetian name." Fourteen months after the child's birth, when requesting that a friend bring him the purchase-deeds of Newstead for signature, he seemed to remember he had some responsibilities for his child. In a letter unequalled for callousness and obviously written to shock the recipient, he wrote, "A clerk can bring the papers (and, by the bye, my *child*, by *Claire* at the same time. Pray desire Shelley to pack it carefully), with *tooth-powder, red only*; magnesia, soda-powders, toothbrushes, diachylon plasters, and any new novels good for anything."

When the Shelleys came to Milan, Shelley had a Swiss nurse bring little Allegra to her father. Discovering the baby really was beautiful and greatly favored by the Venetian women to whom he showed her, Byron was proud of his daughter "who is more like Lady Byron than her mother, she has very blue eyes, and that singular forehead, fair, curly hair, and a devil of a spirit—but that is papa's." On his frequent visits with his child, Byron continued to enjoy her pallid beauty. Yes, she was a real Byron: she could not pronounce the letter *r*, likewise a stumbling block long ago to Byron's sister and himself; her eyebrows were often drawn into a little frown; her voice was soft but her will like iron. He was rearing her in the Catholic faith, to Claire's dismay. When political conditions in Italy became explosive, he placed Allegra in a convent close to Ravenna, where the nuns of Bagnacavallo could look after her. He refused to allow Claire to see her; he was determined Allegra would receive a good, Catholic, moral up-bringing and marry an Italian youth. Claire wrote him frantic letters which seemed only to bring out the cruelty in him. "If Claire thinks she shall ever interfere with the child's morals or education, she mistakes; she never shall," he reiterated.

When Claire was told by friends that the convent at Bagnacavallo was not heated in the winter, and that the climate there was unhealthy, she again implored Byron to place Allegra in a better location. Shelley, distraught by Byron's callous treatment of Claire, tactfully visited Byron at Ravenna where Byron wished to discuss the fate of Allegra should Byron leave Ravenna, near which was located the convent where Allegra was living. Byron's latest mistress wished to live in Switzerland. Could not Shelley describe life in Rome or Pisa as so attractive, Byron implored Shelley, that she would prefer to go there? Shelley, who had never seen the mistress, not only persuaded her to go with Byron to Pisa but to take Allegra also.

Before leaving Ravenna, Shelley visited the five-year-old Allegra. The shy, delicate, pale, little girl with lovely black curls seemed not so vivacious as she had been. When given a gold chain Shelley had brought her, she became less shy, almost friendly, as skipping and running, she led him through the convent garden to her room and showed him her bed and chair.

"What shall I say to your mama?" he asked.

"That she send me a kiss and a beautiful dress."

"And how do you wish the dress to be made?"

"Of silk and gold."

Asked what he should tell her father, Allegra replied, "That he come to see me and that he bring my dear mother with him."

As Shelley talked with Allegra, she recited a great many prayers she knew, spoke of Paradise, of which she often dreamed, and told him of many Saints. Shelley considered her education defective. But she was receiving the kind of training Byron desired. Shelley left, telling her she would soon visit him in Pisa with her father. She did not, for Byron came without her.

Shortly after Byron's visit to the Shelleys, they received word from him that Allegra had died. A typhus epidemic had broken out in Romagna; the nuns had taken no preventive measures; Allegra, always frail, had contracted the disease and died. Byron, never willing to believe he had condemned his daughter to this fate, had loved Allegra in his own way. He had spoken of taking her abroad with him and of her being the companion of his old age. Deeply hurt by her death, he turned to cynicism as he often did, saying, "She is more fortunate than we are; besides, her position in the world would scarcely have allowed her to be happy. It is God's will—let us mention it no more." Shelley wrote Byron that Claire asked to see the coffin "before it is sent to England. . . . She also wishes you would give her a portrait of Allegra, and if you have it, a lock of her hair, however small." Byron immediately sent a pretty miniature and a dark curl.

Byron asked that Allegra be buried "in Harrow Church: there is a spot in the Churchyard, near the footpath, on the brow of a hill looking towards Windsor, and a tomb under a large tree (bearing the name of Peachie, or Peachey) where I used to sit for hours and hours when a boy; this was my favorite spot; but, as I wish a tablet to be erected in her memory, the body had better be deposited in the Church. Near the door, on the left hand as you enter, there is a monument with a tablet containing these words:

> When sorrow weeps o'er Virtue's sacred dust
> Our tears become us, and our Grief is just;
> Such were the tears she shed, who grateful pays
> This last sad tribute of her love and praise.

I recollect them (after seventeen years) not from anything remarkable in them, but because from my seat in the Gallery I had generally

my eyes turned toward that monument; as near it as convenient I
could wish Allegra to be buried, and on the wall a marble tablet placed,
with these words:

In memory of
ALLEGRA
daughter of G. G. Lord Byron,
who died at Bagnocavallo,
In Italy, April 20, 1822,
aged five years and three months.
I shall go to her, but she shall not return to me.
2nd SAMUEL, *xii, 23.*

The churchwardens at Harrow disregarded Byron's careful directions, considering it not fitting to bury a natural child within the
church. In the graveyard crowning the hill was placed in the turf a
rose tree to mark, as it still does, the restingplace of Byron's and
Claire's daughter.

Though scorned by many in England, Byron had his admirers
there. Tom Moore, Leigh Hunt, and many a man of letters recognizing his genius, came to Italy to visit him. While England had found
his *Childe Harold's Pilgrimage* exciting, and others had found it the
work of a real poet, even more enthusiastic, the Italians awaited in
crowds each new canto of his *Don Juan*. Since some seemed to believe the adventures of the hero were the author's, he willingly im-
plied that they were, even assuming thereby the credit or discredit
of murdering a Turkish hero who was a creature of his imagination.
Tasting fully whatever life had to offer, Byron, weary of dissipation,
threw himself into the cause of the Greeks struggling against the
Turks.

He had always been interested in the problems of man's conduct as
an individual and as a citizen, and had sought a solution for the difficulties man faced in his society. Man, he believed, was best in simple,
rural societies; cities, art, and laws made him evil. He wrote of
Daniel Boone and the Kentucky pioneers that they were cheerful in
their toil in America;

> Corruption could not make their hearts her soil;
> The lust which stings, the splendour which encumbers,
> With the free foresters divide no spoil:
> Serene, not sullen, were the solitudes
> Of this unsighing people of the woods.

Believing that society corrupted men, he had contempt for it. Naturally, then, he loved the ruder, more primitive people; he favored the Italians, Greeks, and South Sea Islanders, whom he considered unspoiled. Like his predecessors in revolt, he railed against society, which he felt was often vicious. He wrote:

> Eternal Spirit of the chainless mind!
> Brightest in dungeons, Liberty! thou art,
> For there thy habitation is the human heart.
>
> . . . . They never fail who die
> In a great cause: the block may soak their gore;
> Their heads may sodden in the sun; their limbs
> Be strung to city gates and castle walls—
> But still their spirit walks abroad . . . . .

He was the friend of the poor and oppressed from the time he gave his first speech in the House of Lords, defending the weavers who had taken part in the agitation against the installation of machinery. These men, whose lives, he said, the House of Lords values as "something less than the price of a stocking-frame," are the people of England, not to be dismissed as a mob. "Are we aware of our obligations to a mob?" he asked the House. "It is the mob that labours in your fields and serves in your houses—that mans your navy and recruits your army—that has enabled you to defy all the world and can also defy you when neglect and calamity have driven them to despair. You may call the people a mob; but do not forget that a mob too often speaks the sentiments of the people." Mindful of the fact that he was an aristocrat—and proud of the fact—he disliked popular agitators. Yet, he chided England for caring more for contentment than for truth. In fact, he declared English society "was built on cowardice. It was organized stupidity." England, he said, once stood for freedom; but that day is past. Now England, who once

> . . . . held out freedom to mankind
> . . . now would chain them—to the very mind.

"I," he said, "was born to opposition," and so saying, he despaired.

When Greece struggled against Turkish domination, he set about raising money for the Greeks. He gave unsparingly of his own fortune; he kept in control a rebellious band of Suloites, inspiring the soldiers with enthusiasm and affection. Before he could take active part in the campaign, he died in the swamps of Missolonghi; hardened soldiers, remembering his kindnesses to them, wept. All Greece went into mourning for him. As the Dean of Westminster Abbey denied him burial in that shrine with other poets, he was interred in the family vault at Hucknall Torkard, Newstead, where many of the local gentry held their heads high, still condemning him. Indeed, Byron might have expected their scorn, for he once wrote,

> He who ascends to the mountain tops shall find
> The loftiest peaks most wrapped in clouds and snow,
> He who surpasses or subdues mankind
> Must look down on the hate of those below.

The hero of *Childe Harold* had said, as certainly Byron must often have thought,

> I have not loved the world, nor the world me—
> But let us part fair foes . . . .

Claire spent most of her later life on the continent; for a time she was a governess in Russia. When Shelley's father died, she came into an inheritance left her by the poet, which freed her from poverty. She spent considerable time writing a book in which she intended to point out, using Shelley, Byron, and herself as examples, how essential it was to have only conventional ideas on love. Her last years were spent in Florence, where she became a Catholic, devoting herself to charities. In 1878, when a young man asked Claire if she had ever loved anyone, she smiled and said she had loved Shelley "with all my heart and soul."

Godwin, in the meantime, suffering from the actions of his children and from financial troubles, gained considerable attention when he answered Malthus' alarming statement, well bolstered with statistics to prove its point, that population was increasing more rapidly than the means of subsistence could be made to increase. Godwin contended that with the development of machinery and with more intensive farming, the production of food would multiply. This answer was bitterly assailed by the powerful *Edinburgh Review* as the work of one "showing his age"; Godwin fared better at the hands of critics of *The Quarterly Review*, but even that magazine was convinced Malthus had spoken more wisely. When Mary Shelley returned to England, he saw her several times a week, gaining intellectual stimulus from her as he did from men like William Hazlitt, who were convinced that the ideas in *Political Justice* would be quoted for years. The government, recognizing Godwin's greatness, gave him the position of Yeoman Usher of the Exchequer, which carried with it a house and adequate income to permit him to live comfortably; it brought him financial security and physical comfort. He, who had derided organized government, spent his last years supported by government. He died in his eightieth year from a severe cold and fever. He was buried beside Mary Wollstonecraft Godwin; and on the small monument bearing her name was added "William Godwin, Author of *Political Justice*," and the dates of his birth and death. In 1851, the bodies were moved to St. Peter's, Bournemouth, but the monument still stands at Old St. Pancras.

Young William Wordsworth, admirer of Godwin, was in London in 1793, still unable to secure a position; at length, he tried to find a tutorial job. He was invited in June by a former classmate at Hawkshead, William Calvert, to accompany him, all expenses paid, on a holiday to the West of England. The Calvert boys, William and Raisley, had inherited their father's modest fortune two years earlier. Wordsworth and William Calvert went first to the Isle of Wight. Still harassed by the struggles for French independence, William was troubled at times by the sight of the English fleet, recently returned from France, now lying at anchor nearby. When, each evening passing by the seashore, he heard "the sunset cannon's roar" from the ships in the distance, a "monitary sound that never failed," his spirits always sank as he experienced

> Imaginations, sense of woes to come,
> Sorrow for all mankind, and pain of heart.

He found some peace, however, on the Isle of Wight. For a whole month of "calm and glassy days," he enjoyed long hikes

> . . . along the woody steep
> When all the summer seas are charmed to sleep
> While on the distant sands the tide retires.

Expecting to be in Halifax by October, he continued plans he had secretly made to see Dorothy, whose companionship he had longed for; she agreed to meet him there. He did not reach Halifax, however, until February, 1794.

Meantime, young Calvert and William Wordsworth, leaving the Isle of Wight and traveling in a "whiskey" across the Salisbury Plain, found their tour interrupted when their vehicle broke down. Young Calvert rode north on his horse to the nearest destination, leaving the "whiskey" behind, and returned to London. William, however, now

pleased to have a solitary vacation, walked from Salisbury into Wales.
As he crossed Salisbury Plain, enjoying nature, he reveled in roaming

> . . . . from rock to rock
> Still craving combinations of new forms,
> New pleasure, wider empire for the sight.

Yet, restless, he confided he was

> . . . . more like a man
> Flying from something that he dreads than one
> Who sought the thing he loved.

Within sight of Stonehenge, that great circle of stones used in earlier
days, he believed, by the druids in their worship, he contemplated the
"savagery" of ancient man. Melancholy, he was made more so by the
dreary wheatfields stretching mile after mile, by the whistling winds
that swept the thin grass, and even by the lark singing its "wasted
strain" and the

> Crows in blackening eddies house-ward borne . . .

Going by way of Bath and Bristol, then along the banks of the
Wye, he proceeded to South and North Wales and finally to the
Vale of Clwyd, where he dwelt with the father of his friend, Robert
Jones. As three of the Jones girls were at home, he did not lack
youthful companions.

In October 1793, he probably went to France to see Annette and
little Caroline and to contact his Girondist friends who had been declared outlaws in July. Some Girondists had fled throughout France;
some were in hiding in Paris; others had been guillotined. Annette's
letters telling of her devotion to William still left him distraught.
She told him of the misfortunes her Royalist family was undergoing.
Her brother Paul, accused of complicity, had had to go into hiding;
nine of their Orleans friends had been guillotined; Annette, at risk of
her own life, had aided her brother and their friends. Because of her
"over-generous disposition she and her daughter had to struggle
through many difficulties." Their correspondence made obvious the
fact that many of Annette's letters to Wordsworth and his to her had
not reached their destination. She still wrote of her deep love for him.

To undertake a journey to France at war with itself and with
England was to court trouble. Yet, undoubtedly William went, for he
later told Carlyle he had witnessed the struggle of the Girondists and
"the execution of Gorsas, 'the first Deputy sent to the Scaffold,' and
testified strongly to the ominous feeling which that event produced

in everybody," and of its effect on him. "Where will it *end*, when you have set an example of this kind?" he asked Carlyle. Gorsas was executed on October 7, 1793; the other twenty-eight Girondists in Paris followed their leader to the guillotine on October 31; the following day the Convention passed a decree ordering the arrest of all foreigners; more executions followed; terror mounted. Alaric Watts, a journalist, says "an old republican in Paris told of warning William Wordsworth that his life was in danger and that the young poet 'decamped with great precipitation.' " He had apparently been unable to get to Orleans or Blois to see Annette and Caroline.

Back in England, he relived, not just for days but for years, the carnage he had witnessed in France, as

> The maiden from the bosom of her love,
> The mother from the cradle of her babe,
> The warrior from the field—all perished, all
> Friends, enemies, of all parties, ages, ranks,
> Head after head, and never heads enough
> For those that bade them fall.

These, he said,

> Were my day-thoughts—my nights were miserable;
> Through months, through years, long after the last beat
> Of those atrocities, the hour of sleep
> To me came rarely charged with natural gifts . . .

At times, he dreamed he was imprisoned, awaiting

> . . . sacrifice, and struggling with false mirth
> And levity in dungeons, where the dust
> Was laid with tears. Then suddenly the scene
> Changed, and the unbroken dream entangled me
> In long orations, which I strove to plead
> Before unjust tribunals—with a voice
> Labouring, a brain confounded, and a sense
> Death-like, of treacherous desertion felt
> In the last place of refuge—my own soul.

Whether William suffered because of the deaths and destruction he saw or because of the sense of guilt coming from his relationship with Annette, the fact remains he really suffered. For several weeks he was in Cumberland; he spent some time with the Calverts at Windy Brow, a farmhouse at Keswick they had built, and then with another schoolmate, John Speedings at Armathwaite. In February, he joined Dorothy who brought solace and comfort to him.

CHAPTER IV

"Release from Captivity"

WHEN WILLIAM LEFT FOR CAMBRIDGE, IN 1788, DOROTHY LOOKED FORWARD TO ANOTHER DREARY YEAR WITH HER grandmother at Penrith. Instead, she secured what seemed a release from captivity as in October of that year her Uncle William, just appointed rector at Forncett, told her he was to marry Miss Dorothy Cowper, and wished her and William Monkhouse to be witnesses at the wedding. Moreover, he and his bride-to-be asked her to live with them in Forncett. In the fall, after the wedding breakfast, Dorothy and the newly wed couple set out for Forncett, first visiting friends in Newcastle. Dorothy spent a day with William in Cambridge. Delighted to find him in good spirits, she walked with him in the college courts and groves. She was intrigued by the appearance of the students with powdered hair, wearing gowns similar to those worn by the clergy, "black caps like helmets except that they have a square of wood at the top." "This costume," she said, "may sound very strange, but it is exceedingly becoming." As she and William visited together, for the first time he deeply realized her worth; "she seemed a gift bestowed," for she gave him admiration he craved; her deep appreciation of nature stimulated him as she pointed out scenes and shared her impressions. He became her favorite brother before long, first, because she believed he needed her; John and Richard were happily settled in life, while Kit was still her beloved "little brother." Second, Dorothy realized anew how she and William inspired each other.

The newly-wedded couple and Dorothy stopped briefly at Norwich, a city "with ugly streets, all so ill-paved and dirty as almost to take away the pleasure of walking." In December, when they reached Forncett, a little village, they drove to the rectory through a fine avenue of limes, beautiful even in their bare, leafless state. Their house, spacious and comfortable, Dorothy was certain could be made an excellent home. The "gardens will be charming," she wrote. "I intend to be a great gardener and promise myself much pleasure in taking care of the poultry which we are to have in great abundance . . . we have sketched out a plan of the manner in which we are to spend our time. . . . We are to have prayers at nine o'clock (you will observe it is winter), after breakfast is over we are to read, write, and I am to improve myself in French until twelve o'clock, when we are to talk or visit our sick and poor neighbors till three, which is our dining hour, and after tea my uncle will sit with us and either read to us or not as he and we find ourselves inclined. I enjoy the idea of spending Christmas in the country. We have had many consultations in what manner we are to spend my birthday, but we have at least agreed upon roast beef and plum pudding as the best Christmas day dinner."

Close by the rectory stood the little church of St. Peter where her uncle was to hold services. It had an eleventh-century tower, erected by the Normans, and oak pews, on which had been carved in the fifteenth century, heads of "priest and penitent, falconer and sower, butcher and baker." Yes, the church had seen much of life—and of death, too, for in the churchyard were graves of those who had worshipped at St. Peter's.

Life at Forncett, Dorothy enjoyed, though it was usually uneventful. She, her uncle, and her aunt were invited to teas, card parties, and dances at Norwich, by "the genteelest families in the place," who, Dorothy found, were "so ridiculous as to send invitations three weeks or a month in advance. We had an invitation come on the 26th of November for the 18th of December, for tea and cards,—can anything be more absurd? I cannot help thinking how my grandmother and the old ladies at Penrith would stare at this. They exclaim against the idleness and folly of the age and say it is impossible to secure company unless you send two or three days before you intend to receive them." Occasionally, Dorothy and the Cooksons attended the theatre in Norwich.

At Forncett, in the winter, she and her aunt took long walks, early in the morning and late at night even when it snowed violently, striding through the deep snow in "half boots and spatter-dashes." In spring and summer, Dorothy walked through the woods "full of the melody of birds" and in the fields scarlet with poppies, where thrush, bullfinches, blackbirds and yellowhammers made their nests. Occasionally, she rode her uncle's horse. Indoors, she and her aunt sewed on what seemed mountains of needed linens, while through the open windows came the songs of larks that made their nests in the nearby churchyard. Often at dawn, she was awakened by the singing of a nightingale. She read and reread Pope's works, explored Hume's *History of England*, a book on regeneration, and reread the New Testament with Doddridge's exposition. When Jane wrote of her gay Christmas whirl, Dorothy confessed she had not been to one ball, one play, one concert. Her brother John, with the East India Company, kept in touch with her, despite long trips to Jamaica, the East Indies, and India. Richard, hardworking in London, wrote her frequently and sent her a handsome beaver hat, "a very extravagant gift," she said. William wrote of his life at Cambridge, and of his travels. Kit, she discovered, was more like William than were her other brothers.

In 1789, a visit of the celebrated William Wilberforce, now campaigning to abolish the slave trade, aroused Dorothy who promptly asked Jane to persuade her father to vote for him in the next election. She, in turn, made so favorable an impression on Mr. Wilberforce that he promised her ten guineas a year to distribute among the poor in Forncett and sent her a copy of a volume on regeneration, and Mrs. Trimmer's *Oeconomy of Charity*, a book that gave suggestions on improving Sunday Schools, and told of means of improving the condition of the poor by making them the subject of private benevolence and by forming committees and associations for their relief.

Energetic and creative, she saw that a school was needed. Hence, she organized one with nine pupils whom she taught reading and spelling, prayers, hymns, and the catechism. She had one very bright scholar, some "very tolerable," and one or two very bad. She distributed awards, such as books, caps, and aprons, to encourage incentive. The hours of the school were, on Sundays, from nine to church-time, from half-past-one until three, and in the evening, from four until half-past-five; those who lived near the rectory came also on Wednesday and Saturday evenings. In time, Dorothy and her uncle planned to have a school upon a more extensive plan; Dorothy's was to be only a temporary one. Soon, she hoped to have a mistress who would teach the children spinning and knitting on the week days; Dorothy was to assist her by teaching reading on Sundays. In addition to her teaching, Dorothy visited the poor and did what she could to aid those in need.

The monotony of life at Forncett was broken in 1790 when news came of the wedding of Aunt Threlkeld to Samuel Rawson, a wealthy widower who owned cotton mills. Yet more exciting was the arrival of William, who spent six weeks at Forncett before going to Cambridge to take his degree. The two had not met for eighteen months, for he had spent the previous summer on a walking tour through France and Switzerland. He had written her of his travels and she had traced his trip on maps, often wondering, she told Jane, "that his strength and courage have not sunk under the fatigue he must have undergone"; he says, however, "that they have frequently performed a journey of fifteen leagues, (thirty-nine miles, you know) over the mountainous parts of Switzerland, without feeling more weariness than if they had been sauntering an hour in the groves of Cambridge, they are so innured to walking." He told his sister he had thought of her perpetually on his trip, and "never have my eyes burst upon a scene of particular loveliness but I have almost instantly wished that you could for a moment be transported to the place where I stood to enjoy it." Now that they were together again for a brief visit at Forncett they were as devoted to each other as they had been as children.

As the Cookson family grew, there were increasing demands on Dorothy's time. In 1790, Mary was born; a year later, Christopher; in 1792, another son, William. As Uncle William's family grew, his clerical duties also increased, for in 1792 he was made rector of Windsor, as well as of Forncett. The end of July, the family went to Windsor, where they were to remain three months.

Dorothy was charmed with Windsor; there, she soon made many friends. The Royal Family had come to spend a fortnight. As Dorothy met them on the terrace, she said, "I fancied myself treading upon faery ground, and that the company surrounding me were brought there by enchantment. The King and several of the princesses were advancing, the Queen's band was playing most delightfully, and all around me I saw only well-dressed smart people. What a different scene from that I had quitted a week before! The King stopped to talk with my uncle and aunt, and to play with the children, who, though not acquainted with the new-fangled doctrine of liberty and equality, thought a king's stick as fair game as any other man's, and that princesses were not better than mere cousin Dollys. I think it is impossible to see the King and his family at Windsor without loving them, even if you eye them with impartiality and consider them really a man and women, not as king and princesses; but I own I am too much an aristocrat or what you please to call me, not to reverence him because he is a monarch more than I should were he a private gentleman, and not to see with pleasure his daughters treated with more respect than ordinary people. I say it is impossible to see them at *Windsor* without loving them, because at Windsor they are seen unattended by pomp or state, and they seem so desirous to please that nothing but ill-nature or envy can help being pleased. The king's good nature shows itself in no instance so much as in his affection for children. He was quite delighted with William and Mary. Mary, he considers as a great beauty and desired the Duke of York to come from one side of the Terrace to the other to look at her." Dorothy insisted she was not dazzled with the splendor of royalty; yet, she thought the Princess Royal and Princess Mary were beautiful; the former had "all the dignity becoming her high rank with a great deal of grace"; the latter, "the winning graces of sixteen." At times, Dorothy enjoyed watching the Queen drive in a little park in a phaeton with four white ponies attended by several people on horseback. At this time, William, in France, had no sympathy for royalty, but was aflame with enthusiasm for the French Revolution.

At Windsor, life was gay. Dorothy attended races, monthly balls, and weekly card parties ending in dances. She had not danced for five years, but soon felt at ease, provided she had a good partner. The splendors of society, however, palled in a short time, and she longed for the quiet life in the country.

On her return to Forncett, Dorothy was again, she said, "head nurse, housekeeper, tutoress of the little ones, or rather superintendent of the nursery. I am at present a very busy woman and literally *steal* the moments which I employ in letter writing." Her aunt, who had just borne another child, "does not gain strength so fast as I had expected . . . I am still obliged to sleep in her room, as she goes to bed as early as nine o'clock, which robs me of the most precious hours, as I go to bed at the same time, and as she sleeps very indifferently at nights, I am obliged to lie very long in the mornings for fear of disturbing her."

William, she knew, was soon to return from France. Daydreaming, she remembered his plans that he and she would find a cottage and there live happily together. William had conceived the idea of Dorothy's leading a secluded life with him in a cottage, small and unpretentious, where the golden days together would be tranquil but fraught with inspiration. In her dreams, Dorothy had planned their future until her dreams seemed almost a reality. "When I think of winter," she had written her friend Jane Pollard, "I hasten to furnish our little parlour, I close the shutters, set out the tea-table, brighten the fire. When our refreshment is ended, I produce our work, and William brings his book to our table and contributes at once to our instruction and amusement, and at intervals we lay aside the book and each hazard our observations upon what has been read, without the fear of ridicule or censure. We talk over past days; we do not sigh for any pleasure beyond our humble habitation, the central point of all our joys."

She envisioned their lives together in the spring, when "I have strolled into a neighboring meadow, where I am enjoying the melody of birds, and the busy sounds of a fine summer's evening. But, oh! how imperfect is my pleasure when I am alone! Why are you not seated with me?—and my dear William, why is not he here, also? . . . Our parlor is in a moment furnished, our garden is adorned by magic; the roses and honeysuckles spring at our command; the wood behind the house lifts its head and furnishes us with a winter's shelter and a summer's noonday shade."

Back in London, William sent Dorothy his poems, published in London, as proof that he had not been idle, then told her of his liaison with Annette and asked her to intercede for him with Uncle Cookson, who, having discovered that William had declined the Harwich curacy and had lied about his age, was already ill-disposed toward him. Dorothy's first reaction was shock at having her long-held dream of a home with William shattered. Now, she must share that home with another. Moreover, the Wordsworths were middle-class, a group that always had had high moral principles. How Wordsworth, who had planned to be a minister, could have gotten into a situation where he had an illegitimate child by a Catholic girl, seemed beyond comprehension. Concealing her distress, Dorothy agreed, however, to intercede with her uncle, admitting that perhaps "half of the virtues" with which I fancy William is endowed, "are the creations of my love." She then wrote a warm, friendly letter to Annette. Her intercession with Uncle Cookson was unsuccessful, for that clergyman forbade William to enter his home. Annette, on the other hand, responded warmly to Dorothy's letter, saying that once war between France and England was over, William was going to return to marry her, and telling how, when she did not receive a letter from him for nine days, she worried lest he be ill. She told how the baby resembled William and how proud she was of little Caroline. So graciously did Dorothy write to the French girl, that Annette felt her truly a sister of hers, too. In fact, in a letter to Dorothy and William she said, "When we are there, oh sister, how happy we shall be! And you, my dear (Williams), do you wish for that day as passionately as your Annette? When you are surrounded by your sister, your wife, your daughter, who will breathe only for you, we shall have but one feeling, one heart, one soul, and everything will depend on my dear Williams.

Our days will flow along quietly. I shall at last enjoy the calm I do not find except with you, telling you *aloud* that I love you." Thoroughly aware how Dorothy must have suffered because of the relationship between William and herself, Annette wrote Dorothy, "If you feel so tenderly for my lot, I have equally the unpleasantness of yours. . . . O my dear sister, how unhappy I am to know you are so on my account; never, no never, can I repay you for all you suffer for my sake. My beloved shares my gratitude—he has indeed told me—this dearly beloved one—that he had a charming sister, but how is the picture he drew of your soul inferior to what I see in your letter! No, my dear Williams, you had not told me half enough." Amazingly discerning, Annette, when she enclosed a letter to Dorothy with one to William, wrote her lover, "I beseech you, my darling little one, to pass on this letter to my dear sister, whom I love with all my heart, and to charge her to say nothing to your uncle; it would be a painful fight that she would have to sustain." Uncle Cookson, indeed, was taking a serious view of William's laxity as well as at that of many other young people of the day.

As time passed, Dorothy saw her dream house "still obscure and dark, and there is so much ground to fear that my scheme will prove a shadow, a mere vision of happiness." Yet continuing to hope the dream would become a reality, she wrote her friend Jane Pollard of William's being "so amiable, so good, so fond of his sister," that there was no pleasure he would not have "given up with joy for half an hour's conversation with me." She sensed his discouragement and despair when he wrote her that since he was not welcome at his uncle's home, he wished to see her at Halifax. He wrote her how "each emotion of pleasure and pain that visits your heart" excites "a similar pleasure or a similar pain within me, by that sympathy that will almost identify us when we have stolen into our little cottage! I am determined to see you as soon as I have entered into an engagement: immediately I will write my uncle and tell him that I cannot think of going anywhere before I have been with you. Whatever answer he gives me, I most certainly will make a point of once more mingling my translation with yours." A little later, he wrote her, "with what rapture shall I wear out the day in your sight. I assure you, that so eager is my desire to see you that all obstacles vanish. I see you in a moment running or rather flying to my arms." Finally, he wrote Dorothy to plan to meet him in Halifax. She did plan, expecting to meet him in the fall of 1793. The meeting did not materialize, however, until February, 1794. William wandered about visiting friends, not from choice but from compulsion, for he sought thus to escape the troubles that seemed to engulf him.

Dorothy, in the meantime, found life at Forncett no longer joyous. She was devoted to the little children, Mary and Christopher, William and baby George; but she was distressed at her Uncle William's coldness toward her brother William. As his letters stressed his need for her, she finally told her aunt and uncle that she was leaving to be with William. When she left for Halifax, her Uncle William and her aunt, still reluctant to see her go, told her how they would miss her companionship. The children, whose lives she had always shared, could not understand that Aunt Dolly was going away; even the nursemaid wept.

Going first to Aunt Threlkeld's to await William's coming, Dorothy found this aunt eager to have her remain for a long visit, assuring her that William always would be welcomed. Almost upon her arrival, Dorothy was greeted by the Ferguson and Threlkeld cousins and by the Pollards. Jane, now engaged to "wealthy Mr. Marshall of Leeds," was most accomplished, charming, and even more beautiful than she had been as a child. Dorothy, still exuberant, Jane found, had livelier intelligence than when she first met her, and was wiser than her years. In February, 1794, after a visit in Cumberland, William, visibly shaken by memories of the French Revolution, worried about Annette, came to Halifax. Dorothy, sensing at once his needs, tried to restore him to his usual calmness, but this was not to be accomplished quickly. Her warm, ardent nature, her impassioned intellect, her faith that William would be a great poet, calmed and yet inspired him.

After six weeks at Halifax, brother and sister set out for Windy Brow in Keswick, a farmhouse given them for a time rent free by William's friend, William Calvert. They took a coach to Kendal, then walked two days until they reached their destination. Dorothy could conceive nothing more perfect than the situation of this house on the top of a steep bank below which ran a dashing stream. In the distance, towering over the town, rose a forest-covered mountain. She enjoyed the "neat parlour Mr. Calvert has fitted up" and the comfortable "lodging rooms." For six weeks, sister and brother studied together, read, and walked a great deal. Dorothy, eager to speak Annette's language more fluently again, studied French with William, and began studying Italian.

The older Wordsworths, displeased with William who seemed to be doing nothing to secure a position and with Dorothy who had had the temerity to leave Uncle Cookson's home to be permanently with William, bemoaned Dorothy's unladylike conduct in wandering about the country unprotected. William, unconcerned by the criticism, urged Dorothy to "let them rail" at her.

She wrote Aunt Crackenthorpe that she and William were living inexpensively; "I drink no tea . . . my supper and breakfast are of bread and milk, and my dinner chiefly of potatoes, from choice." She was not, she insisted, unprotected: "I affirm that I consider the character and virtues of my brother sufficient protection." As for her "rambling about the country on foot," she thought it would have given her friends pleasure to hear "that I had the courage to make use of the strength with which nature has endowed me, when it not only procured me infinitely more pleasure than I should have received from sitting in a post chaise, but also was the means of saving me at least thirty shillings." Here, in addition to cooking, washing, ironing, cleaning the house, and mending William's clothing in need of repair, Dorothy began her almost lifelong task of being William's secretary and copyist. The happiness they so cherished they knew must end soon, for William had to find employment. Leaving Windy Brow, the two went to Whitehaven where they spent part of May and June; they visited Cockermouth where they found their former home unoccupied, and to their distress, the garden and the terrace uncared-for. There, they parted for a time.

While William spent the next few months trying to secure a position, Dorothy visited relatives and friends. A favorite with all of them, she found herself beset with invitations. No visit did she enjoy more, however, than the month-long one, in the spring of 1795, with Mary Hutchinson, her close friend of the Penrith days. Mary and her sister Peggy were now keeping house for their brother Thomas at Sockburn, his grazing farm six miles from Darlington. "You cannot think," Dorothy wrote, "what pleasure it gives me to see them so happy . . . they are quite independent and have not a wish ungratified, very different, indeed, is their situation from what it was formerly, when we compared grievances and lamented. the misfortune of losing our parents at an early age, and being thrown upon the mercy of ill-natured and illiberal relations. Their brother has a farm of about £200 a year, and they keep his house. He is a very amiable young man, uncommonly fond of his sisters. The house was built by their uncle, who left them the furniture and eighteen hundred pounds, which, with what they had, makes them very comfortable. It is an excellent house, not at all like a farmhouse, and they seem to have none of the trouble which I used to think must make farmers always in a bustle, for they have very little corn, and only two cows. It is a grazing estate, washed nearly around by the Tees, a noble river, and stocked with sheep and lambs which look very pretty, and give it an interesting appearance. . . . We spend our time very pleasantly in walking, reading, working and playing at ball in the meadow in which our house stands, which is scattered over with sheep and 'green as an emerald.' "

As formerly, Dorothy enjoyed the Hutchinson girls. Tall, dark-haired Mary, twenty-three, had a fair complexion; "radiantly gracious" and calm, she spoke so little that Mr. Clarkson once remarked she could only say, "God bless you." Frail Peggy, the youngest sister, Mary was always concerned about, for Mary was a deeply sympathetic person. Sara, who lived nearby, Dorothy met for the first time. Eighteen-year-old Sara was like Dorothy Wordsworth: small, only about five feet tall; her fair hair framed a delicate face, usually marked with a lively expression. She possessed real distinction of mind and character, and was adventuresome enough to have expressed a desire, later fulfilled, to go to Wales to visit the Ladies at Llangollen.

In the middle of the eighteenth century, long before Sara's birth, Blue Stocking Clubs first flourished in London. Conservative in many ways, these clubs, whose members were women of impeccable social and economic position, rebelled against the current idea that women's brains were not equal to men's. Rebellious, they wrote and published books and articles, conducted literary drawing room meetings, and, like Amazons, defended their cause. Hundreds of girls in remote villages throughout the British Isles heard of the Club's exploits and followed their example. The name "Blue Stocking" came to symbolize a new type of woman.

With the appearance and growing strength of the Blue Stockings, came other types of rebellion among women and girls. Upper-class women, many of whom did not have the intellectuality of the Blue Stockings, restless, felt the urge to break their bonds, also. A growing number of women decided not to marry. The spectacular examples of this type of rebellion were the Ladies of Llangollen, almost as influential as the Blue Stockings.

Lady Eleanor Butler and Miss Sarah Ponsonby, later known as the Ladies of Llangollen, were members of two of the most important and powerful families in Ireland. Behind them were long pedigrees and in their veins ran blood of the bluest. Refined, capable young women, they were expected to marry well and become mothers of broods of children who would carry on the family names and traditions. Sarah's father, Chambré Brabazon Ponsonby, was the grandson of the first Viscount Dungannon and son of Major General the Honorable Henry Ponsonby, and of Frances, daughter of the first Earl of Meath. Chambre Brabazon married three times and each time had a daughter. Sarah was the daughter of the second wife. During the five years following her birth, her mother died, her father married a third time, had his third daughter, and, after begetting a posthumous son, died. The third wife, Sarah's stepmother, daughter and heiress of Sir William Barker of Kilooney Abbey, married again. Thus, almost from infancy, Sarah was an orphan, having no near relatives; she seemed cared for by no one in her home.

Eleanor Butler was a descendant of the Earl of Ormonde who had been created Duke of Ormonde in Ireland in 1661 and in England in 1677. His grandson, the second Duke of Ormonde, was found guilty of high treason and had his honors removed. His Irish earldom of Ormonde and Viscountcy of Thurles were vested in John Butler of Kilcash. On the death of the latter, Walter Butler, Eleanor's father, became "*de jure* sixteenth Earl of Ormonde" and, had the title been then restored, would have assumed it as the sixteenth Earl. It was the ambition of the Butler family to have the title restored. Rich, ambitious and stupid, husband and wife struggled for social position and to regain the title. Extravagant entertaining, attempts to secure advantageous connections through their children having come to naught, Eleanor, the one unmarried child, they believed, remained their last hope. To this end, as a child, she was sent to a French convent for her education; there she mingled with daughters or relatives of France's first families. Letters full of glowing accounts of her popularity, charm, and cleverness, made nervous the priests who had advised this type of education and made jealous Mrs. Butler, who became apprehensive lest the girl wish to remain abroad. Returning home, mature, cultured, aloof, she cared little for the society into which she was rushed. Yet her parents realized they might be able to capitalize on her love of nature and of outdoor life and her interest in politics. They decided to direct her energies into cultivating a hunting clique. In Ireland, though she refused to push herself, her beauty and brains attracted admirers; but she refused suitors at such a rate, despite scenes made by her mother and tirades by her father that she began to be called "eccentric" or "unwomanly." Indeed, she "found she was free to lead a frivolous life, to dress, to spend, to flirt, to run after any man to whom she was attracted, but was not free to read, nor to educate herself, nor to amuse herself out of doors without continual nagging and depreciatory comments of her parents." A gifted young woman, who sang and played the piano well, who wrote and spoke brilliantly, who had a genuine love of good literature and an understanding of politics and government, her narrow world contained no one who shared her interests.

In her home, Sarah Ponsonby also was unhappy. Her father had married two heiresses; her older half sister was an heiress; all of her relatives were rich, but Sarah, somehow, had been deprived of her share of the family wealth. How, remains a mystery; but in the eighteenth century "in Ireland enormous fortunes were made, often lost, or dissipated away, or gambled away, and women by no means always received what was theirs or were able to keep it. No fortune of Sarah's would in future 'tempt' a lover, but only her name and beguiling self." It would pay them, however, her family felt, to bring her up to marry money. Irish families married off their girls early, late, and as often as possible. There were many deaths through childbirth; women seemed always to be dying, leaving husbands to be consoled and remarried. As often there was an inheritance, a fortune, or a good dowry, a family "on the make" married off its daughters to these widowers and thus increased the family wealth. Moreover, few widows were allowed to remain long unwed. Sarah's family planned to introduce her into fashionable Dublin society and find a husband for her. A girl as attractive as she would not long remain unmarried. Clever and observant, quiet and selfcontained, she could also be gay and merry. And though tiny, she was pretty with her clear complexion, blue eyes, and fair hair.

One day, as Sarah stood in the Butler family drawing room, she saw through the window, a hatless young woman, older than she, with a fair complexion, blue eyes, and light thick curly hair, wearing broad-toed shoes, a narrow skirt and broad, flowing cape, crossing the lawn. Coming in, the latter introduced herself as Lady Eleanor Butler. As the two girls met, they instantly liked each other. Sarah later said she felt almost as if her own mother were sitting beside her. Each girl, for the first time, found someone who shared her interests, who felt, moreover, that she could refuse to be married to the highest bidder, that she would not permit her family to force her to marry, that she could remain unwed all her life and enjoy her life; that she cared not whether the world regarded her as "queer" because she chose not to marry. Their friendship, the two girls resolved, would continue.

Meanwhile, extraordinary pressure was being exerted to force Eleanor Butler to marry. The Archbishop of Cashel, Walter Butler's uncle, had been summoned to help arrange a marriage between Eleanor and anyone with social position who would aid Walter in securing the coveted title Earl of Ormonde. Walter promised to do well by the church if it aided him; he agreed to give the prospective husband a dowry of £10,000 to £12,000. When the Archbishop spoke of the matter to his niece, she refused to take part in any such scheme. Threatened by her parents with the prospect of being sent then to a convent, she said she was not made for a religious life. In despair, her parents decided to send her, with Walter's sister, to London for a year. There, at least she would be out of their sight for a time, and she might mention the matter of the title to someone of influence. They gave her £500, thinking they didn't wish anyone to outdress her or to outshine her.

En route from Ireland to London by coach, Lady Eleanor's party stayed for the night at an inn in the beautiful, peaceful valley of Llangollen in Northern Wales. Less fatigued than her companions, and having several hours at her disposal, Lady Eleanor decided to go for a walk. She admired the quiet valley, set at the foot of mountains sprinkled with fir and larch woods; quiet Llangollen village boasted sheep farms, old posting houses, the Hand and Lyon Inns, and the River Dee. It was within driving distance of Shrewsbury and Chester. After a few minutes' walk, she noted a charming four-room cottage with a "For Sale" sign on it. She sought out the agent who said the property had been for sale for some time, that its late owner was dead and that no one wished to purchase it as it was said to be haunted by ghosts. Lady Eleanor said she would give £180 for it and its grounds; at six o'clock that evening the agent and a lawyer came to her and the purchase was complete; the seller agreed to care for it until she decided to occupy it. She kept the key to the house over-night, and early the next morning while her friends slept, she saw her first glowing sunrise from the window of what was to be her and Sarah Ponsonby's home. Meanwhile, none of her party knew of the transaction. She wrote Sarah enthusiastically of what she had done.

As the time drew near for the Rotunda Ball in Dublin, Lady Eleanor decided to return for it. Determined that after it she and Sarah would somehow leave Dublin to lead their own lives, she decided that for this one occasion they should shine as their parents desired. Accordingly, she went to a French coutourier, Madame Rush, to order French dresses for herself and her friend. She arrived to find Madame Rush unpacking dresses that had just arrived from Paris; excitedly, she chose for herself a "narrow ivory gown" with an over-dress of crystal diamenté and a bold touch of black on breasts and shoulders, pale grey gloves, and slippers. For Sarah, she chose a gala rose satin gown and an upright feather ornament for her hair. Both gowns, simple, yet dashingly contrived, she knew would attract attention, for Irish women usually impressed people with the smart, Parisian "daringly cut" gowns "and with their wearers." When it came time to dance the reel, both girls raced to change, as was the custom, to peasant costumes of green skirts and jackets and flat shoes. Then they descended the broad staircase, met their male dancing partners and danced madly as they had never done before. At the conclusion of their dance, they rushed back upstairs and reappeared in their ball gowns. They had been spectacularly successful in their desire to impress and to win suitors. Now, they could put all this behind them.

They returned to their homes with their plans made to run away to Llangollen. What if Sarah had nothing? Lady Eleanor had enough for both of them. Their first attempt to escape their families was a failure, for Sarah Ponsonby fell ill. Aware that their daughters had run away together, both families had sent emissaries for them. Lady Betty had come for Sarah; Eleanor's brother-in-law, Morton Kavanagh, had come for her, for her father refused to permit her to return home. Both families remained adamant about forgiving the girls, though Sarah Ponsonby's family finally gave her an allowance of £200 a year, and Eleanor's, £600.

At Llangollen, the girl's first task was to get their house ready for occupancy. Accordingly, they procured an Irish servant, Mary Carryl, who told the village that she was going to be housekeeper for great ladies who formerly had lived in a castle and a great manor house. It did not take the young ladies long to rebuild their new home, Plas Newydd. Upstairs was a bedroom, a dressing-room, and a guest bedroom; below, a library, an "eating-parlour" or third room, a kitchen, and maids' rooms. Feeling that the place needed atmosphere, they decided to line the walls with oak panelling, which was cheap and plentiful. Indeed, the ancient Abbey of Vale Crucis for two or three centuries had been allowed to crumble away, for the Methodists in the community had no regard for it. Some of its roofing and stained glass had been absorbed by two local churches, but a quantity of valuable material remained. Under Sarah's planning, "oak panels lined the walls and slender pillars and Gothic arches enclosed or outlined windows, alcoves, or doors in the rooms." The little carved saints, angels, or devils, were placed on doors, or walls, or in shaded corners; some seemingly useless carved doors were used for the new home. A lovely old fountain and some stones from the Vale Crucis Abbey the young women made into a drinking fountain, shielded by a Gothic arch; stone seats were placed nearby; and later, on two blocks of stone were carved these lines the young ladies had written:

> Drink gentle pilgrim from the well
> Thus sacred, in this hollow dell.
> Drink deep! Yet ere thy yearning lip
> Touches the draught it longs to sip
> Pray for the souls of those who gave
> This font that holds the liquid wave,
> This holy fount which lay o'erthrown
> Mid Vale Crucis' shadow brown,
> And which the hands of holy men
> Have blest, but ne'er can bless again.
> Drink, happy pilgrim, drink and pray
> At morning dawn and twilight grey
> Pray for the souls of those who gave
> This font that holds the limpid wave.
>
> E.B.   1772   S.P.

They purchased books for their dwelling, for both had come from homes where there were great libraries, and both had read widely. They rented more land and planted flower and vegetable gardens.

Before arriving at their new home, the young ladies had decided to sell their costly raiment and to dress simply. Accordingly, at Birmingham, they had sold all their beautiful, expensive dresses, after first having had made tailored costumes, the nearest approach to what we consider sports clothing. Used for traveling or riding, the habits consisted of full skirts, tight blouses almost resembling waistcoats, cravats, coats that were a great deal like today's riding coats. These, they had tailored in deep blue as well as in black, the cravats, in white, of the finest muslin; they also purchased gauntlet gloves and tall silk hats, then just making their appearance. They cut their hair fairly short. This costume, or others like it, they wore all their lives, thus signifying their freedom.

Happy in this freedom, Sarah Ponsonby and Eleanor Butler enjoyed the respect and admiration of their neighbors and friends in the village. Occasionally, at first, some of their friends from Ireland came to see them. Other women seeking freedom came to Wales to visit them. Their days, however, for the most part, were uneventful. Day after day, in their diaries, one reads merely: "Nov. 21st. A day of peace and delight," or "Jan. 21st. A day of delicious retirement" or "May 7th. A day of sweet occupation and enjoyed retirement" or "March 9th. A day of silent and sweet retirement."

Yes, the two were happy in Llangollen. They entertained at tea and dinner and were entertained. Their friends showered them with gifts of books, curios, pictures, china, carved oak, plants, trees, shrubs, cows, turkeys, fowl, dogs. Occasionally, someone not approving of two females living alone wrote disapprovingly of them in the newspapers. On one such occasion, they wrote to the Right Honorable Edmund Burke, imploring his aid. He regretted to inform them there was no legal remedy then for such an attack in the press and assured them that instead of calumny, they were entitled "to the esteem of all who know how to esteem, honour friendship, principle, and dignity of thinking, that you suffer along with everything that is excellent in the world."

The happy years passed quickly. Mrs. Mary Carry, their housekeeper, died in 1809; Lady Eleanor Butler, aged ninety, died in June, 1829; and Sarah Ponsonby, aged 76, died on December 9, 1831. The three were buried in their plot in the churchyard at Llangollen. After Eleanor's death, her dog continued to keep Sarah company. On the day of Sarah's death, the dog disappeared and was not seen again in Llangollen.

Interested in women's rights, intellectual Sara Hutchinson in 1795 wished to go to Wales where she might derive inspiration from the Ladies of Llangollen. In the evening, by the fireside, near the spinning wheel, the Hutchinson girls and Dorothy Wordsworth sat and talked of current affairs. Dorothy was especially concerned that slavery be abolished. At times they sat quietly reading. During the day, the girls rode, walked, or played ball in the meadow. Dorothy, brown as a gypsy from her life out-of-doors, was perhaps the best liked in the group.

In the spring, William came for a brief visit, finding here an ideal home. He was attracted to Mary Hutchinson; Annette seemed a long distance away. The daughter he had never seen seemed almost unreal.

Leaving the Hutchinsons, William, after trying unsuccessfully to obtain an editorial position, finally became for six months a nurse for William Calvert's brother, Railey, who was dying of tuberculosis in Penrith. When William told the young man of Lord Lonsdale's victimizing the Wordsworths, he so aroused his sympathy that Railey, after having his lawyer investigate the veracity of Wordsworth's story, made a will, first leaving William a legacy of £600, later amending the will and increasing the legacy to £900. Six months after Wordsworth began nursing Railey Calvert, the young man died, and William promptly purchased an annuity with the legacy, then went to London where he lived with Basil Montagu, a young man studying law. He had met Basil through the Reverend Joseph Fawcett, author of *The Art of War*, who shared William's ideas on revolution, freedom, and the happiness of mankind.

Basil, a Cambridge graduate, was the illegitimate son of Lord Sandwich and Martha Ray, a beautiful actress at Covent Garden, who had been killed by a rejected lover. Basil's wife had died leaving a son whom Basil wished Wordsworth to tutor. Why, he asked the poet, not take his son and a couple of boys Francis Wrangham and he were tutoring and earn a comfortable income? Basil had decided to practice law and give up tutoring. He added that Mr. Pinney, the father of one of the boys, had a house in Racedown, Dorsetshire, that could be used by Wordsworth and his sister. The tutoring money plus the sum paid from the annuity William had purchased, and a rent-free house, made it possible for Wordsworth to agree to Basil Montagu's suggestion.

Dorothy thought over the proposition carefully. Financially, the plan was sound. She said, "It will be a very great charge to me, I am sensible, but it is of a nature well suited to my inclinations. You know I am active, not averse to household employments, and fond of children. . . . I am determined to adhere, with strictest attention, to certain rules. In the first place economy and an attention to overlooking everything myself, will be necessary for this purpose. I shall have a great deal of work (needle-work) to do, and I am determined to take the whole care of the children, such as washing, dressing them, etc., upon myself. . . . We may have land to keep a cow and there is a cow of which we may have the use. I think it probable there may be a cottager near us to whose charge we may commit the cow for a share of the milk or some trifling recompense. I mean to keep one maidservant; she must be a strong girl and cook plain victuals tolerably well, as we occasionally shall have both Mr. Montagu and Mr. Pinney with us." One of the chief joys of the plan, she confided, was that "it may put William into a way of getting a more firm establishment." The older Wordsworths agreed the plan seemed good. Young Basil, it developed, was the only pupil, but Dorothy and William were excited over the prospect of living at Racedown, about forty miles from the homes of two poets, Coleridge and Southey. The former's talent appeared very great to Wordsworth; Southey's "manners" and "powers of mind" pleased him exceedingly. Within a month after the offer was made, Dorothy went for Basil, and with William moved to their new home.

Racedown and the surrounding country came up to the expectations of the Wordsworths. Dorothy noted that the hills, which from a distance seemed to be moutains, were almost all cultivated nearly to their summits. The trees on some seemed to suffer from sea blasts; other mountains "in their wild state" were "covered with furze and broom." A little brook ran along one field near their home; from their front door they could view the sea, 150 or 200 yards away. Their house had two parlors, one of which had large bookcases on each side of the fireplace, "very neat furniture," a bath stove, and an oilcloth for the floor; the other, rather larger, bore "a good carpet, side boards in the recesses on each side the fire, and upon the whole, a smart appearance, but we do not like it half so well as our little breakfast room."

Though the servant they hoped to acquire did not arrive for a month, once she came, Dorothy wrote Jane she now had "everything going with the utmost regularity. We wash once a month. I have a woman to whom I give ninepence for one day to wash, on the next we have finished ironing. It is the only time in which I have to do anything in the house, but then I am very active and busy as you will suppose. I have been making Basil coloured frocks, shirts, slips, etc., and I have had a good deal of employment in repairing his clothes and putting my brother's in order." Indeed, a veritable mountain of sewing faced Dorothy. In addition to making little Basil's clothing, she mended William's, in sad need of repair, and in addition made William new shirts. When she discovered that her brother Richard desired some, too, she made them for him, with considerable difficulty but final success, for he had forgotten to tell her the length they should be or the size of the neckband; yet, she still managed to find time to read a great deal of the literature of England, France, and Italy. Every morning, she and William walked for two hours, now to the top of the combs on Pilsdon; again, to Lewis-don or to Blackdown Hill, or to Lowdett's Castle from which they had magnificent views of the surrounding country. At times, William wished to take longer walks, sometimes forty miles. Whenever he wished her to accompany him—and he almost always did—Dorothy donned her "woodland dress" and joined him.

Dorothy was anxious about William, for, noting the change in him, she hoped to be able to restore this restless, distraught brother to his former self. Her deep, though unexpressed affection for him, her calmness, her interest in and love of beauty soothed his spirit. Indeed, he wrote:

> . . . . Methought such charm
> Of sweetness did her presence breathe around
> That all the trees and all the silent hills
> And everything she look'd on should have had
> An intimation of how she bore herself
> Toward them and to all creatures.

William revelled in her "exquisite regard for common things," noting how

> She welcom'd what was given and craved no more,
> Whatever scene was present to her eyes,
> That was the best, so that she was attuned
> Through the humility and lowliness
> And through a perfect happiness of soul—

to flowers, birds, bees, indeed all of nature's wonders; her pleasures were so communicated to him that in time he, too, found pleasure in common things, as he had when a boy. Gradually, his agitation and concern that had left him restless, unable to settle down, much less write good poetry, was now replaced by long periods of calmness. He found real pleasure late one night riding home in finding a glowworm, a creature he believed Dorothy had never seen. Jumping from his horse, he laid the little glowworm on a leaf, bore it home, placed it beneath a tree and all the next day hoped it would remain the same until night. That night, he led his sister to the spot, pointing,

> . . . . "Look here!"
> Oh! joy it was for her and joy for me!

Just as when he was a rough little boy and Dorothy's regard for birds' eggs and butterflies had made William less rough and heedless of these things, so now her interest in nature communicated itself to

ı. Gradually, he realized how she maintained for him a "saving
ɩercourse with my true self," until he agreed with her

> Though impair'd and chang'd
> Much, as it seemed, I was no further chang'd
> Than a clouded, not a waning moon:
> She, in the midst of all, preserved me still
> A Poet, made me seek beneath that name
> My office upon earth, and nowhere else.

Moreover, William now believed that nature so long "foremost in
my affections," which had fallen back into second place, "pleased to
become a handmaid to a nobler than herself," now again seemed of
paramount importance to him. Thus did Dorothy preserve the poet
in William and direct the course of his genius. True, at times, he
still wrote long essays and poetry on controversial topics of the day.
At this time, he composed first the poem *Salisbury Plain*, showing
how poverty and hunger drove a man to commit a crime, and then
the play, *The Borderers*, the account of a man devoid of pity. Yet
Dorothy subtly turned his interest increasingly to poetry and to
Nature's "charms minute that win their way into the heart by
stealth."

Dorothy and William enjoyed their neighbors, having no idea
that William's wandering by day and night with a small telescope
made them suspicious of him, for they were puzzled by his habit of
repeating poetry aloud when he was alone. They thought that perhaps with the telescope, which he carried to view better the distant
scenes, he bewitched their cattle.

The Wordsworths were disappointed that the little girl they expected did not appear, but three-year-old Basil kept Dorothy busy;
William conversed with him and answered his questions only at meal
times. When Basil first arrived, "he lied like a little devil." But
Dorothy, thoroughly cognizant of Rousseau's ideas on education,
managed to cope with that problem. "We teach him nothing at present but what he learns from the evidence of his senses," she told Jane.
"He has an insatiable curiosity which we are always careful to satisfy
to the best of our ability. It is directed to everything he sees, the sky,
the fields, trees, shrubs, corn, the making of tools, carts, etc., etc. He
knows his letters, but we have not attempted any further step in the
path of *book learning*. Our grand study has been to make him *happy*.
... He is certainly the most contented child I ever saw; the least
inclined to be fretful."

When he first came, he cried constantly, as he had been over-indulged. Dorothy finally told him if he chose to cry he must go into a certain room where he could not be heard "and *stay* till he chose to be quiet, because the noise was unpleasant to us; at first his visits were very long and he always came out again perfectly good humored. He found that this rule was never departed from, and when he felt the fretful disposition coming on he would say, 'Aunt, I think I am going to cry,' and retire until the fit was over. He has now entirely conquered the disposition. I dare say it is three months since we have had occasion to send him into this apartment of tears. . . . He had two mornings when he failed to get up when Peggy called him; he came down about an hour after. The second morning Peggy was employed, she could not wash him, we were all engaged and could not fasten his clothes for him, so he was obliged to go to bed again. He has ever since risen at the first call." With the Wordsworths, Basil learned to enjoy gardening. Six months after Basil came to the Wordsworths, Dorothy called him her "perpetual pleasure," adding, "He is quite metamorphosed, a shivery, half-starved plant to a lusty, blooming, fearless boy. He dreads neither cold nor rain."

William and Dorothy were far from well-to-do. William had but £400 of his legacy from Railey Calvert at high interest that was not always paid; often Basil Montagu neglected to pay for the care of his son. William wrote of eating "the essence of carrots, cabbage, turnips, parsley, the produce of my garden" and of "living on air." Dorothy had told Richard that William could use his old clothing.

Yet they welcomed their infrequent guests. When the two Pinney youths, John Frederick, fresh from Oxford, and Azariah, who had had one year in Cambridge, visited them, the young men, Dorothy, William, and often Basil, took long walks. The men hunted, and chopped wood for the fireplaces. They all enjoyed long talks, for the lads were well read and had traveled on the Continent. Little Basil's father also visited them. Dorothy found him pleasant and amiable, and believed everyone must love him. Grieving because of the death by tuberculosis of her sister, Peggy Hutchinson, Mary, Dorothy's close friend, "one of the best girls in the world," came for a brief visit, but lingered on. She had hardly gone when young Coleridge, whom William had met at Bristol a short time before, wrote he was coming to visit. Impressed with Wordsworth's poetry, Coleridge had sent Charles Lamb a manuscript of Wordsworth's, hoping the men would meet and enjoy one another. Later, Wordsworth had visited Coleridge at Stowey; this time again Coleridge was in a mood of "de pression too dreadful to be described," resulting from his trials with an epileptic, Charles Lloyd, whom he was nursing. Coleridge now suffered also from neuralgia. Wordsworth's conversation, however, aroused him somewhat as they discussed poetry. Wordsworth said that Southey wrote "too much at his ease," Coleridge felt Southey's verse lacked "those lofty imaginings that are peculiar to and definitive of the poet." Coleridge believed Wordsworth wrote "poetry of simple diction and strength of expression," equal to the best of his own. Stimulated by Coleridge, Wordsworth had invited him to visit at Racedown, and now he was coming.

Interested in others, not in herself, twenty-five-year-old Dorothy Wordsworth was unaware how attractive she was. Fair-haired, she had skin browned by the sun, grey eyes unusually soft and gentle, but at times "wild and startling," never bold. Her manner was warm, even ardent. Deeply sensitive, some impassioned fire of intellect apparently buried within her at times caused her to become extremely excited; again, trying to yield to the ideas of decorum then prevalent, she suddenly attempted to stifle her thrill over some scene or event and ended by being visibly embarrassed. This, at times, was almost distressing, as "her very utterances and enunciation suffered in point of clearness and steadiness," because of her excessive sensitivity. Her movements were quick; when she walked, at times she stooped forward. Remarkably intelligent, she was, as one friend said, "quick to comprehend, and always profound. Being extremely sympathetic, she could make all that one could tell her, all that one could describe, all that one could quote from a foreign author, reverberate to one's feelings . . . by the magnificent impression it made upon hers."

Twenty-six-year-old William's thick, reddish-brown hair framed his plain face with its high forehead, fiery eyes, and stern, thin mouth. Recently, his face often shone with good humor instead of the glower that had lingered there too long. His tallness contrasted with that of his five-foot sister; yet she could walk as fast as he. Now he was restless and impatient as he and Dorothy waited for Samuel Taylor Coleridge. Indeed, the Wordsworths were not certain at what time twenty-three-year-old Coleridge would arrive on June 5, 1797, for he had preached at Bridgewater on Sunday, as he frequently did, then walked to Taunton, where he spent the night, and left there to walk twenty miles to Racedown. At sunset, they saw the agile young man, striding down the road, then leaping over a gate, bounding down the pathless field by which he cut off an angle, to meet them more quickly.

Coleridge greatly impressed Dorothy. "You had a great loss in not seeing Colerdige," she wrote to Mary Hutchinson who had left just before he arrived. "He is a wonderful man. His conversation teems with soul, mind, and spirit. Then he is so benevolent, so good tempered and cheerful, and, like William, interests himself so much about every little trifle. At first, I thought him very plain, that is, for about three minutes. He is pale and then has a wide mouth, thick lips, and not very good teeth, longish, loose-growing, half-curling rough, black hair. But his eye is large and full, not dark, but grey; such an eye would receive from a heavy soul the dullest expression; but it speaks every emotion of his animated mind; it has more of the 'poet's eye in a fine frenzy rolling' than I ever witnessed. He has fine dark eyebrows, and an overhanging forehead."

Coleridge found Dorothy an "exquisite" person. "She is a woman indeed," he said later, "in mind I mean and heart; for her person is such, that if you expected to see a pretty woman, you would think her rather ordinary; if you expected to see an ordinary woman, you would think her pretty! but her manners are simple, ardent, impressive. In every motion, her inmost soul outbeams so brightly, that who saw her would say,

> Guilt was a thing impossible in her.

Her information various. Her eye watchful in minutest observation of nature; and her taste, a perfect electrometer. It bends, protrudes, and draws in at subtlest beauties, and most recondite faults."

As the two men were interested in each other's poetry, William at once read Coleridge his poem, "The Ruined Cottage," a poem about a simple couple, suffering poverty and famine as the result of their country's going to war, who finally agreed that the husband, to aid their finances, should enlist; while he was in the service his two children died. Coleridge was greatly impressed by the poem, which, unlike much of the verse at the time, had "no mark of strained thought, or forced diction, no crowd or turbulence of imagery." "Yes," he concluded, "Wordsworth is a very great man, the only man to whom *at all times and in all modes of excellence* I feel myself inferior." His praise encouraged Wordsworth and won Dorothy's admiration for she knew her brother needed such approbation. True, she often aided and encouraged him, but she believed her praise was not unprejudiced. Coleridge, commenting on Wordsworth's expressions which he liked nonetheless, taught his fellow-poet how to be more selective; whereas Wordsworth's mind worked slowly, Coleridge's

Percy Bysshe Shelley, from the painting by
Amelia Curran, National Portrait Gallery

Mary Shelley, from a painting by
Richard Rothwell, National Portrait
Gallery

George Gordon, Lord Byron, from the painting by Thomas Phillips, R.A., National Portrait Gallery

Ladies of Llangollen, from an etching in the National Portrait Gallery

Samuel Taylor Coleridge, from a painting by Peter Van Dyke (1795), National Portrait Gallery

lightning-quick imagination and his ability to portray in a few words what Wordsworth took hours to achieve, was a revelation to both the Wordsworths. After tea, Coleridge recited to William and Dorothy two-and-a-half acts of his uncompleted play, *Osorio*, which they praised. The next morning, William read his poetic play, *The Borderers*.

In the following days, as the men and Dorothy visited before the fireplace, or walked together, their friendship was cemented. Both men were rebels; both were radicals, believing firmly in their ideas, that were unlike those of many of their contemporaries; both wrote tragedies; both wrote poetry unlike that of most poets; both had suffered. Indeed, they had much in common. Dorothy, keenly observant, noted beneath Coleridge's seeming gaiety and easy conversation, his anxiety and interest, and from this time added to her concern about William concern about Coleridge.

Later, Coleridge said, "Of all the men I ever knew, Wordsworth has the least femininity in his mind. He is all man! He is one man of whom it might have been said, 'It is good for him to be alone.' " Wordsworth was, in fact, usually cold and reserved.

Coleridge, on the other hand, was gentle, responsive, tender, quick to sympathize, affectionate. Did Dorothy sense this difference and re-evaluate William for the first time? Certainly, the acquaintance of Dorothy and Coleridge ripened rapidly into a close relationship. She referred to him as "dear Col"; he referred to her as "my sister." Just as Dorothy did not conceal her deep affection for William, so did she frankly show her more-than-regard for Coleridge, though she never expressed it in words. Indeed, some of their friends interpreted their regard for each other as merely that of two comrades, but there is much evidence that she loved Coleridge, suppressing for years any expression of that love.

Fascinated by the Wordsworths, Coleridge found his visit lengthening until twenty-four days had passed. Then he tore himself away and returned to his home, only to return four days later in a friend's one-horse chaise, and to insist that the Wordsworths come at once to visit him at his home at Nether Stowey. Dorothy quickly packed some clothing for herself, for Basil, and for William. An hour after Coleridge's arrival, Dorothy and Basil rode with him in the chaise that had room for but three persons, over forty miles of rough, muddy roads, while William walked.

CHAPTER V

Young Rebels "On Fire with Freedom"

AS THEY RODE OVER THE RUTTED ROADS, DOROTHY LEARNED YET MORE OF THE MAN WHO WAS EAGERLY TALKING TO HER and Basil, and who, she realized was no expert horseman.

The chaise bounced up and down hills, through meadows where sheep grazed, through winding village streets, past cottages with gardens abloom with roses, lupins, and sweet williams; Coleridge talked on and on. Dorothy learned that he had come from an old family, always respected, that had become increasingly stronger and wealthier. His father had been a country schoolteacher, "in learning, good heartedness, absentmindedness, and excessive ignorance of the world, a perfect Parson Adams." Capable, he had published a Latin grammar to simplify the study of that subject for beginners, but he had left college without a degree when he was offered a mastership in the grammar school at South Molton. His first wife had died after bearing him three daughters. Then, he had married Anne Bowden. At forty-one, he became the vicar of Ottery St. Mary, near Exeter, and master of its free grammar school.

On October 21, 1772, their tenth and last child, Samuel Taylor Coleridge, was born. His parents spoiled him, and, as a result, he was resented by his nurse and Frank, the brother nearest his age—who deprived him of his goodies, slapped, and scolded him repeatedly. Their condescension was galling to his proud spirit. Once, in late October, in a fit of rage, after having his face slapped, he started after his brother with a knife. Disarmed and reprimanded by his mother, he ran away and hid in one of his secret retreats. At dusk, he fell asleep and awoke to find that a storm had arisen. Wet and cold, he was so stiff he could not move. Early the following morning, he was found by a searching party and his parents, whose joy and relief at finding him were unbounded. "I hope you'll whip him," one lady in the searching party told his parents. They didn't. Later, Coleridge said that "Neither philosophy nor religion has been able to conquer the antipathy I *feel* toward her whenever I see her." Suffering ill effects from the experience, he remained "weakly and subject to ague for many years after." His reaction to the persecution by his brother and his nurse was to seek escape by reading fairy tales and acting them out, often in a nearby churchyard. He read everything that came his way "without distinction." When he was six, his reading of the *Arabian Nights* left him afraid of the dark. At eight, he was considered brilliant and a "character." His lively imagination, his retentive memory, his eloquence, his desire to impress by his cleverness, led to his being "flattered and wondered at by all the old women" and being contemptuous of his contemporaries. When the boy was nine, his father died and he was tutored for a time by a friend of his father. Then another friend, Judge Buller, arranged for him to be admitted to Christ's Hospital, a charity school. Previous to his going there, he visited his uncle, John Bowden, who was devoted to and proud of him. He took the small Coleridge with him to taverns and coffee houses where the child "drank and talked and disputed" as if he were a man. After several weeks of being made much of, he was given the charity boy's costume of blue coat and yellow stockings, and sent to Hertford where, along with other younger boys, he was prepared for entry into Christ's Hospital. Like most boys, so long as he was reasonably well fed he was contented, and at Hertford he was "very happy on the whole," having plenty to eat and drink, and "pudding and vegetables almost every day." When at Christ's Hospital he was less happy, for there "appetites were *damped*, never satisfied" with the scanty portions of dry bread and bad beer, with no vegetables, and meat but three times a week. As the older boys tormented the younger ones, Coleridge, accustomed to the care and devotion of his mother and uncle, really suffered. At night he lay awake in his dark room, trying to picture again his home, and so lulled to sleep, dreamed of it. In the daytime, in classes, he daydreamed of happier days, and as a door opened, often his "heart leaped up" hoping to see entering not the stranger, but "Townsman, or aunt, or sister more beloved."

He made friends among the boys and they soon provided him with "little necessaries" denied many. His uncle, aunt, and cousin visited him and they dined with him every Saturday. Two years later, when his brother George became assistant master of Newcome's Academy, Samuel found him acting as a welcomed father and brother, "everything to me." Over the Christ's Hospital which Samuel attended, presided the Rev. Matthew Field, a dandy and ladies' man, and the Rev. James Boyer, "a proper tyrant, passionate and capricious," a thorough scholar, who taught Coleridge to prefer Theocritus, Demosthenes, and Homer, to Virgil and Cicero, as well as to see the superiority of Lucretius, Catullus, and Terence, over the later Latin poets. He taught Coleridge to appreciate Shakespeare and Milton, and to recognize good style in writing. Coleridge went to Cambridge probably the finest classical scholar among contemporary writers. At times, however, he displeased the Rev. Mr. Boyer; once, when at fifteen he decided to go into trade and become a cobbler's assistant rather than go to the university; once, when, after reading Voltaire, he decided he was an infidel. On both occasions, Boyer flogged him, with the result that Coleridge remained at Christ's Hospital and really studied, though he felt forced "to *love* the Jesus, whom my reason (or perhaps my reasonings) would not permit me to worship."

For a time, he considered being a surgeon, being inspired by his brother Luke, who was working in London hospitals. He read innumerable medical books and acquired further knowledge of medicine by working some Saturdays in hospitals. Though this interest passed, the knowledge he had gained helped him understand his own physical ailments. As his dream of being a surgeon passed, it was supplanted, after his reading *Cato's Letters*, essays on liberty, by a keen interest in metaphysics and theology, to be in turn supplanted, after reading William Bowles' verses, by his desire to be a poet. Bowles had a tremendous effect on him, causing him to revolt against the vogue of artificial poetry.

At that same time, he fell in love with Mary Evans; he and his classmate, Bob Allen, delighted in escorting girls on Saturdays, when they had "oh sixteen to nineteen hours of paradise"; for Mary, Coleridge would pillage flower gardens, wrapping around his bouquet "a sonnet or love-rhyme" he had composed. To affectionate, sympathetic Mary he excitedly recited his verses or confided his opinions on political and ethical matters. His enthusiasm and his personality thrilled her. At times, however, careless of his health, he suffered horribly from jaundice and rheumatic fever. The day he swam across a river and let his wet clothing dry on him caused him to spend half of his seventeenth and eighteenth years in the hospital, where he suffered so horribly that laudanum was the only drug that brought him relief. The deaths of his only sister, of his brothers Luke and Francis, left him to the supervision of his two brothers older than George:

Edward, a school teacher who was too fond of appearing "great to little people," and James, who became increasingly stern. His mother, unable to understand her youngest son, no longer sympathized with him. He felt alone.

A student at Jesus College, Cambridge, he gained friends quickly, though he found Cambridge a "damp place—the very palace of the winds"—and suffered from rheumatism and "a disagreeable tearing pain" in his head that caused him frequently to be "nailed" to his bed despite large dosages of laudanum. He worked hard at his studies and won a gold medal for an ode in Greek on the Slave Trade. Despite the fact that his friend Thomas Middleton had so displeased Cambridge officials by his republican ideas and by upholding the principles of the French Revolution that he had been denied a fellowship he had won, Coleridge wrote an ode celebrating the destruction of the Bastille, and stating that he wished Britain ever to be "first and freest of the free" and the principles of Liberty, Equality, and Fraternity to exist in his country. These ideas William Pitt's Tory government was trying to suppress. An avid reader, Coleridge was able not only to read rapidly but to retain verbatim whole pages of his reading. In his third year at Cambridge, he was one of four contestants for the Craven Fellowship. When Samuel Butler was awarded it, Dr. Pearce, the Master of Jesus College, was so incensed with the award, that he complained that the examination had included no Greek prose and verse, and no English composition. Had it done so, the scholar contended, Coleridge "would have beat them hollow." As a consolation prize, he gave his pupil an appointment as college librarian and chapel clerk, worth £30 a year.

In 1793, when war with France broke out, twenty-one-year-old Coleridge was a pacifist, for he believed that the war could have been avoided had there been any negotiation, and that it was, therefore, unjust and unnecessary. He recognized that Pitt's government, fearing France would spread her democratic ideas to other countries, had chosen to attack France while she suffered internal dissension and had few allies. These arguments the government denied, saying it "could not honorably negotiate with men so stained with atrocious guilt, so avowedly the enemies of religion." Coleridge pointed out his government's insincerity six months later when the restitution of monarchy became its avowed aim. When one of the Cambridge students, openly an enemy of Pitt's government, was tried by the Vice-Chancellor's court and banished from the University for ideas derogatory to theology and socially subversive, hence offensive to University statutes, Coleridge was known to have applauded the offender at his trial.

Coleridge's popularity with his fellows proved expensive, for as they thronged into his rooms, he hospitably wined and dined them. And Coleridge could carry his liquor. He once boasted to his brother George how he and his brother Edward and a friend had "sat from four till ten drinking and then arose as cool as three undressed cucumbers." Coleridge's guests, however, were more interested in conversation than in drinking. With Christopher Wordsworth, he formed a literary society; often, he read to the group papers he had prepared, or recited poetry he had written. At length, he had to confide to his brother George that he was in debt, having extravagantly spent money he should have used to pay his tutor's bills. Knowing that George would speak to Edward and James, and urge them to pay the bills, and knowing how displeased the latter two would be, he was afraid to tell them how much he owed. Telling them he owed a smaller amount, he received what he asked for and paid his more pressing debts; then, when a lottery ticket he'd hoped would bring relief did not, he left Cambridge for London. Drinking to forget his misery, he even contemplated suicide.

While drunk, he met a soldier, and suddenly, on December 2, 1793, enlisted in the Light Dragoons as a trooper, under the name Silas Tomkyn Comberbacke. He was sent to Reading; neither relatives nor friends knew of his whereabouts for two months. Then, impulsively, he wrote friends at Christ's Hospital to give a message to either Mary Evans or her mother. Excited by the secret they were to keep, the boys wrote of it to Tuckett, a Cambridge friend of Coleridge, who, in turn, told it to George Coleridge. Once Samuel Taylor Coleridge learned how rapidly his secret had traveled, he wrote his brother George a contrite letter, saying "My more than brother! What shall I say. . . . I have been a fool even to madness . . . My mind is illegible even to myself. . . . Oh that without guilt I might ask of my Maker annihilation! . . . Pray for me, comfort me, my brother! I am very wretched . . ." George replied at once and asked Samuel if he proposed returning to Cambridge if his discharge were secured. Assured the boy wished to, George got in touch with Mr. Boyer, who was in no mood to allow the escapade to deprive the university of a good student. Equally helpful was Captain James Coleridge, who succeeded after six weeks in securing his brother's release from the Army.

Back at Cambridge, the young man was reprimanded, sentenced

to a month's confinement on the quadrangle and to the task of translating the works of Demetrius Phalareus into English. His scholarship was restored to him. Grateful, Coleridge dropped his frivolous companions, arose at five each morning and studied hard. When college ended, he decided to spend the summer vacation on a walking tour of Wales. En route, he planned to stop at Oxford to visit a friend, a Christ's Hospital boy, Bob Allen, in his third year at Oxford; young Allen had written a paper on the "comparative good and evil of novels," which had brought favorable comments. While at Oxford, Coleridge met a friend of Allen's, Robert Southey, almost two years Coleridge's junior, in his second year at Oxford.

Of Somerset stock, Robert Southey was the second son of Robert Southey and Margaret Hill, the former an employee in a draper's shop. When the boy was two, he went to live with an aunt, Mrs. Hill, during his mother's third confinement. Though Mrs. Hill did not adopt him, she assumed all responsibility for him and paid all his expenses for the next four years. An eccentric, wealthy woman, twice widowed, she adored her nephew, whom she kept in dresses until he was six, gave little exercise, and never allowed "to dirty himself." A beauty, she had a wide circle of acquaintances, among them a London bookseller, Newberry, who gave the boy a complete set of children's books which he read avidly, and works of the dramatists Sheridan, Cumberland, and Holcroft, whose plays he attended with his aunt.

Before he was eight, he was reading Shakespeare, Beaumont and Fletcher, and had begun a play about Scipio. Other plays, among them one on Richard III, followed, for he found it easy to write them and thought it odd other boys did not. After reading Ariosto, Spenser, Pope's translations of the *Iliad* and the *Odyssey*, he began writing epics about Arcadia and Brutus; his reading of Ovid, Virgil, and Horace inspired his making, by his thirteenth birthday, translations of those poets. When his aunt took a house in Bristol, he acquired a companion of his own age, Shadrach Weeks, the brother of his aunt's maid, who taught him carpentry and helped him make a puppet theatre; Shad took him on tramps in the woods where he learned to love nature.

Robert Southey's schooling was frustrating. At six, when he began going to day school, he returned to live with his parents; his teachers had terrorized and bullied him with the result that he did not do good work. When he went to a school at Corston, where he boarded, his master was a negligent fellow who hated the drudgery of teaching and often had the older boys teach the younger ones. Southey says he learned more Latin by helping the younger boys than by preparing his own lessons for the negligent master. He learned so little at another Bristol school that, when an uncle tried to help him attend Westminster, hoping that he could then win a Christ Church, Oxford, scholarship, he proved so ill-prepared that he had to go to a clergyman "crammer" before he was accepted at Westminster. Among the three hundred students at Oxford were a small circle upon whom "nature had set her best testimonials"; those, he enjoyed. Resenting dictatorial discipline and corporal punishment, he rebelled against authority.

Like many, stimulated by the democratic ideals of the French revolution, he found it easy to justify his rebellion against authority. Hence, he and a group of his young friends founded a magazine called *The Flagellant*, in 1792; it was composed of essays. In one number Southey, imitating the style of Voltaire and the ideas of Gibbon, wrote an essay on "Flogging"; this he said had once been part of heathen rituals. Since the Church held the heathen gods to be devils, he concluded that flogging was an invention of the devil, and not fit to be practiced in Christian schools. When the headmaster of Westminster read the article, he instituted libel proceedings against the printer of the magazine; when Southey stated he'd written the article, he was expelled. As school was about to close and as the headmaster said the expulsion would not affect Southey's chance of receiving the Christ Church, Oxford, scholarship the next fall, Southey was not concerned. He was persuaded, however, probably by his aunt, to write the headmaster of Westminster "expressing contrition I did not feel, and apologizing for an action I thought needed no apology." The headmaster, unworthy of his calling, went back on his promise and wrote the Christ Church authorities that a rebel like Southey would be no credit to Oxford. As a result, two weeks before he was to leave for Oxford, he received word that the college had rejected him.

Shortly after this blow, Southey learned that his father was in danger of being arrested for debt. The lad at once went to his father's wealthy brother, asking him to aid his father, who was suffering from a situation "into which the treachery of his relations and injustices of his friends" had thrown him. The uncle refused to save Southey's father from the debtors' prison, though Southey's ever-kind aunt did come to his aid. The father, broken in health, and despondent, died shortly after he was saved from disgrace. Bitterly disillusioned, Southey turned to a young milliner, Edith Fricker, for the comfort and companionship she willingly gave. But nightmares end, and in January, 1793, Southey entered Balliol College, Oxford.

His pleasure at entering Oxford was shaken, however, by the fact that that month war had broken out between England and France. "Isn't it disgraceful," the young man meditated, "at the moment when Europe is on fire with freedom . . . to sit and study Euclid or Hugo Grotius?" He was beginning, too, to be concerned about the future planned for him, that of being a clergyman. "Four years hence," he wrote, "I am to be called into orders, and during that time . . . how much I have to learn! I must learn to break a rebellious spirit, which neither authority nor oppression could ever bow; it would be easier to break my neck. I must learn to work a problem instead of writing an ode. I must learn to pay respect to men remarkable only for great wits and little wisdom." Yet, as a student at Balliol, he was studying to be a clergyman.

Southey found it even less easy to reconcile himself to his country's attitude toward France. The French Revolution, he considered praiseworthy and wise, "defended by the sword of liberty" and "insulted by the proud use of despotism." When the revolutionists committed crimes like the St. Bartholomew Massacre, the torturing of Jean Calas, and the guillotining of Brissot, the King, and Marie Antoinette, he suffered acutely, feeling that France was betraying democracy. "I look around the world," he wrote, "and find the same mournful spectacle—the strong tyrannizing over the weak, man and beast, the same depravity pervades the whole creation; oppression is triumphant everywhere, and the only difference is, that it acts in Turkey through the anger of a grand seignior, in France of a revolutionary tribunal, and in England of a prime minister." He could not condone England's war against democracy any more than France's betrayal of liberty by its atrocities.

When he read William Godwin's *Political Justice*, he found some answers to the questions that so agitated him. Godwin wrote that "no revolution is ever bloodless"; he stated that duty consisted of the best application of one's capacity to benefit mankind; that if a majority agreed to reforms, they might come without violence. These ideas appealed to young Southey. "If this world," he said, "did but contain ten thousand people of both sexes, visionary as myself, how delightfully could we repeople Greece, and turn out the Moslem." The more he listened to the propaganda of Pitt's warmongers, the more he was convinced that the war would be a long and exhausting one, and the more convinced he was that "society requires desperate remedies." Unlike Godwin, he was unwilling to try to leaven society slowly. He saw no hope in Europe. He contemplated America which had thrown off the oppressor and was truly the home of liberty. He read Thomas Paine's *The Rights of Man* and the Reverend Joseph Priestley's *Defense of the French Revolution;* he thought of Abraham Cowley who wished "to retire with books to a cottage in America and seek that happiness in solitude which he could not find in society." Why shouldn't he go to America "where man's abilities would ensure respect; where society was upon a proper footing, and man could be considered as more valuable than money; and where I could till the earth and provide by honest industry the meat which my wife would dress with pleasing care?"

Despite such thoughts racing through his mind, he studied "because it is my duty," reading and writing "till my eyes ache"; he wrote some poetry and translations of Horace and Juvenal; he wrote the first draft of *Joan of Arc*. By January, 1794, he had definitely decided not to be a minister. He contemplated medicine, a profession with "many opportunities of benefiting mankind"; but after suffering nausea in the dissecting room, abandoned that idea. His plan to go into government service also had to be given up because his political ideas, he was told, were too radical. Again, his thoughts turned to America and to Edith Fricker. Why not emigrate to America with Edith and help found an ideal state? So contemplating, he met Samuel Taylor Coleridge.

Almost as soon as Southey met Coleridge, he was charmed by him, writing a friend about Coleridge's genius, clear judgment, and good nature. Heretofore, Southey's friends had been mediocre men, admiring his superiority. Here was a man to whom he could look up. Coleridge, always quick to praise merit, read aloud with enthusiasm parts of Southey's *Joan of Arc*. The two shared kindred theories of poetry and of politics. Southey's plan of going to America appealed, also, to his friend. In fact, Southey's plan grew under Coleridge's vision, for he saw a group escaping from Europe and England, where liberty seemed threatened, where those who opposed the existing government were persecuted or ostracized, where one's very existence depended on lip service. Why could not a group go to America and found a state so ideal that in time Europe and England would emulate it? Coleridge invented a name for his plan, *pantisocracy*, a "scheme" in which all would have equal rights, a creed of individualism, a democracy, as opposed to an aristocracy, by which the people elected the representatives they believed best. As Coleridge elaborated on the plan, two of Southey's friends agreed to emigrate. Southey hesitated; he must first be certain his Edith agreed.

While Southey hesitated, the first seeds of disagreement came. Coleridge, on a walking tour of Wales with his friend Hucks, was dining well with him at a tavern when "a little girl with her half-famished sickly baby in her arms" looked in at the open window and begged for a piece of bread and meat. As Coleridge gave the girl the food, he was angered at the system that permitted such an incident to take place even as he was filled with compassion for the girl. Hucks, on the other hand, was thoroughly annoyed that a gentleman, once he had paid for his meal, could not eat without such a crude interruption. Writing Southey of the incident, Coleridge said that Hucks was a cultivated man, devoid, however, of a genuine fondness for humanity because he suffered from "the lingering remains of aristocracy." Under pantisocracy, Coleridge said, Hucks' reactions and the girl's poverty would be impossible; for, he continued, they would "aspheterize," that is, own everything in common. Southey, on the other hand, sympathized with Hucks' point of view. Yet Coleridge did not doubt Southey's idealism.

Meeting in Bristol, the two young pantisocrats succeeded in securing as recruits for the scheme Robert Lovell and George Burnett. The latter suggested that since they planned to live by agriculture, they should include in their scheme a practical farmer. Tom Poole of Stowey seemed the ideal man.

At twenty-nine, the latter seemed much older to twenty-year-old Southey and twenty-two-year-old Coleridge. Poole had inherited his father's tannery in which he had had an apprenticeship. Although denied an education, he had read widely and founded a lending library at Stowey. He wrote the article on Tanning for the third edition of *Encyclopaedia Britannica;* he introduced improved machinery at Nether Stowey; he managed most of the philanthropic affairs in the community. The wrongs of the people in France had excited his sympathy with the French Revolution; after reading Thomas Paine's *Rights of Man*, Poole had expressed democratic ideas that aroused his Tory neighbors, who believed all the propaganda the government was feeding them. When he prevented their burning Tom Paine in effigy, they were resentful. They thought his hope to visit the Western Republic as stupid as his treasuring a lock of George Washington's hair an admirer had given him. They thought him overzealous in fighting so hotly against slavery. Even his lending library was suspect. Was he using it to distribute seditious pamphlets? Adhering to his principles, he declared "if the French are conquered, Europe is enslaved." He had written a friend, "America seems the only asylum of peace and liberty—the only place where the dearest feelings of man are not insulted." His relatives, who had been concerned about his reputation, worried when some of the local gentry said he "ought to be denounced as a public enemy." They long had agreed that his democratic sentiments "tormented" them, that "he is never happy until the subject of politics is introduced, and we all differ so much from him we wish to have no conversation about it." Impressed with Coleridge, less so with Southey, Poole listened carefully as the enthusiastic young men told him of the plan of *pantisocracy*.

"Twelve gentlemen of good education and liberal education," they explained, were to leave the following April with twelve ladies for America. In the meantime they were to become well acquainted with one another, so that, once they reached their destination, a beautiful frontier settlement on the banks of the Susquehanna River, which they believed to be, not as it is, in Pennsylvania, but in the South in a temperate climate, their procedure would be simple. On arrival, they would be ready to begin at once their new lives. Using an idea gleaned by Southey from Adam Smith's *Wealth of Nations*, that there is not more than one productive man in twenty, they planned to work two or three hours a day; their produce would then be "aspheterized" for the common use. Thus would their livelihood be earned. Their remaining time would be spent using the common library, where they would study, hold liberal discussions, attend to the education of their children. The women, although concerned mainly with educating their children and "other occupations suited to their strength," would spend considerable time improving their minds. Each would be free to enjoy his own religious and political opinions. It had not yet been decided whether divorce, if agreeable to one or both parties, would be acceptable.

Poole liked the idea of settling in America. If their scheme succeeded, he said, they would "realize the age of reason." However, he felt that before a man pulled up his roots and took his family and property to America, he should first see the country. He could not take the risk of going, he said, as the tannery business depended on his management; moreover, his father was old and ailing; if his father died, he could not leave his mother.

Still far from discouraged, Coleridge and Southey continued their plans. The latter felt that each man should have an investment of £125 in the plan. Burnett's father would give him that sum; Southey expected his *Joan of Arc* to yield this amount, and counted on some aid from his aunt. Coleridge believed his "Latin Poems" would provide his share. To swell the fund, Lovell and Southey planned to publish together a volume of their verses; they and Coleridge agreed to collaborate on a poetic drama, *The Fall of Robespierre.*

While the young pantisocrats discussed their plans, Mrs. Fricker and her daughters acted as excellent sounding boards. Mrs. Fricker's husband had died bankrupt, in 1786, leaving her and six children penniless. A determined, aggressive woman, Mrs. Fricker had given the daughters better educations than most girls had, and had stressed the importance of being able to earn a living and to make a successful marriage. May Fricker, recently married to Robert Lovell, was a competent actress and a great reader, not only of the best of Latin and Greek, but also of the English Classics. Eliza and Mary, Edith and Sara were earning good livings as milliners. Southey was engaged to Edith. Burnett and Coleridge spent much time with Martha and Sara. George Burnett proposed marriage to Martha, who rejected him, but Coleridge's sudden proposal to Sara was promptly accepted. She had rejected two suitors, hoping for this proposal. Southey was astonished at Coleridge's announcement of his engagement, "for he had talked of being in love with a certain Mary Evans." Engaged, Coleridge now devoted himself to other matters.

Aware that *The Fall of Robespierre* had been written hastily, the Bristol bookseller refused to publish it; hence, Coleridge went to London, where he still found no publisher. That transaction uncompleted, he went each night to the Salutation and Cat, an alehouse in Newberry Street, where he and friends drank porter and punch. By sheer luck, there he encountered a former classmate who had just returned from America, where he had been five years. He told Coleridge that land in America was cheaper than land in England, assuring him that "twelve men could easily clear *three hundred acres* in four or five months"; for $600, "a thousand acres might be cleared and houses built on them." The Susquehanna was as beautiful, he told Coleridge, as the pantisocrats had envisioned it; it was "secure from hostile Indians" and "the mosquitos are not so bad as our gnats"; there were no bison there. All these facts Coleridge excitedly relayed to Southey.

Two weeks later, back in Cambridge, Coleridge wrote Southey that he thought "incessantly" of Sara Fricker "with unspeakable tenderness." Southey replied by taking him to task for not writing Sara. Coleridge had written Southey weekly and had told him to give messages to Sara. Wasn't that giving her enough attention? Moreover, he had finally succeeded in finding a publisher for *Robespierre* in Cambridge. Still dissatisfied with Coleridge's conduct, Southey wrote a mutual friend of Coleridge's neglecting to write the girl to whom he was engaged. Shown this letter, Coleridge was "beyond measure distressed and agitated" but he had no explanation except that he was "a great tomorrower." He did not realize that Southey, who had abandoned Oxford, was really concerned at Coleridge's returning to Cambridge. Was Coleridge deciding not to be a pantisocrat? Had he not told Coleridge that once a pantisocrat, one should give up everything, father, mother, if necessary, even wife and children for his belief?

Having worked himself up by chiding Coleridge, Southey next decided to go to Bristol to tell his aunt of his plans. Once informed of them, his aunt promptly ridiculed the scheme, derided the Frickers whom she considered far below her nephew socially, ordered Southey out of the house, and told him never to return. Southey went to his mother's home in Bath, and from there wrote Edith Fricker, "Amid the pelting of the pitiless storm did I, Robert Southey, the Apostle of Pantisocracy, depart from the City of Bristol, my natal place—at the hour of five in a wet windy evening on the 17th of October, 1794, wrapped up in my father's old greatcoat and my own cogitations." Equally dramatically, he wrote his younger brother Tom of his treatment, adding that he had "swallowed a glass of brandy and set off" the night his aunt ordered him out. He added, "I am fully possessed by the great cause to which I have devoted myself, my conduct has been open, sincere, and just; and though the world were to scorn and neglect me, I should bear their contempt with calmness."

Coleridge, studying at Cambridge and away from Sara Fricker, found his affections for her lessening. In fact, he became interested in a young actress, Miss Brunton, then appearing in a play in Cambridge. Much taken with her "exquisite beauty and uncommon accomplishments," he saw a great deal of her and accepted an invitation from her parents to visit them at Christmastime. Later, he wrote

Southey he had heard from Mary Evans, attempting to persuade him to give up the idea of going to America. He had no idea of giving up pantisocracy, he said, but, he added, that he loved Mary Evans, "almost to madness. Her image was never absent from me . . . for more than three years." Several days later, he reiterated to Southey that they had not originally planned to have children in the party going to America. "These children—the little Frickers, for instance, and your brothers—are they not already deeply tinged with prejudices and errors of society? Have they not learned from their schoolfellows *Fear* and *Selfishness*, of which the necessary offsprings are Deceit and desultory Hatred? How are we to prevent them from infecting the minds of *our* children?" Assuring Southey "I most assuredly will go to America," Coleridge questioned whether the system on which they were to embark should be "necessarily imperfect." Still later, when he learned that Southey wished Mrs. Fricker to go to America with the group, Coleridge objected. "That Mrs. Fricker! We shall have her teaching the infants *Christianity*—I mean the mongrel whelp that goes under its name—teaching them by stealth in some ague fit of superstition." When Coleridge's brother George wrote objecting to the plan, Coleridge explained his motive in going was "to lead mankind" to a better way of life, "the present is *not* the highest state of society of which we are capable."

In early November, he went to London, where there was much excitement over the acquittal of Thomas Hardy, the shoemaker who had been arrested on the charge of high treason. The government had been trying many for treason, and corrupt judges had sentenced them to be deported. Realizing that Hardy's was a test case, people flocked to the trial. William Godwin, also suspect, free only because he said he objected to "force" in any form, attended the trial, and in an open letter expressed the fallacy of the charges. Hardy and his associates were accused of attempting "to change the form of government established, by publishing or causing to be published, divers books and pamphlets and by belonging to political societies having the same object." Godwin's and Hardy's counsel pointed out that Hardy and his friends had merely advocated radical reform by constitutional means. After Hardy's acquittal, the government worked the harder to convict his friends, but an able lawyer, on the testimony of the dramatist Sheridan, caught Pitt lying, and set the Court in an uproar. Shortly after the trials, Coleridge met Godwin, whose defense of Hardy had led Coleridge to write a sonnet praising Godwin. Godwin found the young poet "one of the four oral instructors to whom I feel my mind indebted for improvement." In London, too, Coleridge met Charles Lamb who had been at Christ's Hospital when he had. Lamb, disappointed in love, haunted by the fear of succumbing to madness that ran in his family, confided his troubles to Coleridge. Nightly, the two met at the Salutation and Cat, drinking "egg hot," smoking "oroonoko," talking, at times writing sonnets together.

For months, Coleridge had intended to tell Mary Evans of his love. Finally, he wrote her, saying that for four years he had "endeavored to smother a very ardent attachment"—and that he had thought of her incessantly. He knew, he admitted, that she regarded him "merely with the kindness of a sister"; he loved her for her kindness, but his love for her had grown until he feared the prospect of losing her. Loving her, he had filled his solitude "with many a delightful daydream." He hoped she might love him; but if she could not, he would not embarrass her "by even a *look* of discontent." On Christmas eve, he received her reply. She blamed herself for not having seen that he might regard her as more than a sister. He, in turn, wrote her that she blamed herself "most unjustly"; he believed, however, that the habit of loving her had made "unalterable" his devotion to her; yet "divested as it is now of all shadow of hope . . . its disquieting power," he begged forgiveness for having pained her. Then, he wrote Southey that Mary Evans had said she could not love him. "But, to marry another, O Southey! bear my weakness. Love makes all things pure and heavenly like itself,—but to marry a woman I do *not* love; to degrade her whom I shall call my wife by making her the instrument of low desire, and on the removal of a desultory appetite to be perhaps not displeased with her absence! Enough! These refinements are the bewildering fires that lead me into vice. Mark you, Southey! *I will do my duty!*" He promised to come to Bath on Saturday, December 27; he was delaying his return, he said, to be with Charles Lamb whose sister was quite ill.

When Southey went to meet the coach on Saturday, "*No S. T. Coleridge* was thereon." Southey decided to go after the man engaged to Sara Fricker; when he did not find Coleridge at the Salutation and Cat, he went to Coleridge's lodging, where he found that his friend was spending much time with Charles Lamb, who seemed to find comfort in no one else. Coleridge pointed out, also, that he'd spent all his money and was contemplating walking to Bath; he owed a considerable bill at the inn; but the owner, feeling that he attracted many customers, offered Coleridge free quarters to stay and talk to his guests. But Southey was adamant. Coleridge must come and see Sara Fricker. The landlord of the Salutation and Cat showed that he, too, could be adamant, and forced Coleridge to leave his clothing, since he would not remain, and could not pay his bill.

Once Southey had Coleridge in Bristol, he took every precaution to see that he did not escape. He informed the captive youth that since war between England and America was threatening, he, Lovell, and Burnett had decided to go to Wales instead. Coleridge objected to having no voice in making the decision, nor could he understand how pantisocracy could be achieved by four men forming a partnership in Wales. If, however, they all agreed to "aspheterize" in Wales, he would join them. He suggested, however, that the group, before making a decision, should determine what capital was required, and whether a house large enough for all of them was available. When Mrs. Lovell said they could not leave for three months, Coleridge decided he would go to London and take a position offered him as a reporter on the *Telegraph*. He would give any money he earned, excepting enough to pay his living expenses, to a common fund. In London, he could complete his *Imitations*. But Southey refused to accept this idea as good. When Coleridge insisted he had to go to Cambridge to explain to the college authorities his reasons for not returning, Southey accompanied him. Though the master of Jesus College, Cambridge, bewailed Coleridge's "visionary and ruinous" idea, he gave him a semester in which to reconsider his decision about leaving the University.

Leaving Cambridge, Coleridge and Southey, soon joined by Burnett, took lodgings together in Bristol. Having no money, since *Robespierre* had had but a small sale, and as Southey had decided to revise *Joan of Arc* before it was published, Coleridge sought newspaper work he could do in Bristol. He and Southey planned, also, a series of lectures; the former to lecture on morals and politics, the latter, on history. Coleridge had a large audience, but one in which many considered his ideas so radical that he had to publish his first lecture to prove there was no treason in it. He had stated that France might well serve as a warning to England. The people, like Samson in the Old Testament, were strong and blind; in pulling down the temple of monarchy and aristocracy, they had buried themselves in the ruins. Those professing to be democrats, he said, condemned constitutions and dispensations without having really examined the natures and capacities of the recipients of democracy. Democrats in France, he believed, demanded equality "of *rights*, not of condition."

Universal education, equal opportunity for aspheterism of raw materials and public services could lead to equality of condition. Religion, too, he believed, would be helpful. Unitarianism seemed to him the ideal religion; hence he became a Unitarian and to that faith he converted Southey. Even William Godwin began agreeing with his religious views.

Southey, in the meantime, showed his instability, first by insisting that he and Coleridge leave Bristol and go to London, then, by deciding that perhaps he had better be a minister after all, also deciding that Wales would not be a good place for pantisocracy. Why shouldn't he and Coleridge settle down in England with the idea of one day emigrating to America? When Southey's uncle said he should study law, but first accompany him to Portugal to get away from radical Coleridge and his ilk, Southey agreed to do so. Secretly, however, he first married Edith Fricker and arranged to support her and have her stay with friends while he was in Portugal. Shocked at his friend's giving up the idea of pantisocracy, Coleridge wrote, "O selfish money-loving man, what principle have you not given up?" Angered at Coleridge, Southey proclaimed with lordly swagger, that Coleridge had done him much good; "I him more."

Coleridge was physically ill—"a devil, a very devil has got possession of my left temple, eye, cheek, jaw, throat, and shoulder"; yet he had given eleven lectures to earn contributions for the pantisocrats; he had aided Southey in the composition of his lectures; he had contributed some lines to Southey's *St. Joan*. He was now harassed by Sara Fricker, who told him her family was disturbed because she had rejected two other suitors, "one of them of large Fortune," for Coleridge. Rebuked by her family, she told him now she was being urged to wed "a third suitor whom she strongly disliked" rather than to wait for Coleridge whom she loved ardently. Deeply moved by her distress, Coleridge pictured her "oppressed with gloom" sitting lonely in a cheerless room, in tears. He must marry her. Having found a suitable cottage for their home, thirteen miles from Bristol, the two were married. George Burnett accepted an invitation to live with them. Coleridge was happy in his marriage, for he wrote his friend Thomas Poole, "On Sunday I was married! . . . We are settled—nay quite domesticated at Clevedon, our comfortable cot!! Mrs. Coleridge— MRS. COLERIDGE! I love to write that name."

The home soon proved to have its disadvantages; as Coleridge needed to see his publisher regularly and to borrow books from the public library at Bristol, where he was lecturing, the twenty-six-mile walk to and from that city in one day proved exhausting. He and Sara moved to her mother's home in Bristol. Mrs. Fricker proved even as difficult as Coleridge had foreseen. Hence, he welcomed a visit for two weeks with Poole at his home in Stowey. Poole, of course, had found Coleridge's lectures brilliant and timely. When Pitt introduced into Parliament bills limiting freedom of the press, and prohibiting public gatherings, in November, 1795, Coleridge gave two lectures opposing these measures. After differentiating between government *by* the people, which he believed France would achieve, government *over* the people, or despotism, and government *with* the people, he contended that Pitt's government, since the members of Parliament belonged exclusively to the propertied, professional, and aristocratic classes, came closest to being a despotism, from which it was saved only by freedom of the press. So popular were these lectures, that Coleridge combined them into one, entitled: "The Plot Discovered; or an Address to the People Against Ministerial Treason."

Happy to have with him a man whom "Providence has been pleased . . . to drop to this globe as a meteor from the clouds," Poole eagerly welcomed Coleridge and his wife as his guests. And Coleridge, revising his poems for his publisher, had a new experience in gardening there. With Poole, he discussed his plans, for he was aware, as never before, of "the wonderful uses of the vulgar article of life, *Bread*"; he was now supporting "my wife, my wife's mother and little brother, and George Burnett—five mouths opening and shutting as I pull the string!" With friends, he was planning a periodical, *The Watchman*. He and several booksellers secured a substantial number of subscribers. Coleridge was the sole writer for it during its brief life, from March 1, 1796, through May 13, 1796, when it expired. *The Morning Chronicle* in London offered Coleridge the position of associate editor. His friends urged him not to take the position, which they felt would not leave him the leisure time to write creatively. As proof of their esteem, Poole began a fund to which other friends subscribed, promising to pay five guineas each year for the next six years, so that the twenty-three-year-old genius could exert his argumentative powers, his forceful eloquence, his keen satire, his learning, in the support and dissemination of what he honestly believed to be the truth. With this tribute and with the financial aid, Coleridge worked the harder. In April, his volume of poems appeared.

Although his friends' aid was helpful, more money must be earned. His brother George wrote praising his poems, but offering no financial assistance. An offer made by Mrs. Elizabeth Evans for them to live at Darley Hall and for him to tutor her children was withdrawn when the Coleridges arrived, as her children's guardians objected to Coleridge's religious and political opinions. Charmed by the couple, Mrs. Evans insited on their remaining as her guests for ten days. When they left, she hurriedly pressed £95 into Coleridge's hands and gave pregnant Sara all her baby clothes. Shortly after returning home to Bristol, Coleridge was persuaded to go to Birmingham, where he agreed to take into his home Charles Lloyd, the twenty-year-old son of a banker. The neurotic and epileptic young man was to be tutored by Coleridge. Then, when Coleridge was offered a teaching position at £250 a year, "with mornings free," he planned to accept it, although Poole felt it would hinder development of his genius.

He was eager to get home to Bristol with Lloyd, for his son had been born during his absence. Sara had urged him to take the Birmingham trip, even though her confinement was imminent, for she liked the idea of his securing a wealthy young man to tutor. Coleridge wrote Poole of how his heart was sad when he first saw his baby son, for in the infant's face he saw all he had been and "all my child might be!" He was thrilled, however, as he kissed his son,

> So for the mother's sake the child was dear,
> And dearer was the mother for the child.

Coleridge named his son David Hartley for the philosopher he so admired.

Despite the happiness of the young parents in their son, Coleridge became ill in November, suffering with neuralgic pains that ran from right temple to right shoulder. The first day of the onslaught of pain, he took from sixty to seventy drops of laudanum; the next day it required twenty-five drops of laudanum every five hours for him to get a measure of relief. His doctor thought the disease was caused by nervousness or excessive anxiety. Small wonder he was nervous: Lloyd's increasing epileptic attacks had brought on acute morbidity from which Coleridge sought to raise him. The physical strength Coleridge had to use to control Lloyd during an attack was great; moreover, the baby cried a great deal; Mrs. Fricker proved irritating. He wrote Lamb, "O my God! my God! when am I to find rest?"

Realizing he must find peace of mind, he wrote Poole to find him a cottage at Stowey. He wrote Lloyd's father his son should return to his home; as Mrs. Fricker was unwilling, he knew, to leave Bristol, he decided firmly she could remain there and he would support her.

Though Poole wrote that he could find only a small and unsatisfactory cottage, Coleridge took it. He must get out of his crippling environment.

In early 1797, the Coleridges and Lloyd settled in the inconvenient cottage at Stowey. Lloyd's father, aware of his son's illness, refused to have him at home, and insisted he remain with the Coleridges. The young couple, however, was happy. The tiny strip of land, half garden, half orchard, and the closeness to Poole's home made up for the cottage's inconveniences. Reading incessantly, trying "to detect what appear to me the defects of all systems of morality before and since Christ," working on a second edition of his poems in which would appear some verses by Charles Lamb and some by Charles Lloyd, Coleridge was busy, indeed. It soon became obvious, however, that Lloyd needed expert treatment. Five times within ten days he had prolonged fits of delirium; as Coleridge sat up all night each time Lloyd had an attack trying to calm him, he himself became exhausted physically in subduing the epileptic's frantic struggles. At the end of March, Lloyd finally went to Erasmus Darwin's sanitarium at Lichfield. Coleridge agreed now to nurse George Burnett for a time, and to tutor Southey's youngest brother.

At last, Coleridge had peace. In the spring, he arose at seven and worked in his garden a short time; then he wrote until noon, when he fed his pigs and poultry; at two he dined, and then wrote until teatime; after tea, he reviewed books until supper. After supper, he chatted with friends. He was proud of his garden, where he raised potatoes, enough corn to supply the family with bread, and all kinds of vegetables. He kept ducks, geese, and two pigs.

As soon as Coleridge had his poems in the form he approved, he sent them, along with Southey's and Lloyd's, to the printer. Then he had visited the Wordsworths at Racedown and had been inspired as never before. Truly, he felt he had much for which to be thankful,—this twenty-five-year-old poet and preacher. He was eager, he told Dorothy Wordsworth again as they drove toward his home, to have her and William meet his nine-month-old Hartley, his wife Sara, and Tom Poole.

CHAPTER VI

Some Friendships Deepen;
Others Diminish

ON JULY 2, 1797, AS DOROTHY WORDSWORTH, YOUNG BASIL MONTAGU, AND COLERIDGE RODE INTO NETHER STOWEY, the gardens, with red roses, pinks, white lilies, sweet williams, and grey lavender seemed to make more cheerful the brown sandstone houses and cottages. They drove the length of the village, for Coleridge's tiny cottage was at the western end of the community, adjoining the larger house of Thomas Poole on the main street; in fact, Thomas Poole had cut a door in his wall so that Coleridge might have easier access to his property. Poole, a bachelor, Coleridge explained, had living with him his aged, widowed mother; a secretary, Thomas Ward; and a French émigré abbé, who earned a livelihood by teaching French. Poole's tanyard, the principal source of his wealth, lay close to his house; Coleridge said Poole also farmed his own extensive acreage. As the chaise stopped at Coleridge's cottage, the poet pointed out the brook running before it and added that his garden and the fine old trees were at the back.

Entering the cottage with its two small, dark, damp parlors and a kitchen on the first floor, the visitors met brown-haired, fair-skinned, plump Sara Coleridge and her exquisite nine-month-old baby, Hartley. Coleridge was very proud of his son whom he called "a minute philosopher." William soon arrived and looked gravely at the baby whom Dorothy held in her arms while Mrs. Coleridge was preparing dinner assisted by Nana, the maid. They learned that upstairs were three bedrooms, really attic rooms. Mr. Poole had spoken truly when he said it was not a desirable house. While dining they talked of poetry, but Sara Coleridge, though she had occasionally written some verse, did not participate in the rapid give-and-take. Later, Dorothy learned that she was more interested in discussing fashions and that she missed the gay life at Bristol. In love with her husband, Sara had no comprehension of his genius. Yet, as she and Coleridge exchanged glances, there seemed to be real affection between them. She was trying to make a home of which he could be proud and in which he would be comfortable—no easy task. After dinner, Coleridge proudly showed the Wordsworths his trees and garden; the weeds showed him to be no expert gardener. Who am I, he queried, to decide whether a weed should grow or not? This same impractical philosophy kept him from setting traps for the mice in his house; he thought it would be unchivalrous to kill them. Before long, Thomas Poole joined the group. They found mutual stimulus in one another. The evening sped by.

The next day, Coleridge, Basil, and the Wordsworths wandered about the country, happier than they had ever been. Sara remained at home, busy with her household chores and caring for her baby. Dorothy found in the region, she later wrote Mary Hutchinson, everything that she loved: "sea, woods, wild as fancy ever painted, brooks clear and pebbly as in Cumberland, villages so romantic; and William and I in a wander by ourselves, found out a sequestered waterfall in a dell formed by steep hills covered with full-grown timber trees. The woods are as fine as those at Lowther, and the country more romantic; it has the character of the less grand parts of the neighborhood of the Lakes."

The second day, Coleridge suffered an injury when Sara accidentally spilled "a skillet of boiling milk" over his foot. This injury kept him confined to the house, the garden and "the lime tree bower" for two weeks, while Dorothy and William, tramping about the countryside, shared with him, on their return each day, their impressions and experiences. They excitedly told him on the first day of his confinement of coming upon a large and beautiful country-house, Alfoxden, and of how they had followed the course of the little brook that ran through the large park surrounding the house, thinking all the while this could well be their dream house.

Later, Dorothy described the house and grounds to Mary Hutchinson. It was, indeed, "a large mansion, with furniture enough for a dozen families like ours," set in "a large park, with seventy head of deer. . . . There is an excellent garden, well stocked with vegetables and fruit. The garden is at the end of the house, and our favorite parlor, as at Racedown, looks that way. In front is a little court, with grass plot, gravel walk, and shrubs; the moss roses were in full beauty a month ago. The front of the house is to the south, but it is screened from the sun by a high hill, which rises immediately from it. This hill is beautiful, scattered irregularly and abundantly with trees, and topped with fern, which spreads a considerable way down it. The deer dwell here, and sheep, so that we have a living prospect. From the end of the house we have a view of the sea, over a woody meadow-country; and exactly opposite the window . . . is an immense wood, whose round top from this point has exactly the appearance of a mighty dome. In some parts of this wood, there is an under-grove of hollies which are now very beautiful. In a glen at the bottom of the wood is the waterfall of which I spoke, a quarter of a mile from the house. We are three miles from Stowey, and not two miles from the sea. Wherever we turn we have woods, smooth downs, and valleys with small brooks running down them through green meadows, hardly ever intersected with hedgerows, but scattered over with trees. The hills that cradle these valleys are either covered with fern and hill-berries, or oak woods, which are cut for clear coal. . . . Walks extend for miles over the hill-tops; the great beauty of which is their wild simplicity: they are perfectly smooth, without rocks.

"The Tor of Glastonbury is before our eyes during more than half our walk to Stowey; and in the park wherever we go keeping about fifteen yards above the house, it makes a part of our prospect."

Coleridge told the enthusiastic Wordsworths that the house standing vacant belonged to the St. Albyn family who had owned it since the fifteenth century. The Rev. Lancelot St. Albyn, the present owner, had recently died, leaving a widow and a minor son. They had rented the house to Mr. John Bartholomew, who, when approached by Thomas Poole who highly recommended the Wordsworths, agreed to rent it to them for £23 a year, "rate and tax-free," and to pay for upkeep of the place. The joy of the Wordsworths at being able to live there was equaled by that of Coleridge and Poole. The Wordsworths had loved Racedown; in fact, Dorothy later wrote, "I think Racedown the place dearest to my recollections upon the whole surface of the island; it is the first home I ever had." Yet, brother and sister thought Alfoxden and the country about more beautiful—and they wished to be near Coleridge.

Wordsworth was aware of how his sister's eyes detected "the most delicate tints—of foliage, the faintest outline of the cloud." Under her guidance, he was recovering his early capacity for "delight and admiration of nature's wonders" and also "regaining, though more slowly, his powers of seeing and loving humanity." She pointed out how after "wet dark days, the country seems more populous. It peoples itself in sunbeams." She observed "the ivy twisting round the oaks like bristled serpents"; she noted on one walk "the blue-grey sea, shaded with immense masses of cloud, not streaked; the sheep glittering in the sunshine" with the morning dew; as she and William returned through the wood, she admired the "trees skirting the wood, being exposed more directly to the action of the sea breeze, stripped of the net-work of their upper branches, which are stiff and erect, like black skeletons"; the ground was "strewed with the red berries of the holly." Only once "while we were in the wood the moon burst forth through the invisible veil which enveloped her, the shadows of the oaks blackened, and their lines became more strongly marked. The withered leaves were covered with a deeper yellow and a brighter gloss spotted the hollies; again her form became dimmer; the sky flat, unmarked by distances, a thin white cloud." One night, as Dorothy and Coleridge walked in the wood and then sat under the trees, she said, "The still trees bowed their heads as if listening to the wind. The hollies in the thick wood unshaken by the blast; only when it came with greater force, shaken by the rain drops falling from the bare oaks above." Impressed with these reflections, William wrote,

> She gave me eyes; she gave me ears.

He realized, too, how Coleridge, with his philosophy and speculation, was providing him with a new philosophical creed.

Coleridge, who had written his friend Joseph Cottle of his admiration for Wordsworth, before whom he felt "little," now wrote Cottle of William's "exquisite sister." "She is a woman, indeed! in mind, I mean, and heart; for her person is such, that if you expected to see a pretty woman, you would think her very ordinary; if you expected to see an ordinary woman, you would think her pretty! but her manners are simple, ardent, impressive. In every motion, her most innocent soul outbeams so brightly, that who saw would say,

> Guilt was a thing impossible in her.

Her information various. Her eye watchful in minutest observation of nature; and her taste, a perfect electrometer. It bends, protrudes, and draws in, at subtlest beauties, and most recondite faults."

Shortly after the Wordsworths' arrival, Charles Lamb, whom Coleridge had invited earlier to be a guest, arrived to spend his week's holiday from the East India House office. Ever since the dreadful day, September 22, 1796, when "dear, gentle Charles' " sister Mary in a fit of temporary insanity had killed their mother, Coleridge had besought Lamb, his old schoolmate, to visit him. Not knowing the Wordsworths were at Nether Stowey, now suddenly Lamb appeared.

On February 10, 1775, Charles Lamb had been born in one of the rear rooms of the ground floor apartment of The Temple, long regarded as an "indestructible symbol" of London's antiquity. Facing the Thames River and the Inner Temple Gardens where Dr. Samuel Johnson lived and where later Oliver Goldsmith moved, The Temple made its own laws and used a legal language heard nowhere else. Walks on which the sun rarely shone ran through the courtyards and on the terraces to secret enclosures. Its sun dials and tombstones fitted well into its cloistral atmosphere. Under Henry VIII, it had passed, it is true, from religious to legal hands. Lawyers acquired the property for very little and converted it to their own use, retaining however, all its churchly privileges, special rights, and exemptions; in the ancient church, among the images of saints and crusaders, beneath stained glass windows, they received their clients. When John Lamb, valet of lawyer Samuel Salt, married handsome, tall Elizabeth Field, who was said to resemble Mrs. Siddons, he and his bride were given lodgings in the Temple, beneath those of Mr. Salt. There, seven Lamb children were born, four of whom died shortly after birth. They were buried in the Temple churchyard. The fifth child, John, suffered so from rickets that he was lame and disfigured throughout his life. Mary, the third child, was born on December 3, 1764; she had a lonely childhood. The quiet, piercingly brown-eyed girl, with well formed features and expressive, white, delicately formed hands, had a smile "that was winning in the extreme."

When she was six, her brother John began attending Christ's Hospital, and was away during most of her childhood. She attended William Bird's Academy in Fetter Lane, where boys went in the mornings and girls in the afternoons to learn reading, writing, and arithmetic. Her formal education seems to have been an afterthought, as she was older than the other children when she went to Mr. Bird's school; educating girls was still a matter of question. Regrettably, Mary's spelling and grammar were far from good when, "as a big girl," she began school. Though the schoolmaster's teaching improved such deficiencies, throughout her life she suffered from these weaknesses. In the brief period she was at school, she enjoyed for the first time the companionship of girls her age. She had one close friend whose brother was an actor. The outstanding event of her childhood was when the two little girls were taken to the theatre. They had gone early so that they might see the people hurrying into the gallery or strolling leisurely into the pit, see the candles being lighted and the musicians coming from under the stage. At length, as the musicians played, the curtain rose and Mary heard a lady on the stage say, "Music hath charms to soothe the savage breast," the opening lines in Congreve's *Mourning Bride*. Finally, they saw *Harlequin and Columbine*.

Sometimes, she visited her grandmother at Blakesware. Life was dull in this home where dwelt her grandmother, another elderly woman, and a number of aged woman servants. There, the days began with morning prayer and Mary's reading aloud the Scriptures for about an hour. Following breakfast, she was allowed to do needlework for a half hour—no longer, lest she strain her eyes. Time hung heavily as she explored the house with its many family portraits, most of them of elderly people, in quaint dress; she lingered long at that of a golden-haired little girl dressed in blue, one of whose arms was about the neck of a lamb; the other, filled with a bunch of roses. She often wished the little girl would come down from the picture and play with her. One day, while exploring the house, she finally succeeded in opening a door she had first thought locked. For days, she went through dusky volumes she found there. The one that most impressed her was about Mahometism. She accepted all the wonderful adventures of Mahomet as fact; she trembled when she read that the souls of the dead would cross a bottomless gulf, over a narrow bridge, no wider than a silken thread, and that those not of the true faith would slip and fall into a bottomless gulf. As her grandmother was not a follower of Mahomet, she worried by day about her falling into the bottomless gulf; she dreamed night after night about this terrible trial and the possible fall. One day, as she saw one of her grandmother's infirm friends totter across a room, she felt genuine panic as she thought of the nice old lady's possible fall into that bottomless pit. Since excessive reading had been forbidden, she dared not tell anyone of her worries.

When she was eleven, her brother Charles was born. Knowing that she was to have a brother, she "thought him a long time coming." From the time of his birth, she cared for the short, thin-legged, black-haired little boy with sad, piercing black eyes. She taught him his letters before he could talk, an accomplishment somewhat delayed because of a speech impediment. She seems to have used the tomb-stones in the Temple Churchyard to help him with his letters. One day, after he had learned to read as well as to talk, the little boy asked her, "Mary, where are the naughty people buried?" Besides playing in the courtyard, they sometimes wandered into the Temple church where "there were curious images on the walls and recumbent statues of the Knights Templar on the floor." They played, too, in the Inner Temple Gardens, from which they could watch the boats on the Thames go by, or where they observed on the walks the old benchers and prominent barristers going to their work or promenading. They noted Joseph Jekyll "of the roguish eye," thrifty Thomas Coventry, burly Daines Barrington, who tried to poison the sparrows, and Baron Francis Maseres, who wore curious, old-fashioned clothes. At times, they visited their great-Aunt Gladman at Mackeray End, where, in the spring, Mary taught Charles to search for the rare violets, blue-bells and double daffodils; when she found him trying to catch a bee, she warned him to keep away from the hive and instead to watch the reapers cut the hay or the shearers clip the sheep. They watched the men sitting at a long oaken table, eating roast beef and plum pudding, or after dinner listened to them singing songs the children had never heard before.

Life at home when the children had to stay indoors, was far from pleasant, as their father had insisted that his sister Hetty live with them in the already overcrowded apartment. With her coming, strife began and never ended. The fact that her favorite books, which she constantly read, were *The Imitation of Christ* and the Roman Catholic *Prayer Book*, was a bone of contention, for though she concealed her Catholicism by attending first the Protestant and later the Unitarian Church on Sundays, had it been known that she and her brother were Catholics, not only would the father have lost his position in the Temple Commons but his sons would not have been eligible for Christ's Hospital scholarships, nor would they have been eligible for positions in the South Sea House and the India House. Furthermore, no young man who was a Catholic could go to the University or practice law; nor could an old man who was a Catholic bequeath property.

The Lamb children, fearful because of their aunt's religious views, which they did not understand, were so nervously upset over their aunt's religion, that one of them once imagined her a witch. They were nervous, too, these war children, about the American Revolution, for they had seen Benjamin Franklin and Thomas Paine going and coming in The Temple. Then had come the French Revolution with its tales of men and women beheaded and cruelty stalking the land.

After Charles was eight and had spent a brief time at Mr. Bird's Academy, his close companionship with his sister for a time ceased, as he entered Christ's Hospital where he remained except for the vacation periods. When he was fifteen, his education stopped, as his stammering seemed to make further education impracticable. Hence, he went to Mr. Joseph Paines' countinghouse to learn the rudiments of business. A year later, he entered his business apprenticeship at the South Sea House, where he received an annual gratuity of £30 a year for three years, but no regular salary while he was learning the essentials of business; again he lived at home.

Meanwhile, Mary became a dressmaker or a mantua-maker, as it was then called. She could not have achieved this position without considerable ability, for Paris set the fashions and the making of a headdress or a fashionable dress of expensive material required a high degree of skill and efficiency. She did her sewing at home in cramped quarters, for John, after attending Christ's Hospital at fifteen, was at home again, having accepted a genteel position with good pay at the South Sea House.

In 1792, after the deaths of Mr. and Mrs. Salt, the Lamb family had to leave their quarters in the Temple for respectable but still cramped ones in Little Queen Street in nearby High Holborn. Long conditioned to the life in the Temple, the older Lambs suffered acutely from the change. Sixty-seven-year-old John Lamb deteriorated rapidly into senility, spending his days in idleness, or begging someone to play cribbage with him. Elizabeth Lamb, fifty-seven, began to break up physically as her arthritis made her a chair-bound cripple. Hetty, older than her brother and sister-in-law, preserved her usual strength and faculties. Mary Lamb, sewing at home all day, was torn by her parents' complaints and her aunt's prayers. As the annuities of her parents and aunt were not sufficient to support them, Mary Lamb went out and solicited extra dress-making orders. So successful was she in acquiring and keeping customers, that she required an apprentice to aid her. At thirty, an established dressmaker, she had a clientele that was noteworthy. Before John acquired an establishment of his own, and Charles was an apprentice in the East India Company, but still at home without wages for three years, Mary was indeed the main support of the family.

In 1792, Mary Lamb read Mary Wollstonecraft's book *A Vindication of the Rights of Woman* which had just appeared, giving the world a shock as she enunciated her theory that women should receive as good an education as men; indeed, she declared "If woman be not prepared by education to be the companion of man, she will stop the progress of knowledge, for truth must be common to all." Mary Lamb agreed with Mary Wollstonecraft's ideas but her agreement did not aid her in her fight to earn a living for a family, most of whom were thoroughly unappreciative of her efforts. The volume gave Mary ideas, however, which she developed later.

Charles Lamb, though devoted to his sister, began seeking male companionship outside the home and became too often a frequenter of ale houses. At one of them, The Salutation and the Cat, he met Samuel Taylor Coleridge, who had deserted his studies at Cambridge, and was deep in troubles of other kinds too, for he was committed to take part in a plan called pantisocracy and was engaged to two young women, Sara Fricker of Bristol and Mary Evans. Not knowing how to face his problems, Coleridge had gone into hiding in London. The friendship of Coleridge and Lamb proved so exciting for both young men that they spent considerable time together talking and drinking. Visiting occasionally at the Lamb's home, Coleridge became fond of Mary Lamb. In fact, he was enjoying life immensely until Robert Southey tracked him down, told the errant male that since Miss Evans had become engaged to another suitor he had better "do the right thing by Miss Fricker," the sister of Southey's fiancé. In October, 1795, then, Coleridge married Sara, and Southey, assured that now all was well, after marrying Edith Fricker, left for Portugal. The Lambs missed Coleridge greatly, though he wrote them frequently.

Shortly before Coleridge's marriage, Charles Lamb had a nervous breakdown and was confined to a hospital for mental diseases at Hoxton. He remained there but a short time, and wrote to Coleridge, "The six weeks that finished last year and began this, your very humble servant spent very agreeably in a mad house at Hoxton; I am got somewhat rational now and don't bite anyone." Though Charles was casual about his illness, his brother John was not; Coleridge, he contended, had been the cause of his brother's insanity, a charge that annoyed Charles exceedingly.

Mary suffered from depression and "a certain flightiness in her poor head." She had suffered these symptoms from childhood. Now, burdened with caring for her parents and overwork in her shop, in December 1794, she was alarmed by a mental illness that seemed to be far worse. From then on, she never passed Bedlam without saying to herself, "Here it may be my fate to end my days." This illness passed, but it had warned Mary that she must not become overtired.

Yet, her elderly relatives proved to be problems: her father, John, now seventy, was in his second childhood, and had to be humored like a sick child. Her mother, sixty, once tall and stately, always austere in her personal relationships, lacking in sympathy toward her only daughter, whose caresses and protestations of filial affection had always met with coldness and repulse, now an invalid, confined to her chair, resented being dependent upon her daughter. Aunt Hetty, old and cross, was insolent, spent her time reading her prayer book; usually she sat silently watching life, at time given to sharp repartee. Mary's responsibilities in the household, as well as those of her job, seemed to increase.

On September 22, 1796, Charles noted she was not well and was showing symptoms not unlike those he had had before his breakdown. Hence, he set out to seek Dr. Pitcairn, a physician whom he wished to consult about her. The physician was not at home. That day, provoked with an apprentice girl who was helping at the table, Mary suddenly became enraged and started throwing forks at her; one struck Mr. Lamb in the forehead; Mary then grabbed a knife and began chasing the girl around the table. As Mrs. Lamb remonstrated with her to stop, Mary turned all her fury upon her mother and stabbed her to the heart. The screaming servant brought the landlord to the door. There he found Mrs. Lamb lying dead in a chair, Mr. Lamb, wiping blood from his forehead and weeping by her side, Aunt Hetty on the floor unconscious, and Mary standing with a bloody knife in her hand. Within moments, Charles Lamb returned, walked to his sister, and quietly took the knife from her.

Up to this time, Charles had stood in awe of his brother John, but now he assumed full responsibility. John, far from sympathetic with Mary, contended she should be placed in an asylum, Bedlam or any other. The very thought of this happening to his sister filled Charles with horror. He had suffered a brief spell of madness and recovered; Mary could, too, he said in a letter he wrote to Coleridge, who offered sympathy immediately. At the coroner's inquest held the following day, the jury found that "the young lady had been once before in her earlier years deranged from the harassing fatigues of too much business. As her carriage toward her mother was ever affectionate in the extreme, it is believed that to the increased attentiveness, which her parents' infirmities called for by day and night is to be attributed the present insanity of this illfated young woman." She was deemed guilty of no crime.

Asylums for the insane at that time were horrible at best. The worst of the lot, of course, was Bedlam, a public charity, for the in-

curable insane, endowed by Henry VIII. There, for a small fee,
visitors could go and see the inmates lying in chairs. Less gruesome
but awful was Hoxton where Charles Lamb had been briefly. There,
it was permissible for one to excite the poor inmates as they paced up
and down, by making faces at them or by threatening to attack them,
until the whole place was in a boiling frenzy. Among the best of the
private hospitals for the insane were those maintained by the Quakers.
One of their doctors, Dr. Pitcairn who cared for Charles and Mary
Lamb, though he knew no therapeutic techniques, realized that the
causes of the abnormal conduct of later life must be sought in the
influences of childhood, and laid a deep responsibility for insanity on
parents and teachers. Mary Lamb, luckily, was guided to this best of
doctors of the time by Charles.

The judge had agreed that Mary could be placed in a private
sanitarium if her brother assumed responsibility for her care. Once she
became sane, however, it decreed she should not live in the same house
as her father. With this arrangement made, Charles' responsibility
began. A new home was sought; a servant procured to care for Charles
and his father; John took separate lodgings; Aunt Hetty went to live
with a wealthy cousin, "a lady of fortune"; and Mary went to the
private asylum at Islington. Charles provided a private nurse for
Mary and visited her or wrote her every day; Coleridge wrote her
almost daily.

Throughout the ordeal, Charles remained calm. "God be praised,"
he wrote Coleridge, "wonderful it is to tell. I have never once been
otherwise than collected and calm; even on the dreadful day and in
the midst of the terrible scene I preserved a tranquillity not of despair
—is it folly or sin in me to say that it was a religious principle that
most supported me? . . . I closed not my eyes in sleep that night, but
lay without terrors and without despair. I have lost no sleep since."
Only once, did he break; in the midst of the carousing that was going
on in his home the night of the customary wake preceding his mother's
burial, he ran from those present and collapsed "in agony of emotion"
beside his mother's casket. The collapse was brief; he soon regained
the amazing self-control that carried him through the following days
with dignity. He wrote Coleridge of how he was going to manage
financially to support himself, his father and Mary: ". . . if my father,
an old maid-servant and I can't live comfortably on £130 or £120 a
year, we ought to burn by slow fires and I almost would, that Mary
might not go into an hospital."

Aunt Hetty, age eighty, stubborn and difficult, was changed by the

Robert Southey in 1796, from a portrait by Robert Hancock, National Portrait Gallery

Mrs. Samuel Taylor Coleridge at thirty-nine, from a miniature in the possession of Mr. Ernest Hartley Coleridge

Charles Lamb, from a painting by William Hazlitt, National Portrait Gallery

'Ride a-cock-horse'!

Mrs Gilpin riding to Edmonton.

drawn after Nature by T. H.

Mary Lamb from a caricature by Thomas Hood and annotated by Charles Lamb, Huntington Library, San Marino, California

Sir Walter Scott, by Sir Edwin Landseer, R.A., National Portrait Gallery

William Hazlitt, from a chalk drawing by William Bewick, National Portrait Gallery

tragedy. Once with her wealthy cousin, she devoted her little income that had paid for her board and room to help defray Mary's expenses at the sanitarium. Before long, however, the cousin tired of Aunt Hetty whom she found "indolent and mulish" and strangely attached to Charles's household. So Aunt Hetty came back to Charles and his father. The once hearty old lady, Charles said, has so wasted away that she "is a mere skeleton" and looks "like a corpse." She did not live long after her return.

Ten days after the tragedy, Mary "regained her senses," with "a dreadful sense and recollection of what had passed, awful to her mind, and impressive (as it must be to the end of her life) but tempered with religious resignation, and the reasonings of a sound judgment," Charles wrote. He kept her well supplied with books; she worked to pay part of her expenses at the sanitarium. "You and Sara are very good to think so kindly and favorably of poor Mary," he wrote to Coleridge, "I would to God all did so too." At the end of six months, Mary was released from the sanitarium and moved into a furnished apartment near Charles's residence. Before long, the old relationship was resumed; Mary again was the leader. She took up sewing as she had before. In June, 1797, she was surprised to received a copy of *Poems* by *S. T. Coleridge, Second Edition, to Which Are Now Added Poems by Charles Lamb and Charles Lloyd.* Charles' part was dedicated "To Mary Ann Lamb, the author's best friend and sister."

All seemed well at first once Mary was released; she and Charles wrote verses, collected them, put them in book form, found publishers —and the public liked their verses. But again and again, Mary's attacks recurred. As they did, Charles, often openly weeping, took her to Islington. Then would follow many months of insanity. Their friends tried to comfort them. Among them were William Godwin, belligerently talking of social justice; and John Hazlitt, the miniature painter; his brother, a portrait painter who was painting a portrait of Charles Lamb in the costume of a Venetian senator and saying he was about to forsake painting for literature; William Wordsworth; and, of course, Samuel Taylor Coleridge. Hazlitt said he "had met with only one thoroughly reasonable woman, Mary Lamb."

Now Lamb, the twenty-two-year-old Londoner, arrived at Nether Stowey in response to Coleridge's long-standing invitation, only to find Coleridge incapacitated by the severe burn and to meet for the first time Dorothy Wordsworth.

Sara enjoyed thoroughly this new visitor with whom she felt more at ease than with the Wordsworths whom her husband seemed to idolize. Wordsworth, she found unapproachable; Dorothy, she considered unwomanly and not at all "exquisite" as her husband had said. She envied Dorothy's freedom that enabled her to go on long walks, while she herself was tied down with her baby and household tasks, made doubly difficult by the stream of visitors her husband constantly invited. Accustomed to small talk about women's games, fashions, and society, she was puzzled and disturbed by her husband's discussions with the Wordsworths, for she simply did not comprehend much of what they said.

Though Coleridge was house-bound by the accident, Dorothy, William, and Charles took short walks of two or three miles during the day, having no idea that they were mystifying the people in the neighborhood. Indeed, they were no ordinary group: tall, gaunt William Wordsworth who wore his hair long, straight and unpowdered in the Jacobin fashion, dark-skinned, spindly-legged; Charles Lamb with his piercing black eyes, and brown-skinned Dorothy with her quick movements and eager eyes, who some natives thought had a "foreign" look.

While his friends roamed the countryside, Coleridge wrote his poem "This Lime-Tree Bower My Prison":

> Well, they are gone, and here must I remain,
> Lam'd by the scathe of fire, lonely and faint,
> This lime-tree bower my prison! They meantime
> My friends, whom I may never meet again,
> On springy heath, along the hill-top edge
> Wander delighted, and look down, perchance,
> On that same rifted dell, where many an ash
> Twists its wild limbs beside the ferny rock
> Whose plumy ferns forever nod and drip,
> Spray'd by the waterfall.

Charles Lamb, who was enjoying his visit, though surprised to find the place he had long held in Coleridge's life usurped by the Wordsworths, wondered whether his friend really did understand him, when Coleridge wrote about Lamb's wandering about the countryside, for he had said:

Ney, gentle hearted Charles! thou has't pin'd
And hunger'd after Nature, many a year
In the great City pent, winning thy way
With sad yet patient soul, through evil and pain
And sad calamity . . . . . .

Did not Coleridge realize, Lamb pondered, how much he really liked the city where he had always lived? Yet, the fortnight with the Coleridges and Wordsworths had brought him greater enthusiasm for life. After his return to London, he wrote telling Coleridge how he had enjoyed his hospitality, adding, "I could not talk much while I was with you, but my silence was not sullenness, nor I hope from any bad motive, but, in fact, disuse has made me awkward at it . . . It was kind of you to endure me as you did . . . I feel improvement in the recollection of many a casual conversation. The names of Tom Poole, Wordsworth and his sister, thine and Sara's, are become familiar as household words." He asked for a copy of Wordsworth's poem "Lines Left Upon a Seat in a Yew Tree" composed while he was there, and regretted he had left behind his great-coat, adding, "is it not ridiculous that I sometimes envy that great-coat lingering so cunningly behind?" Months passed before Coleridge, in midwinter, remembered to return the coat.

On July 14, 1798, the agreement for Alfoxden was signed and William and Dorothy moved into their new home, with an elderly woman as a servant. Thomas Poole had engineered the signing of the agreement for the house and agreed to act as security for the rent. The Bartholomews and Mrs. St. Albyn were glad to rent the estate at the ridiculously low rental, as the war had damaged extensively the prosperity of the country and many families were delighted to get any rent for their houses and to keep them occupied. In August, William returned to Racedown and brought back to Alfoxden, Basil, their servant Peggy, and the Wordsworth clothing and books. Now again, they really were settled in their own home after a prolonged visit with the Coleridges.

The intimacy with Coleridge continued, however, for almost every day the Wordsworths visited the Coleridges; or Coleridge, and at times Sara, visited Alfoxden. After Coleridge's visits, the Wordsworths or more often Dorothy alone, accompanied him half-way home. In her diary, for example, we read "February 3rd.—A mild morning, the windows open at breakfast, the redbreasts singing in the garden. Walked with Coleridge over the hills. . . . 4th.—Walked a great part of the way to Stowey with Coleridge. The morning warm and sunny. . . . 5th.—Walked to Stowey with Coleridge, returned by woodlands; a very warm day. . . . 6th.—Walked to Stowey over the hills, returned to tea, a cold and clear evening, the roads in some parts frozen hard . . . The sea hid by mist all the day. . . . 11th.—Walked with Coleridge near to Stowey. The day pleasant, but cloudy. . . . 12th.—Walked alone to Stowey. Returned in the evening with Coleridge. A mild, pleasant, cloudy day." Often the two enjoyed views near Alfoxden. On the 26th of February, for example, Dorothy tells in her diary of walking nearly to Stowey with Coleridge and on that very clear afternoon, "We lay sidelong upon the turf, and gazed on the landscape till it melted into more than natural loveliness. The sea very uniform, of a pale greyish blue, only one distant bay, bright and blue as a sky; had there been a vessel sailing upon it, a very vision of delight. Walked to the top of a hill to see a fortification. Again sat down to feed upon the prospect; a magnificent scene. . . ." True, she still walked with her brother and with him and Basil, but Coleridge had come to fill an important place in her life and she in his. Before she met Coleridge, she had been almost passionately devoted to her brother. As the mutual attraction of Dorothy and Coleridge developed first into affection, then into love, she found in him a tenderness she had never known before. Yet, she never once considered becoming his mistress nor did he think of asking her to do so. Though each blossomed under the encouragement and understanding of the other, Dorothy sublimated by an even increased devotion to her brother, an affection not unlike that of a wife for her husband. Coleridge, realizing anew how empty his marriage was, became increasingly restless; his daily visits to Alfoxden began to lengthen to five-day visits. As summer passed and autumn came, Sara complained of her loneliness, of her many household chores, of her neglected garden, and of the new baby she was now carrying.

Shortly after Charles Lamb left for London, John Thelwell, a political agitator, long a friend of Coleridge's, accepted the poet's invitation for a visit. On July 17, the day he arrived, Mrs. Coleridge was busy "superintending the wash-tub," as the recent guests had left her with a huge amount of laundry to take care of; Coleridge was at Alfoxden, visiting the Wordsworths. Early the next morning, however, Sara Coleridge and Mr. Thelwell walked to Alfoxden, "to call Samuel and his friend Wordsworth up for breakfast." After breakfast, the Coleridges, Wordsworths, and Thelwell explored the estate, wandering in the woods and dells, admiring the waterfalls and the deer, all the while talking of poetry, philosophy, and government.

Eight years older than Coleridge, Thelwell, who had suffered poverty, was deeply concerned about the French Revolution. Recognizing the importance of awakening the low classes in England to the consciousness of their opportunities, he had gained a position of importance among the more educated members of that group. Feared because of his wide influence, he had been arrested in May, 1794, his house searched, and his books and manuscripts seized, every one, "upon whatever subject—Poems, Novels, Literary and Philosophical Dissertations—all the unfinished labours of ten years' application. Successful or abortive, it matters not; they were the creations of my own industry, and therefore were *absolutely more my property* than the estate of the laudable gentleman or the stock in trade of the manufacturer." His library and writings were never returned to him and he was ordered to await trial on very flimsy grounds. Despite every effort to convict him of high treason, after being held five awful months in the Tower of London and one month in Newgate Prison "where the corpses of such prisoners as died of diseases were placed before burial," he was freed and acquitted of the charge of high treason. Forbidden to speak in public places, he spoke twice a week in his own quarters, at first to large crowds, on the need of electoral reform and of freedom of assembly. He published his lectures in *The Tribune* which he owned and edited. As governmental pressure continued, he gave up his lecturing except on Roman History; the government suppressed publication of *The Tribune*.

Young Coleridge became attracted to Thelwell partly because of Thelwell's revolutionary ideas, but more because he was an atheist whom the young poet and minister hoped to convert. Wordsworth found him stimulating because of his opposition to war and because of his belief that the poor in England were oppressed. Thelwell was one of the first to point out the dangers of the industrial movement which was attracting the population into large centers, where factories and mines had no safety devices and where women's and children's labor was exploited. As England was too rapidly transformed into an industrial nation by improvements in the machinery of manufacturers and the power of the steam engine, many manufacturers who had before been mere operators, had accumulated great wealth, "saw and knew little of anything beyond the demand for their twist or cloth, and the speediest means of production." Children, working in the cotton mills, one manufacturer said to Robert Southey, "get their bread almost as soon as they can run about, and by the time they are seven or eight, bring in money. There is no idleness among us; they come at five in the morning; we allow them half an hour for breakfast, and an hour for dinner; they leave work at six, and another set relieves them for the night; the wheels never can stand still." To his remarks, Southey sighed: "I was looking while he spoke at the unnatural dexterity with which the fingers of the little creatures were playing with the machinery, half giddy myself with the noise and the endless motion; and when he told me there was no rest, day or night, I thought that if Dante had peopled one of his hells with children, here was a scene worthy to have supplied him with new images of torment." The chimney sweeps went to work even younger; as many of the chimneys which these little boys swept to remove the soot were exceedingly narrow, the little boys were often put up the chimney naked lest their clothing get caught and trap them as the soot fell. The skin of these youngsters, one employer remarked casually, became cartilaginous in about six weeks. Others of these poor children were harnessed to small loads of coal and drew the loaded vehicles where there were very narrow passages in the mines. One landlord boasted that the rooms in which such children and their parents lived —for often the entire family toiled—were never vacant, for he rented them to one group by night, another by day.

The war later brought about a great depression, making it necessary to lower wages; taxes were raised; and a protective tariff to aid landowners left the poor with higher prices to pay for food. Adam Smith wrote of the taxes of the middle class, "The school boy whips his taxed top—the beardless youth manages his taxed horse with a taxed bridle, on a taxed road:—and the dying Englishman, pouring his medicine, which has paid 7 per cent., into a spoon that has paid 15 per cent.—flings himself back upon his chintz bed, which has paid 22 per cent.—and expires in the arms of an apothecary who has paid a license of a hundred pounds for the privilege of putting him to death. His whole property is then immediately taxed from 2 to 10 per cent. Besides the probate, large fees are paid for burying him in the chancel; his virtues are handed down to posterity on taxed marble; and he is then gathered to his fathers—to be taxed no more."

Low wages, high taxes, and unemployment brought an increase in pauperism and in crimes. Reformers were advocating increased power for the lower and middle classes, manhood suffrage, and universal education. This new idea that education was a duty of the state puzzled many who refused to believe that "teaching children to *read* tends as much to their happiness, their independence of spirit, their manliness of character, as teaching them to *reap*." And why, they queried, compel a single man to give part of his earnings to teach the married man's children to read and write?

When Thomas Poole's and the Wordsworth's neighbors heard that Mr. Thelwell who advocated such reforms was visiting in their community they were aghast. Thomas's sister wrote in her diary, "We are shocked to hear that Mr. Thelwell has spent some time at Stowey this week with Mr. Coleridge and consequently with Tom Poole. Alfoxden House is taken by one of the fraternity, and Woodlands by another. To what are we coming?"

The concern of the villagers grew the more they talked about the dangerous people in the midst. A former servant at Alfoxden, Mogg, told a woman at Bath who had also been employed at Alfoxden of the suspicious people now there. The woman, in turn, gave an even more elaborate report to her employer, Dr. Lysons, who wrote the Duke of Portland, the House Secretary, about the Wordsworths, "an emigrant family, who have contrived to get possession of a Mansion House at Alfoxden. . . . I am informed that the Master of the house has no wife with him, but only a woman who passes as his Sister. The man has camp stools which he and his visitors take with them when they go about the country upon their nocturnal or diurnal excursions and have also a Portfolio in which they enter their observations which they have been heard to say are almost finished. They have been heard to say they should be rewarded for them, and were very attentive to the River near them. . . . These people may possibly be under-agents to some principal in Bristol." Yet worse, Mogg said that Christopher Trixie and his wife who lived at the dog pound at Alfoxden had been asked "by the French people" whether "the brook was navigable to the Sea, and upon being informed it was not, they were afterwards seen examining the Brook quite down to the Sea." Moreover, the villagers reported the French couple were seen "washing and mending their clothes all day Sunday," wandering "frequently out upon the heights most part of the night." The Wordsworths, it is true, often walked at night; Wordsworth was tracing the source of a brook, as the possible subject for a poem Coleridge had in mind.

Tom Poole was reported as "protecting a mischievous gang of disaffected Englishmen." Coleridge once met a woman from a neighboring village who told him how a Mr. Coleridge at Stowey was a "vile, Jacobin villain" who had "seduced a young woman in our parish."

Listening patiently to the woman's story, Coleridge so won her admiration that he said he had "not courage enough to un-deceive her." Coleridge's and Poole's friends at Nether Stowey, of course, did not believe the gossip about them.

Yet, a detective, Mr. Walsh, was sent down from London by the Home Office to check on the group of people under suspicion. Taking up his residence at the inn at Stowey, the spy used to lie behind the sand-dunes, by the shore, listening to the poets discuss Spinoza; the spy reported they were discussing him and calling him "Spy Nozy." He added that the "inhabitants of Alfoxden are not French, but they are people that will do as much harm as all the French can do. . . . I think this will turn out to be no French affair but a gang of disaffected Englishmen." He reported that Jones, a waiter, said the Wordsworths had had a dinner when fourteen people were there and how a "little Stout Man with dark cropt Hair and . . . a White Hat and Glasses got up and talked so loud and with such a passion that Jones was frightened and has not gone near them since." The Wordsworths' guests were the Coleridges and Pooles and their friends; the man with the white hat, Thelwell. The food for such a repast was a forequarter of lamb sent over by Tom Poole's mother, an unusual treat for the Wordsworths, who lived simply. At length, the spy drifted out of Stowey and back to London.

But the matter did not end then. Mrs. St. Albyn, who owned Alfoxden, was urged to look into the Wordsworth case. She rebuked her former tenant, John Bartholomew, for having rented the house to William Wordsworth and notice was given the poet to leave Alfoxden the next June when his lease expired. Thomas Poole assumed the responsibility of having rented the house to the Wordsworths and he wrote Mrs. St. Albyn that it was he who asked that the house be rented to his friends, the Wordsworths, who, he assured the lady, were of a distinguished family. Wordsworth's uncle, Mr. Cookson, had been one of the Canons of Windsor; William Wordsworth, he pointed out, was in every way a gentleman; his sister, presently living with him, long dwelt with the Canon of Windsor; she, too, was admired and respected. True, he said, Mr. Thelwell had visited the Wordsworths, but he was travelling through the country and came uninvited to Alfoxden. "Surely the common duties of hospitality were not to be refused to any man." He besought her "to hearken to no calumnies, no party spirit, nor to join with any in disturbing one who only wishes to live in tranquility." He urged her to remember she had known him from his youth and had long known the Poole family. His letter to the "incensed aristocrat" was futile; the Words-worths were told they must leave the next June.

John Chubb of Bridgewater, an estate agent, in the meantime, had been seeking to find a cottage for Thelwell in the country, "for it had been found that neither his health nor that of his wife and children can be preserved in London . . . but he has become . . . par-ticularly unpopular through every part of the kingdom." Thelwell wished to settle at Nether Stowey or within five or six miles of that village. In the autumn, young Coleridge warned Thelwell not to come. Without Poole's help, he could not obtain a house and if Poole aided him, Coleridge warned, "The whole malignity of the Aristocrats will converge to him, as to one point. His tranquility will be perpetually interrupted; his business and credit hampered and distressed by vex-atious calumnies, the ties of relationship weakened, perhaps broken; and lastly, his poor old mother made miserable. . . . Very great odium Tom Poole incurred by bringing *me* here; my peaceable manners and known attachment to Christianity had almost worn it away when Wordsworth came, and he, likewise by Poole's agency, settled here. You cannot conceive the tumult, calumnies, and apparatus of threat-ened persecutions, which the event has occasioned about us. If you, too, should come, I am afraid that even riots, might be the consequence. Either of us separately would perhaps be tolerated; but *all three* to-gether—what can it be less than plot and damned conspiracy?—a school for the propagation of Demagogy and Atheism?" Later, young Coleridge wrote Poole, "I am sad about you on many accounts . . . The aristocrats seem to persecute *even* Wordsworth. But we will at least not yield without a struggle. . . ." Thelwell never came to live at Stowey or near it. Though he could not secure a house for Thelwell, Coleridge wrote Cottle that Thelwell "is a very warm-hearted, honest man; and disagreeing as we do, on almost every point of religion, of morals, of politics, and philosophy, we like each other uncommonly well. He is a great favorite with Sara. Energetic activity of mind and heart, is his master feature. He is prompt to conceive and still prompter to execute; but I think he is deficient in that patience of mind that can look intensely and frequently at the same subject. He believes and disbelieves with impassioned confidence. I wish to see him doubting, and doubting. He is intrepid, eloquent, and honest. Perhaps, the only acting democrat that is honest, for the patriots are rugged cattle; a most execrable herd. Arrogant because they are ignorant, and boastful of the strength of reason, because they have never tried it enough to know its weakness. O! My poor country! The clouds cover thee. There is not one spot of clear blue in the whole heaven!"

Meanwhile, the Wordsworths and Coleridges enjoyed Alfoxden; Coleridge hoped to find the brother and sister a house in the district, for, wrote Coleridge, "the hills and the woods, and the streams, and the sea, and the shores, would break into reproaches against us, if we did not strain every nerve to keep their poet among us. Without joking and in serious sadness—Poole and I cannot think of losing him." Fall and winter went by with no further interference from the government; in March, they learned, however, Alfoxden had been leased beginning in June to the Cruikshanks, also friends of Coleridge.

Though the first five months of the Wordsworth and Coleridge relationship were not extremely productive, in the next few months, the poets reached heights they had never reached before nor did later. Coleridge said he, William, and Dorothy were "three persons with one soul." So, indeed, they seem to have been. Gradually, Sara was with them less and less; in July, she had a miscarriage, in September, she was again pregnant and quite unwilling to take the walks over the countryside her husband and the Wordsworths so enjoyed. She no longer tried to understand their discussions.

Coleridge, like Wordsworth, learned to see nature more clearly through Dorothy's eyes. "Nature to him was a conglomerate of color, sound, shape, and movement, in which his fancy revelled with a dreamy voluptuousness." When he looked at a flower, the image soon disappeared beneath his philosophical musing. Dorothy's keen perception was marked by sensitive discrimination. In the continued singing of birds, she could detect the notes of the thrush or blackbird; she expressed in a single adjective exact color tones, as that of the "lively rough green" of a turnip; she was aware how motion changed landscape, as she noted when she sat on the heath one day its "surface restless and glittering with the motion of the scattered piles of withered grass, and the waving of the spiders' threads." Moreover, she brought a transforming radiance and purity to what she saw, as when she spoke of the moonlight lying "upon the hills like snow." Before long, Dorothy's images, as recorded in her journal, made their way into Coleridge's poetry. On January 25, 1798, she had written, "At once the clouds seemed to cleave asunder and left her (the moon) in the center of a blue-black vault," which became Coleridge's

> Yon crescent moon, as fixed as if it grew
> In its own cloudless, starless lake of blue;

Dorothy's February 18, 1798, notation "A sharp and very cold evening; first observed the crescent moon, a silvery line, a thready bow" is reflected in Coleridge's poem as

> For lo! the new-moon winter-bright!
> And overspread with phantom light
>
> (With swimming phantom light o'erspread
> But rimmed and circled with a silver thread).

On January 27, 1798, she wrote of the "sky flat, unmarked by distances, a white, thin cloud," which in Coleridge's poem became

> The thin grey cloud is spread on high
> It covers but not hides the sky;

whereas her description of "One only leaf upon the top of a tree—the sole remaining leaf—danced round and round like a rag blown by the wind" written on January 27, 1798, emerged as Coleridge's

> The only leaf, the last of its clan,
> That dances as often as dance it can,
> Hanging so light, and hanging so high
> On the topmost twig that looks up at the sky.

On March 1, 1798, she reiterated that "spring seems very little advanced. No green trees, only the hedges are budding, and looking very lovely." March 24.—"The spring continued to advance very slowly, no green trees. The hedges leafless." April 6th.—"The Spring still advancing very slowly" became Coleridge's

> 'Tis a month before the month of May
> And spring comes slowly up this way.

Finally, when on February 27, she wrote in her diary of walking with Coleridge from Stowey part way to Alfoxden, "on a very bright moonlight night" when they saw "the sea, big and white, swelled to the very shore," Coleridge wrote in "The Ancient Mariner,"

> The harbour bay was clear as glass,
> So smoothly was it strewn!
> And on the bay the moonlight lay,
> And the shadow of the moon.
>
> The bay was white with silent light,
> Till rising from the same
> Full many shapes, that shadows were,
> In crimson colours came.

The climax of many walking tours the Wordsworths and Coleridge enjoyed came on November 13, after a walking trip to Watchet where they spent the night, returning the next day to Alfoxden by way of Dulverton. "The evening," Dorothy wrote, "was dark and cloudy: we went eight miles, William and Coleridge employing themselves in laying plans for a ballad, to be published with some pieces of William's." Thus, "The Ancient Mariner" and *Lyrical Ballads* were planned. William's account differs a little, for he said, "As our united funds were very small we agreed to pay the expenses of the tour by writing a Poem to be sent to the new *Monthly Magazine* set up by Phillips the bookseller and edited by Dr. Aikin. Accordingly, we set off and proceeded along the Quantock Hills, toward Watchet, and in the course of this walk, was planned 'The Ancient Mariner.'"

They first agreed to collaborate on a single poem, when Coleridge told his friend of a dream his friend Cruikshank had had about a skeleton ship with a skeleton crew. He told, too, of tales he had read, of superstitions gleaned from books of travels. One such story he had come upon in George Shelvocke's *Voyages* about a shipmate, who, convinced that a long period of bad weather was the result of an albatross's continuous pursuit of the ship, had shot the bird, hoping to relieve the horrible weather he and his shipmates had been subjected to. Wordsworth suggested the poem should center about the ghostly navigator who was doomed to a horrible fate for killing the bird. After writing two or three lines while Coleridge, whose imagination was fired, was writing at great speed, Wordsworth decided not to go on with the poem. Coleridge had been excited by various maritime adventures he had read; his experiences with Lloyd had shown him "the morbid hallucinations of an unbalanced mind" and he realized how impressions to an irrational mind become distorted. Writing rapidly, Coleridge showed in his poem how the mariner's mind, "unbalanced by remorse, and fear" was "fanned to frenzy by the awful circumstances of men dying of thirst on a ship becalmed."

Undoubtedly Wordsworth had had a great interest, since his return from France, in crime and the psychology of crime, its consequences, and its effects on the criminal and his victim; of this, he had written in *Salisbury Plain*, *The Borderers* and in *Goody Blake and Harry Gill*, which Coleridge completed. Wordsworth's interests in crime and its psychology undoubtedly influenced Coleridge. Wordsworth's poems, however, were psychological poems having in them nothing of the supernatural. Earlier, the two had planned to write together "The Wanderings of Cain"; Coleridge was to write the first canto; Wordsworth, the second; whoever finished first was to write the third and so they were to alternate cantos until the entire poem was completed. Coleridge hurriedly completed the first canto and took his offering to Wordsworth who had written only a few lines. Years later, Coleridge completed the poem, acknowledging what Wordsworth had written. Now, with "The Ancient Mariner," again Wordsworth, at first enthusiastic, simply could not produce his part of the poem. Realizing that Coleridge could write the poem better, Wordsworth suggested his fellow-poet write it. Truly inspired, Coleridge saw the poem grow and grow beyond the length of a poem for a magazine; its lines of haunting beauty have made it one of the treasures of English literature. Coleridge brought, completed, "The Rime of the Ancient Mariner" to the Wordsworths on March 23.

With approval, Wordsworth read Coleridge's poem of the mariner who casually killed an albatross that had followed his ship bringing it good luck as it came through wind and fog, whose crewmates thereafter felt him responsible for their fates as their ship lay silent in a silent sea, beneath a hot and copper sky. Coleridge's detailed description of the agony of the crew moved the Wordsworths. They read how the crew tied the albatross about the mariner's neck, and how the crew suffered with parched throats, with no water to drink; yet the ship was surrounded by water in which

> . . . slimy things did crawl with legs
> Upon the slimy sea.
>
> About, about, in reel and route
> The death-fires danced at night;
> And water, like a witch's oils
> Burnt green, and blue and white. . . .
>
> And every tongue, through utter drought,
> Was withered at the root;
> We could not speak, no more than if
> We had been choked with soot.

Nor was the crew's agony over; for suddenly they saw, as bars on the setting sun, a spectre ship bearing a Spectre Woman and her Deathmate, who were casting dice. As the spectre bark shot off, one after another, all the mariner's shipmates dropped dead. The ancient mariner lived on, however, for he had further penance to do for killing the albatross. He could not forget the way the dying men looked accusingly at him. Alone, he began to see the beauty in living things; then, for the first time, he could pray; from his neck fell the dead albatross, and he could sleep. Though given a respite from his agony, he had further penance to do. At an "uncertain hour, his agony returned" and he must tell his tale to the man he knew must hear him as he admonished men to have reverence and love for all things that God created and loved. He had found, too, how good it is

> To walk together to the kirk
> With a goodly company.

The Wordsworths did not find, as have later critics, the "Life in Death theme" of "The Loathsome Lady," or the "shadowy, sexual implications in the shooting of the albatross and the reaction of the water snakes," nor any significance in the mariner's drawing "so sharp a distinction between marriage and the church, placing the emphasis on sexual abstinence."

Financial problems still plagued Coleridge, but he refused again the offer of a position writing for *The Morning Post* because he felt he was "not born to be a compiler" and because he could not do his best work with a daily deadline facing him. When "something must be written and written immediately" his creative ability seemed to freeze; moreover, he did not relish the idea of sending something not so well written as he knew it should be simply because it was due at an appointed time. When he was offered the position as minister at Shrewsbury, he hesitated because "becoming a hired preacher in any sect" makes one's "livelihood hang upon the profession of *particular opinions*" and, he feared, tends "to warp the intellectual faculty." True, he often preached at Unitarian churches, but he did so without remuneration.

When Coleridge preached at Shrewsbury, and was considering accepting the pulpit there, among those in the congregation was twenty-year-old William Hazlitt, who had walked ten miles to hear him. The young man with black curly hair, high forehead, wide-set, gentle eyes and sensitive lips, was impressed first with Coleridge's appearance. Coleridge's face, Hazlitt said, was faintly purple; his "forehead was broad and high, light, as if built of ivory, with large projecting eyebrows, and his eyes rolling beneath them, like a sea with darkened lustre"; his mouth "was gross, voluptuous, open, eloquent; his chin, good-humoured and round; but his nose, the rudder of the face, the index of the will, was small, feeble, nothing"; his black, glossy hair "fell in smooth masses over his forehead." When Coleridge gave his text, "And He went up into the mountain to pray, himself, alone," Hazlitt said, "his voice rose like a stream of rich distilled perfumes, and when he came to the two last words, which he pronounced, loud, deep, and distinct, it seemed as if the sounds had echoed from the bottom of the human heart, and as if that prayer might have floated in solemn silence through the universe," so that the idea of St. John "crying in the wilderness" came to his mind. "The sermon was upon peace and war; upon church and state—not their alliance, but their separation—on the spirit of the world and the spirit of Christianity, not as the same, but as opposed to one another." Hazlitt said Coleridge attacked those who "inscribed the cross of Christ on banners dripping with human gore," and "to show the fatal effects of war, drew a striking contrast between the simple shepherd boy, driving his team afield, or sitting under the hawthorne piping to his flock" and to "the same country-lad crimped, kidnapped, brought into town, made drunk at an alehouse, turned into a wretched drummer-boy . . . and tricked out in the loathsome finery of the profession of blood." More than satisfied with the sermon, Hazlitt wrote, "poetry and Philosophy had met together, Truth and Genius had embraced, under the eye and with the sanction of Religion."

The following Tuesday, Coleridge went to dine with Hazlitt and his father at Wem. For two hours, he chatted with Hazlitt's father and young "Hazlitt's forehead," for the lad seemed "shoe contemplative." The following morning, Coleridge received a letter from the Wedgwoods asking him to accept an annuity of £150 for life, "no condition whatever being attached to it." Knowing that Coleridge's acceptance of it meant he would refuse the position at Shrewsbury Unitarian Chapel, Hazlitt "felt little gratitude for Mr. Wedgwood's bounty." He had looked forward eagerly to having Coleridge preach each Sunday in a church but ten miles away.

When the French armies invaded Switzerland and in some cantons instituted military dictatorship under the guise of liberty, Coleridge's faith in the French Revolution vanished. In an ode called "The Recantation," he told how, loving the spirit of liberty, he had welcomed the French Revolution, had regarded the subsequent violent acts and the reign of terror in France as inevitable excesses, how he had opposed England's war against France. Now, he was forced to recognize that the "Rulers of France" had "nothing that distinguishes them to their advantage from other animals of the same species." Indeed, he now had come to the conclusion that aristocrats were more likely to govern for the general benefit. He remained, however, a bitter opponent of Pitt's government, which he believed had forced the French into military aggression and had created unrest in England. In 1798, when the French invasion of England seemed imminent, he wrote

> We have offended, Oh! my countrymen!
> We have offended very grievously,
> And been most tyrannous.

Perhaps, the threatened invasion was just retribution for imperialist ambition and for the war against France. Yet, he suffered as he thought of the agonies of those maimed and wounded, of broken homes, frightened and starving children. His one consolation was his religion, which he believed was the only "universally efficient" cure for social troubles.

Coleridge's peace of mind was suddenly shattered by Robert Southey, recently returned from six months in Portugal where he had learned Spanish and Portuguese, collected material for a book, and so conducted himself that his uncle found him "perfectly correct in behaviour, of the most exemplary morals." Now, Southey had determined to study law. Overwhelmed by the sudden death of his brother-in-law, Robert Lovell, he decided to publish "his best pieces," hoping thereby to purchase for Lovell's widow "at least a harpsichord." Coleridge, more practical, sent her £20 a year toward her support. Southey having been promised an annuity of £160 made plans for his career.

"How does time mellow down our opinions. Little of that ardent enthusiasm which so lately fevered my whole character remains. I have contracted my sphere of action within the little circle of my own friends, and even my wishes seldom stray beyond it," Southey wrote. Though busy with a volume of *Letters from Spain and Portugal*, revising his poems and *Joan of Arc* for second editions, and writing a tragedy on Joan, he was busy indeed. In the latter, Southey was still the rebel. He showed Joan admonishing the king to be a true father to his people, "no common tyrant" in a land where now, at last, oppression is chained, poverty dies, and love and equality exist. Two years later, in *Poems*, one was dedicated to Mary Wollstonecraft; several dealt with slavery; others, with poverty and its crippling effects. He sent Coleridge a copy of the *Letters;* yet, there was no "enthusiasm for friendship" between the two men. Coleridge wrote "We are *acquaintances* and feel *kindliness* towards each other, but I do not *esteem* or *love* Southey as I must esteem and love the man whom I dared call the holy name of *friend*."

Southey felt less kindliness than Coleridge suspected; in fact, he resented Coleridge's friendliness; he had no desire to return to their former relationship, for he blamed Coleridge for the break in their friendship.

When Lloyd, whom Coleridge had long suffered with, and Charles Lamb visited Southey unexpectedly in August, 1797, Southey acted as Lloyd's confidant and friend. Having recently been released from Dr. Darwin's sanitorium, Lloyd had fallen in love with Sophia Pemberton. Her father, feeling Lloyd's wealth did not compensate for his mental illness, opposed the marriage. Southey, on the other hand, encouraged it. He himself had married despite family disapproval. Lloyd should do the same. Moreover, he convinced Lloyd he should not consult Coleridge on the matter, for Coleridge would be an incompetent advisor, said Southey. When Lamb wrote a friend of Coleridge's that he and Southey were going to Birmingham to persuade the girl "to a Scotch marriage," the news dismayed Coleridge. The marriage in Scotland did not take place, as Coleridge suspected it would not; later, however, Lloyd did marry Sophia. For four months, Lloyd remained in Bristol, boarding with Southey's and Coleridge's mother-in-law, Mrs. Fricker. Though her main support and that of her son came from Coleridge, she did not care for him and continually compared him with Southey who, in her eyes, was successful. Lloyd's mind was being turned against Coleridge when the latter proved a very negligent correspondent. Complaining of this neglect to Lamb and Southey, Lloyd magnified the matter until, in his distorted mind, Coleridge became a treacherous enemy, using people to his own advantage. Southey, knowing Lloyd contemplated writing a novel, inspired him to avenge himself on Coleridge in the novel.

In 1798, when the novel, *Edmund Oliver*, appeared, it showed that Southey had done just that. The leading character is Coleridge, whose love for Mary Evans, leaving Cambridge, going into the army, and taking laudanum are largely biographical. The incidents, Lloyd stated in the introduction, were "given me by an intimate friend"; Edmund's very description is that of Coleridge; he has the same "large, glistening eyes," the dark eyebrows, and dark hair. Lloyd exaggerated, however, Coleridge's taking laudanum, neglecting the reasons for his taking the drug and stating he took it for the mental effects it had on him. Edmund in the novel said, "I have at all times a strange dreaminess about me, which makes me indifferent to the future, if I can, by any means, fill the present with sensations,—with that dreaminess I have gone on here from day to day; if at any time thought troubled, I have swallowed some spirits, or had recourse to my laudanum." This novel gave added zest to Coleridge's critics who had known him as a radical; now, they decided, he was a dope addict as well.

After the novel was written, more fuel was provided for Lloyd's anger by the publication of three anonymous sonnets of Nehemiah Higginbottom, satirizing the early poetry of Coleridge, Southey, Lamb, and Lloyd. Southey discovered they were written by Coleridge, who thought he had written goodnatured humor.

When Coleridge read *Edmund Oliver* in May, 1798, he was stunned. To add to his dismay, he learned from Dorothy Wordsworth that not only was Lloyd his enemy but that Southey and Lamb, alienated by Lloyd, intended no further correspondence with him. Lloyd had dedicated *Oliver* to Charles Lamb. Seeking solitude to think things over, Coleridge went to a lonely farm at Culbone. Feeling ill and mentally disturbed, he said he tried to find relief in reading "The Pilgrimage of Samuel Purchas": "In Xamdu did Cublai Can build a stately Palace, encompassing sixteen miles of plaine ground with a wall, soherein are fertile meddowes, pleasant Springs, delightful Streams and all sorts of birds of chase and game, and in the middest thereof a sumptuous house of pleasure." Still feeling ill and mentally over-wrought, Coleridge later recalled, he took two grains of laudanum. While reading, he fell asleep and in his sleep composed a poem. His statements about composing the poem are not believed today. He said that, awakening after two or three hours, he immediately began writing it down; he called the poem "Kubla Khan." Coleridge stated he had written only a few lines when a caller from Porlock told him of the approaching birth of his expected child. Returning to his manuscript after the visitor's stay of an hour, Coleridge asserted he was unable to remember the rest of the dream or to complete the poem. He returned home shortly before the birth of his son, Berkeley. The Wordsworths, distressed by the *Oliver* incident, did their best to bring together again the estranged friends and reconciliation of a sort was made between Coleridge, Lloyd, and Southey. Before long, Lamb again became Coleridge's devoted friend and ally.

By March, the Coleridges and Wordsworths had other plans in mind. Feeling financially secure because of the £150 annuity from Tom and Josiah Wedgwood, Coleridge wrote with increased intensity, in two months completing "Frost at Midnight," "France: An Ode," the first part of "Christabel," "Fears in Solitude," and "The Rime of the Ancient Mariner." This additional money, and that from the sale of a volume to be called *Lyrical Ballads* by Wordsworth and

Coleridge were to finance a trip for the Coleridges and Wordsworths to Germany, where they were to settle "in a village near a University, in a pleasant and mountainous country" for two years, there to study and write. Coleridge was especially eager to explore and assimilate the writing of German philosophers and theologians.

Joseph Cottle, once approached by Coleridge, offered him and Wordsworth each thirty guineas for their two tragedies, *Osorio* and *The Borderers.* This offer, however, was not acceptable to Coleridge. He wished his poems and Wordsworth's to appear in a single anonymous volume, *Lyrical Ballads.* Cottle came down to Stowey in May and agreed to pay thirty guineas for the volume. It contained "The Ancient Mariner" and three short poems by Coleridge as well as nineteen poems by Wordsworth. Against the advice of Cottle, the poems were anonymous. In the introduction, the poets stated *Lyrical Ballads* was an experiment "to determine how far the language of conversation in the middle and lower classes of society is adapted to the purposes of poetic pleasure." The poems, all having "a faithful adherence to the truth of nature," it was pointed out, were of two types: those like Coleridge's "The Ancient Mariner" that dealt with the supernatural, and those like Wordsworth's that dealt with "subjects such as will be found in every village and its vicinity where there is a meditative and feeling mind to seek after them." These included poems that Coleridge said had "the sudden charm which accidents of light and shade which moonlight or sunset diffused over a known or familiar landscape." Wordsworth's poems, a later critic pointed out, read as though he had "turned his back on his personal life and made something like a strenuous voyage of discovery—a sort of arctic expedition—into a region where life was reduced to its elements, the outward trappings to their simplest." Though writing of the joys of nature and his admiration for simple folk, Wordsworth still was something of the crusader, indicating, for example, in blank verse the moral dangers of poverty. Memories of Annette and his desertion of her certainly are evident in some of the poems on motherhood and children.

With *Lyrical Ballads* almost launched, the Wordsworths and Coleridge made plans for the German trip, which they now thought would last four or five months. Coleridge had talked over the proposed trip with dependable Thomas Poole, who agreed it would be intellectually and morally profitable for Coleridge to go with the Wordsworths. Coleridge had made careful financial plans for Sara, who had decided to remain at home; Mr. Poole promised to take good care of her. Agreeing it was best for her to remain at home, Sara still did not relish having her husband travelling with Dorothy and William Wordsworth. When John Chester, a friend of Coleridge from Nether Stowey, asked for the privilege of accompanying the group, Sara was happier about having her husband go. It was eminently more respectable for the four to travel together than for the three, she believed. The £30 Coleridge received from Johnson, his publisher, for any writing he would do while abroad, he gave to Sara. Johnson agreed also to publish a quarto pamphlet, *"Fears in Solitude," "France: An Ode,"* and *"Frost at Midnight."* With the money to be received from these, with 30 guineas received from *Lyrical Ballads*, paid to him and Wordsworth and with his annuity, he felt financially able to go. Meanwhile, Coleridge planned to make "a dart into Wales" with Dorothy and William before leaving for Germany.

In July, in an anti-Jacobin magazine and review, Coleridge and some of his friends were held up to ridicule as dangerous radicals. The cartoonist, George Canning, had shown Lamb as a toad, Lloyd as a frog, singing together, while Coleridge, Southey, and Godwin, as donkeys stood by braying; Tom Paine as a crocodile joined in, while Thomas Wakefield, John Priestly and John Thelwell, as French citizens, sang; at the same time, Justice, Philanthropy, and Sensibility, as hags, joined in the horrible music. In another issue, Coleridge was named and Wordsworth alluded to in a discussion of "The New Morality." Savagely, the band of young Tories, pouring on the abuse, scourged those who had once favored the French Revolution. Coleridge, who said his name "stank," was increasingly eager to go abroad. He always desired tranquility; now, he sought it eagerly away from his native land.

The Wordsworths, in the meanwhile, were making plans to leave Alfoxden. Parting with "good and dear Peggy" was not easy, for, Dorothy said, "She would have gone to the world's end with us. I believe she was much more attached to us than any other human beings in the world." As Peggy had married a blacksmith and was now pregnant, it was essential that she remain at Racedown. Dorothy kept in touch with Peggy for years, as the latter needed aid frequently. Her husband turned out to be a brutal, coarse man; frequent childbearing and poverty made Peggy's life difficult. From time to time, Dorothy remembered her with money, clothing, and more important, with continuing affection.

Young Basil, whose father no longer provided for his care, went to live with his mother's sister; hazardous travel abroad, Dorothy decided, would not be good for Basil; moreover, he was at an age when he needed companions his own age.

Shortly before the Wordsworths left Alfoxden, young William Hazlitt came for a visit. He heard both poets read their poetry. "There is a *chaunt*," he said, "in the recitation of both Coleridge and Wordsworth, which acts as a spell upon the hearer and disarms his judgment." Wordsworth, he described as "gaunt and Don Quixote-like. He was quaintly dressed . . . in a brown fustian jacket and striped pantaloons.

"There was something of a roll, a lounge in his gait. . . . There was a severe worn pressure of thought about his temples, a fire in his eye (as if he saw something in objects more than the outward appearance), an intense, high, narrow forehead, a Roman nose, cheeks furrowed by strong purpose and feeling, and a convulsive inclination to laughter about the mouth, a good deal at variance with the solemn, stately expression of the rest of the face. . . . He sat down and talked very naturally and freely, with a mixture of clear gushing accents in his voice, a deep gutteral intonation and a strong tincture of the northern *burr*, like the crust of wine."

After leaving Alfoxden, the Wordsworths spent a week at Coleridge's; then they visited Mr. Cottle at Bristol, walked up the Wye Valley for three days and back again. Wordsworth was impressed by the beautiful ruins of the abbey on the banks of the Wye, as well as by the "steep woods and lofty banks" of the Wye Valley, and recalled the man he was when he had come there five years earlier. At that time he had been seeking release from his mental torment and enjoying the sensuous pleasure of nature. In "Lines Composed A Few Miles Above Tintern Abbey, On Revisiting The Banks of the Wye During a Tour, July 13, 1798," he told how

> I came among these hills; when like a roe
> I bounded o'er the mountains, by the sides
> Of the deep rivers, and the lonely streams,
> Wherever nature led; more like a man
> Flying from something that he dreads than one
> Who sought the thing he loved. For nature then
> (The coarser pleasures of my boyish days,
> And their glad animal movements all gone by)
> To me was all in all.

Now, he said, he found in nature "the still, sad music of humanity" and a presence that ennobles. In "Tintern Abbey," he paid tribute to Dorothy. Short walking trips about the Wye, a call on John Thelwell near Brecon, a walking tour with Coleridge in Wales, and a short stay in London occupied the tireless Wordsworths until mid-September.

On September 15, 1798, they sailed from Yarmouth to Hamburg with Coleridge and Chester. The trip was not a pleasant one, for the sea was rough, indeed. Coleridge wrote that "Chester was ill the whole voyage; Wordsworth, shockingly ill; his sister, worst of all, and I neither sick nor giddy but gay as a lark." On September 18, they reached Hamburg.

CHAPTER VII

"Partners in Poetry"

✿ DISEMBARKING AT HAMBURG ON SEPTEMBER 18, THE FOUR WATCHED THE CROWDS THAT THRONGED THE QUAYSIDE. Dorothy later wrote of being impressed first by the German women's hats, some, "immense straw bonnets, with flat crowns and rims in the shape of oyster shells, without trimming or with only a flat riband around the crown, and literally as large as a small sized umbrella. Hamburgher girls with white caps with broad over-hanging borders crimped and stiff, and long lappets of riband. Hanoverians with round borders showing all the face and standing upright, a profusion of riband. Fruitwomen with large straw hats in the shape of an inverted bowl, or white kerchiefs tied around the heads like a bishop's mitre." She noted, too, the ladies without hats, wearing frocks of all fashions. Some elderly ladies of considerable means dressed as London ladies did in '80 or '82, had artificial flowers in their frizzed hair. There were many soldiers in "dull-looking red coats and immense cocked hats." Officers, whom she supposed to be Prussians, she observed wore "long coats and leather belts around their waists which pinch in the body and make them look like women." The other men, she said, differed little in their appearance from the English except that they generally had pipes in their mouths. The inns, the English travelers found, were filthy and had "obnoxious smells." Dishonesty and greed, they encountered everywhere; the landlord, the baker, the porters, the coachmen all attempted to overcharge them. They were impressed, however, by the scarcity of beggars and drunken men but amazed at seeing a well-dressed man beating his middle-aged wife in the street, and at the brutal treatment everywhere accorded Jews: "we saw a surly-looking German driving a poor Jew forward with foul language, and making frequent use of a stick. The countenance of the Jew expressed neither anger nor surprise, nor agitation; he spoke but with meekness, and unresisting pursued his way followed by his inhumane driver, whose insolence we found was supported by law; 'The Jews have no right to *reign* in the city of Hamburgh,' a German told us in broken English. The soldiers who were stationed at the drawbridge looked very surly at him and the countenance of the by-standers expressed cold unfeeling cruelty." As Hamburg was a walled city whose gates closed at six-thirty, Dorothy was irked by the fact that "while the sun was yet shining pleasantly" they were obliged to think perpetually of turning their eyes to the church clock, lest after their evening walks they be locked out of the city. In the suburbs, contrasting with the dirtiness of the city, was the bright cleanliness of the merchants' brick and wood homes with the roofs tiled or thatched. All were surrounded by gardens with ever-twisting gravel walks and bending poplars. All had window-shutters, often painted pale green; all, window curtains white as snow. The interiors of these houses "would have done credit to the industry of any English dame of fifty years ago when oak chests were rubbed as bright as looking glasses." Dorothy was delighted that the "English canopies of coal smoke" she found so distasteful in cities were lacking in Hamburg.

Once settled in accommodations far from satisfactory in an inn called "Der Wilde Mann," they found some consolation in talking with Herr Friedrich Klopstock, the father of German poetry, "a venerable old man, retaining the liveliness and alertness of youth." This conversation, though animated, was not entirely effective because of the language barrier, as neither Coleridge nor the Wordsworths could converse in German. Herr Klopstock and William Wordsworth spoke fluently in French; Coleridge, unskilled in that language, for once was silent most of the time. They found the father of German poetry disappointing, for he told them Schiller would soon be forgotten, that Kant's reputation already was on the decline and that Glover wrote better than Milton. Distressed by the dishonesty of shopkeepers, innkeepers, and merchants who seemed determined to cheat foreigners, both the Wordsworths and Coleridge were eager to leave Hamburg. On departing, Coleridge and the Wordsworths decided to separate; the former wished to travel and learn German; the Wordsworths did not feel they could afford to travel; instead, they chose to go to Goslar, a small town where they believed they could live inexpensively and where they would learn German and William would write.

Coleridge, heeding Poole's advice, "Live with the Germans. Read in German. Think in German," went first to Ratzeburg, where he became a favorite with educated, cultured Germans. Then in February, he proceeded, with letters of introduction to the university librarian and to one of the professors, to Göttingen. He matriculated in the university and plunged immediately into work, studying hard and collecting material for a book on Lessing. His hard work did not prohibit him from having a gay, social whirl and being lionized. From Ratzeburg, proud of his ability to speak German, he wrote his wife, Sara, and Poole of long talks with men in a room so smokefilled "the candle nearly goes out," of ice-skating with counts, countesses, barons, and baronesses, of conversing in German with "a very beautiful woman, less beautiful than you (Sara)." To the latter, Sara, burdened by caring for their two little children, bristled, "I am very proud to hear you so forward in the language, and that you are so gay with the ladies. You may give my respects to them, and say that I am not at all jealous, for I know my dear Samuel in her affliction will not forget entirely his most affectionate wife." Coleridge sighed as he read her letter. He had tried to write Sara of these little nothings he thought would interest her: the types of playing cards, women's fashions, and parties.

Nor did Dorothy Wordsworth, lonely without Coleridge, always eagerly awaiting his letters, relish these good times he was having with women, for she wrote him, "You speak in raptures of the pleasures of skating—it must be a delightful exercise, and in the North of England amongst the mountains whither we wish to decoy you, you might enjoy it with every possible advantage. A race with William upon his native lakes would leave to the heart and imagination something more dear and valuable than the gay sight of ladies and countesses whirling along the lake of Ratzeburg. . . . You must come to us at the latter end of next summer, and we will explore every nook of that romantic country (in North England). You might walk through Wales and Yorkshire and join us in the country of Durham and I would follow at your heels and hear your dear voices again." Coleridge, missing the Wordsworths, longed for them. Dorothy had also enclosed some verses her brother had recently written reminiscing of skating as a boy in England one winter at sunset when the precipices rang to the tune of steel and crystal as he speed so fast the world seemed flying past him.

Coleridge enjoyed his friends among the nobility, as well as the students at Ratzeburg and professor friends of his at Göttingen. Among the students, he was considered "noticeable"; with them, he took long walking trips; with them, he engaged in debates, and often in monologue; he read them his poetry and seemed thoroughly irrepressible. He was flattered by being admitted into the circle of professors, some of whom he admired. True, his output of poetry slackened, but his knowledge of German grew.

The Wordsworths, on the other hand, found no intellectuals at Goslar, where they lodged with a widow, Frau Deppermann; their only companions were a French émigré priest and a young apprentice in the drapery business. Coleridge said he might have helped the Wordsworths become acquainted with people of their type had he been with them, for they did not realize that "Sister here is considered only a name for mistress." Hence, many avoided the English couple in their midst. The cold was intense at Goslar that winter; in fact, Dorothy wrote that on Christmas day "when we left the room where we sat we were obliged to wrap up in great coats etc., though we only went into the next room." Wordsworth had purchased a fur coat and a fur cap such as the peasants wore, "in which," Dorothy said, "he looks like any grand Signior." She, too, had purchased fur garments in which she huddled even as she sat beside the black iron stove, "a comfortless oven." Even the residents of the house where the Wordsworths lived said the poet's quarters were so cold they thought the English couple might some night be frozen to death. That cold Christmas day in 1799, Dorothy's twenty-seventh birthday, she tried to enjoy. She had watched with interest the many little fir trees in the market place diminish in number as Christmas day approached, for it seemed every family purchased one to trim with candles, gilt gingerbread, and red apples; the Germans told her that on Christmas eve, the families sang hymns as they sat around their decorated trees. On Christmas night, she and William were invited to join a family in their home and sit around the stove, to eat gingerbread men with currant eyes while the servant girl told the children fairy tales.

In the daytime, Wordsworth walked daily on the ramparts or in a public garden in which was a pond. There, he said, "I had no companion but a kingfisher, a beautiful creature that used to glance by me. I consequently became much attached to it." Sometimes Dorothy walked with him over the frozen plains or in the garden behind the cathedral while the powdery snow seemed to raise up under their feet like smoke.

Their hope to learn German as fluently as Wordsworth had learned French proved disappointing; moreover, Goslar had no library. Forced to be content with the few books he had brought with him, William turned to writing, and prolific he was, though he said had he felt better he would have written five times as much as he did. He enlarged the plan of "The Prelude," an account of "Man, Nature, and Society," really an account of his own youth in retrospect, and planned "The Recluse" that was to state the philosophy and sensations of a poet living in retirement.

He wrote the Lucy poems based on a story Aunt Threlkeld had told Dorothy of a little girl, Lucy Gray, who, on her way to meet her father by Stern Mill Bridge was lost in a snow storm. Searchers traced her footmarks down a steep hill, through a broken hawthorne hedge by a long stone wall, across a field, half way across a bridge, "but further there were none." Dorothy told how, as a child, she had cried when Aunt Threlkeld concluded her story. For days, she had seemed to hear the wind wailing about the house, like a child crying for its mother, "and fancied Lucy was not drowned but lost, and still wandering about in the storm crying for aid." Captivated by the story, William wrote poem after poem about Lucy. He reiterated to Dorothy his gratitude for the inspiration she always was to him, but depressed her when for a time he began talking about how lonely and lost he would be without her. She had no intention of ever leaving him. What if she died? But, she assured him, she was in good health. At times, in her concern about Coleridge she felt almost guilty, as though she was unfair to William even in thinking of Coleridge. As William almost constantly told of not feeling well, she was ever mindful of him, believing he was overactive for his strength. He complained of severe headaches, of pain and weariness in his side and stomach.

In February, Dorothy and William left Goslar on foot, walking through the Harz Mountain and Thuringian Forest, enjoying the fir trees covered with grey and green moss, the songs of larks, and the green hills and valleys.

On April 20th, they met a despondent Coleridge at Göttingen, for he had just received word of the death of his son, little nine-month-old Berkeley. When the child became ill with smallpox, Thomas Poole, who was looking after Sara, had advised her not to tell Coleridge of the child's illness until the baby was better. Berkeley did improve and Sara quickly wrote her husband who wept at the news, "when," he said, "I should be on my knees in the joy of thanksgiving." But the child, weakened by the disease, died soon after; and Sara, grief stricken and full of self-pity, wrote her husband, "You will feel and lament the death of your child, but you will recollect him a baby of fourteen weeks, but I am his mother and have carried him in my arms and fed him at my bosom, and have watched over him day and night for nine months."

Poole, knowing how Coleridge would suffer when he heard of his son's death, unable to persuade Sara not to tell her husband of the sad event until his return to England, wrote Coleridge a letter of sympathy and concluded, "Let your *mind* act, and not your *feelings.* Don't conjure up any scenes of distress which never happened. Mrs. Coleridge felt as a mother did and as all mothers could do. She is now perfectly well."

Sara had written to the tanner: "O! My dear Mr. Poole! I have lost my dear dear child! At one o'clock on Sunday Morning a violent convulsive fit put an end to his painful existence, myself and two of his aunts were watching by his cradle. I wish I had not seen it, for I am sure it will never leave my memory; sweet babe! what will thy Father feel when he shall hear of thy sufferings and death! I am perfectly aware of everything you have said on the subject in your letter; I shall not yet write Coleridge, and when I do—I will pass over all disagreeable subjects with the greatest care, for I well know their violent effect on him—but I account myself most unfortunate in being at a distance from him at this time, wanting his consolation as I do, and feeling my griefs almost too much to support with fortitude. Hartley is better—but still a little feverish towards evening—he is taking some cool physic and I mean to have him carried out every fine day. Southey has undertaken the business of my babe's interment and in a few days we shall remove to his house at Westbury which I shall be rejoiced to do for this house at present is quite hateful to me.

"I thank you for the kind letters you sent me and depend on your writing again—I suppose you will have received from Coleridge the promised letter for me. I long for it—for I am very miserable! ! !"

Coleridge's reply to Poole stated that when he read "Sara's lively account of all the miseries she herself and the infant had undergone, there was nothing to think of, only a mass of pain . . . and I was made to suffer it all again. Death—the death of one's own infant! . . . a very trifle would make me weep—but for the death of the baby I have not wept." Having so written, he went out in the fields to walk; returning, he wrote his reflections on life and death. Then he composed a few verses on Berkeley's death which he sent Sara.

Both Coleridge and Wordsworth had been discouraged at some of the reviews of *Lyrical Ballads*. Robert Southey, believing Coleridge had written all the poems, attacked the volume in *The Critical Review*. Wordsworth's poem "The Idiot Boy," he said, did not deserve "the labour that has been put upon it. It resembles a Flemish painting in the worthlessness of its design and the excellence of its execution." "The Rime of the Ancient Mariner" he said was thoroughly un-

understandable, a lamentable "Dutch attempt at German sublimity." As for the explanation in the introduction to *Lyrical Ballads*, that the poems were written as experiments, "to ascertain how far the language of conversation in the middle and lower classes of society is adapted to the purposes of poetic pleasure," Southey said the "experiment we think has failed, not because the language of conversation is little adapted to 'the purposes of poetic pleasure,' but because it has been tried upon uninteresting subjects."

Charles Lamb, annoyed at Southey, rebuked him for his review; he liked "The Ancient Mariner" and considered "Tintern Abbey," the poem Southey had praised, "one of the finest poems ever written." Later reviews were no better than Southey's. *The Monthly Review* said the style was only an imitation of a bad style of ballad writing, that "The Rime of the Ancient Mariner" is "the strangest story of a cock and bull that we ever saw put on paper," that the whole volume was tinged with a dangerous radicalism and the teachings of Rousseau. The reviewer chided the authors for their hope of better prisons. Did they want palaces for those who commit crimes? He objected to the ideas about miscarriage of justice, mercy for those on trial, and stressed the need of militarism. Mrs. Coleridge wrote to Thomas Poole, "The Lyrical Ballads are laughed at and disliked by all with very few exceptions"; a month later, she reiterated, "The Lyrical Ballads are not liked at all by any. . . . It is very unpleasant to me to be often asked if Coleridge has changed his political sentiments, for I know not properly how to reply. Pray furnish me." Though Wordsworth believed the bad sale and reviews came because of "The Ancient Mariner," he did not so inform Coleridge, but he did not hesitate to inform Mr. Cottle, the publisher, why he believed the volume had failed to please critics and readers.

The reunion of the Wordsworths and Coleridge did much to lessen Coleridge's grief over Berkeley's death. William and Coleridge went for a two-day walking trip; Dorothy, who had been ill in Goslar, was glad to rest for a few days. On the men's return, the Wordsworths planned for Coleridge to live near them once they returned to England and found a home. As usual, each gained inspiration and strength from the others. Though Coleridge wished to return with them, he had work yet to do in Germany on his research on Lessing. After too brief a visit, the Wordsworths went to Hamburg and thence to England.

Without a home, they went at once on April 17, 1799, to Sockburn-on-Tees, the farm house owned by George Hutchinson, who lived there with Mary, Dorothy's closest friend, and Sara. Wordsworth was especially eager to see Mary who had been much in his thoughts while he and Dorothy were in Germany. They planned to visit the Hutchinsons until they found a home of their own. They were thoroughly at home with the Hutchinsons to whom they had felt a close attachment since their childhood. George, a plain, North-country farmer; and good natured, easy-going Mary were pleasant and relaxing to be with. Tall, plain Mary, tender-hearted, tactful, deeply sympathetic, was not intellectual; yet she had a good mind. Unsophisticated and capable, she was restful and pleasant to be with. She spoke very little and was an excellent listener. On the other hand, her sister Sara, short, plump and fair, was lively, fun-loving, cheerful and far from stolid. She was exceedingly frank. Enjoying their visit with the Hutchinsons, the Wordsworths let the days slip by and merely talked of the desire of their own hearth. Since Wordsworth complained of not feeling well, the time did not seem ripe to search for a new home.

Then Coleridge came to Sockburn, concerned about Dorothy's letters telling of her brother's ill health. He had gone home in July, 1799, to Stowey to be with Sara and his son, Hartley, for whom he had "longed and wasted away" during his last days in Germany. But once at home, he found he and Sara had drifted far apart. She never let him forget that while he was enjoying himself abroad she was alone when their baby became ill; she told again and again how she had nursed the sick child and then had suffered alone at his death. She intimated that Coleridge's absence, if it had not caused the baby's death, at least had contributed to Sara's grief and feeling of aloneness at the time. Never did she mention Thomas Poole who had been ever present, ever helpful, considerate and thoughtful. She was quick to point out Coleridge's deficiencies as she showed him a book, *The Beauties of the Anti-Jacobins*, that had appeared during his absence. It attacked those believing in "the new morality," among them Coleridge, saying it was disgraceful he had not been expelled years ago when he was a student at Cambridge. Starvation, it stated, had once compelled him to join the army, and now he had left England, had "become a citizen of the world, left his little ones fatherless and his wife destitute." Sensitive as always to such slander, Coleridge told Poole that it seemed in England he had only "those that hate me, yet here only I have those that I love." When he learned that Southey, too, had attacked his poem "The Rime of the Ancient Mariner," Sara pointed out that now Southey's reputation as a first-rate poet exceeded his. Nor did Coleridge's troubles end there, for his brothers and mother forsook him: George felt his own reputation as a Church of

England clergyman and headmaster was "endangered" by his association with a Unitarian and an opponent of the government; Edward found that only arguments resulted when he was around his younger brother; James, the colonel, was too busy to waste time with him; his mother, hearing him argue with his brothers, knew he must be wrong, and cried, "Ah, if your poor father had been alive he'd have convinced you!" Coleridge concluded to resign any hope of companionship with his brothers and mother. "I have three brothers, that is to say relations by gore," he wrote Thomas Poole, "but alas! we have neither tastes nor feelings in common." Determined to mend his relationship with Southey, his brother-in-law, Coleridge wrote him that when they met, they should not "withhold from each other the outward expressions of daily kindliness; and if it be no longer in your power to soften your opinions, make your feelings at least more tolerant toward me." Southey at first seemed determined to continue to be Coleridge's enemy, overlooking the fact that the latter had ignored the abuse Southey had heaped on "The Rime of the Ancient Mariner." With Poole's aid, a reconciliation finally was effected.

Then, after hearing from Dorothy Wordsworth that her brother was far from well, Coleridge had gone to Sockburn. There, he enjoyed the fond reception the Wordsworths always gave him and relished being told again how often he had been the subject of their conversation and how affectionately. Warmed by their regard and understanding, he relaxed with those he knew admired him; he strove to inspire the Hutchinsons to like him too. Succeeding, he became contented and his self-confidence returned. Dorothy, he believed, was over-concerned about William; he began to find increasing pleasure in young Sara Hutchinson, who, it appeared, had never met anyone so wonderfully accomplished, so thoroughly attractive. He fancied himself in love with her, never once, however, contemplating an illicit affair. There was still Dorothy, of course, to whom he was devoted, but she, more fond of him than he realized, seemed absorbed with her brother. When John Wordsworth, home from a long sea voyage, came for a brief visit, Coleridge and he, too, became friends.

At length, the Wordsworths talked of their desire for a home of their own. But where would they find it? It must be in the North, near their birthplace; it should be near a good library and another house that Coleridge could acquire. Not until November did they find that house. Then, William, Coleridge, and John Wordsworth, who went on a walking tour through Keswick and Grasmere, found the ideal spot and a vacant cottage.

On November 7, as they walked at dusk, through the Lake Country, all three were excited by the beauty "of a world of scenery absolutely new" to Coleridge. William wrote Dorothy, "You will think my plan a mad one but I have thought of building a house there by the lake side [at Grasmere]. John would give me £40 to buy the ground and with £250 I am sure I could build as good a house as we would wish. There is a small house at Grasmere empty which we might take, but of this we will speak." This they did take and old Molly Fisher who lived in one of the cottages at the other side of the road prepared it for them.

As Dorothy and William entered the little dark-wainscoted parlor at dusk on December 17, 1799, reddish cinders glowed in the fireplace to welcome them. Dorothy wrote her friend Catherine Clarkson, "We had returned to our native mountains there to live, so we cared not for any annoyances that a little exertion on our part would not speedily remove." The small stone and plaster cottage several hundred feet from Grasmere Lake had an unobstructed view of the meadows, the lake, and the mountains. Once known as The Dove and Olive Bough, it had been an inn. Downstairs, was a sixteen-by-twelve-foot wainscoted, dark oak room with diamond-paned windows, devoid of curtains, with a stone floor, a kitchen needing paint and curtains, and another stone-floored room, a bedroom, also in need of repair. One of these, Dorothy planned to make a general living room; the other, her bedroom. Upstairs were three rooms, one of which she planned to make a living room for William; there, uninterrupted, surrounded by his three hundred books, he could compose his poetry. Another room upstairs would be his bedroom. Here, two rooms required papering, painting and curtains; one upstairs fireplace smoked; some doors needed mending. Yet, Dorothy began eagerly this task of making a home, delighted when John, who arrived for a visit, helped, for William was not good at household tasks. As the piles of material heaped up for curtains lessened, as the cottage took on personality from the touches Dorothy gave it, as William and she unpacked their books, she began planning the honeysuckle and climbing roses that she would plant in front of their home in the spring, thinking how she and William would enclose the orchard at the back, and of the seat they would place there. She planned to plant French beans, peas, broccoli, spinach, and kidney beans in their back garden in the spring.

Though at first both brother and sister suffered from severe colds, soon William purchased a pair of skates and really enjoyed the nearby lake; Dorothy was busy with household tasks. She had old Molly's aid

The wares of Josiah Wedgwood (1730–1795) were amazingly diverse. A sampling of his lifetime production shows hand-painted plates for Catherine the Great (*upper left*) next to 1788 jasper plaque, *Sacrifice to Love*. Agate glazed urns flank shell-shaped dessert service. Beneath are flower holder shaped as bamboo, classic black jasper urn, medallion, strapware urn and cupid-decorated vase. Between brace of pearlware *putti* statuettes is unusual creamware jelly mold of 1790s; central spindle supported colorless gelatine through which peeped the elegant floral pattern. Photographed by Robert S. Crandan for *Time* Magazine, May 20, 1965, Courtesy, *Time*

Sara Coleridge, the Poet's Daughter, with Her Cousin Edith, daughter of Robert Southey, from a Portrait by an unknown artist, National Portrait Gallery

John Keats, a Painting by William Hilton, from a Miniature by Joseph Severn, National Portrait Gallery

Dorothy Wordsworth, from a Portrait by Samuel Crosthwaite, made in 1835, Owned by Mrs. Dorothy Dickson, The Stepping Stones, Ambleside, Westmorland

A Marble Bust of William Wordsworth at Fifty, by Sir Francis Chantrey, R.A. Owned by Indiana University

but two hours a day, and she was never idle for she washed, ironed, papered two rooms, painted some of the walls, made curtains, cooked, cleaned the house, and copied William's poems. Yet, at times she found leisure to walk with William, to enjoy the mountains and the lake with two swans on it; once, she watched Jupiter shining above Rydal Mountains. "Grasmere," she wrote one day, "calls home the heart to quietness."

Dorothy's warmth attracted to her their neighbors. High spirited old Mr. Sympson, over eighty years of age, his quiet, reserved daughter, and Mrs. Sympson who made her cottage a delicate thing of beauty, often brought Dorothy plants like London Pride for her garden; the Sympsons were as agile as a couple of fifty. Old Mr. Sympson enjoyed hiking with William and fishing. Their son managed their land, read a little and fished a great deal. Molly Fisher and her brother lived nearby. Sixty-year-old Molly was not an ideal servant; yet, she aided Dorothy two hours a day, despite the fact that Dorothy found her "very ignorant, very foolish, and very difficult to teach." Honest, and devoted to the Wordsworths, Molly once would not permit Coleridge in any part of the house but the kitchen until he cleaned his boots; she amused Hazlitt because ten years after the French Revolution she had never heard of it. Molly's brother John often talked about how times had changed. He said that before long there would be only two ranks of people, the very rich and the very poor, for "those who have small estates are forced to sell, and all the land goes into one hand." Nearby, lived John and Mary Hodgson, both over eighty, who had a hard existence as the old man was bedridden. His wife cared for him, and with the help of the neighbors, fetched the wood and water and kept her house in order. They constantly feared they might be separated and sent to board among some other poor of the village. Mrs. Hodgson said this disaster "would burst her heart." Wealthy Charles Lloyd and his wife Sophia, who soon became neighbors of the Wordsworths, Dorothy found it difficult to treat courteously as Lloyd had been so rude to Coleridge; yet she was gracious to them, for her brother Christopher had become engaged to Priscilla Lloyd. Mr. and Mrs. Clarkson of Eusemere she enjoyed, for she shared their fierce pity toward slaves and their concern about the poor; Julius Caesar Ibbetson, boisterous and gay, a landscape painter, reported to know every inn and bar in the district and to be "a wild one," both Wordsworths often conversed with; and he had a charming fifteen-year-old son. Thomas Ashburner, a statesman in reduced circumstances, his wife and five children visited the

Wordsworths almost daily, and Thomas brought the Wordsworths monthly a cart of coal from Keswick. The Ashburner girls, "clean and neat and rosy," in the winter spun and sewed as they sat about the glowing fire in their home, while in the spring they sometimes helped in their garden, picking apples, planting and weeding the vegetable and flower gardens; one of the girls even brought pieces of quartz to set on the stone wall around the family property. Theirs had once been a large estate, but hard times had forced them to sell most of the land except the little plat on which their home stood. Some distance away lived George Green, his second wife, the five children by his first wife and two by the new wife. Though poor—their farm was heavily mortgaged—they were proud. The parson, Edward Rowlandson, curate for the insane and absentee vicar, was a heavy drinker, who lived in a house next to the schoolhouse. He owned some land in the village and, being dilatory though thrifty, often gathered his hay in November by moonlight.

On the wanderers, and the Wordsworths encountered many the next few years, they had compassion. There was the white-haired old man, whose once fine hat was now brown and shiney, whose good shoes were badly worn; whose once good coat of dark blue and whose fustian trousers lacked buttons and were badly faded. An elderly woman still showing signs of beauty, now stooped and wearing threadbare clothing, passed by, one cold, snowy day, with her pale son who wore a shabby coat much too large for him. The old lady said, "We have all been ill. Our house was nearly unroofed in the storm and we lived in it for more than a week." The Wordsworths gave the two assistance. One day, Dorothy wrote in her Journal that she and William on a walk near their home, met a dark-eyed, long-nosed old man, bent almost double, a coat thrown over his shoulders, carrying a huge bundle. He wore an apron and a nightcap. His parents, he told the Wordsworths, were Scotch; his wife, now dead, had been a " 'good woman,' and it pleased God to bless us with ten children." All these were dead but one, of whom he had not heard for years, a sailor. His trade was to gather leeches; they used to sell for two shilling sixpence a hundred but now they sold for thirty shillings; leeches were scarce, partly because of the dry season and partly because they did not breed fast. He had been hurt driving a cart, "his leg broken, his body driven over, his skull fractured. He'd felt no pain until he recovered from his first insensibility. It was then late in the evening when the light was just going away." Now he lived partly by begging, for he had not the strength to work as once he had, and partly by selling books and by selling leeches when he found them.

There were so many beggars that once Dorothy simply passed by an old man. But her heart "smote" her. "I suppose you are a beggar?" she asked. He said he was, that he had been a sailor for fifty-seven years; he was now seventy-five. He'd been twelve years aboard a man-of-war under Sir Hugh Palmer. He had no pension, he added, "because all my officers are dead." His clothing, faded, patched and re-patched, had been that of a gentleman. Unlike him, a well-dressed young man, faint and pale, but resembling John Wordsworth, once knocked at the cottage door. Invited to come in, he confessed he was weary, as he was walking from Liverpool to Whitehaven. As he sat by the fire, he told Dorothy and William he was a sailor, that he had been "pressed," that twice he had escaped by swimming from a king's ship by night, that his last trip had been to the coast of Guinea. He had been on a slave ship commanded by Captain Maxwell. "Oh he's a rascal, sir, he ought to be put in the papers." The lad told of how one boy had had no place to rest except with the pigs and had been "half eaten," and of how one man had been set to watch in the blazing sun until he died violently. Rested, refreshed, and well fed, the sailor went on his way, but his memory lingered on. Dorothy thought of how soon John would have to go to sea again.

After neighbors had told the Wordsworths the tale of an old man unable to complete the stone fence about his sheepfold, one afternoon when the mountains were "soft and rich with orange fern, the cattle pasturing upon the hilltops, kites sailing in the sky, sheep bleating and feeding in the watercourses," Dorothy and William walked up Green-head Gill, searching for that half-finished wall, for William thought that it and the accounts of beggars he and Dorothy had met were subjects for poems. And poem after poem he wrote about them. From observing these poor people, William was forming, too, social and political philosophies. Some years later he wrote Charles James Fox telling him how he believed excessive industrialization, heavy taxes, Work Houses of Industry, and the invention of soup kitchens had contributed to excessive poverty. Prices, he pointed out, were high; wages paid laborers, low; prices for crops, low; many of the farmers, unable to pay the taxes on their farms, had lost them. "You have felt," he told Fox, "that the most sacred of all property is the property of the Poor." He affirmed his contention that the poor long to be in-dependent, cherish their farms "for which they feel a real affection."

William and Dorothy had hardly settled down in their new home when the stream of visitors began. In late January, John came and remained until the end of September. A blessing he proved to be, as he helped Dorothy make their home habitable. Whereas she always waited on William, John insisted on doing things for her. Gentle, kindly, he proved an expert carpenter as he made the shelves for William's books, cupboards, and even chairs. He helped with gardening of which he knew a great deal; he also planted trees about the cottage. As Dorothy sewed, he regaled her with tales of his travels in the China Sea, in Malaya, Java, and India. He said he had received the scar on his arm from a Malayan "who ran amuck." With Dorothy, he often rowed upon the lake; in the evening, at times he called her out-of-doors to look at the moon, or the stars, or the sky on a moonlight or on a cloudy night. With William and Dorothy, he took long walks. Though he enjoyed society, he also loved solitude and at times would wander among the hills with his fishing rod. Coleridge said John had "the solitary musings of his own intellect, with a subtle tact, and swift instinct of Truth and Beauty." Mary Hutchinson came and stayed six weeks while John was there. She helped Dorothy make curtains and gave her several new recipes; she was a better cook than Dorothy. At Easter, Coleridge came for a month and, again enchanted with the Lake Country, decided he should live in the Lake District. Before long, their guests found the Wordsworths had a delightful habit of naming places they loved for their friends. A pool in the woods they named for Mary; a rock where William enjoyed resting became William's Rock; soon there was John's Grove, Mary's Rock on which William carved her name, and the Rock of the Names.

The end of November, 1799, Coleridge had gone to London where he had accepted a position on the *Morning Post;* on December 9, Sara and Hartley had joined him. "I am employed from I-rise to I-set (that is, from nine in the morning to twelve at night), a pure scribbler," he wrote Southey. He found the work fatiguing, for during debates in Parliament the hours were yet longer; one debate kept him "twenty-five hours in activity"; another, from ten in the morning till four the next morning. After he had covered a long speech made in Parliament by Pitt justifying continuing the war with France, Pitt, Coleridge said, "is much obliged to me; he never talked half so eloquently in his life-time. He is a *stupid, insipid* charlatan, that *Pitt*." Pitt had seemed brilliant in the published report because Coleridge had so abbreviated his talk that the statesman's logic had appeared greater than it was. After four months, weary and exhausted, Coleridge resigned his position with the *Morning Post* but continued to write articles for the paper, working from morning to night. After a few weeks, he wrote Wedgwood, "I shall have completed my purpose, and then adieu to London forever." He had, indeed, "sweated" at the "bread-and-beef occupations" made necessary by the "Dunning Letters, etc. etc.—all the hell of an Author."

Though working incredibly hard, he had found time to renew his acquaintanceship with Charles Lamb; Mary Lamb was again in a sanitarium. He and Sara enjoyed, too, William Godwin and his children. Coleridge found Godwin "in heart and manner . . . all the better for having been the husband of Mary Wollstonecraft," though he found the "cadaverous silence of Godwin's children" really "quite catacombish" and felt oppressed by the thoughts of their dead mother. Godwin, on the other hand, found young Hartley somewhat too "rough and noisy" and when the young boy one day gave him a "rap on the shins with a saucepan," Godwin was so angered that "in huge pain" he lectured Sara on her son's boisterousness.

When, in February, 1800, Hartley and Sara left London for a visit, Coleridge went to share Charles Lamb's home at Chapel Street, Pentonville. Lamb enjoyed his guest, "*a very good man*," thoroughly, and Coleridge, too, found peace at Lamb's. In a dilapidated dressing gown, all day he worked at his translation of *Wallenstein*. Occasionally, he and Lamb enjoyed themselves at night as they had at the Salutation and Cat; once, Coleridge confessed to Godwin, he was tipsy as the result of drinking "punch after the wine."

With *Wallenstein* still imcomplete, Coleridge joined his wife at Bristol and set about finding a home, a difficult task, for the location "which suits my wife does not suit me, and what suits me does not suit my wife." Thomas Poole had found a house some distance from his at Stowey but, Coleridge rationalized, it was too far from the village. Much as he wished to be near Poole, he longed more to be near the Wordsworths. When he visited the Wordsworths in April, he was still looking for a house. There was none available near Grasmere but when the owner of Greta Hall, an almost completed house in nearby Keswick, offered Coleridge half the residence he was building, Coleridge took it. Set on a high hill, the tall, yellow, three-storied, frame house, of classical proportions, with Corinthian pillars, boasted a yellow and white parlor with a marble fireplace, a breakfast room with shelves to the ceiling for books, a study for Coleridge; upstairs, were a dozen rambling rooms. Coleridge named the living room and breakfast room Peter and Paul; he pointed out with pride the many views from his study. On June 29, 1800, the Coleridges moved into their new home; in September, when their son Derwent was born, Dorothy served as the godmother at the christening. As soon as Coleridge's possessions were at Greta Hall, he had begun work on some poems to be included in a new edition of *Lyrical Ballads*, and on *The Life of Lessing*. Though the damp climate at Keswick, where it seemed to rain incessantly, left him feeling ill and rheumatic, he still enjoyed from his study window the beauty of "the two lakes, the vale, the River, the mountains," and the occasional sunshine in "endless combinations, as if heaven and earth were forever talking to each other." Frequently, he visited the Wordsworths.

As thirteen miles separated Keswick and Grasmere, the former daily meetings of the Wordsworths and Coleridge were not possible, but Coleridge came frequently and his visits lengthened into days and weeks. When he first came, he was beset with financial worries, listless and despondent, and so ill that at times he could hardly stir from his bed. One Sunday evening, while he and his family were with the Wordsworths, he seemed content just to lie under the trees, watching his son Hartley collect pine cones and wood for the fire, above which Dorothy had swung the tea kettle from the branch of a fir tree. Little Hartley, his father said, was "like a spirit dancing on an aspen leaf." Later, Coleridge, rested by watching the fire and its reflection in the lake, helped his son build a rousing bonfire. Dorothy and William never knew what time of night he would arrive for a visit. On August 31, 1800, he came at eleven at night, when William and John were in bed but Dorothy was walking "in the clear moonlight in the garden." William and John arose, and sitting in their dressing gowns before the glowing embers in their fireplace talked with their guest and Dorothy until three-thirty in the morning. Again, a little later, he arrived unannounced and very wet, as the Wordsworths were at dinner, bringing the second part of his poem "Christabel," which he read to the fascinated Wordsworths at once; once more, they talked away most of the night; the next evening, he and Dorothy walked to Ambleside to mail a letter; the following day, she and Coleridge again walked to a nearby village.

Despite spasmodic bursts of physical energy, Coleridge's health was not good; the rainy climate of the Lake Country aggravated the weaknesses of a constitution never strong. Swelling of his joints, lumbago, gout, and rheumatism in every part of his body left him in almost constant pain. Having read that laudanum was an excellent remedy especially for swelling of the knees, he began taking it in increasingly large dosages. Dorothy, unaware of his taking laudanum, became alarmed as she noted his bloodshot eyes, the recurrence of boils on his neck and shoulders, the arthritis in his knees, his extreme nervousness and melancholy. During one visit, a knee was swollen until it seemed as large as the thickest part of the thigh. One night, arriving at the Wordsworths' soaking wet, he changed his clothing immediately, but rheumatic fever developed and he lay ill with a high temperature for two weeks, nursed by Dorothy, until a chaise came to take him home, where he remained ill for weeks. His doctor recommended horseback riding and sea bathing; Dorothy thought a warm, mild climate was the solution. Added to his troubles was the lack of harmony at home. Dorothy wrote, after a visit with the Coleridges at Keswick, that Sara Coleridge was "a bad nurse for C. but she has several great merits. She is much, much to be pitied, for when one party is ill-matched the other necessarily must be so, too. She would have made a good wife to many another man, but for Coleridge!! She is an excellent nurse to her suckling children (I mean to the best of her skill, for she employs her time often foolishly about them). Derwent is a sweet lovely Fatty—she suckles him entirely—he has no other food. She is sure to be a sad fiddle faddler. From about ½ past 10 on Sunday until two she did nothing but wash and dress her two children and herself, and was just ready for dinner."

Despite his illness, Coleridge pushed himself, writing, writing. When Wordsworth wished him to add further poems to a second edition of *Lyrical Ballads*, he again wrote poetry. When Thomas Poole asked him to write some articles on wartime trickery in the corn trade, he did so under the title *Monopolists and Farmers;* he also prefixed an essay to the publication. At long last, he began work on *Wallenstein*. As his ill health continued and the rain at Keswick fell without cease, Coleridge realized he had chosen the wrong location for his home. He cherished the Wordsworths, but he longed for the happy hours in Poole's parlour, where daily he had found refreshment in Poole's healthy, manly affections and understanding. Too many days he could not go to the Wordsworths' but sat lonely in his study while the rains poured, dimming the mountains through a mist.

Almost constant physical pain led him to take increasing amounts of laudanum. At Keswick, he was taking daily doses of from eighty to a hundred drops. Later, he took as much as two quarts a day. Concerned about the after-effects of the drug, as early as 1801 he asked Humphrey Davy for details of a drug that did not have the "after fatigue" of opium. Years later, a postmortem examination emphasized not only the pain he had suffered but a dropsical condition that had had its commencement nearly forty years before his death. Yet, except Dorothy Wordsworth, all his friends, even Poole, believed he had exaggerated his illness.

Still attempting to continue his study and writing, in the late summer Coleridge had gone to Durham to do metaphysical research in the Dean and Chapter's Library in the Cathedral. He dined with "a large parcel of priests" and talked with a librarian who had never heard of Leibnitz, whose books Coleridge sought. The librarian had loftily informed him "We have no museum in this Library for natural curiosities"—he had thought Coleridge asked for "live nits." The poet shuddered and decided the priests at Durham were all "thoroughly ignorant and hard hearted."

He received real encouragement and joy from Sara Hutchinson, who was now living with her brother Thomas Hutchinson nearby at Middleham. While at Middleham, he became ill and his knee began swelling. As the doctor had recommended baths, he went to Scarborough where he could receive the recommended medical baths. Nearby was Gallow Hill, where Sara Hutchinson's brother George lived. She and Coleridge visited there frequently. Association with Sara for five weeks strengthened his determination not to continue his married life on its present terms. He had long ago faced the fact that he and his wife were not suited to one another; yet, he had tried to draw her nearer to him.

Her constant reproaches agonized him until her lack of sympathy engendered antagonism which soon developed into aversion. He could have endured her stupidity had it been accompanied by any sympathy; her nagging snapped the frail bonds of their marriage. Yet, Coleridge never considered divorcing Sara. Indeed, he said, "When I love her least, then most do I feel anxiety for her peace, comfort, and welfare. Is she not the mother of my children?" He wrote Southey of his unsuccessful marriage, never dreaming that Southey, too, was unhappy, in his marriage. Coleridge felt the obligation of contributing all he could to the support of his children and he wished them to have many advantages. "If I separate," he said, "I do it in the earnest desire to provide for Sara and for them, that while I live she may enjoy the comforts of life and that when I die, something may have been accumulated that may secure her from degrading dependence." Back home at Keswick, he still found Hartley an amazing little philosopher and enjoyed little Derwent. He tried again to make a success of his marriage but Sara's nagging was a habit now. Grasmere, with William and Dorothy, provided the usual escape.

In November, 1802, far from well, he went to London to work again for the *Morning Post*. The day he left was a beautiful autumn day. "The birches on the crags beautiful, red-brown and glittering. The ashes glittering spears with their upright stems. The hips very beautiful and so good!! dear Coleridge!" Dorothy wrote in her diary. He wrote the Wordsworths frequently. One letter Dorothy "took to my bosom, a safer place to keep it," she rationalized. The letter Dorothy received from Coleridge on the thirteenth of December left her concerned; two she and William received on the twenty-first told of his being very ill; that on the twenty-fifth left her so "uneasy" she was glad she was not alone when she received it; that of January 29 was so "heart-rending" that William talked of going to London to see him; that of February 6 left Dorothy ill and William with a bad headache. Coleridge was considering a new climate where he might be better; two days later, he wrote he was better.

Despite the discouraging letters to the Wordsworths, Coleridge had had good days when he visited with the Godwins and with Charles Lamb, and he had done a vast amount of work for the *Post;* his research had progressed wonderfully. On March 13, 1802, his work in London was completed and he returned to Keswick, first visiting Tom and Sara Hutchinson for two weeks at Gallow Hill. Again enjoying his children, his joy was short-lived, for Sara went into a tantrum about his having visited the Hutchinsons and his eagerness to see the Wordsworths. After only a few days at home, he walked one night through a pouring rain to Grasmere where he arrived soaking wet, "half stupified," with swollen eyes. He went to bed early at the Wordsworths', but Dorothy and William sat up until four in the morning talking. It was probably then that William told her of Coleridge's taking laudanum.

While Coleridge was considering changes in his life, William Wordsworth was also contemplating changes. Once it was possible for letters again to come from France to England, William had received frequent disturbing letters from Annette, still in France. Dorothy was perhaps the first to realize a crisis had come. Years before when she first heard of Wordsworth's liaison with Annette and of the illegitimate child, she had believed that her brother and Annette would marry and she would share their home. As the years passed and it became obvious that William did not care to marry Annette, but was interested only in making amends to the French girl, Dorothy at first thought he would be content while she made a home for him. And at first he was contented just to be with her; there was real devotion between sister and brother. In the beginning, Dorothy idealized him; as she found she cared deeply for Coleridge, she tried to shut out that love by over-devotion to William, who always had depended upon her. He became, indeed, "the pivot of her life." As he went over the mountains on a trip, she looked anxiously at the mountains hoping he would have a safe passage; she put the cottage in order so that everything would be pleasant when William returned, and made up her mind "to look well and be well when he comes back to me . . . Blessings on him." And William? Missing her, though he had been visiting Mary Hutchinson, he returned a day early. On another occasion when he was away, Dorothy collected "a few mosses" to make the chimney gay "against my darling's return." One quiet night, as the two sat before a flickering fire, she wrote in her diary she heard only the ticking of the clock and "nothing else save the breathing of my Beloved as he now and then pushes his book forward, and turns over a leaf." She aided him in writing his poems, suggesting subjects or changes, copying revised drafts, aiding him with revisions. Sometimes, they would send off a poem and then William would decide to change parts of it. Mrs. Nicholson, the Ambleside postmistress, had told how, frequently, after a letter containing a poem was mailed, late at night the Wordsworths would come to ask to retrieve their letter. The obliging postmistress, aroused from her sleep, would give it to them and then, she says, "they would sit up in our parlour or in the kitchen discussing over it and reading and changing until they had made it quite to their minds, and then they would seal up the packet & say, 'Now, Mr. Nicholson, will you bolt the door after us? Here is our letter for the post. We'll not trouble you any more this night.' And oh, they were always so friendly to us and so loving to one another." Whenever William wished her to walk with him—and he did so frequently—Dorothy went with him, whether it were a mile or a twenty mile jaunt. His wishes were commands, she seemed to believe.

One evening, after walking in the orchard until dinner time, William read her a poem he had written and, after dinner, she wrote in her diary, "we made a pillow of my shoulder. I read to him, and my Beloved slept." Another evening, after her household tasks and a long walk with William, Dorothy went to bed early, for, she says, "I was tired to death." William sat alone completing a poem and then, Dorothy writes, "came down to me, and read the poem to me in bed."

Devoted as brother and sister were to one another, Dorothy seems to have been aware, beginning while in Germany, that her brother's morbid moods and illnesses arose from sex repression and that he should marry. When he seemed interested in her closest friend, Mary Hutchinson, the latter appeared to be the ideal wife, for she would satisfy his sexual and domestic requirements without upsetting William's way of life or supplanting Dorothy's intellectual bond. Dorothy was perfectly satisfied to be a "self-effacing third party"; she longed only to be with them. At length, on March 21, 1802, she and William talked of his future. They agreed he should see Mary, and if she agreed to marry him he and Dorothy would go to France and make whatever amends were agreeable to Annette. Then Mary and William could be married.

One fine sunny February day when the snowdrops were beginning to peep through the ground, William, who had been strolling in the orchard, called to Dorothy that he must go at once and see Mary Hutchinson before he could settle down to work. Hastily helping him pack, making a copy of "The Pedlar," a recently completed poem, for him to take with him, writing a letter to Mrs. Clarkson whose home William would pass en route to the Hutchinson's, and a letter to Mary, Dorothy was busy, indeed. Old Molly went for a horse for him and thought William very smart in "his blue spencer and new pantaloons fresh from London." This time, he visited Mary but a few hours. On April 7, he went again to see Mary; on the twelfth, Dorothy received a letter from Mary and William saying they expected Dorothy always to live with them and that they planned to be married in October. Dorothy wrote Mary an affectionate letter, telling her again how she would enjoy her new home and its many views.

On William's return, as William and Dorothy walked by the lake, Dorothy wrote of their seeing "a few daffodils close to the waterside. We fancied that the lake had floated the weeds ashore, and that the little colony had so sprung up. But as we went along there were more and yet more; and at last, under the boughs of the trees, we saw that there was a long belt of them along the shore, about the breadth of a country turnpike road. I never saw daffodils so beautiful. They grew among the mossy stones, about and about them; some rested their heads upon these stones as on a pillow for weariness; and the rest tossed and reeled and danced, and seemed as if they verily laughed with the wind that blew them over the lake: they looked so gay, ever glancing, ever changing. This wind blew directly over the lake to them. There was here and there a little knot, and a few stragglers a few yards higher up, but they were so few as not to disturb the simplicity, unity and life of that one busy highway." Later, as William read the description in Dorothy's Journal, he composed his poem, "The Daffodils," using some of Dorothy's very words or a paraphrase of them as he wrote of the "host of golden daffodils,"

> Beside the lake, beneath the trees,
> Fluttering and dancing in the breeze,

spoke of their stretching

> . . . in never ending line
> Along the margin of the bay:
> Ten thousand saw I at a glance
> Tossing their heads in sprightly dance.

Though he added little in imaginative concept, he did add the emotion when the sight was recollected in tranquility:

> For oft when on my couch I lie
> In vacant or in pensive mood,
> They flash upon that inward eye
> Which is the bliss of solitude;
> And then my heart with pleasure fills
> And dances with the daffodils.

In poem after poem, William was dependent upon Dorothy, not only for inspiration but often for phraseology. When they passed Westminster Bridge early one morning, Dorothy found in the sleeping city something of Nature's calmness. "The houses," she wrote in her Journal, "were not overhung by their cloud of smoke, and they were spread out endlessly, yet the sun shone so brightly, with such a fierce light, that there was even something of one of Nature's own spectacles." In his sonnet, "Composed Upon Westminster Bridge, September 2, 1802," Wordsworth wrote,

> This city now doth, like a garment wear
> The beauty of the morning; silent, bare,
> Ships, towers, domes, theatres, and temples lie
> Open unto the fields and to the sky;
> All bright and glittering in the smokeless air.
>
> Never did sun more beautifully steep
> In his first splendour, valley, rock, or hill.

On the 27th of June, 1800, Dorothy wrote, "we saw a raven very high above us. It called out, and the dome of the sky seemed to echo the sound. It called and called again as it flew onwards, and the mountains gave back the sound, seeming as if from their centre; the musical bell-like answering to the bird's hoarse voice. We heard both the call of the bird and the echo, after we could see him no more." Years later, in a poem, "The Excursion," William first used Dorothy's picture as he wrote,

> . . . the solitary raven, flying
> Athwart the concave of the dark blue dome,
> Unseen, perchance above the power of the sight!—
> An iron knell! with echoes from afar
> Faint—and still fainter—as the cry, with which
> The wanderer accompanies her flight
> Through the calm region, fades upon the ear.
> Diminishing by distance till it seemed
> To expire; yet from the abyss is caught again,
> And yet again recovered.

In like fashion, William seems to have been impressed with Dorothy's January 25, 1798, entry about the sky which, she noted as she and William went to Poole's for tea, was "spread over with one continuous cloud, whitened by the light of the moon, which, though her dim shape was seen, did not throw forth so strong a ray of light as to chequer the earth with shadows. At once the clouds seemed to cleave asunder, and lift her in the centre of a blue-black vault. She sailed along, followed by multitudes of stars, small, and bright, and sharp. Their brightness seemed concentrated, (half-moon)." William used the description in "A Night Piece," writing of the overcast sky "whitened by the Moon," yielding so feeble a light that not a shadow falls "chequering the ground"; suddenly, he says, the clouds "split asunder" and a traveler saw

> The clear Moon, and the glory of the heavens,
> There in a black-blue vault she sails along
> Followed by multitudes of stars . . . .

The image he used again in "Peter Bell"; Coleridge used it in "Dejection, An Ode."

Dorothy's conversations, too, inspired lines in poems more than once; for example, she writes in her Journal, she told William that when she was a child she would not pull a strawberry blossom. He wrote in "Foresight,"

> Here are daisies, take your fill;
> Pansies, and the cuckoo-flower:
> Of the loftiest daffodil

> Make your bed, or make your bower;
> Fill your lap and fill your bosom;
> Only spare the strawberry blossom.

He used, too, Dorothy's recollections about fearing as a child to brush the dust from a butterfly's wings and of watching a redbreast chasing a butterfly.

Innumerable times, we find her exact words in his poems. She described that "a bright silver stream inlaid the flat and very green meadows, winding like a serpent"; in September 1802, William wrote in "The Excursion,"

> The mightier river winds from realm to realm;
> And like a serpent, shows his glittering back;

Dorothy's "cottages lurking under the hills" became William's

> Villa, or cottages, lurking among rocks
> Throughout the landscape . . . .

Dorothy writes of "struggling clouds"; William, of fleecy clouds

> . . . struggling through the western sky.

Dorothy hears "a sweet sea-like sound in the trees over our heads"; William's

> . . . fir grove murmurs with a sea-like sound.

Dorothy describes a village that "straggles down both sides of a mountain glenn"; William says

> The dwelling of this faithful pair
> In a straggling village stood.

Dorothy narrates that she and William "passed through one or two little villages, embosomed in tall trees"; William says

> Among steep hills and woods embosomed, flowed
> A copious stream . . . .

Dorothy found that "trees, still fresh and green, were magnified by the mists," whereas William wrote of

> Mists that distort and magnify.

Often Dorothy's influence is seen in poems in which no exact parallels are found. She writes, for example, of "little birds busy making love" and a short time later William tells of

. . . birds, and butterflies and flowers,
Make all one band of paramours;

she says, "The lake was now most still, and reflected the beautiful yellow and blue and purple and grey colours of the sky," while William writes that

Within the mirror's depth, a world at rest—
Sky streaked with purple, grove and craggy field.

In Dorothy's Journal are many references to times she and William corrected lines of his poems; frequently she was conscious of imperfections of his work; but once a poem was published she usually was not critical. Yet, when William's *An Evening Walk* and *Descriptive Sketches* were published, she was severely critical. She was shrewd enough to realize that Coleridge's poetry had far more merit than Southey's, and that Coleridge's "Christabel" was vastly superior to Scott's "The Lay of the Last Minstrel." Of course, she had not Wordsworth's gift of expressing her ideas in verse; yet, like her brother, she saw "nought common on this earth"; often she pointed out to him more than he would otherwise have seen.

The next three months were months of pleasure and anguish for Dorothy. William, attempting to prove by his actions that she was still dear to him was more tender than he had been; yet his very devotion showed her there was something he needed that Mary, not she, could give him. Coleridge, too, spent much time with her, telling of his unhappiness at home and of his growing belief that if he had married Sara Hutchinson his life would have been different. He read Dorothy the poems he had written to and about Sara Hutchinson, thoroughly unaware that he wounded Dorothy. Tortured, Dorothy was convinced Coleridge's feeling toward young Sara was not real; yet, outwardly calm, she comforted him and sought to relieve his unrestrained emotions. Rarely did she find the old companionship she had had with Coleridge. Yet, she cherished these days, like the one when, as she and Coleridge walked, he stopped to make a miniature lake while she watched; and the May day when she, William, and Coleridge had lingered in the shadow near a lofty purple crag by a waterfall to eat their dinner and drink a little brandy as they sat on a moss covered rock. Then, they had lain in the sun while Coleridge and William alternately repeated poems. To Dorothy all was beautiful. A bird flying around the top of the crag was like a moth; the sheep browsing nearby were silver-like. Later, as they walked toward Keswick, they stopped at the rock where earlier Coleridge had carved his initials,

S.T.C. As Coleridge left them, Wordsworth took out his knife and deepened the T; Dorothy kissed the letters. Happy times like these were few.

Richard, concerned about Dorothy's future, had written to her asking how much money she required a year, for he believed her brothers should each contribute a yearly sum to insure her independence. She replied she would always live with William and Mary and that £60 a year would be adequate for her needs. Before William's marriage, however, Lord Lowther, the heir, agreed at long last to pay Lord Lonsdale's debt of £8500 to the Wordsworths. As this sum was to be divided among all of the Wordsworths, Dorothy was provided for without her brothers' contributing to her expenses.

All that summer Dorothy prepared for the coming of her future sister. The house was made immaculate; the garden, always lovely, received extra attention so that it might be as beautiful as possible when Mary came. Yet as Dorothy strove, she was always conscious she was making it ready for another. The day before she and William were to leave first for France to see Annette and then to return for William's wedding, she wrote in her Journal, "O, beautiful place! Deary Mary, William. The hour is come. *Friday morning*—so I must give over. William is eating his broth—and I must prepare to go. The swallows, I must leave them, the well, the gardens, the roses, all. Dear creatures! they sang last night after I was in bed; seemed to be singing to one another, just before they settled to rest for the night. Well, I must go. Farewell."

After two days visiting Mary and Sara Hutchinson at Gallow Hill, where Dorothy replenished her wardrobe with some of Sara's gowns, the two Wordsworths set out for France. At Calais, Annette and ten-year-old Caroline met them and visited with them at Calais for four, hot, sultry weeks. The evenings were pleasant; at sunset they walked by the ocean, enjoying the distant view of England and at night the phosphorescent lights on the ocean, which especially delighted lively little Caroline. Wordsworth found, to his sorrow, his French daughter lacked the mystical ecstasies in nature that he, John, and Dorothy shared. Smiling tenderly as he heard her scream in delight at the phosphorescent waves, he wrote,

> Dear Child! dear Girl! who walkest with me here
> If thou appear untouched by solemn thought
> Thy nature is not therefore less divine:
> Thou liest in Abraham's bosom all the year
> And worshipp'st at the Temple's inner shrine,
> God being with thee when we know it not.

Dorothy had been deeply stirred by these summer evenings, seeing the coast of England "like a cloud crested with Dover Castle, which was but like the summit of the cloud—the evening star and the glory of the sky . . . the purple waves brighter than previous stones forever melting away upon the sands." One hot, stormy night as lightning flashed, the waves were "interfused with greenish firey light. The more distant sea always black and gloomy. It was also beautiful . . . to see the little boats row out of harbour with wings of fire and the sail boats with the firey track which they cut . . . with a hundred thousand sparkles, balls, shooting and streams of glow-worm light. Caroline was delighted."

Annette and William both realized their love was a thing of the past. Tall, stern, serious Wordsworth was not the lonely, passionate lad Annette had loved; nor was Annette, still aflame with ideas that had not altered in ten years, one William now could love. Annette's hot, rebellious tears had long ago been shed; William had aided her financially; he still would. She no longer desired his love any more than he, hers. Yet, she believed Caroline should be cared for, and he agreed to make his daughter a yearly allowance as soon as the Lonsdale estate was settled. The year after Waterloo, he settled £30 yearly on her and in 1834 gave her a lump sum of £400, no small sums for one in his position. Dorothy so endeared herself to Caroline and Annette that years later when Caroline was about to wed, she postponed her marriage hoping world conditions would become so stabilized that Dorothy could come to her wedding. Then some years after her marriage, she named her baby for Dorothy. But Caroline and her husband became demanding as the years passed, and in time the Baudouins continued seeking money from the Wordsworth family, in 1850 practically blackmailing Wordsworth's heirs, saying his French granddaughter was in distress financially. Eventually, Christopher Wordsworth and Crabb Robinson, fearing "the French people will try to get money from the family as the price of silence, and failing in that, they will make up and publish a revelation which will be as romantic as French ingenuity can make it," apparently paid them off.

In France, Wordsworth was convinced that Napoleon's rise to power and the "establishment of a Consulate based on military force and government by decree" had destroyed the hope of France's recovery after the fall of Robespierre. At Calais, Wordsworth felt the atmosphere of the new revolution was so tainted it was bringing the death of liberty. The French no longer felt free; their greeting, "Goodmorrow, citizen," seemed as hollow "as if a dead man spoke it." The public holiday when Napoleon was proclaimed consul for life seemed more a day for the French to enjoy individual outings than a day of national rejoicing, quite unlike that other day, when in his youth, Wordsworth, "in a prouder time" bore witness to the pride the French had in the Revolution for

> The senselessness of joy was then sublime.

The Wordsworths were indignant as they watched crowds of Englishmen, "men of prostrate mind" and "feeble heads, to slavery prone," en route home, come to Paris to visit the Louvre, filled with "the spoils from Italy," and to catch even a glimpse of Napoleon. Wordsworth was enraged that Toussaint L'Ouverture, the captured leader of the insurgent Negroes of St. Domingo languished in prison. In a poem to that captive Negro Wordsworth wrote,

> Live and take comfort; thou hast left behind
> Powers that will work for thee: air, earth and skies,
> There's not a breathing of the common wind
> That will forget thee.

Indeed, he affirmed,

> Thy friends are exultations, agonies,
> And love, and man's unconquerable mind.

The captive Negro died in prison.

Wordsworth and Dorothy, returning to England with pleasure and relief, said this was the happiest homecoming they had ever had. As Wordsworth heard the church bells chiming, watched the boys playing cricket, he said "This, this is England," his land. After three weeks in London, where he and Dorothy stayed in Basil Montagu's rooms, they had a family reunion with their brothers Richard, Christopher, and John, the latter just returned from sea. They enjoyed Charles and Mary Lamb; they visited two days with the Cooksons. In London, Wordsworth's spirits dampened as he saw evidences of the English suffering from "too much prosperity" and "undisturbed wealth." The vanity and parade in London, he contrasted with the desolation the revolution had produced in France and the poverty he saw about him at Grasmere. Wages, he knew, were disastrously low, while large landowners were increasing their wealth as corn prices rose and demands of the navy and the war were lining the pockets of industrialists. He bemoaned the fact that England refused to abolish the slave trade. When he and Dorothy had gone with Charles Lamb to Bartholomew Fair, they, unlike their host, had not enjoyed the mountebanks and buffoons, the freaks, the ventriloquists and the fire-swallower. Indeed, William thought the spectacle "a hell for eyes and ears"; Dorothy thought it ugly, depressing, and exhausting.

On Friday, September 27, they reached Gallow Hill, eagerly welcomed by Mary, Sara, and Joanna; Tom was shucking corn in the sunshine. The next week, the household was busy with wedding preparations.

The day before the wedding Dorothy, attempting to be tranquil amid all the bustle and gaiety, became almost ill. That night, she longed for rest. The emotional wish for her brother's happiness, yet her consciousness that after the next day their lives would not be as they had been, all the strain of meeting Annette and Caroline and smoothing the relationships between them and William, the struggle of remaining calm while Coleridge told her of his love for Sara Hutchinson suddenly overwhelmed her. She had written Jane that she had "long loved Mary Hutchinson as a sister and she is equally attached to me. This being so, you will guess that I look forward with perfect happiness to this attachment between us; but happy as I am I half dread that concentration of tender feelings, past, present, and future, which will come upon me on the wedding morning. There never lived a better woman that Mary H and I have not a doubt but that she is in every respect formed to make an excellent wife to my Brother and I seem to myself to have scarcely anything left to wish for but that the wedding was over, and we had reached our home again."

Exhausted by her emotions, Dorothy did not go to the church with the others to see her brother and Mary wed, nor did Mary's sisters; no relative of William's was at the service. The only wedding gift the couple received came from John Wordsworth. In Dorothy's Journal she writes, "On Monday, 4th October, 1802 . . . at a little after eight o'clock I saw them go down the avenue towards the church. William had parted from me upstairs. When they were absent, my dear little Sara prepared the breakfast. I kept myself as quiet as I could but when I saw the two men running up the walk, coming to tell me it was over, I could stand it no longer, and threw myself on my bed where I lay in stillness, neither hearing or seeing anything until Sara came upstairs to me and said, 'They are coming.' This forced me from the bed where I lay, and I moved, I know not how, straight forward, faster than my strength could carry me, till I met my beloved William and fell on his bosom. He and John Hutchinson led me to the house, and there I stayed to welcome my dear Mary. As soon as we had breakfasted, we departed."

On October 9, 1802, this announcement of the wedding appeared in the London *Morning Post:* "Monday last, William Wordsworth, Esq, was married to Miss Hutchinson of Wykeham, near Scarborough, and proceeded immediately with his wife and sister for his charming cottage in the Paradise vale of Grasmere. His neighbor, Mr. Coleridge, resides in the Vale of Keswick, 13 miles from Grasmere. His house (situated on a low hill at the foot of Skiddaw, with the Derwent Lake in front and the romantic River Greta winding round the hill), commands, perhaps, the most various and interesting prospects of any house in the island. It is a perfect *panorama* of that wonderful vale, with its two lakes, and its complete circles or rather ellipse of mountains." Just who wrote the notice—was it Lamb or Coleridge?—remains a mystery. Suffice it to say, its wording offended the Wordsworths who felt they were being advertised as attractions of a tourist resort. On reading it, John Wordsworth told Dorothy the notice was "not quite so bad as I thought it would have been from what you said."

The honeymoon was as strange as the wedding, for it consisted merely of the journey to Mary's new home, a journey made by Dorothy, William, and Mary. Dorothy writes that "We had sunshine and showers, pleasant talk, love, and cheerfulness." As they traversed routes often taken by Dorothy and William, Mary was shown places dear to them and told of ecstatic pleasures they had had there. Once back at home, Dorothy says, "Molly was overjoyed to see us; for my part, I cannot describe what I felt and our dear Mary's feelings would, I dare say, not be easy to speak of. We went by candle light into the garden, and were astonished at the growth of the brooms, Portugal laurels etc etc. The next day, Thursday, we unpacked the boxes. On Friday, May 8th Mary and I walked first upon the hillside, and then in John's Grove, then in view of Rydal, the first walk that I had taken with my sister."

Thus, at last tranquil and happy, Dorothy resumed her new life with Mary and William, a relationship of devotion and understanding that was to continue fifty years without any disagreements or jealousy. The walks of brother and sister, sometimes with Coleridge, continued. Under less nervous strain than she had been for years, Dorothy confided less and less to her Journal until January, 1803, after which she wrote in it no more except to give accounts of tours and expeditions she had taken with William. Her letters to her good friend Mrs. Clarkson indicate she was happier, calmer than she had ever been, triumphant proof of the magnificence of her spirit.

CHAPTER VIII

"*Pleasure and Anguish*"

THE FIRST FEW WEEKS AFTER MARY'S AND WILLIAM'S WED-
DING WERE BUSY ONES. THE YOUNG WOMEN UNPACKED
Mary's possessions, and Dorothy and William, eager to show Mary
their favorite spots near Grasmere, took many a walk; they were
eager, too, for her to get to know their neighbors, and shortly after the
wedding invited thirteen to tea. Coleridge visited them often, until
the middle of May. As he slept in a bed in the living room, did not
rise usually until noon and liked his meals at unusual hours, he kept
Dorothy occupied, indeed. Yet, she spent much time out-of-doors, for
the winter was so mild that in December she found strawberries,
yellow turf flowers, and buttercups, daisies and even a foxglove still
blooming. Coleridge returned from Wales the day after his little
daughter, Sara, was born. Still restless, he talked of going to a warmer
climate, Italy or Sicily or Malta. He left Keswick shortly after the
first of the year and returned in the spring.

On June 18, 1803, Mary's first son, John, was born. Dorothy and
Peggy Ashburner had been with Mary the night before the baby's
birth. The following beautiful morning with swallows singing in their
nests in the garden, the rose bushes aglow with their abundant flowers
and the mountains bathed in sunshine, Mary's ordeal was over after
hours of labor.

On June 29th, Dorothy wrote Mrs. Clarkson, "Oh my dear friend
how happy we are in this blessed Infant! He sleeps sweetly all night
through, loves the open air—he has been out two hours today at one
time and by snatches at different times all the day through. He is a
noble looking Child, has a very fine head, and a beautiful nose, and
thrives rarely." Two weeks later she describes "our own darling
Child" who she says, has "blue eyes, a fair complexion (which is already very much sunburnt) a body as fat as a little pig, arms that

are thickening and dimpling and bracelets at his wrists, a very prominent nose which *will* be like his *Father's* and a head shaped upon the very same model. I send you a lock of his hair sewed to this letter. Today, we have all been at Church—Mary was *churched* and the Babe christened—Coleridge, my brother Richard, and I were Godfathers and Godmother, old Mr. Sympson answered for my brother Richard and had a hearty enjoyment of the christening cake, tea and coffee, this afternoon.—I wish you could see him in his little Basket, which is neither more nor less than a meat Basket which cost half a crown. In this basket he has (Not like Moses in his cradle of rushes, but in a boat, mind that.) floated over Grasmere water asleep and made one of a dinner party at the Island, and we often carry it to the orchard where he drops asleep beside us."

Although William cautioned Dorothy not to talk too much about the baby lest she become tiresome to others, she continued to say a great deal about little John. "I feel very deeply," she explained, "every hour of my life the riches of the Blessings which God has given us, and you who have nursed your own Babe by a cottage fire know what peace and pleasure, wakefulness and hope there is in attending on a healthy infant, and that one's thoughts are never tired when so employed." Indeed, caring for the baby brought Dorothy a calmness and peace that her devotion to Coleridge and her brother William never gave her.

Absorbed as the Wordsworths were in little John, they also enjoyed two new friends, Sir George and Lady Beaumont, who had taken the unoccupied half of Coleridge's house at Keswick. Among London's intelligentsia, they knew Coleridge before coming to Keswick, but they had not heard of Wordsworth. Before long, realizing that the tiny Wordsworth cottage was overcrowded when Coleridge lived with them as often as he did, Sir George purchased a small plot of land at Applethwaite at the foot of Mount Skiddaw, where the Wordsworths might build a house and be near Coleridge. On expressing his desire to present it to the Wordsworths, Sir George said that as he "thought with pleasure on the increase of enjoyment you could receive from the beauties of Nature by being able to communicate more frequently your sensations to each other; and that this would be the means of contributing to the pleasure and improvement of the world, by stimulating you both to poetical exertions." Though Sir George's plan did not materialize, for Wordsworth chose not to build, Wordsworth was deeply appreciative of the gesture. A warm friendship developed among the Beaumonts, Coleridge, and the Wordsworths.

On August 15, William, Dorothy, and Coleridge went on a six weeks' trip to Scotland. Though they expected to walk most of the way, they purchased an Irish dog cart and horse so that they might ride if they so chose. Lightheartedly, they passed through Carlisle, a town all abustle, to desolate Solway Moss, a vast waste broken by an occasional grass hut, through Dumfries, where they visited Burns's grave in the red stone quarry of a cemetery where footstones were the size of ordinary headstones. The good people of Dumfries seemed to vie with one another to see who would have the largest grave markers of hideous red stone; they were in "all sorts of fantastic shapes—obelisk-wise, pillar-wise, etc." Burns's grave lay at the corner of the churchyard, with no stone to mark the spot. "A hundred guineas have been collected to be expended upon some monument," the Wordsworths were told. Little did they dream that one day a glittering white marble mausoleum would be erected to mark Burns's grave, complete with a life-size statue of a man plowing, and near the plough a field mouse and a mountain daisy—a white monstrosity that would stand out sharply from the dark reddish rock monuments, this tomb to a simple man who disliked the ostentatious. The Wordsworths and Coleridge visited Burns's home, a white-washed cottage, "dirty about the doors as almost all Scotch houses are," with flowering plants in the windows. Mrs. Burns and the children were at the seaside, but the servant invited the Wordsworths and Coleridge into the house whose "walls were coloured with a blue wash; on one side of the fire was a mahogany desk, opposite to the window a clock and over the desk a print from *The Cotter's Saturday Night* which Burns mentions in one of his letters having received as a present. The house was cleanly and neat inside; the stairs of stone, scoured white, the kitchen on the right side of the passage, the parlour on the left. In the room above the parlour the poet died." Mrs. Burns's youngest son, the servant told the Wordsworths, was at Christ's Hospital. "We were glad," Dorothy says, "to leave Dumfries, which is no agreeable place to them who do not love the bustle of a town that seems to be rising up to wealth. We could think of little else but poor Burns, and his moving about on that 'unpoetic ground'." They then went to Wanlockhead, where they met three barefoot boys with honeysuckle in their straw hats, on through wide stretches of treeless moors, marked at times by exquisite heather, through Leadhills and toward Lanark where they encountered a lone shepherd, draped in a grey plaid, on a moor with his sheep. At Lanark, "The evening sun was now sending a glorious light through the street, which ran from west to east; the houses were of fire red, and the faces of the people were almost like a blacksmith when he is at work at night."

On and on, the tireless Wordsworths went, going to Hamilton, to Glasgow, to Dumbarton with its majestic castle and Rock of misty yellow, deeply stained by wind and weather, with its stupendous view of sea storms, of mountain winds and water winds. Near Dumbarton, they examined a small pillar erected to the memory of Dr. Tobias Smollett, who was born in a little village nearby. "There is," wrote Dorothy, "a long Latin inscription which C. translated for my benefit. The Latin is miserably bad—as Wm. and C. said, such as poor Smollett, who was an excellent scholar, would have been ashamed of." Then they drove and walked to Loch Lomond, a paradise with its steep purple banks on which grew high trees, with its little green wooded island having a single hut on it set in a natural garden; before the cottage, boys played with their kites. At Loch Ketterine, they met an old woman who spoke no English; on they went to the Trossachs. Three weeks had passed since they left Grasmere; Coleridge, finding the Wordsworths too strenuous for him, decided to leave them. The brother and sister went to Gencoe, thence to Callender, then back for a second visit to the Trossachs. There, this time, they climbed to a burying-ground where they were told Rob Roy, Scotland's prototype of Robin Hood, was buried. They found several tombstones but "the inscriptions were worn out or unintelligible to us, and the place choked up with nettles and brambles." Wordsworth composed a poem to Rob Roy, whose name kindled "with instantaneous joy" almost all who heard it, this

> Wild chieftain of a savage clain

who

> Hadst this to boast of—thou dids't love
> The Liberty of Man.

Leaving Rob Roy's grave at dusk, they descended to the lake and rowed some distance under cloudless skies where everything seemed at rest. That night, "I slept as soundly," Dorothy said, "on my chaff bed as ever I had done in childhood after the long day's playing of a summer holiday." While breakfast was being prepared the next morning, Dorothy, strolling in the fields, encountered a paralyzed old woman who said she had traveled far in her time. She had married an English soldier and lived at the garrison; they had had many children, all now dead or living in foreign countries. The widowed old woman had come home to her native land and was now looked after by her neighbors, who provided her with peat for fuel and other necessities. "I could but think of the change of things," Dorothy says, "when the shrill fife sounding from the Garrison made a merry noise through the echoing hills." Leaving the old lady, after breakfast, the Wordsworths walked through more fertile land, though much of it was uncultivated. It was harvest time and often they met small companies of reapers, occasionally, a single person so employed. William's "Solitary Reaper" was occasioned by seeing such a girl and by a line in Thomas Wilkinson's *Tour in Scotland*.

They journeyed next to Edinburgh, where they went to Holyrood Palace, climbed the hill called Withers, looked down on grey, misty Edinburgh, which William said seemed built on crags. They climbed up till they came "to St. Anthony's well and *chapel*, as it is called, but it is more like a hermitage than a chapel, a small ruin, which from its situation is exceedingly interesting, though in itself not remarkable. We sat down on a stone not far from the chapel, overlooking a hollow as wild and solitary as any in the heart of the Highland mountains; then, instead of the roaring of torrents, we listened to the noises of the city, which were blended in one loud indistinct buzz, a regular sound in the air, which in certain moods of feeling, and at certain times, might have a more tranquilizing effect upon the mind than those which we are accustomed to hear in such places. The Castle Rock looked exceedingly large through the misty air: a cloud of black smoke overhung the city, which combined with the rain and mist to conceal the shapes of houses, an obscurity which added much to the grandeur of the sound that proceeded from it. It was impossible to think of anything that was little or mean, the goings-on of trade, the strife of men, or everyday city business; the impression was one, and it was visionary, like the conceptions of our childhood of Bagdad or Balsora when we have been reading the Arabian Nights' Entertainments. Though the rain was very heavy we remained upon the hill for some time. . . ."

Leaving Edinburgh, they set out for Lasswade where they hoped to see Walter Scott, an Edinburgh advocate and poet with whom William had had some correspondence. William had been invited to call upon the Scotch writer if ever he came north. Just now, Walter Scott, a ruddy-faced, blue-eyed, stout, broad shouldered man in his thirties who walked with a decided limp, was spending his honeymoon with his bride in Lasswade. The Wordsworths arrived at their home before the Scotts had arisen, and waited for some little time in a large sitting room. When the Scotts appeared, Walter Scott introduced his young wife, a brown-eyed, dark skinned, vivacious girl of French extraction, elegantly dressed. They had breakfast together and talked until two o'clock when Walter Scott accompanied the visitors back to Roslyn, promising to meet them at Melrose two days later. This first visit with Scott, the Wordsworths long remembered.

They learned that Walter Scott was proud that he came from "gentle stock," being related to such border families as the Murrays, Rutherfords, and Haliburtons, and having some Celtic blood from the MacDougals and Campbells. He was, indeed, so proud of the fact that he was descended from border chieftains whose exploits won him a coat of arms, that, in 1820, when asked by the Heralds' Office to prepare his escutcheon, he wrote that his ancestors for three hundred years before the union of the Kingdoms had "murdered, stolen, and robbed like other border gentlemen"; and, from James's reign to the revolution, "held commissions in God's own parliamentary army, canted, prayed and so forth; persecuted themselves during the reign of the last Stuarts; hunted, drunk claret, rebelled, and fought duels down to the times of my father and grandfather." At fifty-four, he wrote in his journal, "What a life mine has been!—half educated, almost wholly neglected or left to myself, stuffing my head with most nonsensical trash, and under-valued in society for a time by most of my companions—getting forward and held a bold and clever fellow contrary to the opinion of all who held me a mere dreamer. Brokenhearted for two years—my heart handsomely pieced again—but the crack will remain to my dying day. Rich and poor four or five times, once at the verge of ruin, yet opened new sources of wealth almost overflowing. Now taken in my pitch of pride and nearly winged. . . ."

His father, Walter Scott, Sr., son of a farmer, had been a lawyer, an upright man, zealous in winning cases for his clients, but so occupied with causes that he did not bother to keep books, with the result that many, less scrupulous than he, never paid their debts to him. It took fifteen years to settle his estate. His mother, daughter of a professor of medicine at Edinburgh University, was fond of ballads and tales; like her husband, a strict Calvinist, she made every Sunday a day of penance; husband and wife found their recreation in studying theology and attending funerals.

Their son, Walter, it seemed at first would not survive childhood; at eighteen months, his right leg was powerless. Not knowing a cure for infant paralysis, someone suggested that whenever a sheep was killed for food, the baby should be placed naked within the skin, raw and warm as the skin came from the carcass. Even at the end of his life, Scott still recalled the terrible odor, the awfulness of touching that skin in which he was forced to lie. This treatment continued through his third year. Attempts were made to get him to crawl and to stand; he was kept much out of doors. Finally, he was able to stand, to walk, and even to run, but throughout his life he suffered from the shrunken leg and lameness. At four, he went to Bath, sent by a doctor who hoped electrical treatments and the waters at Bath would cure his leg. A devoted aunt and grandmother read him ballads and told him of border-frays. The most exciting event of his year at Bath was his trip with an uncle to see *As You Like It*. It was even more exciting than had been his visits while in London en route to Bath, to the Tower of London and Westminster Abbey. Back at home with his family, he was thrilled at the exciting tales his older brother told him when the former was not kicking and beating him; his second brother, a disagreeable child, ignored him; his sister snapped at him; his lazy youngest brother, he did not respect; but he did have real affection for his brother Tom, a spirited boy.

His disability, however, left him feeling lonely; he recalled for years a maid's unkindness as she helped him over steps his brothers traversed easily. Self-conscious, he compensated by reading a great deal. At six, he was genuinely fond of Pope's translation of Homer, and of Milton's *Paradise Lost*. Since the waters at Bath did not cure his infirmity, he was sent to try the waters of the Firth of Forth. Regularly bathing in the sea, he met a little girl who, ignoring his limping, made life joyous for him, as did an old soldier who recounted his exploits, and a friend of his father's who introduced him to Shakespeare and made Falstaff and Hotspur live. Back at home, he discovered in his mother's room, copies of Shakespeare. By firelight, he read and re-read the bard's plays when he was supposed to be asleep. His scholastic career, when he entered Edinburgh High School, was undistinguished, but here he was popular with boys who enjoyed the tales he told. Moreover, his limp was ignored, as his companions admired his intelligence and bravery.

Not in robust health, at the close of his years at Edinburgh High School, he was sent to his Aunt Janet's home at Kelso. There, he attended a school, where two pupils, James and John Ballantyne, considered him the best storyteller they had ever heard. He often recited to the boys ballads he was reading in Percy's *Reliques of Ancient Poetry*, which he had discovered in his aunt's library. Forsaking the companionship of boys, he sat frequently in his aunt's garden "beneath a huge platanus tree in the ruins of what had been intended for an old-fashioned arbour in the garden. . . . The summer day sped onward so fast, that notwithstanding the sharp appetite of thirteen, I forgot the hour of dinner, was sought for with anxiety, and was still found entranced in my intellectual banquet. To read and to remember was in this instance the same thing, and henceforth I overwhelmed my schoolfellows, and all who would hearken to me, with tragical recitations from the ballads of Bishop Percy . . . Nor do I believe I ever read a book half so frequently, or with half the pleasure." In this garden of seven or eight acres, "with its hedges of yew and hornbeam, which rose close and tall on every side," its long walks, almost a labyrinth, with its huge old trees and its orchard with fruit trees, he became acquainted, too, with Spenser, Smollett, Richardson, and Fielding.

When he entered Edinburgh University in 1783, his Greek professor, at the end of one term, called him a dunce who would never amount to anything. Uninterested in the Greek classics, Scott read widely in books that interested him more, and when several illnesses compelled him to leave the university, promptly forgot even the Greek alphabet. In 1786, an apprentice in his father's law office, he began to realize as he did increasingly that he should have spent more time on the classics and science. On one business trip to the Highlands, he met Robert Burns who impressed him greatly, but the accounts he had heard of the bard's revolutionary views and drinking exploits caused young Scott not to seek to know the man better.

At seventeen or eighteen, he fell in love with a tradesman's daughter, Jessie, whose gentleness, goodness, and kindness, he said "fill me with the sweetest feelings I have ever known." Reluctant to tell her parents of Walter Scott's interest in her, Jessie insisted they meet secretly, which they did. Her praise of his poetry emboldened him to write more verse. Although Jessie continued to encourage the lovesick young man who wished to "labor" in her service, she finally told him she was in love with a young medical student, whom she later married. Though he must have realized, as he mingled with his friends in the social life of Edinburgh, that she would not have been a suitable wife, he long resented her marriage to his rival.

At twenty, he began a love affair with Williamina Belsches, which he once said consisted of "three years of dreaming and two of awakening." As young Scott with the rest of the congregation was leaving Greyfriar's Church one Sunday morning in 1791, it was raining. The chivalrous youth offered his umbrella to the fifteen-year-old brown-haired, hazel-eyed beauty, and escorted her home. Her father, Sir John Belsches, was a barrister; her mother, a daughter of the Earl of Leven. He carved her name on the turf beside the castle gate at St. Andrews; while he longed for his "adorable," he strove to do well in his profession so that he might marry her. When he told his mother of his love, she passed on the news to his father, who, in turn, relayed it to Sir John, to whom it came as a surprise. The latter did not think the matter serious. Yet, the two young people continued to see each other, and Walter Scott to hope his affections were returned. When he learned that William Forbes, the son of a rich banker and the heir to a baronetcy, was also courting his love, he said that "blue Devils, and white black Devils and grey" insisted upon plaguing him. A few months after he learned of his rival, he was told that Williamina was going to marry young Forbes. Angered as she told him the news, Scott informed her he would be married before she was. The intensity of his love for her continued for some years, so strong that once when someone merely mentioned her name, he broke in his hand the wine-glass he was holding. Twenty-two years later, after her death, he wrote, "Scarce one person out of twenty marries his first love and scarce one out of twenty has cause to rejoice that he has done so. What we love in those early days is generally rather a fanciful creation of our own rather than a reality. We build statues of snow and weep when they melt."

Trying to brace himself after his refusal by Williamina, Scott worked hard forming the Royal Edinburgh Light Dragoons. Fearing a French invasion after the Revolution, troops of volunteers were being raised throughout Scotland. Energetic, conscientious, and capable, Scott became quartermaster of the Light Dragoons, drilling daily at five each morning and always arriving at the rallying point during the many war scares, though he once rode a hundred miles without a break to do so. In the midst of his military training, on a vacation at Gilsland, having made up his mind to marry, he flirted with pretty girls who struck his fancy, and shortly decided that a handsome brunette, dark-eyed girl with a pale complexion, much like Williamina in appearance, though gayer than she, was the girl for him.

Charlotte Charpentier, of French parentage, was a ward of Lord Downshire. She spoke English fluently though with an accent, was sympathetic, good-natured and so cheerful that Scott wrote her, "I admire of all things your laughing Philosophy, and shall certainly be your pupil in learning to take a gay view of life." At first she felt she could never marry a man who limped, but when he told her of his love and of his previous love affair with Williamina, he won her compassion and then her affection. He explained that he must earn his livelihood and that he felt certain he could do so and achieve success as well. When Scott told his mother of his new love, she told his father, who insisted upon knowing the background of the girl. Charlotte provided the needed information, which satisfied Scott's parents. His devotion, he told them, was based, not so much on her personal charms as on her "good sense and sweetness of character." He told his aunt that Charlotte was "not a beauty by any means, but her person and face are very engaging." Lord Downing consented to the marriage and settled £400 a year on his ward; Walter Scott, angered that his parents were giving him no financial aid, executed a deed settling Charlotte's money on herself; he was earning but £125 a year. He took a house for ten guineas for six months, confident "We shall do very well . . . I really do not think I was born to stick in the world. . . ." They were married December 22, 1797, in Carlisle Cathedral. The marriage was a good one. A dozen years after it was consummated, Scott confessed "Mrs. Scott's match and mine was our own making and proceeded from the most sincere affection on both sides, which has rather increased than diminished during twelve years of marriage. But it was something short of love in all its fervour, which I suspect people feel only once in their lives. Folks who have been nearly drowned in bathing rarely venture a second time out of their depth."

Charlotte's high spirits soon endeared her to Scott's friends whom she loved to entertain; she was eager to dress fashionably, to dance, and to attend the theatre frequently; she shocked her mother-in-law by using the drawing room as a sitting room, whereas Scotch custom decreed this room was used only on special occasions. The death of Scott's father, who left him a considerable legacy, and Scott's appointment as Sheriff-deputy of Selkirk enabled the ambitious man to renounce the practice of law and to devote himself to writing. In 1802, the Scotts moved to Edinburgh, where they resided twenty-two years. Saddened by the death of their first son a month after his birth, they rejoiced in the birth of a second son three years later, "a fine, chapping boy whose pipe, being of the shrillest, is heard amid the storm, like a boatsman's whistle in a gale of wind." The duties of a sheriff were slight, and Scott spent more time collecting and composing ballads than in all his other activities. In this, he was encouraged by many, among them, Monk Lewis whose Gothic romance, *Ambrosia or The Monk*, excited the reading public and won him acclaim; and George Ellis, critic and writer, who, Scott said, "had more wit, learning, and knowledge of the world than would fit out twenty *literati*." For recreation, Scott loved to work in his garden and to tramp with his dogs, a black and tan terrier and an English bulldog. He enjoyed his children, Sophia, Walter, Anne, and Charles, though Walter was often a problem.

The Lay of the Last Minstrel made him famous and lionized at thirty-three; he then began work on an edition of Dryden, and in haste completed his poem *Marmion* to aid financially his brother Tom who was deeply in debt. Whereas he had hitherto been considered a border poet, *Marmion* raised him to the stature of a national poet. The poem, however, received severe criticism from Francis Jeffrey, the caustic critic of the *Edinburgh Review*, who had pilloried many a writer. Good-natured Scott said that he and Jeffrey dined together "and had a hearty laugh at the revisal of the flagellation." Not so charitable, Charlotte, who had treated the critic politely during dinner, said to him as he was leaving, "Well, good-night, Mr. Jeffrey—de tell me you have abused Scott in de *Review*, and I hope Mr. Constable has paid you very well for writing it." Later, Scott, a frequent contributor to the *Edinburgh Review*, refused to continue writing for it. Two years later, its Whig writers, praising Napoleon and asserting the French were invincible, were preaching nonintervention in Spain and urging peace with France at any price; they even declared that a revolution in England was inevitable if the war continued. Scott knew there could be no peace with Napoleon and believed that the Spanish war, if fought vigorously, would cause Napoleon's defeat. He recognized the greatness of Arthur Wellesley, later the Duke of Wellington, long before others did. Angered at the Whig writers in the *Edinburgh Review*, Scott canceled his subscription to the magazine. Ceasing either to read or to write for it, he began writing for Murray's new *Quarterly Review*, which grew rapidly. His *Lady of the Lake* not only delighted critics but also brought tourists to Scotland. Though idolized by many readers, Scott remained modest, replying, when asked how his genius compared with Burns, "There is no comparison, we should not be mentioned in the same day."

His acquaintanceship with Lord Byron started off badly. When Jeffrey attacked Byron's poetry in the *Edinburgh Review*, Byron retorted by attacking Scott as a "hireling barb" and "Apollo's venal son." Byron's abuse hurt Scott who said to Southey, "It is funny enough to see a whelp of a young Lord Byron abusing me, of whose circumstances he knows nothing, for endeavoring to scratch out a living with my pen. God help the bear, if, having little else to eat, he must suck his own paws. I can assure the noble imp of fame it is not my fault I was not born to a park and £5,000 a year, as it is not his lordship's merit . . . that he was not born to live by his literary talents or success." When *Childe Harold* appeared, Scott was impressed and, though he considered the poem somewhat immoral, thought it "very clever, poetical, and powerful." This opinion he expressed boldly; moreover, he wrote Byron praising his genius. Byron replied, and the two met in John Murray's rooms in London. Handsome Byron with his club foot and his limp and Scott with his decided limp came together down stairs, the descent making their disabilities the more marked. Though they did not agree politically, though Scott thought chastity would improve Byron, and Byron thought a little adultery now and then would do Scott some good, each found the other's company stimulating. When Lady Byron parted from her husband and accused him of insanity and incest with his sister, public disapproval of Byron affected the acceptance of the third canto of his *Childe Harold*, which was coldly received. Scott came to Byron's defense, writing a generous review of it for the *Quarterly*. When Byron thanked him for his review, Scott replied, "I have been too long an advocate for fair play to like to see twenty dogs upon one, were that one their equal—much less to see all the curs of the village set upon one noble staghound who is worth the whole troop." Byron replied, "I wish it had been my good fortune to have had such a mentor." Had he done so and found even a half-dozen others like Scott in the world, he declared he would have believed in human nature. When Stendahl stupidly said that Scott's character was not all it should be, Byron wrote Stendahl that "Walter Scott is as nearly a thoroughly good man as now can be, because I *know* it by experience to be the case."

In 1812, Scott purchased Abbotsford on the Tweed, where one of the last great Border battles had been fought. Happy with this estate, he continued to add to it, in three years doubling his acreage; by 1816, his estate had grown from a hundred acres to nearly a thousand; in 1817, he added yet more acres. About five hundred acres were planted with trees—poplars, filberts, laburnums, Scotch elms, horse-chestnuts, sweet briar, and birches. He revelled in planting his trees. "You have no idea of the exquisite delight of the planter; he is like a painter, laying on his colours at every moment he sees his efforts coming out. There is no art or occupation comparable to this; it is full of past, present, and future enjoyment. I look back to the time when there was not a tree here, only bare heath; I look around and see thousands of trees growing up, all of which, I may say almost each of which, have received my personal attention. Unlike building or even painting, or indeed any other kind of pursuit, this has no end, and is never interrupted, but goes on from day to day and from year to year, with a perpetually augmenting interest . . . I promise you my oaks will outlast my laurels." As his grounds increased, his house gradually grew also. In 1822, he wrote, "I have been busied all this season in finishing a sort of a Romance of a house here built in imitation of an old Scottish manor house, and I think I have attained not unsuccessfully, the scrambling style of these venerable edifices." And proud was he, indeed, of "the Grand Babylon I have built" and of the fact that it was lighted by gas, then a novelty. There were many assemblies, dances, feasts, football games, shooting and fishing parties at the manor. Over these festivities, Charlotte presided, not demurring even when there were, once, in addition to the guests, thirteen ladies' maids, though she remarked that at times Abbotsford was a hotel in all but name and pay. Visitors came, invited and uninvited, in droves, to meet the famous man. Among them were Dorothy and William Wordsworth. The latter, Scott said, "was a gentleman, every inch of him unless he is mounted on his critical hobby-horse, and tells us Pope is no poet. He might as well say Wellington is no soldier because he wears a blue greatcoat and not a coat of burnished mail." Maria Edgeworth, the novelist, and her two sisters, came to visit and so enjoyed their visit that they wept at parting.

Only one visitor left in a huff: Mrs. Counts, the wealthy widow of a banker, who arrived with three coaches, containing in addition to the owner, two doctors, various servants, the Duke of St. Albans and his sister. Despite her wealth, the lady was thoroughly snubbed by the guests because she had once been an actress, and was ridiculed because of the way the stupid Duke make ardent love to her. Scott, disturbed by the behavior of his guests and liking the "Dame of Diamonds," though he considered the Duke very "spoony indeed," rebuked his guests, reminding them they had been told of the expected arrival of the lady two days earlier and that they could have left had they not desired to meet her. They, therefore, treated her well after this; the next day, however, she left, though she had expected to remain three days longer. She still respected "kind Mr. Scott" but could not stay in the same house as his "horrid women" guests.

A master of his house, Scott also rebuked some who resented the poor coming to Abbotsford for assistance. To one of his employees he said, "If you have nothing to give them in the way of alms, always give them civility, and for this reason: you do not know what you are to come to yourself, although you are under my roof. Just now there is no certainty either for you or for me how soon we may be dismantled." Scott was on good terms with everyone: his servants, his neighbors, the nobility.

Busy with his estate, with his duties as sheriff, and with his entertaining, he continued to write. Novels followed one another in rapid succession. Nor did illness long keep him from writing. Ill with "cramps" that lasted from six to eight hours at a time, with jaundice, then with paroxysms that blinded him for a time, he was at the mercy of doctors who administered opiates, bled him, blistered him, once within a few hours giving him six grains of opium, three of hyoscyamus, and two hundred drops of laudanum without relieving his agony. Many strange remedies were suggested and tried in vain. Finally, he took small quantities of calomel over a long period and seemed cured. He had barely survived this illness, when he was saddened by the death of his mother, his uncle, and his aunt; yet he continued to write. Some, amazed at the quantity he wrote, insisted that two men, Scott and some unknown person, were together writing the novels *Kenilworth* and *Ivanhoe* as well as others Scott wrote. He laughed off these critics, saying, "no brain but a madman's could have invented such stuff."

In May, 1818, he met at a dinner party, a barrister and journalist, John Gibson Lockhart. Haughty, thoroughly unsociable, Lockhart, son of a minister, an Oxford man, who with John Wilson wrote scurrilous and malicious reviews for *Blackwood's Monthly Magazine*, had taken delight in using his powerful invective against Keats, Leigh Hunt, and Hazlitt. When after a short courtship, Lockhart wished to marry Scott's daughter Sophia, Scott did his best to persuade the young man first to find "worthier work" than "this species of (verbal) warfare" in which he was engaged. The young couple were married and Scott was gracious to his son-in-law. When two of Lockhart's friends, angered at one another's verbal attacks, finally fought a duel in which one was killed, Lockhart listened more courteously to his father-in-law's advice. Urged by Benjamin D'Israeli to take the editorship of a Tory newspaper, Lockhart accepted this position as well as the editorship of the *Quarterly Review*, giving up the connection Scott hated with *Blackwood's Magazine*, though Scott did not relish a gentleman's editing a newspaper. A great admirer of Scott, Lockhart eventually wrote a ten volume biography of him.

Though in 1813 Scott had refused the poet laureatship of England, a position he thought of recent years to be "absurd" and of no consequence, he had suggested for the position a man whom he considered a better poet than himself, Robert Southey, who was proffered the position and took it gladly. When, however, five years later, Scott was offered a baronetcy, he was pleased to accept the honor. Illness prevented his going to London until 1820, when he had lots of fun out of the investiture. He was impressed at his gracious reception by his Sovereign, but thoroughly amused at those who made before him "five hundred scrapes and cougees as I retired," and at the servants who now "bowed two inches lower" and opened doors "three inches wider." Soon, he was tired of being lionized, weary of "fine company and fine living, from Dukes and Duchesses down to turbot and plovers' eggs. It is all very well for a while, but to be kept at it makes one feel like a poodle dog compelled to stand forever on his hind legs."

His patriotic fervor had reached its height five years earlier when he had received royal permission to search the Crown Room in Edinburgh Castle where he believed the Royal Regalia of Scotland, long missing, was hidden. In 1818, a Commission was formed to search for the Regalia. Scott was present when a chest, unopened for a hundred years, had its lid broken open. As the lid was lifted, there reposed the Royal Regalia in perfect condition. Scott succeeded next in securing the appointment of a friend as Custodier of the Scottish Regalia—and a knighthood as well.

Honors poured upon him from throughout the British Isles. He journeyed with Lockhart to Cork, Dublin, and Holyhead in Ireland, and to Llangollen in Wales, where he met Lady Eleanor Butler and Sarah Ponsonby; in the English Lake Country, he met William and Dorothy Wordsworth, who made a bad impression on Lockhart. Lockhart believed Wordsworth "old and pompous, and fine and absurdly arrogant beyond conception," and said the English poet continued "spouting his own verses very grandly all the way . . . never once quoting Scott, all the way from Windermere to Keswick where they met Southey." Whenever Wordsworth for a time "dried up," Lockhart added, Scott quoted Wordsworth's verses. Scott, unlike Lockhart, enjoyed Wordsworth's "manly sense and candour" and found his conversation "like a fountain in the desert." Though he did not agree with Wordsworth's theories of poetry, Scott never considered his own verse as good as Wordsworth's. Back at Abbotsford, he was visited by the Irish bard, Thomas More, whose singing fascinated Scott.

In 1825, when inflation was at its height, Arnold Constable, the publishing house, like many other firms, was in dire financial trouble. Scott, never too careful in his business, raised, by a mortgage on Abbotsford, £10,000 to aid the firm, in which he was a partner. When this company and another in which he had extensive interests failed, Scott found himself in debt £116,838 plus the £10,000 mortgage on his property and £40,000 in debts owed by Constable and Son. Life for Scott had almost always been pleasant; now it seemed ghastly. Though within a month he realized money was of little concern to him, luxury and social position meant much to his wife and family. Some of Scott's servants refused to leave, though they would have to receive small wages. Many were quick to recognize that Scott's financial collapse was not exceptional, for, before long, others were in a similar plight as the result of a country-wide monetary crisis. From this time on, work at his writing occupied Scott, determined to pay off his debts by his pen. At the time of his death in 1832, he had cleared all debts but £22,000—the latter, a questionable balance, as one of Scott's partners had cleared £60,000 by 1836 on Scott's writing. Ten years later, on the agreement that Scott's family turn over to this man fifty percent of all the copyrights of Scott's work, the family estate was freed of all debt. This had been accomplished by the long hours Scott worked each day, writing, writing.

After the death of Charlotte in 1826, he wrote on the day of her funeral, "A kind of cloud of stupidity hangs over me, as if all were unreal that men seem to be doing and talking about." Nor did this feeling soon leave, for days later, as he sat in his study, overwhelmed by a feeling of loneliness, he wrote, "The solitude seems so absolute— my poor Charlotte would have been in the room half-a-score of times to see if the fire burned, and to ask a hundred kind questions. Well,— that is over. . . ." Still later, he wrote in his Journal that his son, Charles, came into his study and found him weeping. "I do not know what other folks feel, but with me the hysterical passion that compels tears is of terrible violence—a sort of throttling sensation—then succeeded by a state of dreaming stupidity, in which I ask if my poor Charlotte can actually be dead. I think I feel my loss more than at the first blow."

A month later, his novel *Woodstock* was published. Continuing his hard work, he saw his best-selling *Life of Napoleon* appear fifteen months later, bringing him £18,000 toward paying off his debts. That same year, two of his sermons were published. And still the *Waverley* novels flourished when they sold in an extremely popular Collected Edition.

In 1830, he suffered a stroke, not a severe one, but one which for fifteen minutes prohibited his speaking. Yet, he continued to write, for without writing life would have been empty. Moreover, he still had work to do. In '31, he noted that at times his speech was confused and he seemed weak. Finding writing difficult, he dictated his next novel, arising at 6:45 to get in a full day's work. When his family visited him in May, they noted how haggard his face was, how loosely his clothing hung upon him. Yet, he took an active interest in politics, and traveled, accompanied by his daughter and Lockhart, to the Lake Country in England where again he visited Wordsworth, who composed a poem calling him a "wondrous Potentate"; he went then to London and on to Italy. En route home, he suffered yet another stroke at Cologne. In London, seriously ill, he was forced to remain three weeks; but, as he grew better, he persuaded his doctors to allow him to be brought home to Abbotsford. At times conscious, he was wheeled about his garden. Once, he asked to sit at his desk, but he was too weak to hold his pen. On September 21, 1832, Scott died and was buried near Charlotte in what he had once called "the lap of beauty," but which others call the ruins of Dryborough Abbey.

In an age of controversy, Scott was born a Tory and died a Tory; like the Major in *Old Mortality*, Scott could easily have said, "I am no politician and I do not understand nice distinctions. My sword is the king's, and when he commands, I draw it in his cause." He was an opponent of Reform, humanitarian as well as political. Prison reform, he could not approve "except it imitate the ways of a captain reforming a mutinous ship by discipline of the strictest sort." He was willing to grant Catholic Emancipation for "since we tolerate the Roman Catholics at all, there is no need to bother about little pin-pricks as deprivation of political rights. The great mistake was in not rooting the Roman Church out completely; but that mistake is now irretrievable." He had little faith in democracy, which he was convinced would only end in disorder to be quelled by military dictatorship. He opposed reform, some say not only because "as a gentleman he was satisfied with a society in which he held so enviable a position but because as a romantic he could not be happy in a society without gradations and interesting prejudices." Lacking sympathy with workmen who had revolted against their employers, Scott gave a sermon on the virtues of the capitalistic employer and the rewards of proper submission to his benevolent rule. Scott's conservatism was that of a new middle class.

After leaving Walter Scott, the Wordsworths found that being a friend of his brought them every possible civility. Dorothy wrote, "indeed, Mr. Scott is respected everywhere. I believe that by favour of his name one might be hospitably entertained throughout all the borders of Scotland." At Melrose, where the Wordsworths had gone to see Melrose Abbey, they met Scott as planned; he insisted upon being their guide. An admirable one he was, showing Dorothy many pieces of beautiful carving in obscure corners that otherwise she would have missed.

At Jedburgh, where Scott in his capacity as sheriff had come for the assizes, the Wordsworths met him again, as had also been arranged; he spent all of his available time with them. William told later how Scott's conversation had been lively, entertaining, "full of anecdote and free from disquisition," how he had partly recited for them, "sometimes in an enthusiastic style of the chant, the first four stanzas of 'The Lay of The Last Minstrel,' and the novelties of the manners, the clear picturesque descriptions, and the easy glowing energy of much of the verse, greatly delighted me." The Wordsworths noted with dismay the similarity of parts of Coleridge's unpublished "Christabel" to "The Lay"; Scott, they knew, had heard a friend, Stoddard, recite Coleridge's poem; in fact, Scott said he had been glad that Coleridge had employed "so happy a specimen of the kind of irregular metre" and that Scott had used it in "The Lay"; he had memorized "Christabel." The Wordsworths were convinced that Scott's was an unconscious imitation, and William wondered whether he should tell Scott he was plagiarizing. He decided, however, not to say so, as he had not known Scott long; when "The Lay" was published before "Christabel" was, Wordsworth regretted he had not done so, for he feared "The Lay" with its new meter would "tarnish" the freshness of "Christabel" and considerably injure the first effect of it; Dorothy, on the other hand, was so convinced of the superiority of Coleridge's poem that she did not in the least fear the effect of Scott's poem would lessen appreciation of Coleridge's.

The following day, Scott took a long walk with the Wordsworths after the court adjourned. It was a beautiful sunny day, with just enough wind to toss the branches of the trees. Dorothy's remark,

"What a life there is in trees" delighted him. The three dined together that evening and, being in a festive mood, the Wordsworths ordered a bottle of wine for the occasion. The talk flowed on and on and Scott was persuaded to repeat some of his poems for them. The following day, the last day of the assizes, the Wordsworths went with Scott to Court to hear the Judge's speech, which Dorothy declared was "the most curious specimen of old woman's oratory and newspaper loyalty that was ever heard." When all was over the members of the court "returned to the inn in procession as they had come, to the sound of the trumpet, the Judge first in his robes of red, the Sheriffs next, in large cocked hats, and inferior officers following, a sight not much calculated to awe the beholders . . . Mr. Scott was very glad to part from the Judge and his retinue, to travel with us in our car to Hawick; his servant drove his own gig. The landlady very kindly had put up some sandwiches and cheese cake for me," Dorothy wrote; "and all the family came to see us depart." She had given Dorothy also a quantity of pears, telling her that the Jedburgh pears were famous. The Wordsworths found them delicious. Lockhart says the Wordsworths and Scott "met as if they had not been strangers and they parted, friends."

Scott's local attachments, Dorothy recalled, were "more strong than any person I ever saw—his whole heart and soul seem to be devoted to the Scottish Streams, Yarrow and Tweed, Tiviot and the rest of them, of which we hear in the Border Ballads, and I am sure there is not a story ever told by the firesides in the neighborhood that he cannot repeat. . . . He is a man of very sweet manners, mild, cordial, and cheerful."

One remark of Scott's Wordsworth pondered. Scott had said, "he could, if he chose, get more money than he felt he should ever wish to have from the booksellers." His profession, law, he said, was not profitable. As Wordsworth was making almost nothing from his writing and his brother Richard and his friend Basil Montagu were prospering as lawyers, Wordsworth was inclined to question his friend's statement. In the end, however, he had to admit Scott was right. Wordsworth noted, too, Scott's keen interest in "bodily sports, exercises, and social amusements . . . fishing, duck-hunting, and riding about the countryside—his Liddesdale raids as he called them, when he explored every ruined peel-tower—and was welcomed at every remote farm house in all the wide Border." Most of Wordsworth's poems about Scotland were written two or three years after his return from that tour.

Two days after leaving Walter Scott, the Wordsworths arrived home, to find Mary in perfect health "and little John asleep in the clothes-basket by the fire." Dorothy wrote her friend Mrs. Clarkson that the baby "looks as if he was not the child of ordinary parents. . . . It is very affecting to us to see how much he is beloved in the neighborhood. Peggy Ashburner dotes on him as if she were his grandmother, and Molly Ashburner and Sally are never more happy than when John smiles at them. . . . By the bye, his eyes are not fine ones, they are small; but that, you know, makes him seem more like father, and they have frequently the very same expression as his father's— that same mild light when he smiles . . . if it were possible to tire you with a long story of him you would be tired now. But oh that you should see him!"

Dorothy was happy, too, when the Coleridge children, Derwent and Sara, were christened, and she was asked to be Derwent's godmother. Though she did not attend the christening because she was not well, she did consent to be the chubby little boy's godmother. After the christening, there was a gala party, of which Dorothy was told every detail. Fat, roly-poly little Derwent had always been regarded with affectionate amusement by his father, who many a time had called to Dorothy, "Come and look at his darling mouth when he shouts out q," as the child was learning the alphabet. Inclined to overeat, Derwent, then ill, would come crying for comfort to Dorothy, saying "My belly is full." And comfort him she did. Often she walked with him and a group of neighbor children. That autumn, Coleridge said, had all the colors of unripe lime, the ripe lemon, the bright orange, even the depth of dried orange peels; the leaves of the birches were a lovely lemon color. It was a beautiful time to be out-of-doors.

Shortly after the Wordsworths' return, Coleridge came with his son Derwent to visit. Though Derwent remained only a short time, Coleridge's visit lengthened into one of more than three weeks, for he became ill, nursed he says, "by Mary and Dorothy who tended me with a sister's and mother's love, and often, well I know, wept for me in their sleep and watched for me even in their dreams." Once well, he went first to London and then in April to Malta. Before his departure, Dorothy dutifully copied for him all of William's unpublished poems including the poem of his life the two wished Coleridge to have. Mary soon assisted Dorothy in this task, which was a tremendous one, not only because of its length but because of the difficulty of transcription, for, as Dorothy said, the poems were "scattered about in this book and that, one stanza on one leaf, another on another, which makes the transcribing more than twice the trouble." Dorothy and Mary decided to make two copies of the poem, one for Coleridge who was insistent on having one and one for William. It is well the task was begun, for otherwise one half of the last three books on his own life might have been lost through illegibility. "I shall never, I hope," said William, "get into such a scrape again." Dorothy was busy, too, on her Journal of the tour of Scotland. Her thoughts, though, were of Coleridge whom she entreated, "Write us yet once again, dear friend; and never, dearest friend! never miss an opportunity of writing while you are abroad." When she heard from Coleridge, a letter "concluded in the moment when the ship was going to sail," it was, she said, "like another parting to us, when we were assured that the last step was taken, and that he was really gone." The Wordsworths heard almost no word from him for three years.

On their arrival from Scotland, the Wordsworths had learned that the Southeys had taken the vacant half of Coleridge's home; there they lived the next forty years. Southey, after fourteen months in Portugal, had returned in 1801 with *Thalaba* complete, had begun an epic poem, and was now talking of going to the Mediterranean. Restless, he next had suggested to Coleridge that the two of them and the Wordsworths go to the West Indies and form a pantisocracy, an idea which Coleridge had promptly refused. After a short visit with his wife and family, Southey went to Wales to gather material for a book, *Madoc*. While there, he accepted an offer to become secretary to the Chancellor of the Exchequer of Ireland, to be stationed in London.

He was beginning to adopt an attitude of detachment from politics. While in Portugal, he had seen a woman carrying on her head a heavy burden of wool she herself had cut and was spinning as she went along. "A melancholy picture of wretchedness," he said, adding, "I have learned to thank God that I am an Englishman, for though things are not so well there as in El Dorado, they are better there than anywhere else." Contemplating France in 1801, he said, "I still have faith enough in God and hope enough of man, but not of France. Freedom cannot grow in that hotbed of immorality; that oak must root in a hardier soil—England or Germany." Resigning his appointment as secretary to the Chancellor of the Exchequer of Ireland, he went to live first in Bristol and then, in 1803, in Keswick, in the house from which Coleridge longed to escape. He enjoyed increasingly staying at home, traveling little, "revelling in conversation with books." Coleridge, his brother-in-law, realized finally that Southey was not happy in his marriage, that Edith Fricker, his wife, "sympathizes with nothing, she enters into none of his peculiar pursuits—she only loves *him;* she is therefore a respectable Wife, but not a companion. Dreary, dreary would be the Hours passed with her." Weary though Southey was of her, he was content finally to enjoy her society as recreation and relaxation, "devoting most of his intellectual energy to increasing authorship, never interrupted," Coleridge said, "from morning to night but by eating and sleeping." When Walter Scott refused England's highest literary award, the poet laureatship, once held by such luminaries as Dryden and Pope, and suggested that the honor be bestowed upon Robert Southey, it was tendered him and he accepted it. Whether weariness of fighting losing battles for causes or rigid self-discipline brought him to cease attacking policies distasteful to him, is a question. At any rate, he ended his life compromising, and found an inner peace. He was convinced that "if faith in liberty, equality, and fraternity results in licentious misdeeds, some things are good, some faiths result in virtuous actions." Therefore, he decided to cling to what gave him comfort, to be disinterested in systems and dogmas "for their fixity is a delusion." Though he no longer fought for causes, he could not refrain from making in *The Quarterly* political suggestions that showed his wisdom. He advocated a national grant for education, the spread of inexpensive editions of good literature like the English classics and the Bible, child labor restrictions, allotments of land to laborers, changes in the factory system to aid those working in the factories, government aided savings banks in market towns, better trained hospital nurses, a cooperative movement. A true humanitarian, he always believed in the goodness of human nature, and that human vice could be lessened by improving political conditions. He was certain that the industrial worker could be raised from degradation. Impatient with those who disagreed with him, he had contempt for them. Thomas Carlyle said his facial expression showed "a mixture of sorrow or of angry contempt, as if his indignant fight with the world had not yet ended in victory but also never should in defeat." William Hazlitt, too, found in his expression that of one trying to compromise, "a hectic flush upon his cheek, a raving fire in his eye, a falcon glance, a look at once aspiring and dejected." Some felt this struggle of prudence "sapped his poetry of spontaneity and his political thought of strict integrity."

The chief conversation in the district that fall was the expected invasion of French troops. William, along with his neighbors, in October went to Ambleside to volunteer his services. Two or three times a week the Grasmere volunteers drilled and marched past the Wordsworth home in their red coats. Dorothy thought the valley seemed far removed from war.

The village was shocked when Miss Sympson, aged thirty-seven, suddenly married young Ibbetson, half her age. The general opinion was that she'd done a "crazy thing"; Dorothy pitied the young woman who, in a sudden fit of passion, had married. A year later, after a long, painful labor, she bore a girl "a little waxen thing who seemed to have no strength." Several months later, the mother died. Every time Dorothy passed the grave, she questioned "Why the swift flame to end in darkness? Why the brief ecstasy of the blood to lead to a huddle of tortured days? Why the barter of a life for the strange, late flowering? Truly, Life drove a cruel trade."

The Wordsworths were excited when on August 16, Mary's second child, a little daughter, was born. She was named for her Aunt Dorothy. The gay little girl, William almost worshiped, and little John was always eager to hold her or be near her. Sara Hutchinson, who had come to help care for her sister; Lady Beaumont, who was the baby's godmother; and Miss Monkhouse and Mary Monkhouse, long friends of the Wordsworths', were at the christening. Dorothy became ill from the strain of entertaining the many visitors, some of whom remained a week. It was imperative, she, Mary, and William felt, that they have a larger house, for they had long ago outgrown the cottage which, when crowded, was now most inconvenient.

On February 11, 1805, Dorothy had hardly finished a letter to Mrs. Clarkson telling of her brother John's having written in high spirits from Portsmouth of his being captain of the *Abergavenny* that would sail the first of the month for Bengal, India—a trip he felt would make him a fortune—when news came that the ship had struck on The Shambles of the Bill of Portland and that John and the entire crew had perished. Devoted as the Wordsworths were to one another, the news came as a great shock. John, they had somehow always taken for granted, good-natured John, who helped Dorothy about the house, who quietly advised William or accompanied him on his walks. There were many reminders of him: the chairs he had made, the cupboards, the bookshelves; the trees and flowers he had planted; the grove they had named for him. The Wordsworths longed for Coleridge to comfort them.

Gradually, they learned the details of the disaster, how the ship had struck early in the afternoon and sunk at eleven at night. Then came newspaper accounts criticizing Captain John Wordsworth for the disaster, telling how the ship had struck an hour-and-a-half before the guns were fired, and how the life boats had not been hoisted down. Some accounts said that the Captain had not tried to save himself. Dazed and made half sick by these new reports, the Wordsworths wrote Charles Lamb, who was in the offices of the East India Company, to ascertain the truth. Lamb replied quickly, stating that the company's investigation showed that the disaster had been caused by the incompetency of the pilot, not by Captain John Wordsworth. After the boat struck and just before the vessel sank, Lamb wrote, John had seemed "like one overwhelmed with the situation, and careless of his own safety . . . Perhaps he might have saved himself but a Captain who under the circumstances does all he can for his ship and nothing for himself is the noblest idea." Later, Lamb wrote that Gilpin, the fourth mate, who had seen the captain after the ship went down, said that though overwhelmed by waves and half dead, "John had tried to save himself." John's body was found on March 20, lying beside his ship. He was buried the following day in Wyke Churchyard.

Wherever the Wordsworths were, indoors or out-of-doors, the constant reminders of John remained with them. Dorothy, writing to Lady Beaumont says, "Wherever we go we shall know what would have been John's sentiments and feelings, as if he had been at our side for he was true and constant as the light of heaven—he seemed to be made for the best sort of happiness which is to be found in this world, for his whole delight was in peace and Love and the beautiful works of this fair Creation. . . . I have begun again to attend to the children; the quietness of the little girl is very soothing to me, and I have great delight in her but John is too boisterous. We walk out whenever the weather is tolerable—these walks feed our melancholy, but in the end they are tranquillizing, and we are the better for them —but this vale is changed to us, it can never be *as* it has been. . . . We have had many fine days since we heard the dismal tidings; but sunshine and darkness, starlight and moonlight, calm weather and fierce winds are all doleful to us." Later, she wrote, "I did not know what sorrow was till now, which made me oversecure in what I loved and rejoiced in, and I think it too good and too perfect." Gradually, however, she took up the threads of her old life. Assured that Dorothy could now bear to speak of her brother's death, on May 10, Mary Lamb expressed her sympathy to her in verse, writing,

> Why is he wandering on the sea?
> Coleridge should now with Wordsworth be.
> By slow degrees, he'd steal away

Their woe and gently bring a ray
(So happily he'd time relief)
Of comfort from their very grief.
He'd tell them that their brother dead,
When years have passed o'er their head,
Will be remember'd with such holy
True, and perfect melancholy,
That ever this lost brother John
Will be their heart's companion.
His voice they'll always hear,
His face they'll always see,
There's naught in life so sweet
As such a memory.

Even as Mary Lamb was composing the poem, she was aware that she was becoming ill again. Less than a month later, Charles Lamb again had to take her to an asylum.

CHAPTER IX

"Not Through Action But Through Suffering"

AS THE WILLIAM WORDSWORTH FAMILY INCREASED, DOROTHY FOUND HERSELF BUSIER THAN SHE HAD THOUGHT POSSIBLE. Thomas was born in June, 1805; Catherine, in September, 1808; and William in May, 1810. As most of the household chores except cooking were done by Dorothy, she had her hands full. Not only was the family large, but often there were two to four guests for several weeks. She did find, locally, a girl who helped her; but cleaning an overcrowded house, doing all the washing and ironing, copying William's poems, helping care for the children, taking entire responsibility for them at times when William and Mary were away for two, three, or four week periods, or taking a sick child away for a week or two months, taxed her strength. As they had no baby carriage, she carried one of the smallest children on outings until she began physically to suffer from the strain. William inevitably became alarmed when contagious diseases appeared in the village and insisted on Mary's taking away those children old enough to play with others until the disease had disappeared, leaving Dorothy with the responsibility of the home and the other children. Often, too, Hartley and Derwent Coleridge spent weeks with the Wordsworths.

Dorothy was devoted to all these children. Boisterous little Johnny, with his "shy looks of gladness and beautiful blushes when anything pleased him," full of good and noble feelings, was loved by his playmates. When he was a baby, Dorothy often left him on "the carpet with a good store of play-things. . . . Give him but a work-basket full of tape and thread and other oddments and he riots among them like a little pussycat. He can sit upright on the carpet, and so we leave him—sometimes he gets a good bump on his head and lustily he roars, but no matter, he cannot hurt himself seriously, so we are not afraid of him and he will soon learn to take care of himself," she wrote. When he was learning to walk, he insisted on Dorothy's watching him trudge in manly fashion up and down the half dozen steps in the back garden; later, at Dorothy's approach, he would come bounding down the steps to greet her. Happy as a bird in the open air, he enjoyed the sounds of the out-of-doors; he laughed and clapped his hands as he heard two crows high up in the sky; he laughed and showed his two teeth as he listened to the wind in the trees. Dorothy insisted that he recognized a fine view. Did he not call out "Hooy, hooy, hooy" when, as she carried him, they came upon one? One of the first words he learned to say was "happy"; proud of his new word, he went through the house repeating it. Often, he slept with Dorothy, and awakening in the middle of the night, would cry out, "Happy." When Johnny was hurt, he inevitably came running to Dorothy crying, "Anny! Anny!" At times, resourceful, though he was crying, he would come bringing a basket with thread in it for her to sew a bandage on his burned arm. A vigorous, noisy little boy, Johnny often when crossed had temper tantrums; but, gently, every night came to kiss his Aunt Dorothy good night. At times, he became jealous of his little sister, Dorothy; just let her take one of his possessions, no matter if he had almost forgotten it, and a fury of anger ensued until it was restored to its rightful owner.

He was extremely fond of old Mary Fisher and often wandered over to her cottage, where he was a welcomed visitor. Busy writing to Mrs. Clarkson, "Perhaps you will remember this is my thirty-fourth birthday," Dorothy suddenly heard loud cries of anguish. Going outside, she found little Johnny in the rain clad in his great coat and a black cap half over a very dirty face, outside Mary Fisher's cottage, sobbing bitterly and crying, "Is Mary Fisher my wife? Is Mary Fisher my wife?" Wherever he got such a notion remains a nice question. Suffice it to say, he had decided to go to visit Mary. When no one answered his repeated knocks at the door or his calls, he had became panicky and more determined to see his friend. Dorothy believed he had slipped out of the warm kitchen where he was about ten minutes before. Told that Mary was not at home, he had insisted, "Then let's go and seek her." He was not content until Dorothy took him to the door, which she proved would not open, and lifted him to the window through which he could see for himself that Mary was not there. Back again in the house, with Johnny divested of his wet clothing, Dorothy was in the midst of her letter to Mrs. Clarkson

when there were cries of "Aty," little Dorothy's name for Aunty. Upstairs, Dorothy went to pacify her namesake, who then helped her
aunt write her letter by holding the pen, too, in her tiny fingers.
Later, Johnny, ably assisted by his sister, developed a sudden passion
for constructing houses of stone, bricks, and slates, which his brother
Thomas admired and then knocked down.

When Johnny was six, he was seriously ill for a time, with all the
symptoms of water on the brain. "We resigned ourselves to his loss,"
says Dorothy, "and contemplated the poor innocent's sufferings with
awful dread." But the crisis passed and soon Johnny was sleeping
quietly, "beautiful as an angel, though different from himself, his
features enlarged, as he is grown so thin; but his countenance is divine; he more resembles his father than ever. Nothing remains of the
disease but the weakness."

When Johnny went to school, he seemed to learn nothing and to be
terribly backward. Dorothy was certain he "was not a dunce in soul,"
for when she read to him and his sister Catherine, though his sister
was mentally quicker than he, she yawned and grew sleepy whether
Dorothy read them poetry, history, natural history, or stories, whereas
Johnny's "attention would be kept continually awake if you read until
midnight." When, to conquer his laziness and shyness among boys
his own age, Johnny at nine, was sent away to Mr. Dawes' school, his
scholarship improved. Dorothy was not surprised, for she recalled
how, when he was younger, he had heard much talk among his elders
about printing. He would be a printer when he grew up, he declared.
When Dorothy told him he would have to be a good scholar before
he could be a printer, he had worked at his lessons with great energy
and with results.

Young Dorothy, often called Sissy, was a beautiful, rosy-cheeked
youngster, with lively, almost wild eyes, a mixture of wildness and
elegance, quick in her movements, bright and alert, wayward, and
difficult to subdue. Quick-witted, high-spirited little Dorothy, Coleridge called "the wild cat of the wilderness," adding "none so fair as
she." As a baby, she was happiest in her father's arms; when she began to talk, she called him, "dear Ather." Enchanted by his "sweet
chatterer," William could refuse her nothing. When her Aunt Dorothy made her a coat, she insisted on wearing it all day, spiritedly and
independently trotting up and down stairs by herself with pride, admiring herself in her new garment. When she was two, William insisted on his and Dorothy's taking her to Park House because of a
whooping cough epidemic at Grasmere. The little girl seemed not to

mind leaving home at all and was happy as a bird with strangers, greeted the sheep in the village with "Baa, Baa, Black Sheep" and called after the cows, "Curly Cow Bonny, let down thy milk." Yet, she kept an eye on her father and aunt, and when she thought they had gone far enough from her, cried out, "Ather, turn back again; Anny, turn back again." William, as usual, melted at her demand. Liking a certain stool, she immediately proclaimed it was hers; and so it remained during their stay. Mary, who had preceded them with Johnny, was at Park House when they arrived. Little Dorothy was apparently asleep when her Aunt Dorothy said she'd like to see little Johnny's "blue britches" again, chuckling over the little boy's pride in his trousers. The seemingly sleeping little girl was wide awake at once, crying out, "Johnny breeches! Johnny breeches!" Indeed, there seemed no quieting her until she had seen them. Johnny slept undisturbed while his sister danced with joy exclaiming as she saw them "Johnny breeches! Johnny jacket! Johnny shoes! Johnny stockings!" Then, quietly, she danced back to bed and in no time was sound asleep.

It was easier to let the child have her way than to try to pacify her, Dorothy knew well. She recalled the horrible boat ride at Ullswater, which she and William had looked forward to. Impatient of confinement, Sissy had screamed and struggled from the time they got on the boat until they landed. Fond of Johnny, she liked to provoke him to anger, and seemed to enjoy it when he in a fury would start after her with a stool, a chair, a stick, or a poker.

When her aunt returned from a visit, Sissy's first question was about her gift. It was well Aunt Dorothy had come bearing gifts and remembered that Sissy wished a doll. All summer, Sissy's main subject of conversation was that doll. She adored sleeping with her aunt and was a perfect barometer, as she woke Aunt Dorothy on cold mornings with, "Anny, it is time to get up, it is a blasty morning, it does blast so" or "Anny, it is a haily morning, it hails so hard."

Sissy was five when Johnny was so critically ill that it was thought best to have his exuberant little sister away for a time. Mrs. Charles Lloyd offered to take her to her home at Brathay; and so excited was the little girl over a visit that the day she left she was in almost giddy ecstasies of delight. When Mrs. Lloyd came for her, she danced up and down "as if there were quicksilver in her veins"; so eager was she to leave that she hardly had time to give anyone a parting kiss. Throughout her stay at Brathay, she continued in a rapturous state, paying little attention to the other children except when they all had lessons together. The cook, she quickly adopted, calling her "my Mary Dawson"; she was enchanted with the gardener and never wearied of going with him round and round the garden, "hearing that this tree would bear plums, that, cherries, and this bush, gooseberries." She said she never wanted to go home. How different, Aunt Dorothy thought, from Johnny who would have been unhappy a day away from home without his friends.

When it was time for Sissy to go to school, her mother and aunt hoped then her manners would improve, that she would be steadier, less excitable and tempestuous. It was not so. After much persuasion by his wife and sister, William agreed that Sissy should go to Miss Weir's Boarding School at Appleby. At ten, Sissy went to this school, where Dorothy said, "Much good we are sure she will get . . . there was never a girl who would be more easily led to industry by following others, or to whom it would be more difficult to learn to sit still when she has no companions." When Sissy returned from her first half-year at school, Dorothy, though eager to see her, arranged to be away when she arrived so that her father and mother first should have her to themselves. When Dorothy, eager to see her namesake, came back, she was told that they were pleased with the progress Sissy had made and had decided to send her back another half-year. Sissy was still wayward, but, Dorothy says, "tender hearted, affectionate, and very lively as ever. . . . I wish you could have seen the animated countenance with which this instant she looked up at me when she came to something in her book which amused her." When at Christmas time the village fiddlers came around to the Wordsworth house, she was in her element as she called Aunt Dorothy in to join the dance. All the children had a joyous Christmas, as usual.

Three years after Johnny's birth Thomas was born, also in June, on a beautiful morning when the birds were singing in full chorus in the orchard outside Mary's window. The "dove eyed" little boy, a very affectionate child and a great chatterer, was a frail baby. Dorothy loved him intensely as did Sissy, who thought so much about her new little brother that she talked of him in her sleep, murmuring, again and again, "Baby! Baby!" As a little boy, he so enjoyed playing in the kitchen with the pots and pans that the family called him Potiphar, a name he disliked, always saying, "Me no Potiphar. Me no Potiphar." He loved playing with Johnny's Noah's Ark while Johnny was at school. On November 1, when he first walked alone, he was proud of his accomplishment, and trotted after Dorothy from room to room all day calling "Any, Any, look." Dorothy worried about

Thomas, who picked up colds readily and suffered from them; he did not seem to grow as fast as he should; he was far too delicate, she feared. Coleridge once said, Thomas "is nearest my heart—I so often have him before my eyes, sitting on a little stool while I am writing my essays; and how quiet and affectionate the little fellow would be if he could but touch one and now and then be looked at." After Thomas was ill with whooping cough at age six, he went with Dorothy to Hackett for a change of air. He was still frail and in December he became ill. Hot and feverish, he was distressed with a cough that tore at his aching chest and lungs. The following day the doctor thought he had measles; though still feverish, he seemed better; six days later, though he was still bedfast, his condition seemed improved to Dr. Scambler. Thomas chatted with his mother about some profiles of Mr. and Mrs. Clarkson on the mantlepiece facing his bed.

"Mother," he said, "they have been bad picture-makers; they have made no legs."

Mary explained why.

"Ho," came his reply.

An hour later, following a spell of coughing and choking, trembling, he told his mother, "I shall die; I shall die!" Mary, stricken at his words, summoned the doctor who bled him. His pain seemed relieved but toward evening his strength ebbed gradually until he died. His last words were, "I am getting better." Dorothy, who was away at the time, hurried home and later wrote a friend, saying that she had started home as soon as she heard he was ill, for she had been concerned about a cough he had had for two years, and knew he was frail. William met her when she was part way home and told her the boy was dead. "Oh, my dear Friend!" she wrote, "he is an unutterable loss to all of us . . . as you rightly say it is a selfish grief when we pine after the pure spirit of a child returned to the Heaven from whence it came—pure and unspotted as when it came from its Maker. Yet this child seemed so fitted to give and to receive happiness, to calm the thoughts of those who looked upon him, to enjoy the best things of this life from the virtuous ardour which he possessed, without the anguish of regret, which nothing can ever wholly repress, save the Christian's faith in another world. . . . It has been a cruel stroke for William. He loved Thomas with such a peculiar tenderness." Later, she wrote, "My brother is grown very thin and at times I think he looks ten years older since the death of Thomas." Sorrowful, too, was Coleridge, who, Dorothy says, "loved the darling the best of all our little ones."

Born three years after Thomas's birth, Catharine, named for Dorothy's good friend Mrs. Clarkson, not so handsome as the other children, had blue, blue eyes and "the funniest laugh you ever heard peeping through her eyes." Wordsworth called her his "little Chinese maiden"; her expression, from babyhood, was droll and once she began to talk, she "set everyone in a roar"; she was the wittiest of the children. Wherever she was, almost always there was laughter. For a long time, she had very little hair, so that she seemed almost bald. Too young to walk, she made an art of crawling rapidly any place she chose to go. When she was a year old, left to play on the kitchen floor while Sally Green, in charge of her, was making porridge, Catharine suddenly discovered a whole "hill" of fresh carrot pellets that her brother and sister had made and proceeded to swallow many of them. Not until she became seriously ill with convulsions did Sally realize what had happened. Mary and Dorothy, expert at administering aid, did so to no avail while Sally Green summoned the doctor. When the violent convulsions subsided, Catharine's right hand, side, and leg were paralyzed; the doctor thought the paralysis came from some brain damage. Later, though the child could move her hand and leg a little, she was weaker than a new born babe. Dorothy spent many hours massaging Catharine's limbs to stimulate the nerves; noting that the hot sun seemed to bring the child relief, Dorothy took her out several hours each morning and afternoon. Before long, Catharine could just manage, holding onto a chair, to stand on both legs. Dorothy then took her for short walks several times a day. Though she could not walk alone, by holding on to things she could stand on both feet, though she could not rest long on her lame leg. At first the Wordsworths were encouraged; but as time passed they noticed that she dragged the right leg after her, and at times had no control of the leg; nor could she bend her knee freely. Eager to help the child, they asked their doctor if sea bathing would be beneficial. At first, he said no; later, he added that if the water were warm it might prove helpful. Accordingly, Catharine and Mary set out for the seashore. When they returned, Dorothy was shocked to find the child paler than she had ever been, so thin that her cheeks were hollow and her mouth seemed to protrude. Gone were all traces of the gaiety, the efforts at being playful, the sweet smile; suffering now marked the child's face. Catharine, who needed much care, wanted always to be near her mother. Now her mother massaged her limbs several times a day. When in February, she was ill and the doctor decided a change of air would be beneficial, Dorothy took her to Green Bank for several months. The child continued to be in bad health; she did not sleep well, being ill two or three times a night. They were away from home two months.

Young Thomas De Quincey took quite a fancy to Catharine and asked that, once she was old enough, he be allowed to be her tutor; Catharine in turn was fond of this new friend, whom she called "Kinsey." Catharine, he declared, was "an impersonation of the dawn and the spirit of infancy"; he walked with her, and when she tired put her to bed, feeling, he said, as if he had entered into an ideal world of tenderness where he found peace and happiness. When he was away and Catharine tired of being massaged, Dorothy and Mary sang her a chant that kept her amused about "riding away to London to meet Mr. De Quincey."

In May, while William and Mary were away, five-year-old Catharine suddenly had convulsions such as she had had before her first stroke. Applying such remedies as they had before, Dorothy sent Sara Hutchinson, who was visiting, for the doctor, who came at once but gave them no hope. As the convulsions continued, Dorothy realized that the paralysis was total and that if the child lived she would not have control of her limbs; her brain, it seemed, too, was affected. Death, Dorothy thought, was preferable to a child deprived of understanding and a helpless invalid; hence, she prayed for Catharine's death. Just at dawn, she died. She was buried beneath a hawthorne tree that was a favorite of hers.

Young William, whom the family called Willy, born May 11, 1810, had a difficult birth. As Mary had naturally been anxious and nervous about Catharine, it was not surprising that she had some difficulties while carrying Willy; her labor was easy until the actual birth, and then difficult because "the child was somewhat entangled." The little boy, who resembled Johnny, was cared for from the first by Dorothy, as Mary was busy caring for Catharine. Two months after he was born, William and Mary left for a month's vacation, leaving Dorothy in charge of the children. Not so husky as Johnny, at times young William was ill, and his illnesses alarmed everyone. Precocious, he was sent to school when he was three. Dorothy was a disciplinarian, and Mary, though gentle and tender with the children, guarded against foolish indulgence. But their father! William's nervous anxiety about his children having increased a hundredfold after Catharine's and Thomas's deaths, petted and pampered Willy until he was thoroughly spoiled. Dorothy, distressed about Willy's future, wrote Sara Hutchinson, "it is a thousand pities he should be so spoiled! It is impossible, unless you have seen it to have an idea of the father's folly respecting this child—we strive against it as much as possible, but it is all in vain." When Dorothy was away for a vacation, she returned more "astonished at Willy's babyishness—and really his father fondles over him and talks to him as if he were but a year old." Willy was then seven. Dorothy hoped that in time Willy would recover from being treated as "the little darling," for "when he is among his schoolmates, none is more active, independent, and manly than he, and he disdains all notice from Father, Mother, or any of us at such times."

When he was nine, Dorothy saw a campaign she had tactfully maneuvered to "save" Willy, succeed, for Willy was sent to London with their friend Tom Monkhouse, to go to school under Mr. Johnson, master of Central School, Baldwin Gardens, to prepare for Charterhouse. Two months after Willy left for school, Dorothy wrote Catharine Clarkson, "I had long been convinced that nothing but a removal from home would save the Boy from ruin, but his Mother could not be brought to this conviction till it was forced upon her; and long did his Father waver and despond from fears for his health; but happy am I to tell you that his health and looks have visibly improved; and this I believe to be solely owing to a cheerful submission to unbending laws, and activity of mind *fixed*, not wandering, as it ever used to be."

Stern a disciplinarian as Dorothy was, she was as fond of Willy and as anxious about him as his parents. She, therefore, asked Charles Lamb to visit her nephew and give her any news of him. On November 25, 1819, Charles Lamb wrote her he had found Willy "a lad of promise. He is no pedant or bookworm . . . . But he has observation and seems thoroughly awake. . . . Being taken over to Waterloo Bridge, he remarked if we had no mountains, we had a fine river at least, which was a Touch of the Comparative, but then he added, in a strain which augured less for his future abilities as a Political Economist, that he supposed they must take at least a pound a week Toll. Like a curious naturalist, he inquired if the tide did not come up a bit *salty*. This being satisfactorily answered," he had a host of other questions. He amazed Lamb at the quickness with which he could add and subtract. "Willy," the essayist concluded, "is a well-mannered child, and though no great student, hath a lively eye for things that lie before him." Later, in the spring, Dorothy went to London for three months, taking quarters in Lambeth, overlooking the Archbishop's garden grounds, to have some dental work done and to see Willy. She found the boy "very sweet and interesting—in all respects wonderfully improved—no better boy can be—and he can well take care of himself among the 400. I went once to him at school. The boys were at play without hats and he and I wandered about the large Square like two forlorn things—nobody noticing us— but I doubt not he is quite at home there when he is playing with the rest." One day, she took him to Kensington Gardens; a week of his vacation, he spent with her at Lambeth. Much as she wished to see him more frequently, she denied herself the privilege, for she had no desire to unsettle him "and I assure you," she wrote Tom Monkhouse, "I have no disposition to spoil him." Later, she was concerned with Willy's extravagance, when he spent most of his allowance on a tie-clasp which he at once broke. She was horrified when another undergraduate promptly replaced it with a new one costing ten shillings, a large sum then. Dorothy immediately confiscated it, to Tom Monkhouse's amusement. Nevertheless, at the end of her stay she was able to return home encouraged about young William.

While all England rejoiced in Lord Nelson's great naval victory at Trafalgar in 1805, when bells were tolling and crowds excitedly gathering, Dorothy and William were sad, thinking more of the fact that, at the time of his naval triumph, Lord Nelson had been shot. They found it difficult to believe that people could so rejoice when Lord Nelson was dead. They believed him "a truly *brave* man, in the highest sense of the word . . . tender and humane in all the daily acts of life."

In 1806, Sara Hutchinson came to live with the Wordsworths. Mary was her favorite sister; Dorothy, a close friend; and she was eager to help in the work the growing family made. The rest of her life she lived with the Wordsworths. This newcomer added to the overcrowding of Dove Cottage; the Wordsworths, however, hesitated at deciding on a new home until Coleridge could be consulted on his return from Malta. Yet not one word came from him. The Beaumonts had offered the Wordsworths the use of their house-farm in Coleorton in Leicestershire and they were eager to accept it; yet, as Coleridge often had been with them for months they felt he should be consulted. In late summer of 1806, they expected him to come walking in any day. On August 15, finally came word that he was in quarantine off Portsmouth, and on the twenty-first, news that he was with Charles and Mary Lamb in London. He had been gone two years and eight months. Days passed and no letters came from him nor did he appear.

The Wordsworths finally moved for the winter to Coleorton. This cottage, owned by Sir George and Lady Beaumont, had been lent partly because of friendship and partly because Sir George was building on a large scale at Coleorton and wished Wordsworth's advice as a professional student of the relationship of natural beauty and the works of man. Both Coleridge and Wordsworth had stated how stupid many had been in building large houses and then trying to make the surrounding country conform to the style of the mansions. "Indeed," Wordsworth wrote, "I see nothing interesting either to the imagination or to the heart, and, of course, nothing which true taste can approve, in any interference with Nature." Wordsworth had studied the lives of trees; he knew their manner of growth and how they as well as hedges would look years after planting. He knew how a house with the wrong proportions, even a badly shaped chimney, would distort a view. Accordingly, for a year, he advised the Beaumonts on their building and landscaping, giving weeks of time to careful and methodical planning of groves, hedges, fences, cottages, and the manor house, with excellent results.

Finally, a letter came from Mary Lamb, a letter she had hesitated to write lest she seem to betray Coleridge's confidence. Her fears for him, she believed justified her writing the Wordsworths to say that he was sick in mind and in body. The thought of returning to his wife, to whom he refused to write, threw him literally into a "stupor of misery." Mary wished either that William Wordsworth would come to London to see him or that Mr. Southey would try to persuade Mrs. Coleridge to consent to a separation. William blamed himself for not having gone to London as soon as Coleridge arrived. When William wrote he was coming, Coleridge said he was preparing to come North. By the end of October, he was still not there; the Wordsworths hesitated to go to London lest they pass him on the way. After much confusion, Dorothy, William, Mary and Sara Hutchinson finally met him at an inn at Kendall. "Never", writes Dorothy, "never did I feel such a shock as at first sight of him. We all felt exactly in the same way—as if he were different from what we had expected to see; almost as much as a person of whom we had thought much, and of whom we had formed an image in our own minds, without having any personal knowledge of him. . . . His fatness has quite changed him—he is more like a person in a dropsy than one in health; his eyes are lost in it . . . the divine expression of his countenance. . . . I never saw . . . as it used to be—a shadow, a gleam there was at times, but how faint and transitory! I think, however, that if he has the courage to go through the work before him, William's conversation and our kind offices may soothe him and bring tranquility; and then the only hope will be applying himself to some grand object connected with permanent effects."

The Wordsworths, Dorothy says, "have long known how unfit Coleridge and his wife were for one another; but we had hoped that his ill-health and the present need his children have of his care and fatherly instructions, and the reflections of his own mind during this long absence would have so wrought upon him that he might have returned home with comfort, ready to partake of the blessings of friendship, which he surely has in abundant degree, and to devote himself to his wife and his children. . . . Poor soul! he had a struggle of many years striving to bring Mrs. Coleridge to a change of temper, and something like communion with his enjoyments." Coleridge, however, was steadfast in his refusal longer to live with his wife or to make any pretense of doing so. He talked to his brother, the Rev. George Coleridge, and explained that Sara's bad "temper and general tone of feeling I have found wholly incompatible with even an endurable life, and such as to preclude all chance of my ever developing the talents which my Maker has entrusted to me." Furthermore, his two years in Malta had convinced him he was really in love with Sara Hutchinson. While in Malta, he said, "talking of government or war, or chemistry, there comes into my bodily eye some tree beneath which we have rested, some rock where we have stood on the projecting road edging high above the Crummock Lake when we sat beneath the Rock, and those dear lips pressed my forehead—or . . . when they laughed at us as lovers." Repeatedly, he wrote Dorothy Wordsworth that he could not endure the thought of life with his wife, and Dorothy writes that finally Mrs. Coleridge fully agreed to a separation "and consented that he should take Hartley and Derwent, and supervise their education, she being allowed to have them at the holidays"; she would keep their daughter Sara. "I say she has agreed to the separation but he tells us that she breaks out into outrageous passions, and urges continually that one argument (in fact the only one that has the least effect upon her mind), that this person, and that person, and everybody will talk. . . . My brother has written him to bring the boys to us." A few days before Christmas, he arrived with little Hartley and stayed with the Wordsworths two months.

At first, Coleridge seemed more like his old self, as he relaxed and was contented; but before long, the Wordsworths realized Coleridge really had changed. The narcotics he took so frequently seemed to have undermined his will, his affections, and his moral sense. Always subject to moods, now he was yet moodier, often resentful, suspicious, even jealous. He felt keen remorse at his failure to have or achieve a goal. The talkative man was now silent and morose. More and more, Dorothy says, "he shrank into himself." Though Mrs. Coleridge had fully agreed to a separation, at times she wrote her husband as though she had made no such agreement. These letters Coleridge would read to Dorothy who tried to console him, but finally she confessed neither she nor the others in the household seemed to have the "power to make him happy."

There are understandable reasons for Sara Coleridge's not wishing a separation. Her father had died bankrupt, leaving his wife and six children penniless; her mother, who had taught school and given her daughters better education than most girls had, had emphasized to her girls the importance of being able to earn a living or to make a successful marriage. Mary Fricker, who became Mrs. Lovell, had been a competent actress and, until her death at ninety, kept up her Latin by reading Horace, and her French by reading Mme. de Staël. Eliza and Martha always earned good livings; Edith, in her marriage with Robert Southey, lived comfortably and in the reflected glory her husband achieved. Sara feeling alone with her children, deserted by Coleridge, did not wish the world to know her marriage had failed. Her husband believed her "self-encouraged admiration for Southey" was "a vindictive feeling in which she delights herself while satirizing me." Though friends continued to help her financially, though Coleridge gave her financial aid when he could, though friends surrounded her, almost always considerate, often devoted to her, she could never forget that in the eyes of the world she did not have the status enjoyed by a woman surrounded by her children and husband. She began, however, to compensate by making a business of motherhood. Coleridge wished she had been as considerate of him as she was of their children. "The one main defect of female education is that everything is taught but reason and the means of retaining affection," he wrote. "This—this—O! it is worth all the rest told ten thousand times: —how to greet a husband, how to receive him, how never to recriminate . . . the love-killing effect of cold, dry uninterested looks and manners."

The Coleridges' friends, naturally, talked of the separation. Mr. Poole and Mr. Cottle, liking Sara, sympathized with her, though they admitted her main reason for not wishing the separation was that "everybody will talk" and "it will not be respectable." Others sympathized more with Coleridge. Shelley found Sara "stupid and her sister worse"; De Quincey found her "prettiness of a rather common order"; Dorothy Wordsworth, "the lightest silliest woman" whom "nothing hurts"; Walter Scott found her a "pleasing person who has been pretty."

At the end of February, Coleridge went off to London with Hartley to stay with Basil Montagu. William and Mary joined him there for the month of April. In the summer, they all went back to Dove Cottage for a brief time.

One of the gala events of the year was William Hazlitt's visit to the Wordsworths when he painted a portrait of Coleridge for Sir George Beaumont, "in the Titian manner." He also painted a portrait of William Wordsworth which Southey said made that poet look so dismal that one of his friends on seeing it "exclaimed, 'At the gallows —deeply affected by his deserved fate—yet determined to die like a man'; and if you saw the picture you would admire the criticism."

William Hazlitt, the Wordsworths learned, was born on April 10, 1778, at Maidstone, Kent, the son of the Unitarian Minister, William Hazlitt, and of Grace Loftus, an ironmonger's daughter. A friend of Benjamin Franklin, the older William Hazlitt had left Maidstone when his son William was eighteen months old, to go to Ireland, a move the rebellious man, openly supporting American independence, found prudent. In Ireland he found it just as dangerous as it had been in England to speak his views about freedom and democracy. Hence, he and his family left Ireland for America when young Hazlitt was six. There, the Rev. William Hazlitt founded the first Unitarian Church in Boston. He settled at Weymouth, fifteen miles from Boston, walking to Boston most of that first cold winter to give lectures on "The Evidence of Christianity." The parsonage at Weymouth was a joy, but the village had only a few homes, the meeting-house, a mill, and a shop; there was neither a grocer nor a butcher. Often, little William accompanied his father when he went to speak before various Unitarian groups; as Weymouth was strongly Calvinistic, he preached but once in the village where he lived—and that was before a group in his own home. At length, realizing that there seemed no opportunity for him to preach in the land of his choice, he moved his family to Dorchester, nearer Boston, and returned to England, leaving his family for a time in America. Young William was then nine. Shortly after the elder Hazlitt left, two positions in the Ministry, either of which he would gladly have accepted, became open.

The nine months the father was in England and his family in

America, his two sons were busy indeed. Young William, his sister said, "nearly killed himself" studying Latin grammar; but he confessed he did "not cypher any at all." Twenty-year-old John was aiding the family finances by painting portraits of prominent Americans; his sister Margaret spent her time helping their mother around the house.

Once back in England, the family went first to Walworth, a suburb of London, for their mother's health, and at the end of the year to Wem. Young John, now twenty-one, remained in London, studying under Sir Joshua Reynolds and painting miniatures. Eleven-year-old William wrote his brother John of his attempts to draw portraits, of reading "Ovid's *Metamorphoses* and Eustropius. I shall like to learn all the Latin and Greek I can. I want to know how to measure the stars. I shall not, I suppose, paint the worse for knowing everything else. I began to cypher a fortnight after Christmas, and shall go into the rule of three next week. I can teach a boy of sixteen already who was cyphering eight months before me; is he not a great dunce? I shall go through the whole cyphering book this summer, and then I am to learn Euclid. We go to school at nine every morning." Among the boys who were his classmates he found some "so sulky they won't play; others are quarrelsome because they cannot learn and are only fit for fighting like stupid dogs and cats. I can jump four yards at a running jump, and two at a standing jump. I intend to try you at this when you come down. . . . I wish I could see all those paintings that you see. . . . I don't want your old clothes. I shall go dancing this month." He took pleasure in a flower garden and a kitchen garden of his own, watering them carefully when his day's tasks were done; he flew a kite, and did some hiking over the nearby hills.

When he was eleven, the French Revolution began and the Bastille fell, but these events interested the young Hazlitt less than his visit to Liverpool where he had a spirited argument in which he informed his opponent that the Catholic Church was far older than the Established Church, and the Presbyterian better than either. He went to church there, for the first time, "and I do not care if I should never go into another one again . . . . (The) sermon had neither head nor tail. I was sorry that so much time should be thrown away upon nonsense." After going to dinner at the house of a gentleman, he wrote his mother, "He is a very rich man—but the man who is a well wisher to slavery is always a slave himself. The king who wishes to enslave man is a slave to ambition. The man who wishes to enslave all mankind for his king, is himself a slave to his king."

At fifteen, at the Unitarian College at Hackney, his favorite writers were Edmund Burke and Rousseau. He, with the other students, enjoyed Tom Paine when the latter came to the college and dined and chatted with the students, for Paine reflected the stormy times of the French revolution. It is doubtful, however, whether Burke was correct when he found the college "an arsenal" for fabricating revolutionary weapons and a breeding place for revolutionary ideas, "a volcano of sedition," a "nursery of riot," and a "slaughter-house of Christianity."

True, New College at Hackney was more liberal than most English universities. Young Hazlitt as a Freshman wrote his parents it was not the best place to acquire politeness: "the behaviour which suits a set of young fellows, or boys, does not suit any other society." Homesick, young Hazlitt learned discipline the hard way when he told a tutor he had not written a required paper and was told to write it immediately. An hour later, when the paper was still unwritten, his tutor found a nervous boy with swollen eyes still staring at blank paper. The tutor, realizing this was no ordinary case of disobedience, talked with the boy, found he had written "a number of things" which he showed the interested questioner. Then the boy confessed he had been planning several essays, "but I could not write any of them in a week, or two or three weeks." Then he informed the tutor after the latter had read "the things" Hazlitt had already written that he planned to enlarge and improve upon the Essay on Laws. Given leisure for his writing, the boy did his other work on schedule, but all his thoughts, as before, were on his writing. His classes included Greek Grammar, Greek and Latin Literature, and Antiquities, Hebrew, History, Geography, Logic, Mathematics, and Shorthand. He studied and recited from seven in the morning until after eleven at night, injuring himself "irreparably" by overstudy.

Every two weeks he spent a weekend with John in London, finding his chief relaxation in the theatre. Mrs. Siddons' acting excited him and stirred his "inmost soul" as she aroused in him a capacity for emotion he did not know he possessed. Mrs. Jordan, another actress, had a voice that gladdened him like wine and he enjoyed her physical appearance "large, soft, and generous as her soul." Two actors intrigued him: King, "whose acting left a taste on the palate, sharp and sweet like quince" and Jack Bannister "shining like a gilded pill." Just as exhilarating to him as these actors and actresses was his discovery of a translation of Schiller's *The Robbers*, which had a profound effect on him. Its effect was like that he experienced the first time he saw Mrs. Siddons act. "We do not read the tragedy of *The*

Robbers twice"; he said, "if we have seen Mrs. Siddons in Lady Macbeth once it is enough. The impression is stamped there forever."

At the end of his second year at Hackney, he withdrew, as his father could not afford to keep him at the college longer. Although young Hazlitt was independent enough not to give up Christianity as some of his classmates did, he decided he would not become a minister; therefore, he was ineligible for any of the special grants given divinity students, though one had been set aside for him.

The next two years, at home in Wem or in London with his brother John, he read and read. *Tom Jones* and *Peregrine Pickle*, *Pamela*, *Don Quixote*, and *Faustus* became friends of his. Among English authors, his favorites were Spenser whom he read "with a sort of voluptuous indolence"; Chaucer, he liked even better; then came Pope, Dryden, and Goldsmith. Edmund Burke, he found an admirable stylist, possessing "true eloquence," as he poured out his mind on paper. "All other styles," Hazlitt said, "seemed to me pedantic and impertinent. Dr. Johnson's was walking on stilts; and even Junius's (who was at that time a favorite with me) with all his terseness, shrunk up into little antithetic points and well-trimmed sentences. But Burke's style was forked and playful as the lightning, crested like the serpent. He delivered plain things on a plain ground, but when he rose, there was no end of his flights and circumgyrations." Hazlitt was exhilarated by Milton; he spent two years reading Rousseau's works.

The high point in his literary career came when he met Coleridge. He had heard Coleridge speak at the Unitarian Church at Shrewsbury and had been tremendously impressed by hearing the poet preach.

When Coleridge visited the Hazlitts, young William, now twenty, said "No two individuals were more unlike than the host and his guest. A poet to my father was a sort of nondescript; yet whenever he added grace to the Unitarian cause, he was welcome. He could hardly have been more surprised or pleased, if our visitor had worn wings. Indeed, his thoughts had wings, and as the silken sounds rustled around our little wainscoted parlour, my father threw back his spectacles over his forehead, his white hairs mixing with its sanguine hue; and a smile of delight beamed across his rugged cordial face, to think that Truth had found a new ally in Fancy! Besides, Coleridge seemed to have taken considerable notice of me, and that of itself was enough. He talked very familiarly but agreeably, and glanced over a variety of subjects. At dinnertime, he grew more animated, and dilated in a very edifying manner on Mary Wollstonecraft and Mackintosh." The conversation turned to other important people of the day. The following morning when young Hazlitt learned that Thomas Wedgwood, as we have seen, had just written Coleridge offering him £150 a year as an annuity so that he need not preach, he was disappointed, for he had looked forward to having Coleridge reside at Shrewsbury, but ten miles away; now the poet would "inhabit the Hill of Parnassus" and "Alas! I knew not the way thither and felt very little gratitude for Mr. Wedgwood's bounty." When, on leaving, Coleridge wrote on a card his name and address, invited young Hazlitt to see him in a few weeks' time, and offered to meet him halfway, the lad was no more surprised than the shepherd-boy "when he sees a thunder-bolt fall at his feet." Stammering his acceptance of the offer, he accompanied the departing poet six miles on the road back to Shrewsbury.

The visit to Coleridge proved a happy one and its pleasure increased when Coleridge took Hazlitt to Alfoxden. Wordsworth was away but Dorothy greeted the visitors, gave them supper, and showed Hazlitt *Lyrical Ballads*, still in manuscript form. The following day, Wordsworth, back from a trip to Bristol, came to Coleridge's home. For three weeks, young Hazlitt visited Coleridge and his friends; then, he went south to Lynton with Coleridge and a friend, John Chester.

As a boy, William Hazlitt had planned to be a painter, as his brother was; his father, however, wished him to enter the ministry. When he firmly declined that profession, he considered turning to his brother's. In December, 1798, a collection of old Italian paintings from the collection of the Regent Orleans in Paris was placed on sale in London. From the time William Hazlitt saw this collection, he said, he was staggered "and looked at them with wondering and longing eyes. A mist passed from my sight; the scales fell off. A new sense came upon me, a new heaven and a new earth stood before me . . . . From that time, I lived in a world of pictures. Battles, sieges, speeches in Parliament semed idle noise and fury, 'signifying nothing,' compared with these mighty works that spoke to me in the eternal silence of thought." After seeing his first Titians and Raphaels, he knew he must be a painter.

He was as meticulous about his painting as he had been about his writing. "The first head I ever tried to paint," he says, "was an old woman with the upper part of her face shaded by her bonnet, and I certainly laboured it with great perserverence. It took me numberless sittings to do it . . . . If art was long, I thought that life was too at that moment. I got in the general effect the first day; and pleased and surprised enough I was at my success. The rest was a work of time—of weeks (if need were) of patient toil and careful finishing. I had seen an old head by Rembrandt at Burleigh House, and if I could produce a head at all like Rembrandt in a year, in my lifetime, it would be glory and felicity, and wealth and fame enough for me." Another of his early portraits was that of his father with his spectacles on, reading. With a throbbing heart, the young artist sent the portrait to the Royal Academy Exhibition in 1802, where it was hung beside a portrait of the Honorable Mr. Skeffington.

Having made some progress in painting, he went to Paris to study in the Louvre and to paint five copies of the old masters for a Liverpool patron. The four days of the week when students could go to the Louvre, he was there at half-past nine or ten o'clock and worked until three or four. The Titians, Raphaels, and Rubens interested him especially.

Back from Paris in 1803, he saw Coleridge briefly, for the poet, returned from Germany, was in London having his portrait painted by John Hazlitt. Then William Hazlitt, on a commission from Sir George Beaumont, went to the Lake Country to paint portraits of Coleridge and of his son Hartley, now seven. When Thomas Wedgwood wondered if Hazlitt would be a good companion to travel abroad with him, Coleridge replied that "William Hazlitt is a thinking, observant, original man of great power as a Painter of Character Portraits, and far more in the manner of the old Painters than any living Artist, but the objects must be *before* him; he has no imaginative memory. So much for his intellectuals. His manners are 99 in 100 singularly repulsive; brow-hanging, shoe-comtemplative, strange . . . He is, I verily believe, kindly natured; he is very fond of, attentive to, and patient with children; but he is jealous, gloomy, and of an irritable pride. With all this, there is much good in him. . . . he says things in a way that are his own; and though from habitual shyness, and the outside and bearskin at least, of misanthropy, he is strangely confused and dark in his conversation, and delivers himself of all his conceptions with a Forceps, yet he says more than any man I ever knew (yourself only excepted) that is his own in a way of his own and often-times . . . he will gallop for half an hour together with real eloquence." Coleridge added he was glad to recommend Hazlitt as a portrait painter and hoped his friend would commission him; but "To be your Companion, he is, in my opinion, utterly unfit."

The portrait of Coleridge in the Titian manner, Sir George Beaumont and Coleridge considered excellent; one of Wordsworth, they liked not at all. Before Hazlitt left the Lake Country, as the result of some sort of affair with a local girl, he so aroused the people of the district that he had to go for help to Wordsworth, who came to his assistance. Just what Hazlitt did remains a mystery. Lamb, commenting on the tale he heard of Hazlitt's almost being ducked by the people because of "a gross attack" on a girl, wrote "The scapes of the great god Pan" who was almost "submerged by the local swains, afford me much pleasure. I can conceive the water nymphs pulling for him." At any rate, Hazlitt left in haste, and Wordsworth, who had aided him, was not eager later to have Lamb entertain the two of them at the same time.

Back in London, living with his brother John, William Hazlitt, in 1804, met Charles Lamb at William Godwin's. The evening had been sparkling as Coleridge and Holcroft were disputing whether Man was best *as he was*, or *as he is to be*. "Give me," said Lamb, "man as he is not to be."

Interested in Charles Lamb, then twenty-nine, a little over three years his senior, Hazlitt spent much time with him and with his sister, Mary, whom he called "the only reasonable woman" he had ever known. Before long, he painted a portrait of Charles Lamb in the dress of a Venetian senator. He enjoyed thoroughly the Lambs' Wednesday social evenings; he adored Mary Lamb; when he was absent on Wednesdays, Mary said, "All the glory of this night is gone." At the Lambs' home, he met Mary's close friend, Sarah Stoddard, of whom Coleridge, then in Malta, had written earlier when he met her there. Sarah Stoddard, who had been with her brother, the Advocate General, had left Malta and come to live in a cottage in Winterslow, near London. Her father, a retired Navy officer, was dead; her mother was mentally ill. "No longer in her first youth," Sarah had set about acquiring a husband while she was in Malta. "The vile wretch" who said he loved her had tired of her. Now, still desiring a husband, she wrote to Mary Lamb, telling of her desires. Mary gave her advice on the subject when Sarah came to London. The latter had been in Winterslow briefly when her name was linked with that of a Mr. White; next, she seemed to be in love with a Mr. Dowling of that village. John Stoddard, Sarah's brother, who had been one of the pantisocrats, wrote Mary Lamb, asking that she meet the young man and see if he would make an acceptable husband for his sister.

Mary Lamb, in turn, wrote Sarah Stoddard telling her that "your brother . . . says, that if Mr. D. is a worthy man he shall have no objection to becoming the brother of a farmer, and he makes an odd request that I shall set out for Salisbury to look at and examine into the merits of the said Mr. D. and speaks very confidently as if you would abide by my determination. You have gone too far in this affair for any interference to be at all desirable, and if you had not, I really do not know what my wishes would be. When you bring Mr. Dowling at Christmas, I suppose it will be enough for me to sit in judgment upon him, but my examination will not be a very severe one. If you fancy a very young man and he likes an elderly gentlewoman, if he likes a learned and accomplished lady, and you like a not very learned youth, he may need a little polishing which probably he will never acquire; it is all very well, and God bless you both together and may you both be very long in the same mind." But this love affair seems to have floundered and died.

In the meanwhile, William Hazlitt had for some time been looking for a suitable wife. Charles Lamb obligingly introduced Hazlitt to many pretty young girls, who, unfortunately interested Hazlitt not at all. True, they were all eminently eligible, but with them Hazlitt was miserable; finally, he confessed to Lamb that he could not bear young girls. He once said that, up to his twenty-ninth year, "I never fell in love but once; and then it was with a girl who always wore her handkerchief pinned tight about her neck, with a fair face, gentle eyes, a soft smile, and cool auburn locks . . . . It was not a raging heat, a fever in the veins: but it was like a vision, a dream, like thoughts of childhood, an everlasting hope, a distant joy, a heaven, a world that might be. The dream is still left, and sometimes confusedly over me in solitude and silence, and mingles with the softness of the sky, and veils my eyes from mortal grossness."

When one day, by chance, at the Lambs' he encountered Sarah Stoddard, in her thirties, then considered past the marriageable age, he met in her a young woman quite unlike the first recipient of his love. Sarah's brother, Dr. John Stoddard, who had lived through her stormy love affair in Malta, found her manners hoydenish; her good taste and discretion, lacking; her high spirits which seemed to thrive on excitement and amusement which she demanded, deplorable. Mary Lamb, he hoped, would make a lady of his sister. Hazlitt, on the other hand, admired wholesome Sarah with her sandy, closecut hair and red cheeks, who loved to prop her feet up on the fender of the fireplace, who loved her brandy and water, who was cordial, well-read, and a highly skilled needlewoman. The fact that she was three years his senior mattered not at all; nor did he find her opinionated and aggressive as others did. He knew how Sarah and Mary enjoyed chatting and drinking together, discussing writers and women's fashions. The idea of William Hazlitt and Sarah Stoddard being seriously interested in one another amused Charles Lamb. Yet, before long the two were secretly engaged, though settlement of details of the considerable estate which Sarah was to inherit and William's poverty caused some delay in their plans. Once news of the approaching wedding leaked out, Sarah's brother insisted that the couple be married with "proper decorum" from his home. After much discussion, the young couple and Sarah's brother agreed the wedding would take place on May Day, 1808, the party leaving from Dr. John Stoddard's home after being married at St. Andrew's Church at Holborn. The wedding proved a gruelling experience for the Lambs because of its associations; for it was from this church that their mother had been buried. Mary Lamb, the bridesmaid, had made her dress of China silk and had wished to embroider and make the wedding dress for Sarah. The bride, however, had preferred to make her own white satin bridal gown.

The newly married couple went to live in Hazlitt's lodgings in the Southampton Buildings. But these proved cramped and they moved, first to Sarah's cottage in Winterslow, then to John Milton's gloomy house in London. Their first son soon died; then, Sarah suffered a miscarriage. The third son, William, brought general rejoicing at first both to the Hazlitts and their friends. As the child grew older and the Hazlitts brought him to the Lambs' Wednesday evening parties, most people found him a forward and thoroughly disagreeable little boy. Often finding his wife boring, Hazlitt took a room nearby his residence, where he could be alone to write. His fame as a writer was increasing.

Then he fell in love with Sarah Walker, the daughter of the man in whose house he had taken the room where he might write. Twenty-year-old Sarah, who waited on the lodgers in her father's house, was described by one of Hazlitt's friends as being petite, with "a steady unmoving gaze," seeming never to look at one but to look down; she walked "in a sort of wavy, sinuous manner, like the movement of a snake. She was silent or uttered monosyllables only and very demure." Hazlitt wrote, "The truth is, I never had any pleasure like love, with any one but her . . . . She came (I know not how) and sat by my side and was folded in my arms, a vision of love and joy—as if she had dropped from the heavens, to bless me by some special dispensation of favouring Providence, to *make me amends for all.*" With her, he "recaptured the bliss of childhood"; he was happier than he had ever been. Sarah Walker, he decided, must be his wife; hence, the first step he must take was that of securing a divorce. Resourceful, he discovered one could easily procure a divorce in Scotland by "the oath of calumny" once one established residence there. Hence, he asked his wife for the divorce, and said that she as well as he must spend three months in Scotland for him to secure it. Although in a friendly, matter-of-fact way Sarah Hazlitt agreed to the divorce and to assist her husband in securing it, she was still in love with him and, once in Scotland, used any excuse to see him. When she donned a veil as a disguise and went to his lodgings to collect her allowance for living expenses, her husband was indignant. When she encountered him drinking in the public room at The Black Bull, she was so "fluried at meeting him" she forgot many things she was going to tell him. After they had been in Scotland three long months, the divorce was granted and Hazlitt returned to London to find "Miss Walker" engaged to another man.

Though he seemed distraught over the girl's jilting him, a few months later, in the spring of 1822, he met and married Mrs. Isabella Bridgewater, the widow of a barrister, who had an income of nearly £300 a year. Considerably younger than Hazlitt, she was, said one of Hazlitt's friends, "one of the loveliest girls I had ever seen"; Mrs. Bridgewater was a charming, gracious woman, fair skinned, with very delicate, fine features. She said she had fallen in love with Hazlitt "because of his writings." Shortly after their marriage, they went abroad, visiting France and Italy. Blissfully happy, though Hazlitt was aging, they remained abroad until the autumn of 1827. Then suddenly, Hazlitt returned without Mrs. Hazlitt. It seems that when the essayist's fifteen-year-old-son had visited the couple at their invitation, he was exceedingly rude to the second Mrs. Hazlitt. The lad felt keenly that his own "mother had been ill-used—in which there was a considerable amount of truth, no doubt; and when he joined his father and step-mother abroad, he . . . seems to have been very pointed and severe in his remarks on the matter. This probably gave Mrs. Hazlitt a foretaste of what she might have to expect on her return to England. . . ." Accordingly, she left Hazlitt, who, having had to make a choice between his second wife and his son, chose the boy, of whom he had always been very fond, tending to overprotect the lad. Hazlitt had called his son "Dear Baby" when the lad was thirteen.

Hazlitt's reputation for being disagreeable did not lessen as his

fame as a critic grew. When in 1816 Coleridge, on Byron's recom-
mendation, decided to have published "Christabel," "Kubla Khan,"
and a number of prose works on social panaceas, even Wordsworth
was doubtful about how the public would receive these unusual
poems. In "Kubla Khan," Wordsworth said, Coleridge "repeats so en-
chantingly that it irradiates and brings heaven and Elysian bowers
into my parlour while he sings or says it, but there is an observation,
'Never tell thy dreams,' and I am almost afraid that Kubla Khan is
an owl that won't bear daylight, I fear lest it should be discovered
by the lantern of typography and clear reconducting to letters, no
better than nonsense or no sense." Hazlitt, now considered a critic of
note, reviewed the poems for *The Examiner*, stating that Coleridge
"is a man of that universality of genius, that his mind hangs suspended
between poetry and prose, truth and falsehood, and an infinity of
other things, and from an excess of capacity he does little or nothing.
Here are two unfinished poems and a fragment." "Kubla Khan," Hazlitt
said, was "not a poem but a musical composition. We could repeat
the opening lines to ourselves not the less often for not knowing the
meaning of them." Coleridge said later that Hazlitt had praised
"Christabel" as "the finest poem in the language" and had ridiculed
"the public for their want of taste and discrimination in not admiring
it." Yet, some months later, Hazlitt is said to have reviewed the three
Coleridge poems, "Christabel," "Kubla Khan," and "The Pains of
Sleep" in the *Edinburgh Review* as "one of the most notable pieces
of impertinence of which the press has lately been guilty; and one of
the boldest experiments that has been made on the patience and
understanding of the public." He added that "the other productions
of the Lake School have generally exhibited talents thrown away upon
subjects so mean that no power of genius could ennoble them." The
present poems, he contended, have "not a ray of genius, and we defy
any man to point out a passage of poetical merit in any of the three
pieces." When questioned about the review, Hazlitt said he had been
asked to write it, and that he had had to write it in accordance with
the style of the magazine, says George Gillman. Others say Hazlitt
denied writing the review.

With Coleridge's prose pieces Hazlitt was less generous. When
Coleridge's publishers announced publication of "A Layman's Ser-
mon on the Distresses of the Country Addressed to the Middle and
Higher Orders," Hazlitt attacked the work even before he read it.
At the time, Hazlitt was writing on "Speeches in Parliament on the
Distresses of the Country." Vehemently, he said that "the expenses of

the war might as well have been sunk in the sea; and so they might, for they have been sunk in unproductive labour, that is, in maintaining large establishments, and employing great numbers of men in doing nothing or mischief; for example, in making ships to destroy other ships, guns and gunpowder to blow out man's brains, swords and pikes to run them through the body, drums and fifes to drown the noise of cannon and the whizzing of bullets; in making caps and coats to deck the bodies of those who live by killing others. . . . We have paid . . . and we must pay . . . out of our own pockets. The price of Restoring the Pope, the Inquisition, the Bourbons, and the Doctrine of Divine Rights is half of our nine hundred millions of debt. That is the amount of the Government bill of costs, presented to John Bull for payment, not of the principal but of the interest; that is what he has got by the war. . . . War in itself is a thriving, sensible traffic only to cannibals." Once started, Hazlitt was hard to stop. Next, he wrote, "The rich and the poor may at present be compared to the two classes of frequenters of pastry-cooks' shops, those on the outside and those on the in. We would seriously advise the latter, who see the gaunt faces staring at them through the glass-door to recollect that though custard is nicer than bread, bread is the greatest necessary of the two."

Aroused when he heard that Coleridge whom he had once admired unreservedly was the author of "A Lay-Sermon on the Distresses of the Country, Addressed to the Middle and Higher Orders" soon to appear, Hazlitt reviewed not the book, which he had not seen, but the announcement of publication. "We see no sort of difference between his published and unpublished compositions," wrote Hazlitt. "It is just as impossible to get at the meaning of one as the other. No man ever yet gave Mr. Coleridge 'a penny for his thoughts.' His are all Maiden ideas; immaculate conceptions." Coleridge, he continued, is not the author of a single "intelligible passage" in other prose works. His paper, *The Friend*, is "but an enormous title-page; the largest and most tiresome prospectus that ever was written; an endless preface to an imaginary work; a table of contents that fills the whole volume; a huge bill of fare of all possible subjects, with not an idea to be had for love or money . . . One number consists of a grave-faced promise to perform something impossible in the next; and the next is taken up with a long-faced apology for not having done it . . . He is the Dog in the Manger of literature, an intellectual Mar-Plot, one who will neither let anybody else come to a conclusion nor come to one himself."

Having ripped into Coleridge, he then took on Southey, the poet laureate. Southey had refused the editorship of *The Times*, saying he could not give up the joys of country life for any emolument; moreover, he did not wish to be in the public eye, for he was embarrassed when a radical bookseller, without his permission, had republished his "Wat Tyler." In fact, Southey had tried by legal means to stop the publication of this work of his youth. Now grown conservative, he said, "We are in danger of an invasion of the Yahoos: — it is the fault of governments that such a cast should exist in the midst of civilized society, but till the breed can be mended, it must be curbed, and that too with a strong hand." On March 9, 1817, Hazlitt reviewed Southey's new article on "Parliamentary Reform" and also his "Wat Tyler." With vitriolic zeal, he wrote, "The author of 'Wat Tyler' was an Ultra-Jacobin; the author of 'Parliamentary Reform' is an Ultra-royalist; the one was a frantic demagogue; the other is a servile court-tool . . . . the one vilified kings, priests, and nobles; the other vilifies the people; the one was for universal suffrage and perfect equality; the other is for seat-selling and the increasing influence of the Crown: the one admired the preaching of John Ball; the other recommends the Suspension of the Habeas Corpus Act and putting down *The Examiner* by the sword, the dagger, or the thumbscrew; for the pen, Mr. Southey tells us, is not sufficient . . . A changeling is your only oracle." When Coleridge attempted to defend Southey, saying in *The Courier* that Southey had written "Wat Tyler" when he was but nineteen, Hazlitt replied, "A person who forgets all the sentiments and principles to which he was most attached at nineteen, can have no sentiments ever after worth being attached to." Southey, seeking to defend himself, said some "had turned their faces toward the East in the morning, to worship the rising sun, and in the evening were looking eastward still, obstinately affirming that the sun was still there. I, on the contrary, altered my position as the earth went round." Hazlitt replied, "The sun, indeed, passes from the East to the West, but it rises in the East again: yet Mr. Southey is still looking in the West—for his pension."

Having spoken his mind on Coleridge and Southey, he turned to Wordsworth who, he contended, "tolerates nothing but what he himself creates; he sympathizes only with what can enter into no competition with him, with 'the bare earth and mountains bare, and grass in the green fields.' He sees nothing but himself and the universe. He hates all greatness and all pretentions to it but his own. His egotism is in this respect a madness; for he scorns even the admiration of himself, thinking it a presumption in anyone to suppose that he has taste or sense enough to understand him. He hates all science and all art . . . he hates logic, he hates metaphysics, which he says are unintelligible, and yet he would be thought to understand them; he hates prose, he hates all that others admire and love but himself." Wordsworth did not answer Hazlitt, but his friend Crabb Robinson, meeting Hazlitt the day the attack on Wordsworth appeared in *The Examiner* told Hazlitt the article was "scandalous." The essayist replied he was not in the habit of defending himself but added "It may be indelicate, but I am forced to write an article every week, and I have not time to make one with so much delicacy as I otherwise should."

Indeed, Hazlitt had been immensely productive, as he wrote political and literary articles as well as drama and art criticism in turn for *The Chronicle, The Examiner*, the *Edinburgh Review, The Times, Blackwood's Magazine, The London Magazine, The New Monthly Magazine*, and *The Liberal*. In addition, volumes of essays poured from his pen; he wrote an article on "The Five Arts" for the *Encyclopaedia Britannica* and a four-volume *Life of Napoleon*. He was busy, too, as a lecturer. When he delivered his first lecture in 1812, his friend Crabb Robinson found him a poor lecturer; he spoke in a "low, monotonous voice with his eyes fixed intently on his book, not ever daring to look at his audience. He read, too, so rapidly that no one could possibly follow him . . . ." When Hazlitt's friend, Dr. Stoddard, left him a letter of advice on how to lecture better, Hazlitt was hurt and at first considered giving up lecturing. That he heeded his friend's advice, however, seems obvious, for ten days later when Robinson heard Hazlitt's second lecture, he reported that the lecturer "delivered himself well; that is, loud, and with a tone of confidence which being forced had sometimes the air of arrogance; this however, did not offend (except perhaps a few) and he was interrupted by applause several times." A month later, Robinson finds him giving an "animated lecture." From then on, his ease as a lecturer continued and he became sought after as a speaker. Crowds now attended his lectures.

Though Hazlitt quarreled with many of his friends, with some his friendship, though at times forced, continued. Charles Lamb believed Hazlitt at fault in his savage attacks on Coleridge, Southey, and Wordsworth; he broke with him for a time, when Hazlitt insisted on divorcing loyal Sarah Stoddard, but before long the two men were friends again. When Southey, in an essay "On the Progress of Infidelity," said that the only trouble with Charles Lamb was the company he kept, meaning William Hazlitt, Lamb replied that he did not know what had "soured" Hazlitt and "made him suspect his friends of infidelity towards him . . . . I stood well with him for fifteen years (the proudest of my life) and have ever spoke my full mind of him to some of whom his panegyric must naturally be at least tasteful. I never in thought swerved from him; I never betrayed him; I never slackened in my admiration of him; I was the same to him (neither better nor worse), though he could not see it, as in the days when he thought fit to trust me . . . . I think W. H. to be, in his natural state, one of the wisest and finest spirits breathing . . . I think I shall go to my grave without finding or expecting to find, such another companion." Reading Lamb's comment, Hazlitt said, "I think I must be friends with Lamb again"; he was. Mary Lamb had never wavered in her devotion to him.

Young John Keats, who met Hazlitt in 1817, found the essayist brilliant, and wrote of his intentions, after studying Greek and perhaps Italian for a year, of finding out from Hazlitt "the best metaphysical road I can take." The young poet went to lectures with Hazlitt, attended at least one art exhibit with him, admired the brilliance of his criticism—"he has a demon in him,"—and came to him for advice which Hazlitt gladly gave.

Twenty-eight-year-old Leigh Hunt, eminently successful, Hazlitt met when he was thirty-four and had not yet won a name for himself. A year after their meeting, in 1814, Leigh Hunt was arrested because of an article against military flogging, a reprint in *The Stamford News;* the essay had appeared earlier in *The Examiner.* Annoyed at Hunt's views which were contrary to those of the government, the ministry had eagerly sought to imprison the young man they considered a rebel. Suit had been brought against *The Observer* and *The Examiner* because of Hunt's views. After the government lost its suit against the first paper, it dropped that against *The Examiner.* When an article criticizing the Prince Regent's morals and figure appeared, the government this time brought suit against its authors, Leigh Hunt and his brother John, and won. Both young men were sentenced to two years in prison. Leigh Hunt in Surrey Gaol, and his brother in Coldbath Fields; in addition, each was fined £500. The conviction made *The Examiner* an important paper and Leigh Hunt famous. Shelley, then a student at Oxford, offered Hunt his aid; Byron brought him food and copies of his poems. Dramatically, Hunt had had his gaol room gaily painted: the ceiling, like a blue sky in which clouds seemed to float; the walls, like those in a garden with trellises on which a multitude of roses seemed to climb. There, Hunt sat, editing *The Examiner* and writing the political news for that paper; he was also writing a poem, *Rimini*. To this amazing room, Hazlitt came to exchange amenities with Hunt, to whom he deferred. As his two year imprisonment neared its close, Hunt also wrote the theatre section for *The Examiner* and instituted a new feature: "The Round Table," in which he and Hazlitt alternately presented points of view. Though this venture went well for some time, by 1821 Hazlitt was attacking Hunt, not as "dull and monotonous" but as an "excessive" egotist, who, whether he talked of country, poetry, or politics, "it comes to much the same thing." People like this, he contended, "are, in fact, in love with themselves; and, like lovers, should be left to keep their own company." At the same time, Hazlitt attacked Shelley who, he said, "has a fire in his eye, a fever in his blood, a maggot in his brain, a hectic flutter in his speech, which mark out the philosophic fanatic. . . . Bubbles are to him the only realities: —touch them and they vanish. Curiosity is the only proper category of his mind, and though a man in knowledge, he is a child in feeling." Hunt wrote a letter to Hazlitt asking if he might not have "found a better time, and place, too, for assaulting me and my friends in this bitter manner. . . . In God's name, why could you not tell Mr. Shelley in a pleasant maner what you dislike in him? If it is not mere spleen you make a gross mistake in thinking that he is not open to advice or so willfully in love with himself and his opinions. His spirit is worthy of his great talents. Besides, do you think that nobody has thought or suffered, or come to conclusions through thought or suffering but yourself?" In time, the three became friends again, Hunt writing Hazlitt after visiting him and Mrs. Hazlitt in Florence in 1826 that he was "more at ease with you in your house than anywhere else." Yet, two years later, in "A Farewell to Essay Writing," Hazlitt complained about Leigh Hunt's description of him. Resentful of Hunt's description of his "standing upright, speaking loud, entering a room gracefully," wearing "a prim and self-complacent air as if I were 'the admired of all observers,' " at times wearing "a little hat stuck on the wrong way," Hazlitt asked if he should try to look nervous and uneasy. As to his hat, "I commonly wear a large slouching hat over my eyebrows; and if I ever had another, I must have twisted it about in any shape to be rid of the annoyance." He resented, too, Hunt's references to his "strange gestures and contortions of features in argument, in order to look energetic." Before Hazlitt's death, however, he sought out Leigh

Hunt, telling a friend he met in Soho he hoped Hunt had forgotten their differences; "if he has not, I have."

At fifty-two, Hazlitt seemed an old man; he was writing less than usual, but he was still productive. As fond of the theatre as in his youth, he went frequently to plays, now centering his praise on both Mrs. Siddons and her niece; and it was great praise, for no one had lauded Mrs. Siddons more than vitriolic Hazlitt; Fanny Kemble, too, he admired, but remarked, "There will never be another Mrs. Siddons."

A stomach disorder of many years' standing finally caused Hazlitt to be bedfast, though his mind was as keen and alert as ever. Physically shrunken and helpless, he had his friends Charles and Mary Lamb, Bryan Proctor and his son with him much of the time. As he lay dying, he asked for his mother, aged eighty-five, who was in Devonshire, and then said, "I have had a happy life." He was buried at St. Anne's, Soho, on September 30, 1830. His wife, Sarah Stoddard Hazlitt, still in love with him, still loyal, recorded details of his death and burial.

Wordsworth wrote his friend Francis Wrangham in 1804, "I have great things in meditation but as yet I am doing little ones. I am at present engaged in a poem on my earlier life which will take five parts, or books, to complete. My other meditated works are a philosophical poem and a narrative one. These will occupy me some, I ought to say several years; and I do not mean to appear before the world again as an author until one of them at least be finished." "The Prelude," the work on his own early life, he told an admirer, young Thomas De Quincey, in March 1804, would only be a tributary to a longer and more important one, "The Recluse." "Of this larger work I have written one book and several scattered fragments; it is a moral and philosophical poem; the subject, whatever I find most interesting in Nature, Man, and Society, and most adapted to poetic illustration. To this work I mean to devote the prime of my life and the chief force of my mind." On September 8, he wrote Sir George Beaumont that he had written one book of "The Recluse", "nearly a thousand lines, then had a rest. Last week I began again and have written three hundred lines." He "tinkered" with what he had written and added new lines until, on Christmas day, 1804, he wrote Walter Scott he had completed "two thousand verses in the last ten weeks."

In "The Recluse," a long narrative poem, Wordsworth's two principal characters both have in themselves something of himself; one, the Wanderer, is a Poet, who, Wordsworth says, represented "an idea of what I fancied my own character might have become in the circumstances"; the Wanderer stands for that "active and happy life" to which he aspired; the Solitary is the conflicting, frustrated part of himself in extreme consciousness of failure to achieve an active, vigorous life; the latter is portrayed as having lost his faith in the French Revolution. Though Wordsworth worked long on "The Recluse," it was never completed. "The Prelude," the account of his earlier life, on the other hand, grew until it was more than twice its intended length; it was completed in May, 1805. One of the longest poems in English, it deals with Wordsworth's boyhood and youth, his experiences in France, and sets forth a speculative theory of the mind and nature and of their mutual relationships.

In the meantime, he wrote a number of shorter poems inspired by the danger of the French invasion. With England threatened, he believed now his country was a symbol of liberty and national independence, just as in his youth he had believed France was. He loathed what Robespierre and Napoleon had done to France. It was imperative, he felt, that England present a "united front" against France in which he now found

> . . . . nothing great:
> Nothing is left which I can venerate;

his patriotic fervor was mingled with sorrow—sorrow for the state into which France had fallen and at the imperfections of his own country.

Coleridge, of a religious bent, sorrowed too, and in print wondered whether the expected invasion came as a judgment for England's national sins, especially for the slave trade. Though Wordsworth wrote a considerable number of shorter poems and, two years after his return from Scotland, a number of poems inspired by that trip, he spent considerable time, too, on *The Excursion*, with its accurate analysis of mental sickness and with "its psychological penetration that points unerringly to the cure."

Believing that narrative poetry such as Scott was popularizing could be equally or more successful by subordinating the action to some spiritual meaning, he wrote "The White Doe of Rylstone." It was suggested by an old ballad "The Rising of the North," describing an attempt to restore Catholicism. The father, who is the central figure of Wordsworth's poem, and seven of his eight sons devote their lives to the cause, whereas the elder son, Francis, and the daughter, Emily, though loyal to their father, belong to the new faith, opposed to Catholicism. The tragedy of the poem lies in these divergent interests: Emily, for example, though opposed to her father's point of view, makes for him, at his bidding, a banner of the Cross, which the father carries in a fatal battle, and which the dying father asks Francis to carry back to the shrine of Bolton Priory. Though this wish is contrary to his own desire, the obedient and loyal son carries the banner and in so doing loses his life; he had tried in vain to tell his father that all that could result from the latter's attempt to restore Catholicism would be the extinction of a family. Only Emily survived to witness the utter emptiness and ruin of fortune. Yet she, though lonely, remained

> Undaunted, lofty, calm and stable,
> And awfully impenetrable.

Returning one day to her father's domain she was surprised by the visit of a white doe that, when she was a child, had been her playmate. From this faithful creature who now remained with her, she drew comfort and peace even on that "trouble-haunted ground." Some critics have said that "a note of almost oriental renunciation runs through the poem." Human endeavor and human deeds will pass away; only "Nature and Mind and the Peace of God endure. Salvation is found not through acting but through suffering."

While Wordsworth was working on the Scottish poems and the longer ones, which were then far from ready for publication, an edition appeared of his earlier poems and of those inspired by the expected French invasion. *Poems In Two Volumes* brought a flood of adverse reviews from Francis Jeffery in the *Edinburgh Review*. The savage critic had earlier pilloried Coleridge and Southey and "the Lake School of Poets," maintaining there never was any justification for the term "Lake School"; Coleridge, Jeffrey contended, had lived only a short time in the Lake Country and "his poetry shows hardly any trace of that residence." Moreover, Jeffrey despised the poetry of these "*dissenters* from the established systems in poetry and criticism . . . . Their most distinguishing symbol is undoubtedly an affectation of great simplicity and familiarity of language. They disdain to make use of the common poetical phraseology, or to enoble their diction by a selection of fine or dignified expressions . . . . A splenic and idle discontent with the existing institutions of society seems to be at the bottom of all their serious and peculiar sentiments. Instead of contemplating the wonders and pleasures which civilization has created for mankind, they are perpetually brooding over the disorders by which progress has been attended. They are filled with horror and compassion at the sight of poor men spending their blood in the quarrels of princes and brutifying their sublime capabilities in the drudgery of unremitting labour. For all sorts of vice and profligacy in the lower orders of society they have the same virtuous horror and the same tender compassion. While the existence of these offences over-powers them with grief and confusion, they never permit themselves to feel the smallest indignation or dislike toward offenders. . . . The present vicious constitution of society alone is responsible for these enormities." Jeffrey continued, allowing his sarcasm full vent: "the poor sinners are but the helpless victims or instruments of its disorders, and could not possibly have avoided the errors into which they have been betrayed. Though they can bear with crimes, therefore they cannot reconcile themselves to punishments; and have an unconquerable antipathy to prisons, gibbets, and houses of correction, as engines of oppression and instruments of atrocious injustice. . . . No sort of indulgence is shown to the rich and powerful. Their oppressions and seductions and debaucheries are the theme of many an angry verse; and the indignation and abhorence of the reader is relentlessly conjured up against those perturbators of society and scourges of mankind." At this time, poor men were savagely punished for poaching and other small offenses, whereas embezzlement, bribery, and purchasing promotions were practiced by the powerful and rich "with comparative immunity."

Wordsworth, of all the Lake poets, Jeffrey considered a menace and the grand conspirator against society as it was and as Jeffrey wished it to remain. Hence, he lashed out against him with special fury, poking fun at Wordsworth's "affectation of infantine innocence and simplicity, an affectation of excessive refinement and preternatural enthusiasm; and an affectation of certain perverse singularity of learning, taste, and opinions." Some of Wordsworth's poems, he announced were "an insult to the public taste"; others of the poems he said made so little sense that they merely left the reader "bewildered." In conclusion, he branded Wordsworth's poetry "trash," except, "when by accident he is led to abandon his system, and to transgress the laws of that school which he fain would establish on the ruin of all existing authority."

In 1808, Byron attacked Wordsworth in "English Bards and Scotch Reviewers," when he wrote of

> That mild apostate from poetic rule,
> The simple Wordsworth, framer of a lay
> As soft as evening in his favorite May
> ....
> Who both by precept and example shows
> That prose is verse, and verse is merely prose
> Yet let them not to vulgar Wordsworth stoop,
> The meanest object of the lowly group,
> Whose verse, of all but childish prattle void
> Seems blessed harmony to Lambe and Lloyd.

William described these comments as "a miserable heap of spiteful nonsense"; Dorothy declared they were worse than anything she had thought possible. They effectively stopped the sale of Wordsworth's poems.

When William completed "The White Doe of Rylstone," he was certain the poem would find acceptance. Dorothy said she could never expect any poem of his to be immediately popular, like Scott's *The Lay of the Last Minstrel*, "but I think the story will help out those parts which are above the common level of taste and knowledge, and that it will have a better sale than his former works and perhaps help them off." Encouraged by Dorothy, he left for London with his poem, expecting to show it to Charles Lamb and Coleridge and then publish it and "ask 100 guineas for an edition of 1,000." In London, he changed his mind and decided not to publish it, for Lamb did not like it and Coleridge, though he thought the part about Emily exquisite, believed it had some weakness of construction, which he pointed out. Coleridge believed the poem was unlikely to please the general public.

Dorothy was dismayed at his not publishing the poems; she believed he should defy his critics. Moreover, the Wordsworths needed the money the poems would bring. With need of a new house and new furniture, with the necessity of an additional servant for the large family, she rebelled at working "the flesh off our poor bones. Dear William," she entreated him, "do pluck up your courage and overcome your disgust at publishing." But he could not be persuaded; the poems lay in manuscript form eight years.

While William was in London, a tragedy came to their neighbors,

George Green and his wife, whose little daughter Sally helped the Wordsworths and was then living with them. On a cold Saturday morning, the father and mother had left their little children at home to go to a sale at Langdale. They left Langdale between five and six in the evening, but never reached home. The children sat up until eleven o'clock at night waiting for their parents, then went to bed satisfied that their parents had remained at Langdale because of bad weather; a little snow had fallen; there was a deep mist, and it had turned bitterly cold. On Monday noon, the eldest child went to a neighbor, George Rowlandson, and said her parents had not yet come home. The older man suspected they were lost and immediately spread the word. Fifty or sixty set out to search for them. When some women went to the Green home, they were amazed at the self-reliance of the little children, though when they came in all were crying together. Sally, of course, was grief stricken. The neighbors found that the Greens were even poorer than the community thought; they never made tea; the only food in the house was two boilings of potatoes, a very little meal, little bread, and three or four legs of lean, dried mutton. Their cow gave less than a quart of milk a day. The children were well-provided-for at once. A fund was opened for the orphans and in less than six weeks £300 had been raised in sums ranging from ten guineas to the threepence given by the poorest laborers. Six ladies were on a committee to place the children in suitable homes. Here, the only spirit of discord entered when a newcomer, Mrs. North from Liverpool, whose husband had just bought Rydal Mount, without consulting the committee arranged for the children to board with an old woman who, Dorothy protested, "was totally unfit to look after them." When Dorothy protested, Mrs. North was, Dorothy said, "very rude and impertinent to me and in my person to the whole committee." The bodies of the father and mother were not found until Wednesday. The day after the funeral, there was a sale of their furniture "and the next day the house was left empty and silent." In the end, Dorothy had the satisfaction of seeing all the children placed in homes where they were "hospitably welcomed."

The end of May, 1808, the Wordsworths moved into Allan Bank, a large mansion, which both William and Dorothy thought "the only object that is not cheerful and in harmony with the sheltering mountains and the quiet vale . . . . But if any ugly house is built in a beautiful and commanding situation, it is at least better to be inside it than outside it." At any rate, this large "temple of abomination," the only vacant house in Grasmere, solved their housing problem for a time. The Wordsworths had decided to make a home for Coleridge and his two boys, for though he had custody of his sons, it seemed obvious to the Wordsworths that he could not take care of them by himself. They realized their decision might provoke criticism; yet their decision was final. Realizing full well they might not make Coleridge happy, well aware of his vacillation, they were concerned that he and his sons have some permanent abode, though, Dorothy wrote, "If Coleridge makes our house only an *occasional* residence, there is no objection whatever on our side."

|"*What Man Hath Made of Man*"

THE BULK OF THE WORK OF MOVING TO ALLAN BANK IN MAY, 1808, RESTED ON DOROTHY. KNOWING WILLIAM WOULD BE troubled by the confusion of moving, she hoped to get him out of the way; Henry Hutchinson, Mary's sailor brother, came to help them, just as John Wordsworth had years before. He "is the handiest person in the world," Dorothy found; "—can sew, cook, wash dishes, put up beds, —anything you can name. Being very poor we are determined to do everything ourselves; for [Henry] is as good as a tailor, and at the same time a very pleasant companion and fellow labourer. Judge how busy I must have been this fortnight past—papers, linen, books, everything to look over in the old house and put by in the new—besides curtains to make etc etc etc. In another fortnight all will be over, we hope, for Henry and I work body and soul, and with less we should never be done." The new house delighted her now, for it provided a safer place, farther from the street, for the children to play without fear of horses and carriages. The larger house, too, provided further privacy for the older people. "Sara and I have a delicious view from our several windows—both look to the East—the mighty mountains of Fairfield and Seat Sandal, now green to their very summits. Oh! that you could see that mass of clouds now resting on the pass which we used to traverse in our visits to you, that pass where William and I were near being lost for ever. Oh that you could see the bonny cottages and their tufts of trees and sweet green fields. It is a soothing scene, and I trust you will one day behold it," she wrote.

The Wordsworths had hardly settled in their new home when guests began to arrive. Mary's cousin, Mary Monkhouse, an attractive twenty-one-year-old girl, was much feted at picnics, which Dorothy said "our Windermere gentlemen have almost every day." Young John Wilson, later known as Christopher North, an Oxford graduate and "a man of fortune, of good understanding and most affectionate heart and very pleasing manners," who admired Wordsworth's poems, was building a house above Lake Windermere. He found Mary Monkhouse most attractive and seemed almost to be courting her. After Mary left the Wordsworths, Sara Hutchinson, a veritable matchmaker, wrote her, "You must have him, if you can get him; he is a nice creature and would fain be better than he is. I am sure if he were near William he would never seek those wild companions of his any more." Coleridge and Thomas De Quincey came in September; the former to make his home with the Wordsworths in the drawing room and bedroom they had reserved for him; the latter to remain until February and then to return for another visit in the following November. De Quincey a short time later settled in Dove Cottage which he had rented from the Wordsworths and which Dorothy Wordsworth had made ready for him, furnishing it at his expense. Hartley and Derwent Coleridge, in school at Ambleside, came to spend weekends and holidays with the Wordsworths and their father. At times, little Sara Coleridge came to visit her father. Regularly, there were thirteen in the Wordsworth household; on Sundays, fifteen.

De Quincey, the Wordsworths soon learned, was born of solid, middle-class stock. His father, De Quincey said, had had little influence upon the development of his character, but his mother had had an enormous amount. A merchant who was denied a college education, his father had great respect for those who had one; his mother, who considered herself superior to her husband, had a passion for building or rebuilding houses, and for social standing. Moving eight times in nineteen years, she remodeled each house in which she dwelt. Nor were her alterations trifling. At the Priory, for example, she "immediately threw out a drawing room in suitable proportion to the dining room, and about six little bedrooms" at a cost of £1000; for her next home, she paid £12,500 plus the inevitable cost of alterations. She lost money on every house she sold. Small wonder is it that her husband was so busy providing a living for his family that De Quincey remembers little about him. His estate amounted to £1600 a year, from which each son was to receive £150 a year, and each daughter, £100. Though four guardians were to supervise the estate, Mrs. De Quincey was so strong-willed she did exactly as she chose. Indeed, as she continued moving and building, often the money due her six children simply was not available.

Thomas De Quincey was born on August 15, 1785. He suffered

acute shock at the age of five when his sister Jane died and when a year later his sister Elizabeth died. After Elizabeth's death, he felt he must have one last look at her. Choosing to go when the servants were at their mid-day meal, he crept up the stairs to her room. As he gazed on her face, an awe fell upon him and he believed he heard "the sound of a wind that might have swept the fields of immortality for a thousand centuries. Many times since, upon summer days, when the sun is about the hottest, I have remarked the same wind arising and uttering the same hollow, solemn, Memnonian but saintly swell: it is in this world the one great audible symbol of eternity." Two years later when his father was dying, though the boy was not in the room, he heard the dying man cry to his wife, "Oh, Betty, Betty! Why will you never come and help me to raise this weight?" The memory of that call and the vision he had had of his dead sister never left him.

A frail youth, who suffered with ague from his second to fourth years, who lived in almost exclusively feminine surroundings, he was ill-prepared to defend himself against his "horrid, pugilistic," energetic older brother William, who had spent some years at Louth Grammar School in Lincolnshire. When Mrs. De Quincey sent the two boys to Salford to the Grammar School run by the Rev. Samuel Hall, the route from their home in Greenhay to the school lay past a cotton factory where they encountered factory boys with whom William waged a battle twice each day. Stones, pieces of slate, and brickbats flew until the hostilities ended, always with Thomas a prisoner. As the factory boys knew William was the aggressor, they, Thomas said, "were not disposed to be too hard upon me. But at the same time they clearly did not think it right that I should escape altogether from the calamities of war." Hence, they were content merely to kick him with legs "that ranged through all gradations of weight and agility." The lad's troubles increased when one day he was handed over to the factory girls for punishment. The girls were so entranced by the yellow-curled, blue-eyed, pink-and-white-cheeked little boy that they picked him up and kissed him. Before long, Thomas was freed from the bondage to William who, having shown ability as an artist, was sent to London to study. He died in London of typhus at eighteen.

After attending a number of schools and being taught at home by a French émigré, De Quincey spent some time in school at Manchester. Determined to leave there before his seventeenth birthday, he met opposition from his mother who was equally determined he should stay. Nor would she give him money to go to Oxford. Borrowing £5, he left school, aided in his escape by a porter. Shortly before leaving, he had received an envelope addressed to "Monsieur Monsieur [sic] de Quincey, Chester." Upon opening it, he discovered a letter in French which he deciphered, and a draught on Smith, Payne, and Smith for forty guineas. At first, the boy tried to convince himself the letter was intended for him; but his better judgment told him it belonged to another De Quincey. On leaving school, he planned to take the letter and draught to the postmaster at Chester; he planned then to go to see William Wordsworth, whose *Lyrical Ballads* had impressed him greatly. He later said that at Chester, he gave the letter and draught to a woman to give to the postmaster; yet, four years later when he came of age he or his family had to pay £150 because of its not having been received by the right De Quincey. Many believe he destroyed it, throwing the remains in the lake. At any rate, the draught had not been cashed.

As he wandered about northern England, finding it not at all difficult to borrow twelve guineas from two lawyers he met, he decided to go to London. Seeking to borrow money there, he went to the large, ramshackle house of a moneylender, a big hulk of a man named Brunell who lived in Greek Street in Soho. He permitted young De Quincey to live in one of his unfurnished rooms; without food for days, the boy was tormented by sad dreams. His companion at night was a timid, frightened ten-year-old girl, Ann, probably an illegitimate child of Brunell's, to whom the older man paid little attention. Together, they would wander through the empty rooms seeking a place to sleep comfortably. On cold nights, lying on the floor with a bundle of papers for a pillow, they huddled together under an old horseman's cloak. By day, he wandered aimlessly about London's streets and parks; his only friends were prostitutes who took pity on him and defended him against the night-watchman who tried to hurry the boy and keep him from loitering or sitting on the steps of houses. Among them, his favorite was a sixteen-year-old-girl, later immortalized as Ann, whom he never forgot. Seduced and then abandoned by a man who had left her to her fate, she believed she had no future. One night when she and De Quincey were walking in Oxford Street, he suddenly became faint, and asked Ann to help him get back to Soho; as they reached that destination, he fell down unconscious. Ann rushed back to Oxford Street, procured a glass of port and worked over him until she revived him.

De Quincey had been drifting. Now, he realized he must secure money and change his way of life. A friend of his family whom he encountered gave him £10 with which he purchased needed clothing

—he was almost in rags. A journey to Eton and to Oxford proved futile, as those he sought to aid him were away. Returning to London, he was unable to find Ann. The two had agreed to meet, but when she did not appear, De Quincey was at a loss to find her as he knew not her last name and knew only the street on which she lived. Whether Ann decided it was best for him to forget her, we do not know; but she remained for him a symbol of a love that was pure and good. Suddenly, some opening was made by a friend for a reconciliation between the seventeen-year-old boy and his family. With health undermined by the poverty he had experienced, a changed boy met his family. Yet, the letter he subsequently wrote to William Wordsworth telling how he enjoyed the latter's poetry and craved his friendship was extremely adolescent.

Wordsworth admonished him not to neglect the older poets for him, regretted that he himself was leaving on a Scotch tour with Coleridge and Dorothy Wordsworth but invited the young man to visit him later at Grasmere. Excited over receiving an answer, De Quincey wrote at once begging Wordsworth not to bother to write him more often than he felt disposed. Wordsworth did not reply for eight months.

Meanwhile, months passed while arguments raged about what should be young De Quincey's future; his guardians, his mother, and De Quincey all had different points of view. At length, they agreed he could go to Oxford. His mother offered to allow him £100, hardly enough for his expenses. Yet he went to Oxford, having chosen Worcester College because it was the least expensive.

He found the university curriculum far from stimulating. Stressing classical studies and theology, it was narrow, permitting no new ideas. Even the scholars were so ill-read in English literature that De Quincey did not consider them worth cultivating. Scorning his fellow students, he spent endless hours reading, working harder than he ever had before, acquiring the habit of concentration and developing the inexhaustible memory that proved valuable assets the rest of his life. He chose to read Latin and Greek classics, English, French, and German literature, and the ancient and modern philosophy necessary for him to receive a degree. His most important intellectual discovery was Kant, who later cast "a gloom of something like misanthropy upon my views of human nature."

Wordsworth influenced him, too, answering De Quincey's second letter and warning him "against being seduced into unworthy pleasures." Wordsworth told him how when he was a student at Cambridge, the manners of the students were "very frantic and dissolute."

He reminded De Quincey that there was no true dignity but "in virtue and temperance, and let me add, chastity; and that the best safeguard of all these is the cultivation of pure pleasures, namely those of the intellect and affections." Then he advised his young friend to love "nature and books; seek these and you will be happy; for virtuous friendship, and love, and knowledge of mankind must inevitably accompany these, all things ripening in their due season."

In 1805, De Quincey visited London several times, hoping to find Ann and to meet Charles Lamb. Ann, he did not find; Lamb, whom he did see, the serious young man thought disturbing. Talking of Wordsworth as though he were sacred, De Quincey was shocked when Lamb slyly remarked, "If we are to talk in this strain, we ought to have said grace before we began our conversation." Later, De Quincey learned to appreciate Lamb's humorous vein and to see the often profound seriousness than underlay it.

Despite his enjoyment of reading and acquaintanceship with Lamb and Wordsworth, De Quincey was unhappy. A sick young man, probably suffering from a duodenal ulcer, he was at times almost out of his mind because of acute pain. When a fellow-student recommended opium, De Quincey took a dose. "In an hour, oh! heavens! what a revulsion! what a resurrection from the lower depths, of the inner spirit! What an apocalypse of the world within me. That my pains had vanished, was now a trifle in my eyes; this negative effect was swallowed up in the immensity of those positive effects which had opened before me—in the abyss of divine enjoyment thus suddenly revealed." Not for nine years did he feel any ill effects of the drug, probably because he took small quantities and exercised a great deal. Even in times of crisis, he never took more than a doctor would have prescribed. Laudanum and opium, the commonest remedies for all kinds of pain at that time, were obtainable without druggists' prescriptions. Laudanum, the tincture of opium, was drunk by the poor almost as much as alcohol. It varied in strength. Opium, much stronger, varied in cost; the East India product sold, in the raw state, for three guineas a pound; Turkish, eight. De Quincey's relief from grinding pain, his sense of feeling well and a consequent new intellectual stimulus kept him from realizing that the ecstasies he felt at times were danger signals.

In August, 1806, he finally met Coleridge and, in December of that year, William and Dorothy Wordsworth. His shyness had kept him from meeting the Wordsworths a year earlier, for he had gone to the Lake Country and was within sight of the Wordsworths' "little white cottage" in "this loveliest of landscapes, [when] I retreated like a guilty thing, for fear I might be surprised by Wordsworth, and then returned" faint-heartedly to Oxford.

While visiting relatives in Bristol in 1806, he called on Thomas Poole at Nether Stowey, seeking Coleridge. Poole took the lad to Alfoxden where the Wordsworths had once lived and thence to Coleridge's, but Coleridge was away at Bridgewater. There, De Quincey went alone to meet him. Riding horseback down the main street, he saw a man in whose eyes was a "peculiar appearance of haze or dreaminess." This man must be Coleridge, he decided. As he introduced himself, he found Coleridge very easy to speak with; in fact, Coleridge invited the newcomer to accompany him to a large dinner party at Mr. Chubb's that evening. Then, as the two chatted, De Quincey said Coleridge swept "into a continuous stream of eloquent dissertation, certainly the most novel, the most finely illustrated, and traversing the most spacious fields of thought by transitions the most just and logical, that it was possible to conceive." That night at the dinner, Coleridge seemed tired and talked little. De Quincey, however, was so stimulated that after the dinner party, he walked for hours.

When Mrs. Coleridge and her children Hartley, Derwent, and Sara were traveling north to visit the Wordsworths, en route to Keswick, where they were to live with the Southeys, De Quincey offered to escort them, as Coleridge was away lecturing at the Royal Institution in London. When De Quincey and this party reached the Wordsworth home, De Quincey was too awed by Wordsworth to look at him. Mrs. Wordsworth, who welcomed him, made him feel at home; he noted she had a "tolerably good" figure and eyes that squinted. Dorothy impressed him tremendously. Wordsworth, he compared to a Venetian Senator or a Spanish monk. The following day he met Robert Southey, who, De Quincey believed, had "an air of reserve and distance about him—the reserve of a lofty self-respecting mind, but perhaps a little too freezing." The twenty-two-year-old student returned to Oxford, planning to make Dorothy, not William Wordsworth, his chief confidant.

Though technically a resident at Oxford University from 1804 to 1808, De Quincey moved about the country a great deal. His ill health, which often left him sleepless for nights and days, and his traveling caused him to fall behind in his studies. Then, in one instance, with thirty-three Greek tragedies to read in one week, with "collections of unassorted details" to memorize, with needed explorations into several literatures specified as required by his school, he read eighteen hours a day, sleeping on a couch only when he could stay awake no more. In the first day of tests following this strenuous period of study De Quincey did so well that one of his examiners called him "the cleverest man I ever met with." The second day, when he was to face an oral examination in Greek, at the last minute changed to Latin, De Quincey did not appear. Annoyed at the change, contemptuous of the method of examination which he considered no real test of knowledge, he left Oxford never to return as a student.

Having come into his inheritance and hearing that Coleridge was in financial trouble, he sent Mr. Cottle £300 to be given the poet anonymously. Then he went to London to study law. This decision was swept aside when he visited the Wordsworths at Allan Bank. Living with them were Sara Hutchinson and Coleridge. De Quincey's favorites among the children were Wordsworth's five-year-old Johnny and six-weeks-old Catharine; he adored, too, Thomas and little Dorothy. De Quincey won the affections of all the children. Won over, also, by the countryside, he decided to rent Wordsworth's old home, Dove Cottage, vacant since the Wordsworths had left it.

When he returned to London in February, 1809, Dorothy set about making needed repairs on the house, adding bookshelves for De Quincey's large library and the necessary furniture. The spring, summer, and fall of that year Dorothy wrote the young man of the progress in getting his new home ready, and of the Wordsworth household and their neighbors. She told him she had had mahogany bookcases made, since De Quincey preferred them; she had obtained "all the rest of the furniture of mahogony." She had also tried to help Catharine pronounce De Quincey's name; the child called it "Ah! Kinsey." Dorothy chided De Quincey for buying a new toy cart for Johnny; his old one would have done quite well. Coleridge, she said, disorganized the household by staying in bed all morning and sitting up most of the night. Financial matters, she confided, might make it necessary for William to turn to journalism.

De Quincey at this time edited for publication Wordsworth's *The Convention of Cintra*, a tract favoring nationalism. After spending a hectic summer in his mother's home in Westbay at Wrington in Somerset, which was almost uninhabitable because of the "stonemasons, carpenters, painters, plaisterers, bell-hangers etc" who were remodeling it, De Quincey was relieved, in November, 1809, to come to his new home, Dove Cottage, and to find that Dorothy had employed a maid to care for his house. He enjoyed the tranquility of the village, the view of Lake Windermere from his study window, and in the distance, the village of Grasmere, the church with its tower and, to the left Wordsworth's home, Allan Bank. Here, De Quincey read for hours; a decanter of laudanum sat nearby, but from it he drank moderate portions. He took long walks by day or by night. He enjoyed tutoring little Johnny Wordsworth.

Not until March, 1812, did he go to London. There, he met Lady Hamilton, heard her recite a scene from *Macbeth*; he thought the rumors of her illicit relations with Nelson quite unfounded. He still considered becoming a lawyer. In June, he was distraught when Dorothy wrote him of the death of three-year-old Catharine. For five months, he grieved over the child's death. Grieving, he suffered physical pain and began taking larger doses of laudanum. The next few years, he divided his time between Dove Cottage, London, and Edinburgh; his dosage of laudanum he had increased to eight thousand drops a day.

The year 1816 brought strained relations between the Wordsworths and De Quincey because of a misunderstanding. Old Mary Dawson, who cared for Dove Cottage while De Quincey was away, did not know that an agreement had been made that the Wordsworths, if they had guests, could use Dove Cottage in De Quincey's absence. Hence, she refused to allow the Wordsworths access to the house. Thirty-one-year-old De Quincey, once he returned, lonely without his close friends, sought new ones, among them William Parke, the latter's son-in-law John Sympson, Sympson's wife, Mary, and their eighteen-year-old daughter Margaret. Before long, De Quincey sought the farmhouse primarily to visit with Margaret. Then, in November, 1816, the unmarried girl bore De Quincey a son; in February, 1817, the two were belatedly married. Undoubtedly, De Quincey loved the girl, although Charles Lamb wrote Dorothy Wordsworth of De Quincey's talking "to me about her, in terms of such mild quiet whispering speculative profligacy."

Dorothy Wordsworth, usually kind and forgiving, wrote her friends the Clarksons: "Mr. De Quincey is married; and I fear I may add he is ruined. By degrees he withdrew himself from all society except that of the Sympsons of the Nab. . . . At the up-rouzing of the Bats and the Owls he regularly went thither, and the consequence was that Peggy Sympson, the eldest daughter of the house presented him with a son ten weeks ago, and they are now spending their honeymoon in our cottage at Grasmere. This is in truth a melancholy story! He uttered in raptures of the beauty, the good sense, the simplicity, the angelic sweetness of Miss Sympson, who to all other judgments appeared to be a stupid, heavy girl, and was reckoned a dunce at Grasmere School and I predict that ere this all these witcheries are removed, and the fireside already dull. They have never been seen out of doors, except after the day was gone. As for him, I am sorry for him—he is utterly changed in appearance and takes largely of opium." Wordsworth made no comments; but registered silent disapproval. Dorothy Wordsworth was unfair in her description of Margaret De Quincey, for most people found her beautiful, possessing "solid peasant virtues" and a "wistful and pathetic charm." When chided by his mother about his marriage, De Quincey replied that his wife "is all I could desire, and has in every way dignified the position in which she stands to me." This opinion, De Quincey never changed throughout his married life.

The disapproval of De Quincey's friends drove him away from people. Not wishing to expose themselves to the displeasure of their neighbors, the young couple kept within their cottage. During the cold winter, it was pleasant to be with his pretty wife in his cozy house with "Candles at four o'clock, warm hearth-rugs, tea, a fair tea-maker, shutters closed, curtains flowing in ample drapery on the floor, whilst the wind and rain are raging inaudibly without. . . ." Nearby was "a sublunary wine-decanter" with "a quart of ruby-coloured laudanum; that, and a book of German metaphysics placed by its side."

The year De Quincey met Margaret he had decreased his opium from eight thousand drops a day to one thousand. The close confinement in his cottage and his feeling the world was against him caused him to increase the dosage. Before long, he suffered horrible visions: incidents of his childhood appeared in distorted form; ladies dressed as in the days of Charles I "danced stately minuets on tapestries of darkness; beige palaces, ruins of Piranesian grandeur moved restlessly and changed their shapes only to disappear before quiet lakes" and "silvery expanses of water"; faces, innumerable faces, imploring, despairing, wrathful. His "mind tossed, as it seemed, upon the billowy ocean, and weltered upon the weltering waves." The horror of these visions was that De Quincey seemed really to *see* these things with physical eyes. Time expanded until he seemed to have lived "seventy or a hundred years in one night." Then came a period when he seemed to be "stared at, hooted at, grinned at, chattered at, by monkeys, by paroquets, by cockatoos. I ran into pagodas, and was fixed for centuries at the summit, or in secret rooms; I was the idol; I was the priest; I was worshipped; I was sacrificed." In one vision, he saw Ann, sitting under a palm, outlined against the dim background of Jerusalem. "And I said to her at length, 'So, then I have found you at last.'

I waited but she answered not a word." She seemed the same Ann, and yet not the same, for her beauty was not the unseizable beauty of long ago. Suddenly, he seemed to be back on Oxford Street eighteen years before with the Ann he once knew. Then, suddenly, there were horrible farewells and he awoke. At length, he grew afraid to sleep, sitting up whole nights. As he finally slept, again these visions appeared, more real than life. Often, he awoke to hear Margaret calling to him, "Oh, what do you see, dear? What is it you see?" Distressed by his cries of agony, she told him his cries began almost as soon as he fell asleep.

His taking over the editorship for a time of the *Westmorland Gazette* aroused him and brought him renewed friendship with Wordsworth. In 1818, De Quincey wrote vitriolic editorials against Henry Brougham, competing in the Whig cause against Colonel Lowther. An arrogant, unscrupulous man who ran roughshod over everyone, Henry Brougham used campaign tactics which were certainly questionable. The fact that Brougham was defeated won some prestige for De Quincey. When a firm in which De Quincey money was invested went bankrupt, De Quincey believed he must earn additional money, though he had not lost much. *Blackwood's Magazine* in Edinburgh had been insistent that he write for it. In December 1820, he went to Edinburgh and began to do so. He returned to Dove Cottage in the spring. By now, the De Quinceys had three children—William, Margaret, and Horace. Feeling they needed a larger house, De Quincey took Fox Ghyll at nearby Rydal. There and in London he lived for some years; in the city, he was now employed by the *London Magazine. Confessions of an Opium Eater*, appearing at this time, brought wide comment. Trying desperately to overcome the opium habit, he now took only 130 drops a day; finally, 30 drops; then 25 drops one day and none another. He suffered horribly as he tried to break the habit; yet his mind was clearer and his work better when he did.

In 1825, when Margaret was bearing their fourth child, De Quincey, whose work in London allowed him only short visits to Rydal, wrote asking Dorothy Wordsworth to visit his wife who was feeling dejected, and try to "raise and support her spirits; beg her not to lie down too much as she is prone to do in states of dejection but to walk in the fields when it is cool; and to take some *solid* food, which she is very apt to neglect." He concluded his letter, "God bless you, my dear Miss Wordsworth,—stand my friend at this moment."

Shortly after this letter was written, De Quincey's work took him to Edinburgh. Dorothy then wrote him on July 16, 1825: "I called at your cottage yesterday, having first seen your son William at the head of the schoolboys, as it might seem a leader at their noon-tide games, and Horace among the tribe—both as healthy looking as the best, and William very much grown. Mrs. de Quincey was seated by the fire above stairs with her Baby on her knee. She rose and received me cheerfully, as a person in perfect health, and does indeed seem to have had an extraordinary recovery, and as little suffering as can be expected. The Babe looks as if he would thrive, and is what we call a nice child,—neither big nor little.

"Mrs. de Quincey seemed on the whole in very good spirits; but with something of sadness in her manner, she told me you were not likely very soon to be at home." Dorothy told him how Mrs. De Quincey was disturbed at the news that his work would necessitate his being in Edinburgh so much, but stated she had explained to Mrs. De Quincey that "you could never regularly keep up your engagements at a distance from the press; and, said I 'Pray tell him so when you write.' She replied, 'Do write yourself.' Now I could not refuse to give her pleasure by so doing, especially being assured my letter would not be wholly worthless to you, having such agreeable news to send of your Family. The little cottage and everything seemed comfortable.

"I do not presume to take the liberty of advising the acceptance of this engagement, or of that—only I would venture to request you well to consider the many impediments to literary employment to be regularly carried on in limited time, at a distance from the press, in a small house, and in perfect solitude. You must well know that it is a true and faithful concern for your interests and those of your Family that prompts me to call attention to this point; and, if you think I am mistaken, you will not, I am sure, take it ill that I have thus freely expressed my opinion.

"My brother and sister do not know of my writing, otherwise they would send their remembrances." Dorothy's letter probably settled this question for De Quincey, though he did not live in Edinburgh permanently until 1830. Between 1828 and 1830, he took his two older children, eleven-year-old William and ten-year-old Margaret, to be with him, to lessen his loneliness and give him a semblance of home life. When his father-in-law suffered business reverses, De Quincey raised some money to send him and mortgaged his father-in-law's home to help him. When further funds were needed, Mr. Sympson gave up the home and came with his daughter and her children to join De Quincey in Edinburgh in 1833, though the tenancy of Dove Cottage was retained another year. Despite financial troubles, De Quincey wrote brilliant essays for the *Edinburgh Review* on subjects as diverse as Jean Paul Richter, Lessing, Lamb, Pope, Shake-speare, Herodotus, Greek Tragedy, and the "Education of Boys." In the latter essay, he advocated reforms in teaching and in school government, some of which did not come into use until well in the twentieth century. Rules, he said, should be made by students for students; a school court should be established for students trying one of their classmates; corporal punishment should be abolished. Teaching should be improved to make subjects more interesting; love for knowledge must be generated; cribs should be permitted to those studying classical texts; memorization of useless facts should cease. So well received were De Quincey's essays in *Blackwood's* that he was invited to write for *Tait's*, a Whig magazine.

The years 1833–35 were a period when De Quincey suffered many bereavements: in '33 the death of his four-year-old son, Julius; in '34, of close friends, including Blackwood; in 1835, of his brilliant eldest son, William. At this time, too, his uncle died, leaving his estate of £400 a year to De Quincey's mother, to pass at her death to her two other children, William and Jane. In notifying De Quincey of the bequest, she chided him for taking opium and thus destroying himself, for writing for *Tait's*, which she had heard was a "disreputable magazine," and for neglecting his children's education. The latter accusation, of course, was an untrue as her evaluation of *Tait's*. The untruth about De Quincey and his children, he learned later, came from Coleridge's daughter Sara, who, in a moment of anger, had written to Mrs. William Wardwell that "little Maggy manages all Papa's (De Quincey's) concerns. She and the other children are sensible and good looking but have no regular education and are brought up in a bad shifting way, allowed to sit up late, to help themselves to laudanum and so forth. 'How can you keep your eyes open, Maggy,' said a gentleman to the little girl, 'when you are kept up so late?' 'O we get an opium pill and that makes us all brisk and lively.' However, she added that this would have been displeasing to Papa, had he known of it." This whole story was untrue. The origin of the gossip probably came from the fact that when the eldest daughter Margaret was sleepless as a child, De Quincey would bring her down to his study, give her bits of sugar soaked in coffee and let her cut the leaves of a book.

The death of his wife in 1837 left him in despair. He knew hers had not been an easy life: she had watched at his bedside while he had his horrible opium dreams; she had borne eight children and had seen two of them die. She had been extremely lonely while she and her husband had had to be separated; she had been overworked caring for her children. Now De Quincey became prematurely old, at times re-living his first meetings with Coleridge, Lamb, and the Wordsworths.

With financial problems facing him, De Quincey relied on his older children, twenty-two-year-old Margaret and twenty-one-year-old Horace, to help him bring up his other children, Francis, Paul Frederic, Florence, and Emily. It was they who decided the family should move to a more restful and peaceful spot, to Mavis Bush, a small house in Lasswade, seven miles from Edinburgh. This remained his permanent home. Later, Florence assumed the upper hand in managing her father's life and that of the family. Given a small allowance for family expenses, she handled it well. The sons soon led quite independent lives, though their father corresponded with them and aided them to the best of his ability. Francis, for a time a clerk in a mercantile house, later pursued a medical education in Edinburgh and practiced in Brazil, where he died in 1861 of yellow fever. Horace, who was an officer in the 26th Cameronians, died in the China campaign of 1842; Paul Frederic, likewise in the army, served in the Sikh War and later in the Indian Mutiny; he became a military secretary to General Galloway in the Maori War and received a grant of land in New Zealand. There, he died in 1894.

Between 1840 and 1848, depressed, De Quincey again turned to opium, sometimes taking five thousand drops a day. Again, the visions, horrible or beautiful, came in abundance. Finally, believing he was losing his mind, he once more abstained from its use almost entirely and achieved a lasting peace.

His mother died in 1846 without realizing how great a man her son was. Many visitors, including Ralph Waldo Emerson, sought out the aged man, who never took care of his appearance. Always untidy, perched on the edge of a chair with a cup of tea or a small glass of laudanum in his hand, he would converse brilliantly, leaving long, dreamy pauses during which his face would be expressionless, with his eyes closed. Suddenly his eyes would open and again the "silver thread tapestry" of his talk would shine; his talk was often sheer poetry.

Most of his writing was done at night; occasionally, he stopped to get cups of tea or coffee. At daybreak, he retired and at midday awoke, and after dressing and having breakfast he took long walks. As he grew older, music was a necessity; despite the fact that the long journey to Edinburgh tired him, he went there to hear concerts. Cimarosa, Cherubini, and Mozart were his favorite composers. The violin he loved; bagpipes, he hated.

When in 1859 he began the task of revising his *Collected Works*, he found himself often weary. Overwork was at last taking its toll. Yet, in 1857, despite the fact he had had influenza several times and suffered from minor ailments, he visited his daughter, Mrs. Craig in Ireland. The last six weeks of his life, he saw only his daughter Emily, his landlady, and three friends. As death approached, he seemed to see again his wife and children. Suddenly, at daybreak on December 5, 1857, the feeble old man threw up his arms, as though surprised at a sudden meeting, and cried out, "Sister! Sister! Sister!" Then his arms fell back; his breathing stopped; Thomas De Quincey was dead.

Like De Quincey, William Wordsworth, always interested in national affairs, was troubled when, by the Convention of Cintra, England seemed to have thrown away an opportunity to free Spain and Portugal and to strike a blow at Napoleon. Deeply concerned over the struggle of the Spanish and Portuguese to deliver themselves from French oppression, "many a time," he said, "I have gone from Allan Bank to the top of Raise Gap as late as two in the morning to meet the carrier bringing the newspaper." Throughout the winter, he worked on a pamphlet to arouse his countrymen to the need of England's helping the Spanish. He finally completed several short articles on the subject for *The Courier*, and then set to work on a longer one which De Quincey edited. In 1809, the longer work on the Convention of Cintra appeared under the title *Concerning the Relations of Great Britain, Spain, and Portugal, To Each Other and to the Common Enemy, at This Crisis*, and *Specifically Affected by the Convention of Cintra; the Whole Brought To the Test of Those Principles By Which Alone Independence and Freedom of Nations Can Be Preserved or Recovered*. The conquests of Napoleon in Germany, the Low Countries, and Italy, Wordsworth contended, were against governments; those in Spain and Portugal, against the people and therefore against freedom. All England was happy when the British sent an army under Sir Arthur Wellesley to oppose the French in Portugal. In August 1808, he defeated Junot, but when Sir Arthur Wellesley was superceded by Sir Hew Dalrymple and Sir Harry Burrard, a convention or military treaty was signed at Cintra whereby the French army was allowed to return with all its booty; thus England, Wordsworth said, lost a chance both to free Spain and Portugal and to cripple Napoleon. The news was received in England with indignation. Now,

Wordsworth said, Napoleon could be defeated only by arousing the dormant national spirit of the subject nations under his domination. *The Convention*, signed by Dalrymple and Burrard, in which Junot and his army were allowed to go free with all their booty, Wordsworth stated was a heavy blow to the popular movements in Portugal and Spain. Nationalism, he insisted, was important, for it is the true sign of the general will of a society; it springs from the simple feelings that fill the breasts of all men. The chief function of politics should be that of giving man the opportunity for this part of his nature to develop. The nation made by men, is somehow exalted and better than its makers, he contended. The Spanish patriot not only has a country to love but one to save from foreign tyranny. A crusader, he lives in no ordinary time, "for these are times of strong appeal—of deep-searching visitation." That which today is Spain's strength, Wordsworth asserted, is the potential strength of all nations; moreover, patriotism, though purest and best in times of stress, can exist also in times of peace. Germany and Italy, he believed, should unite, for the good of Europe, their scattered fragments into a true state. It was national honor that drove England to oppose the aggressions of France, national honor that drove Spain and Portugal to resist the attacks on their independence. If the honor among all nations were raised high enough, all nations could live in peace and with true understanding. As the ethical principles of a people control their governments' actions, satisfactory international relations will be brought about, he concluded. "In the last thirty years, we have seen two wars waged against Liberty—the American war and the war against the French people in the early stages of their Revolution." Then showing his distrust of industrialism, he said that in Spain "manufacturers and commerce have there in far less degree than elsewhere, by unnaturally clustering the people together, enfeebled their bodies, inflamed their passions by intemperance, vitiated from childhood their moral affections, and destroyed their imaginations. . . . The paradoxical reveries of Rousseau and the flippancies of Voltaire are plants which will not naturalize in the country of Calderon and Cervantes." Believing in the essential goodness of mankind, "the dignity and intensity of human desires" to uplift mankind, Wordsworth reiterated, he looked forward to the future with hope; in fact, he said, "There is a spiritual community binding together the living and the dead; the good, the brave, the wise of all ages. . . . We would not be rejected from this community: and therefore we do hope." Wordsworth emerged from the Napoleonic wars with the conviction that men could not be freed at a stroke without preparation and that too great haste in bestowing a nominal freedom upon the uneducated and unready would lead to one form or another of despotism.

Shortly before this, he had written a letter giving advice to a friend about the education of his gifted daughter. Wordsworth advised that this talented child not be too much noticed and praised; he urged that she acquire knowledge without measure, knowledge interesting for its own sake, knowledge that would "lead her out of herself."

Meanwhile, Coleridge's behavior concerned the Wordsworths greatly. William told Thomas Poole Coleridge "has no voluntary power of mind whatsoever, nor is he capable of acting under ordinary constraint of duty or moral obligation." The Wordsworths had tried to make Coleridge forget his troubles by undertaking something of value; they realized, however, that they were fighting a losing battle. Coleridge tried to help, it is true, by reducing to one sixth his dosage of opium. As a result, his general health was better. "This change," he said, "was due to the blessed effect upon my spirits of having no secret to brood over"; he resolved "henceforth never to conceal anything from those who have loved me and lived with me." Dorothy wrote that he was "well and in good spirits, writing letters to all his friends and acquaintances, dispatching prospectuses and fully prepared to begin his work." Yet, she was fearful for him, "seeing him so often obliged to lie in bed more than half the day—often so poorly as to be utterly unable to do anything whatever. Today, though he came down to dinner at three perfectly well, he did not rise till near two o'clock, but however ill he may have been in the mornings he seldom fails to be cheerful and comfortable at night." Two months passed and no copy for *The Friend*, a magazine Coleridge had decided to publish, was written. When the Kendall firm that was to print it went out of business, Coleridge went to Penrith to make arrangements with a printer there. Dorothy was fearful of what would happen to him away from William and herself. The first copy of *The Friend* was to appear April 1; yet April and May passed with no publication nor any word from Coleridge, to whom the Wordsworths wrote repeatedly. Finally, on June 1, the first issue made its appearance and on June 8, the second. Later the Wordsworths learned Coleridge had stayed briefly at Penrith; then, realizing he needed help, had gone to visit the Quaker, Thomas Wilkinson, whose quiet home Coleridge enjoyed. There he had done no drinking and had been happy as well as productive. On June 14, Coleridge was back at Grasmere, where he surprised everyone by being up at six A.M. and asking

Dorothy if he could be of any help. The fourth issue of *The Friend* came out on August 5, on schedule. Coleridge, working by fits and starts, dictated every word of the magazine to Sara Hutchinson. Sometimes, he dictated a whole issue in two days; then nothing for days. In December, he wrote not only *The Friend* but also a series of essays on Spain for *The Courier*. The first of the year he began to flag. On February 28, Dorothy wrote Lady Beaumont his spirits had been "irregular." Discouraged at the slow arrival of payments for *The Friend*, he was half persuaded not to continue it. He became increasingly lethargic, so that no entreaties could arouse him. In March, Sara, worn out, trying to drive him on, left for a visit with her brother. Now again Coleridge was in bed half the day. He never worked out-of-doors; he joined the family only at tea, sometimes at supper, always "impatient to get back to his solitude. He went the minute he swallowed his food. Sometimes he did not speak a word. . . . The boys come every week and he talks to them, especially Hartley, but he never examines them in their books," Dorothy wrote. "He speaks of *The Friend*, always as if it were going on. . . . Do not think it is his love for Sara which has stopped him in his work. Do not believe it. His love for her is no more than a fanciful dream. Otherwise he would prove it by a desire to make her happy. No! he likes to have her about him as his own, as one devoted to him, but when she stood in the way of other gratifications it was all over," Dorothy told her friend, Mrs. Clarkson.

In May, 1810, he went to Keswick for ten days, but stayed five months. Mrs. Coleridge reported him to be in better health, spirits and humor than she had found him in years. He could face with ease Mrs. Coleridge for whom he had no love, but felt his friends whom he loved were a constant reproach when he failed. At the end of October, he went to London with the Montagus, passed through Grasmere and spent the night at Allan Bank; Dorothy was not there, but in London. Before Montagu and Coleridge left the Wordsworths' home, William had told Montagu of Coleridge's addiction to opium, a fact which sometimes made him difficult to understand. Ten years passed before Dorothy saw Coleridge again. These years, she said, were the saddest in her life. Not until May 11, 1811, did the Wordsworths know why no one at Grasmere or Keswick heard from him. At that time, Robert Southey had met Coleridge, who explained his silence and absence. It seems that Coleridge told his brother-in-law that when he and Montagu reached London, Montagu had said Wordsworth had authorized him to say that Coleridge was a perfect nuisance and that William had given up all hope for him. Hardly believing his ears, Coleridge had left Montagu's home at once, had disconsolately walked London's streets until he was exhausted. Then, he had gone to the home of his friends, the Morgans, in Portland Place, Hammersmith. That night, he dreamed Wordsworth had come to give him away like a piece of useless lumber. Without doubting or even questioning Montagu's veracity, he accepted his statement as literally true. "Wordsworth saw no hope for you. You are a perfect nuisance," he kept repeating, at times trying to justify himself, again denying the accusation. The more he thought of Wordsworth's so-called words, the more he exaggerated them. If Wordsworth saw no hope for him, who would?

The Morgans, deeply sympathizing with him, finally brought him back to a realization that he had to face the world and be at his best. John Morgan, a not too successful lawyer, and his sisters Mary and Charlotte Brent encouraged him so greatly that he thought their home a veritable paradise. At times, he felt himself not worthy of the happiness and would leave and go secretly into other lodgings. But always John Morgan sought him out and led him back. In August 1810, Charles Lamb saw him while he was staying briefly at Brown's Coffee House. "Coleridge has powdered his hair, and looks like Bacchus, ever sleek and young," Lamb wrote Dorothy. "He is going to turn sober, but his clock has not struck yet; meantime, he pours down goblet after goblet."

Lamb did not know that Coleridge was considering placing himself under a doctor's care that he might be cured of the opium habit, though he dreaded the ordeal. The death of George Burnett, a friend whom Coleridge had seen walking in Lincoln's Inn Fields, with stupidly wild eyes, caused by addiction to opium provided an awful warning. When Mary Lamb became unbalanced because of Burnett's death, here was another warning of what one's excesses could do to one's friends. Coleridge realized how lucky he was that the Morgans cared so tenderly for him; they knew he was unfitted to be in lodgings alone. Determined on his rehabilitation, he approached Daniel Stuart about procuring a position on the staff of *The Courier* with regular hours. He worked steadily there from April until September, leaving the Morgan home at Hammersmith at seven-twenty each morning, reaching *The Courier* office at eight-thirty and, to save nine shillings coach fare a week, walking home each evening. His articles were mostly on foreign affairs. When Dorothy Wordsworth heard of his writing the articles, she regretted "the waste and prostitution of his fine genius, at the sullying and perverting of what is lovely and tender in human sympathies, and noble and generous." In December, he gave a series of lectures before the London Philosophical Society. About a hundred and fifty attended the lectures, which proved financially rewarding; money was a necessity, as there was a small debt lingering from printing *The Friend*. Katherine Byerly Thompson said Coleridge's "locks were . . . trimmed, and a conscious importance gleamed in his eloquent eyes"; as he began "He was *so eloquent*—there was such a combination of wit and poetry in his similies—such fancy, such a finish to his illustrations; yet, as we walked home, I recall we could not call to mind any real instruction, distinct impression, or new fact imparted us by the great theorist." Henry Crabb Robinson called the lectures "brilliant."

After these lectures, he went to Liverpool to arrange for some further ones that did not develop, and then went to Ambleside to pick up Hartley and Derwent from their school. "Derwent," he said later, "is the self-same, fond Samuel Taylor Coleridge as ever. He inherited his father's tenderness of bowels and stomach, and consequent capriciousness of animal spirits. He complained that Dr. Dawes, his schoolmaster, scolded him because he was not such a genius as Hartley. 'A gentleman who took a third in the chaise from Ambleside . . . said . . . that the two boys would make a perfect representation of myself.'"

Still angered at the Wordsworths, he took the children, not as usual to the Wordsworths', but to their mother's home in Keswick. There, he was delighted at his ten-year-old daughter Sara's educational progress. She was reading French fairly well, Italian fluently and English with genuine feeling and comprehension. He told how when, in reading a passage that included the word "hostile," he asked her the meaning of the word. "Why! inimical," she replied, "only that 'inimical' is more often used for things and measures, and not as 'hostile' is, to person and things." Coleridge wrote that she was "a sweet tempered, meek, blue-eyed fairy and so affectionate, trustworthy, and really serviceable."

Taking his sons back to Ambleside, in a chaise—this was in January 1812—he had passed through Grasmere without stopping to see the Wordsworths. Mrs. Coleridge wrote Thomas Poole how "poor Hartley sat in speechless astonishment as the chaise passed the turning point to the Vicarage, where W. lives, but he dared not hazard one remark—and Derwent fixed his eyes full of tears upon his father who turned away to hide his emotions . . . H . . . turned white as lime, when I told him Mr. W. had a little vexed his father by something he said to Mr. Montagu . . . these children in the habit of going weekly to Grasmere could not comprehend how things were . . . he would not go to *them* and they could not come to him. . . ."

On his return to London, Coleridge wrote to Morgan: "I have had four letters in 3 days about my not having called on Wordsworth . . . and this morning a most impassioned one from Mrs. Clarkson—Good God! how could I? how can I? I have no resentment unless grief and anguish be resentment . . . but unless I meet them as of yore what use is there in it? . . . A nuisance and then a deliberate Liar!"

Dorothy Wordsworth, in the meantime, still puzzled about Coleridge's not writing her or William, wrote Mrs. Coleridge several times while he was in Keswick asking her to have Coleridge write her. A business letter she had written him earlier in London had never been answered; it lay unopened on Coleridge's desk. Whether Mrs. Coleridge delivered Dorothy's messages we do not know. She did say, in a malicious vein, that her husband had been taught "a very useful lesson—that even his dearest and most intelligent friends, even those persons who have been the great means of his self-indulgence, when it comes to live wholly with them, are as clear-sighted to his failings and much less delicate in speaking of them than his wife." She probably knew that Coleridge's good friend Josiah Wedgwood, who with his brother Timothy had given Coleridge his annuity, was so concerned with the poet's addiction to opium that he had said, "I fear Col. is a lost man. . . . I see the wreck of genius with tender concern, but without hope."

The Coleridge boys, at school at Ambleside, continued to spend their week-ends and holidays with the Wordsworths. Except for the brief two weeks with their father they, like the Wordsworths, heard not a word from him. "It would pity anyone's heart to look at Hartley when he enquires (as if hopelessly) if there is any news of his father," Dorothy wrote Mrs. Clarkson. She said that, concerned about Coleridge, she "had spent an anxious winter."

The Wordsworths had always been devoted to the Coleridge children. They, like Coleridge, had sensed when Hartley was a little boy that he was half-jealous of his brother Berkeley for a short time after Berkeley's birth, for the new baby was receiving the admiration usually accorded him as an only child. During one of Coleridge's illnesses, Hartley, "a dreamy little boy," had spent some time with the Wordsworths. Now that Berkeley did not command so much attention, he was full of chatter and admiration for his little brother and "Wilsey" as he called the Coleridge housekeeper; an imaginative child, he had many quaint fancies which he shared with the Wordsworths. Coleridge had told them how he had held a mirror so that a view about Keswick was reflected in it; he had been interested in watching Hartley try to distinguish between the view and the image. Dorothy, observing how Coleridge treated his son as an adult, had observed little Hartley sitting near the men with the quaint air of a little man. When Coleridge and his wife separated and the boys, now older, were given to the custody of their father, they spent their weekends and holidays away from their school at Ambleside with the Wordsworths. Dorothy loved having them. Their "cries, caresses, and needs" caused the days to flee. Hartley loved being with the Wordsworths, for on arriving he'd skip "around the room with great joy." After the Wordsworths decided to take their children to Sunday school, the Coleridge boys went also. In the two years the Wordsworths and Coleridge's family did not hear from the poet, Dorothy was apprehensive about the way young Hartley seemed to suffer because of the absence of his father. Dorothy and William gave more time to his sons and were now planning their college education. Dorothy was greatly concerned one day when, as it was time for the boys to walk back to their school at Ambleside, suddenly the sky became black; thunder roared and lightning flashed, "a beautiful and terrible" sight. Then suddenly, the blackness lifted, vivid sunbeams emerged, and a perfect rainbow appeared. As the storm subsided and all seemed calm, Dorothy permitted the boys to leave for their school. A short time later, a drenching rain poured down, causing Dorothy to worry about the children who not yet had reached their school.

While the Wordsworths were at the parsonage, that was smaller than Allan Bank, the Coleridge boys came only for the day. Always Hartley asked if there was any news of his father, only to be met with a negative answer. When Coleridge finally did return to Keswick, the boys were there for a visit with their mother. Mrs. Coleridge said that on seeing his father briefly Hartley had turned pale, trembled all over and at first had been unable to speak. Then, he had asked some questions about the connections between Latin and Greek; Derwent, on the other hand, had come up dancing with joy. At sixteen, Hartley, though smaller than his father, resembled him in manner, but his voice was deeper. His mother, who found it as difficult to understand him as she had his father, said he always did the wrong thing at the wrong time. On the other hand, Derwent, a chubby boy, was an extreme extrovert. An affectionate little boy, he had come many times a day to tell Dorothy his stories or to sing her a song. He still loved to eat, to play, and to talk.

The Wordsworths now saw less of little Sara, named for her mother. She was a beautiful child, though at times a little vixen. At her birth, Coleridge, who had never dreamed of having a daughter, called her "Coleridgella." Fair-skinned and delicate, almost too delicate, beautiful little Sara was a contrast to little Dorothy Wordsworth, also beautiful but wild and reckless. When little Sara had visited the Wordsworths, she had stood amazed as she saw little Dorothy, in her kittenish way, begin to skirmish with Coleridge. She had been jealous of little Dorothy, and when asked by Coleridge if she did not think little Dorothy had grown pretty, vehemently had shouted "No." When the Coleridges separated, she had been given to the custody of her mother, but the stipulation had been made that she would visit her father at stated intervals. Coleridge had maintained she was better away from her mother. On her visits with him at the Wordsworths', he had taken her in his arms and told her fairy tales which she repeated to the others. Though she had enjoyed her father briefly, she had longed for her mother. Her mother always had postponed as long as she could the evil day when her little Sara "who has nothing about her of the natural wildness of a child," had to pay these periodic visits to the Wordsworths for, said Dorothy, she dreaded "the contamination which her ladylike manners must receive from our rustic brood more than she would dread illness. I may almost say *death*."

When gossips in London literary circles heard of the trouble between Wordsworth and Coleridge, talk buzzed. Finally, in April, 1812, William, exasperated about the matter, decided to go to London and confront Coleridge and Montagu with the whole business. Mrs. Clarkson had written him there "has been downright lying somewhere, not mere misrepresentations and dressing up of facts but inventions against you." Wordsworth first asked Lamb to be an intermediary; but Lamb offended Coleridge who remained silent. Finally Crabb Robinson interceded. He told Coleridge that Wordsworth had never told Montagu that Coleridge was a nuisance and that he had not commissioned Montagu to say anything to Coleridge. He said he had tried only to prevent Coleridge's living with Montagu and that in this he probably had done wrong. He refused to break off relations with Montagu, regardless of what he thought of him. Crabb Robinson praised Wordsworth's "integrity, his purity, his delicacy" in handling the matter. Their friendship was resumed, but there was a difference; they never again had the same intimate feeling; yet Coleridge wrote of coming to visit the Wordsworths as soon as his play was produced if it was successful. The play was successful, but Coleridge did not come for the visit.

In April, Dorothy wrote Mrs. Clarkson that Coleridge "little knows with what tenderness we have thought of him, nor how softened we are to all sense of injury. We have no thought of him but such as ought to have made him lean upon us with confidential love, and fear not to confess his weakness." They showed their regard by doing all they could for the Coleridge children. "The boys," Dorothy wrote her close friend, "come to us almost every week . . . William will now be able to assist in sending Hartley to college; but of course this must not be mentioned. The best thing that can happen to his father will be that he should suppose that the whole care of putting Hartley forward will fall upon himself." William attended the second series of Coleridge's lectures. Though well received, they were not remunerative.

Then Coleridge suffered a real blow when Josiah Wedgwood wrote requesting permission to withdraw his half of the annuity. Tom Wedgwood had died in 1805 and his half had been made secure by his will. But Josiah had lost some £121,000 and probably this business loss was the real cause for his asking to be relieved of his paying his part of the annuity. Some people thought, however, he had been distressed that Coleridge had not written the biography of his brother Tom, which he had requested.

Josiah and Tom Wedgwood were the sons of the first Josiah Wedgwood, a pottery maker who had been born in 1730 at Burslem, Staffordshire. The first Josiah, like his father, had been a potter, as had his forefathers before him. One of thirteen children, he was a mere "toddler" when he was sent to a dame's school to learn his ABC's; he was sent more to keep him out of the way of the older children and to keep him out of mischief than for any learning. Hardly any children in Burslem learned more than to read and write until 1750 when the free school was established there to teach young people to read the Bible, "write a fair hand and know the primary rules of arithmetic."

At seven, he went across the moors to Mr. Blunt's school, which he left when he was nine and his father died. For the most part, the rest of his education was self-taught. His father's estate was not large; he was left but £20 to be received on coming of age. He immediately went to work in his brother Thomas's factory, where he early displayed a talent for modeling, imitating in clay many objects, among them a mountebank's stage, the doctor, and his suite; he drew elaborate designs on paper, too. Tom was making molded glassware; but he did not achieve distinction in its manufacture until Josiah began designing pieces for the tea table and dessert service; he modeled some in the shape of leaves, shells, and pineapples. Josiah was likewise successful in the manufacture of jasper models. When he was fourteen, he almost died from smallpox; even after his partial recovery, he suffered acute pains in his right knee, which, for a time, left him unable to walk except on crutches; he was lame for many years.

At fourteen, Josiah was bound to his brother for five years as an apprentice by the ceremony of indenture. According to the terms, he was to "learn the Art, Mystery, Occupation or Imployment of Throwing and Handling, which he, the said Thomas Wedgwood, now useth, and with him as an Apprentice, to Dwell, Continue, and Serve" until the expiration of the term agreed on. He was to be given his meat, drink, washing, and lodging, with suitable apparel "of all kinds, both linen and woollen, and all other necessaries, both in sickness and in health," in return for which his master was to teach him "the art of throwing and handling." Nothing was said about the payment of any wages. The thrower was the person who sat near the potter's wheel and formed by hand, from the moist clay, as it revolved, "the crock, the butter-pot, the porringer," or other objects. A workman weighed a portion of clay and handed it to the thrower, seated before a revolving disk; another boy turned the wheel to cause the disk to turn horizontally. Before the thrower were patterns of or guides to the object he was to execute. Other workmen finished the product: one formed the handles and attached them when still moist to the cup or porringer; another decorated the ware with various colors.

Despite the fact that his leg still pained him greatly and that he could work only with it extended before him on a stool, Josiah Wedgwood continued with his experiments. He created an ornamental teapot, made from the ochreous clay of the district; he designed and produced plates, knife-shafts, and snuff boxes in imitation of agate, marble, tortoise-shell, and porphyry; he studied the chemical and mechanical parts of the potter's art, extended and developed their classification. When, in 1749, his apprenticeship with his brother ended, his brother, impatient with his experiments, refused to have him as a partner. On arriving at maturity, he received his father's small legacy of £20 and went into partnership with John Harrison of Cliff Bank Pottery, near Stoke-upon-Trent. This partnership lasted five years; he then went into partnership with Mr. Whieldon of Fenton Hall, near Stoke. Here, free to experiment, he designed dessert plates in the form of leaves, beautifully ornamented, and snuff boxes mounted on metal. These, jewelers purchased in large quantities. He experimented with various colored glazes, attempted to make red china, worked for "a cutting color to trace flowers *etc* upon plain biscuit-ware and to bear a lead gloss over it." After five years, his partnership with Whieldon was dissolved and he set up his own pottery workshop at Burslem. While continuing his experiments, he read widely in arithmetic, geography, literature, and chemistry. Now he first introduced his white medallions; he began to decorate his glass and pottery with flowers and foliage, gold or colored. He prided himself on producing unusual tea services. He trained his workmen in new methods. His great ambition was to rival the works of the Etruscans and to raise the Staffordshire potter's art far above the current standard of excellence. He studied and worked to produce fine earthenware with a beautiful finish; he created a cream ware. As the materials used in his pottery came from many far-flung districts of England, he saw to it, though more than once Parliamentary action was necessary, that roads were improved and canals built so that he could receive his materials more easily and market his wares more efficiently. As his fame grew and the demand for his product increased, he opened offices in London, Liverpool, Europe, and America.

At thirty-four, a prosperous young man, he married Sarah Wedgwood, distantly related, a young woman who was both handsome and accomplished. To them were born three sons and five daughters; the oldest daughter, Susannah, became the mother of Charles Darwin, author of *Origin of the Species*. Of the sons, the most distinguished were the second Josiah, and Thomas.

Eager to improve his glassware and pottery, Josiah Wedgwood introduced the black ware, the jasper, the cane-ware; he made innumerable chemical experiments. After Queen Charlotte of England ordered a "cream service," she was so pleased with it that she asked that similar services Wedgwood produced should be called "Queen's Ware." Under this royal patronage, the ware became extremely popular and was soon copied by other potters. King George III then ordered a service for himself of the same material—to be decorated differently, however. This design became known as "The Royal Pattern." Encouraged by this recognition, Wedgwood opened a warehouse in London to exhibit Queen's Ware, Etruscan vases, and other fine pieces of his famous manufacture. Later, he opened elegant shops to display it, shops usually as crowded as the Royal Academy. In 1766, he produced unglazed black porcelain to which he gave the name basaltes, "from its possessing the properties of that stone, a variegated terra-cotta, a white wax-like porcelain and other inventions adapted to different purpose." Knowing that the Etruscans had painted their vases with durable colors, burned in by fire, Wedgwood, by continued experimentation and skill, revived this lost art. The colors he produced were considered as beautiful as those in the original vases he copied; his colors, he discovered, could be of greater variety. His order from Catherine, Empress of Russia, for a set of 952 pieces of Queen's Ware, to have, on each piece, in black enamel, a different view of a palace or seat of the nobility or other notable place in Great Britain, took eight years to complete. Three years were spent making the designs for each piece. The Empress paid £3000 for the set, but the amount hardly paid the expenses involved in its production. Its exhibition, when completed, in one of Wedgwood's London shops, was an excellent advertisement, not only in England but throughout Europe. Eagerly, he sought for and obtained sculptors and painters to work for him. One, John Bacon, had received from Sir Johsua Reynolds the first gold medal in sculpture given by the Royal Academy. For Wedgwood, he designed a statue of Mars and one of Apollo and Daphne; he also designed vases and candelabra. Other artists who assisted him included James Watt, who modeled gems and cameos; David Power, a flower painter of distinction; and Wedgwood's finest sculptor of all, John Flaxman, who did, among others, a bust of Sarah Siddons, a cameo of Benjamin Franklin, and a set of chessmen, the first executed in modern times of pottery. Flaxman, too, had exhibited at the Royal Academy.

As Wedgwood's business grew, he purchased an estate, calling it Etruria, thus showing his love for the Etruscans and their craftsmanship. On the estate, which he landscaped beautifully, he constructed a factory, a school and houses for workmen and their families. It lay near the Grand Trunk Canal, thus making transportation easy. In the midst of building Etruria, Wedgwood decided that his leg, which had caused continual pain night and day for many years, should be amputated. Had doctors known more of conservative surgery at that time, his leg might have been saved. As it was, the only way Wedgwood's surgeons knew to relieve the young man from the constant pain that at times hindered his peace of mind, interfered with "tired nature's sweet restorer, 'balmy sleep,'" and at times prevented his attending to his business or even his correspondence, was by amputation. There were no anesthetics in those days; in fact, Wedgwood watched the operation, which a friend also present called "an execution." He was ill for some time after, but within a month he was dressing the wound himself and walking with crutches. Before long, a wooden leg arrived for him to wear; but he was so active that he required a whole succession of wooden legs.

Once Etruria was completed he acquired a partner, Thomas Bentley, a successful businessman and linguist who had traveled widely on the continent. The two set up more elaborate showrooms in London on Pall Mall, as elegantly clad ladies and gentlemen wishing to examine and purchase his wares in his other shops had sometimes to wait outside, so crowded were his places of business. Continually experimenting since his illness, he strove now to introduce the highest art in the production of earthenware. Wherever he heard suitable clay was to be found, he sent emissaries to secure it. He even sent travelers to Charleston, South Carolina and to Pensacola, Florida to procure tons of pure white earth or clay. He backed inventors James Watt and Matthew Boulton, and installed one of their first industrial steam engines; he invented a pyrometer for measuring extremely high temperatures, an accomplishment that won his admission into the Royal Society.

When Sir William Hamilton, Ambassador at Naples, published his book on Etruscan Art, Wedgwood found models for his patterns of Etruscan vases. He had previously experimented successfully until he could produce colors and glazes like those of the Etruscans. Now, he took out a patent on this process, the only one he ever registered. Next, he began producing cameos of jasper paste, a chalk white substance capable of receiving colors through its whole substance. In 1784, Flaxman wrote Wedgwood of Sir William Hamilton's vase, "made of dark blue glass with white enamel figures. The vase is about a foot high and the figures between five and six inches, engraved in the same manner as a cameo, and of the grandest and most perfect Greek sculpture." This, Wedgwood studied and duplicated; he then began making gems and cameos for rings, bracelets, and tablets. "The whole assemblage," he wrote a friend, "of white, blue, gold, and black have a striking effect. . . . They are really a most liberal and notable collection of objects, very rare and most difficult to come at. The white Muses seem to me even finer things than those with colored grounds." That same year, he began to make china and porcelain.

When Ireland imposed high taxes on manufactures imported from England, whereas England imposed no duty on manufactures imported from Ireland, Wedgwood was one of the leaders in the movement in 1785 to establish a Chamber of Commerce to protect the interests of British manufacturers. The Chamber of Commerce petitioned Parliament for free interchange on equal terms. Having succeeded in this effort, the Chamber of Commerce extended its interests. When Wedgwood heard that the celebrated Barberini or Portland Vase, the finest work by the ancient Greeks, a vase in which the ashes of the Roman Emperor Alexander Severus and his mother were deposited about 50 A.D., was to be sold, he determined to possess it. When it was put up for sale, Wedgwood bid £1000 for it; the Duke of Portland overbid him and then before the bidding resumed asked Wedgwood what his desire was in endeavoring to possess this vase. "I wish only to copy it," came the prompt reply. "Then if you, the only one now bidding against me, will give over bidding, I will let you have the vase as long as you like, that you may accomplish your object," the Duke answered. Wedgwood agreed; the Duke paid £1028 for the vase and Wedgwood took it with him to Etruria to copy. The vase of deep blue glass, he concluded as he studied it, had been coated over in part, while red-hot, with a semitransparent enamel, and the figures of Leda with the swan, Cupid with a bow, and a man, said to be Paris, formed by cutting through the coating to the blue ground in the manner of real cameos; the effects of light and shade had been achieved by cutting the parts to various thicknesses.

After twelve months, the imitation vase was completed; the presidents of the Royal Society, of the Society of Antiquarians, and of the Royal Academy of Arts declared it "a faithful imitation both in regard to the general effect and the most minute detail of the parts." Wedgwood made fifty copies of the vase, each of which sold for 50 guineas. A hundred years later, they sold for 205 guineas. In 1964, one of Wedgwood's copies of the Portland vase sold for $8,600. In 1845 a lunatic came into the British Museum where the Portland vase stood and smashed it into many pieces. It was restored and today, along with one of Wedgwood's copies, rests in the Museum in the medal room. To perfect jasper ware, he made more than 10,000 experiments in his kilns; in cauk, a form of barium sulphate, he found just what he wanted. Though the white classical relief on blue jasper was his most popular product, he also produced jasper in unfading colors of green, lavender, yellow, and maroon.

Among Josiah's friends were Sir Joshua Reynolds, who painted his portrait and that of Mrs. Wedgwood, William Wilberforce, and Benjamin Franklin. To the latter, Wedgwood once sent a medallion his firm had made showing a chained negro pleading, "Am I not a man and brother?" He and Thomas Clarkson were active in efforts to abolish the slave trade; Clarkson had spent £1500 in his efforts and Wedgwood gave considerable money and time to the cause. When he knew the people of Poland were oppressed, he and his sons sent substantial sums to aid them. He assisted the French émigrés who flooded England after the outbreak of the French Revolution; he supported the American Revolution; he started a Free Public Library and a sick fund for the benefit of his workers. He urged and worked for Parliamentary reform. He died in his sixty-fifth year and was buried at the old Parish Church of Stoke.

Wedgwood's large fortune was left to his family, to which he was devoted. He had taken his sons John (born in 1766), Josiah (born in 1769), Thomas (born in 1771), and his nephew Byerly into partnership with him in 1790; the latter was to have an eighth share of the profits. He had sent John and Tom to the University of Edinburgh. John had there been introduced to Dr. Joseph Black, lecturer on chemistry and the discovery of latent heat which helped Dr. Watt in his development of the steam engine. John had then gone to France to perfect himself in the French language. Young Josiah, who likewise went to the University of Edinburgh later, and Tom were sent to Geneva for further instruction; the three boys went to Rome and to Naples at their father's request to study ancient Greek sculpture and to see Sir William Hamilton's collections of antiquities. The youthful Josiah toured Wales and England with an excellent mineralogist. Finding his father's business not to his taste, young John retired to become a partner in the London and Middlesex Bank.

Tom Wedgwood, after a few terms in the University of Edinburgh, worked energetically a number of years in the potteries, but his bad health compelled him to retire and to lead a wandering life in France, Wales, Switzerland, and the West Indies in the vain search of cure. Like his father, however, he was an experimenter, though his chief interest was in photography. It was he who first made practical use of the well-known fact that nitrate and chloride of silver are affected by light under certain conditions by showing that a copy or silhouette of any object could be obtained when its shadow was thrown on a piece of white paper or leather which had been sensitized by being moistened with nitrate of silver. He wished to "obtain photographs in a camera obscura" but his efforts were unsuccessful, for he failed "to discover any method of fixing his picture, and the copies made had to be kept in the dark." To him goes the credit for first conceiving and publishing a statement of "utilizing the chemical action of light for the purposes of making pictures either by contact or in the camera and of taking the first steps necessary toward the realization of this project." At twenty, he read before The Royal Society two papers on "The Production of Light from different Bodies by Attrition," the result of his research embodying "the earliest suggestion of the general law since established, that all bodies become red hot at the same temperature."

Josiah, in the meantime, was busy with the various commercial and manufacturing concerns of the business his father had set up. Byerly, who for a time managed the London business, also took an active interest in the commercial part of the concern at Etruria. Josiah, in 1792, had married Elizabeth Allen, who bore him eight children. The two brothers, Tom and Josiah, were extremely devoted to one another and "Bessy" Allen Wedgwood shared her husband's fondness for her brother-in-law. The two young men, however, were quite unlike one another. True, Josiah, as high-minded and upright as his brother, was a man whom everyone trusted. He, too, had intellectual tastes but they were secondary to his business. That his judgment was excellent is borne out by the fact that when his nephew Charles Darwin, at twenty-one, wished to go as a naturalist on the *Beagle*, his father, Dr. Robert Darwin, strongly opposed the idea. When the young man appealed to his "Uncle Jos" to aid him, Josiah, having inquired into the young man's reasons for going on the expedition, agreed with young Charles that he should go, and so convinced the boy's father that he gave his permission. Thus Charles Darwin became a naturalist rather than a preacher as his father had hoped. Young Darwin said of Josiah, "I greatly revered him; he was silent and reserved so as to be rather an awful man; but he sometimes talked openly with the clearest judgment. I do not believe any power on earth could swerve him from what he considered the right course."

As Tom never married, he spent much time at the homes of John and of Josiah. Indeed, Josiah's was almost his home; in it, a room had been soundproofed for Tom. Deeply sympathetic with Tom's physical suffering, Josiah, Coleridge, and Tom Poole did everything in their power to cheer him up. Tom writes of finding in Josiah's home a "love more than mortal, which cannot flourish in this chilling world, and must survive it. Your deep affection, and Sally's angelic kindness, give a certain value to life in its trying moments." Bessy writes Tom that she feels "toward you as sister in full, with all rights and privileges, and, also, with a claim on you for duties and attentions as such. After ten years intimacy, I am less inclined than ever to love you by halves. You must not judge always of my feeling to you by halves." Josiah's absorbing attachment to Tom might have made some wives jealous. Assuring her husband she was not, Bessy wrote "there are no sacrifices I would not make to be of any use to him compatible with my other duties."

At times, Tom must have been troublesome, as he made Bess's and Josiah's children's nursery a field of study for working out his philosophical and educational theories. If little Bess misbehaved or little Joe was disobedient to his governess, Tom would note the incident as illustrating some type of child training and propose a plan, based on the theories of Locke, Hartley, or Rousseau, for correcting the child's "evil tendencies." Always eager to improve the world, he worked to spread the knowledge of inoculation as a preventive of smallpox; after corresponding with scientists engaged in this same effort, he had a thousand copies printed of an address to parents on this subject to be distributed to workers in the Wedgwood potteries.

A young radical, Thomas Wedgwood in 1792 was one of the first out of England to make a flying visit to Paris to be present at the great "Federation" fête to be held on July 14 to celebrate the fall of the Bastille. In 1793, he met William Godwin, among the "friends of liberty," and became so fond of him that at one time the two, Mary Shelley later said, "contemplated making a common household together." Interested in improving the education of "the labouring poor" in his neighborhood, he commissioned a Quaker bookseller to send him a supply of books fit for popular reading. A severe judge of books, he found none of the novels sent him good, as "few of them are true pictures of life. The best of them fill the mind with dreams of imaginary happiness not to be enjoyed in this life."

Through Thomas Poole, he met and became a close friend of Coleridge and William and Dorothy Wordsworth. He introduced Josiah to the group. When, in 1797, the brothers heard that Coleridge was considering accepting the position of minister at the Unitarian Chapel at Shrewsbury at a salary of £150 a year, they were distressed for they felt Coleridge's gift of writing would be hampered by his responsibilities as a minister and they believed he had a very real gift. Hence, they hastened to send him a present of £100 to relieve his immediate needs and to give him an opportunity to write. Coleridge returned the check, saying that that sum would only relieve his poverty temporarily and "prospectless poverty" would recur. He then went to Shrewsbury to preach. Preceding that day, Josiah penned a letter to

Coleridge saying that "Writing is painful to me. I must endeavor to be concise, yet to avoid abruptness. My brother and myself are possessed of a considerable superfluity of fortune; squandering and hoarding are equally distant from our inclinations. But we are earnestly desirous to convert this superfluity into a fund of beneficence, and we have been accustomed for some time, to regard ourselves as Trustees rather than as Proprietors. We have canvassed your past life, your present situation and prospects, your character and abilities. As far as is compatible with the delicacy of the estimate, we have no hesitation in declaring that your claim upon the fund appears to come under more of the conditions we have prescribed for its disposal, and to be every way more unobjectionable, than we could possibly have expected. This result is so congenial with our heartfelt wishes, that it will be a real mortification to us if any misconception or distrust of our intentions, or any unworthy diffidence of yourself, should interfere to prevent its full operation in your favour.

"After what my brother Thomas has written, I have only to state the proposal we wish to make to you. It is that you accept an annuity for life of £150 to be regularly paid by us, no condition whatsoever being annexed to it. Thus your liberty will remain entire, you will be under the influence of no professional bias, and will be in possession of a *'permanent income not inconsistent with religious and political creeds,'* so necessary to your health and activity. . . . we shall only say that we mean the annuity to be independent of everything but the wreck of our fortune, an event which we hope is not very likely to happen, though it must in these times be regarded as more than a bare possibility. . . ."

Coleridge accepted the proposal at once, writing Wordsworth of "the magnificent liberality of Josiah and Thomas Wedgwood" and telling Thelwell, "Astonished, agitated, and feeling as I could not help feeling, I accepted the offer in the same worthy spirit, I hope, in which it was made." Though Josiah wrote the letter to Coleridge offering the annuity, the letter was written at Tom's initiative. Wordsworth called granting the annuity an act of "unexcelled liberality"; it sprang from the same impulse that prompted dying Raisley Calvert to leave Wordsworth a legacy of £900; Raisley's gift, however, was a bequest; the Wedgwoods' an immediate gift. Among the first things it made possible was Coleridge's trip to Germany with the Wordsworths.

From Göttingen, Coleridge wrote Josiah six lengthy letters telling what he had accomplished there. One letter said, "What have I done in Germany? I have learned the language, both high and low German; I can read both and speak so fluently that it must be a torture for a German to be in my company—that is, I have words enough and phrases enough and arrange them tolerably; but my pronunciation is hideous. 2ndly, I can read the oldest German, the Frankish, and the Swabian. 3rdly, I have attended the lectures on Physiology, Anatomy, and Natural History, with regularity, and have endeavoured to understand these subjects. 4thly, I have read and made collections for a History of the Belles Lettres in Germany before the time of Lessing; and 5thly very large collections for a Life of Lessing, to which I was led by the miserably bad and unsatisfactory Biographies that have been heretofore given, and by my personal acquaintance with two of Lessing's friends." Coleridge then elaborated on this general summary.

In 1799, the brothers' long hunt for a place of abode was settled when Josiah took Gunville House at Tarrant Gunville, where he planned to live most of each year, going to look after the Wedgwood Works at Etruria during the three summer months. Tom bought the Eastbury Estate nearby and was soon joined by his mother and sisters. Josiah's life at Gunville became that of a country squire. "He hunted, shot, did his share of country business, and became deeply interested in improving his sheep." Tom spent part of his time on his estate, part in London, part with Josiah, part abroad. Tom and Coleridge saw a great deal of each other. At length, incredibly ill, Tom went to live with Josiah in a room Josiah had soundproofed. When he wrote Coleridge in 1804 that he was giving up hope of recovering his health, Coleridge wrote him, "It is idle for me to say to you, that my heart and very soul ache with the dull pain of one struck down and stunned . . . You *must hope*, my dearest Wedgwood; you must act as if you hoped! Despair has but that advice to give you. . . ." Eight weeks later, Coleridge was en route to Malta. At length, Tom Wedgwood resorted to opium as a relief from his pain. In July, 1805, while planning another trip to the West Indies which he thought would bring him better health, he died. For fourteen years, he had been in wretched health, his friends remembered, feeling that death was a blessed release. For only twenty years during his childhood and youth had he been well. In his will, he bequeathed Coleridge £75 a year, his half of the annuity. Josiah, who asked Coleridge to write a biography of his brother, remained a friend of Coleridge and of the Wordsworths. He died in 1843, leaving his son Josiah to carry on the Wedgwood business. In 1965, a great, great, great grandson of the first Josiah is carrying on the business, "keeping pace with the twentieth century," but stating that his firm today makes many of the wares the first Josiah created. The same careful craftsmanship that he insisted upon continues today.

Coleridge's news that Josiah Wedgwood had asked permission to withdraw his half of the annuity was relieved somewhat by the fact that Sheridan's directorship of Drury Lane Theatre had been succeeded by a committee of which Lord Byron was a leading member and that this committee had decided to produce Coleridge's play *Osorio*. The title was changed to *Remorse*, because a prominent London family bore the name Osorio. The play ran twenty nights; it was "a good thing for the Theatre," Coleridge wrote Thomas Poole. "They will get £8,000 or £10,000 by it, and I shall get more than all my literary efforts put together." He received about £300 and disposed of the copyright, edition by edition, on advantageous terms.

He then set out for Bristol to give a series of lectures; he did not arrive there, having gone instead to Wales. His friend Joseph Cottle had worked hard selling tickets for the series and informing Coleridge's friends. The first lecture was postponed three days. On the opening day, not one of his friends had seen Coleridge; finally, in late afternoon, Cottle found him, again a slave to opium. Coleridge arrived at the lecture hall an hour late without notes, but spoke brilliantly on his subject, "Hamlet." Despite his tardiness, the lecture was a great success, as were the others. A second series he was persuaded to give, however, was poorly attended.

Cottle did not suspect that Coleridge was taking opium until he took him to see Hannah Moore. Then he noted how his friend's hand had shaken so that he could not hold a glass of wine without spilling it. A friend told Cottle what caused Coleridge's trouble. Alarmed, Cottle wrote the poet a long, moral letter, telling him how "the baleful use of opium" has "thrown a dark cloud over you and your prospects." He reminded Coleridge of the sight of opium addicts: "the wild eye! the sallow countenance! the tottering step! the trembling hand! the disordered frame! and yet you will not be awakened to a sense of your danger, and I must add, your guilt?" He reminded him of his family, of Southey who would aid him; he offered to pay for the return trip to Keswick.

Coleridge replied: "You have poured oil in the raw and festering wound of an old friend's conscience, Cottle! But it is *oil of* vitriol. . . . I have prayed with drops of agony on my brow; trembling, not before the justice of my Maker, but even before the mercy of my Redeemer. 'I gave thee so many talents, what hast thou done with them?'" He told how he had begun taking opium to allay the pain of his disease, how he had tried, seemingly in vain, to cure himself of the habit and concluded, "Had I but a few hundred pounds, but £200—half to send to Mrs. Coleridge, half to place myself in a private mad-house where I could procure nothing but what a physician thought proper . . . then there might be hope." Cottle, horrified at the thought of Coleridge going to a private sanitarium, pled with him to pray earnestly for help. He was convinced that any money sent Coleridge would be spent on opium. Determined, however, to aid his friend, Cottle was prepared to secure funds for an annuity. In the midst of his plans, he burst a blood vessel and had to cease his activities. In the meantime, Coleridge lived for a time with Josiah Wade at Bristol under the medical supervision of Dr. Daniel and had procured a meek, elderly but strong man to accompany him everywhere with instructions to knock him down if he ever tried to get opium. Cottle tells how Coleridge and "his keeper" were out walking one day when Coleridge said to the man, "I think that's an American ship over there; go over and see if it is." While the unsuspecting man went on the errand, Coleridge quickly slipped into an apothecary's shop and filled a bottle he carried in his pocket with laudanum. Afraid that he might, under its influence, commit suicide, Coleridge had razors, pen-knives, and all possible methods of suicide removed from his room. When the Morgans moved first to a cottage at Ashley near Bath and then to Calne, Coleridge went to live again with them. The Morgan sisters, devoted to him, were beginning to take the places of Dorothy Wordsworth and Sara Hutchinson. Despite ill health, he wrote to one publisher about translating *Faust*, to another about translating the lesser works of Cervantes, wrote letters to Daniel Stuart on the political situation, and began *Christianity, the One True Philosophy*, which was to occupy him the rest of his life. The *Faust* translation did not materialize. Again, he gave a series of lectures, one of which brought about his final break with the Unitarian Church. Coleridge said that Milton represented Satan as "a sceptical Socinian" and substantiated his statement by a passage from *Paradise Regained* where Satan was tempting Christ. An important Unitarian minister, Dr. Estlin, was offended when he heard of the comparison and concluded that Coleridge had said the Unitarians and Socinians were Satanic. Though Coleridge sought to explain what he had said, his Unitarian friends, aroused by Dr. Estlin, would not be reconciled.

Again he was ill, first with erysipelas and then with "a kind of mortification of his leg"; on his forty-fourth birthday he wrote he was "in all but brain an old man." Yet, urged by John Morgan, he began work on *Biographia Literaria* which expanded into a two-volume work, in which he reminisced on his school days, on the University, remarked on men of genius, and critics, defended Southey's works, told of the creation of *Lyrical Ballads* and the theories behind it, discussed Fancy, Imagination, Hartley's law of Association, Dualism, Materialism, his indebtedness to Kant, Shakespeare's poetic power, German drama, and told anecdotes of literary life. Aroused by the Corn Bill, he spoke in the market place against it, standing on a butcher's table before "a very ragged but not butcherly audience, for by their pale faces few of them seemed to have had more than a very occasional acquaintanceship with butcher's meat. Loud were the huzzas," he said, "and if it depended on the inhabitants at large, I believe they would send me to Parliament." When his play *Remorse* was produced at Calne, Hartley Coleridge came down to see it. Crabb Robinson said Hartley had "the features of a foreign Jew, with starch and affected manners. He is a boy pedant, exceedingly formal and I should suppose clever." Early in 1816, because of the financial troubles of the Morgans, Coleridge came to London.

There, Dr. James Gillman, a surgeon, received a letter from Joseph Adams, a physician: "Dear Sir, A very learned, but in one respect an unfortunate gentleman has applied to me on a singular occasion. He has for several years been in the habit of taking very large quantities of opium. For some time past, he has been in vain endeavoring to break himself off it . . . and has proposed to me to submit himself to any regimen, however severe. With this view, he wishes me to fix himself in the house of some medical gentleman who will have the courage to refuse him any laudanum, and under whose assistance, should he be the worse for it, he may be relieved. As he is desirous of retirement, and a garden, I could think of no one so readily as yourself. Be so good as to inform me, whether such a proposal is absolutely inconsistent with your family arrangements. I should not have proposed it, but on account of the great importance of the character as a literary man. His communicative temper will make his society very agreeable and interesting." Dr. Gillman, who knew Joseph Adams only slightly, had no intention of receiving anyone into his home; yet, feeling a strong sympathy for the victims of opium, he asked Adams to drive Coleridge over the following evening. Coleridge, however, came alone to find Dr. Gillman visiting with a friend he had not seen in many years. Coleridge sat down and the three began to talk; at length, Dr. Gillman's friend excused himself, saying, "I see by your manners an old friend has arrived, and I shall therefore retire." Within a few minutes, there was deep understanding between the two men. Dr. Gillman later said, "I felt, indeed, almost spellbound, without the desire of release. My situation was new and there was something affecting in the thought, that one of such amiable manners, and at the same time so highly gifted, should seek comfort and medical aid in our quiet home." The following day, Coleridge came to the Grove, Highgate, to spend the rest of his life with Ann and James Gillman.

He endured the new regime with fortitude; the fasting times between doses, he walked his room in pain for seventeen hours at a time. He had, however, made an arrangement with Dr. Dunn, the chemist, should he fail. On Dr. Gillman's advice, he had a brief visit by the sea at Muddiford in Hampshire. He performed "miracles of self denial" to please Ann Gillman. When he was better, he walked in the Gillman garden; his habit of weaving from side to side, as if avoiding obstacles, now was exaggerated. The Gillmans had the ceiling of his room raised to afford space for all of his books. At peace, Coleridge believed his self-castigation would enable him to "lay the final stones of his life work." The publication of *Biographia Literaria*, of "Christabel," with "Kubla Khan" and "Pains of Sleep," of the *Sibylline Leaves*, of his *Lay Sermons* and *The Statesman's Manual* which he published under the title *The Bible, the Best Guide to Political Skill and Foresight*, he thought would bring a return to literary life "after a long exile."

It seemed, however, as if the literary world did not wish his return. Hazlitt damned these last publications in *The Examiner*. Up in arms against the "school of hypochondriacal poets who haunt the lakes," Coleridge, he said, had written better "*Nonsense* verses than anyone in England." The *Edinburgh Review*, where Hazlitt also had a hand, called "Kubla Khan" and the "Pains of Sleep" the "most notable pieces of impertinence of which the press has lately been guilty." In "Kubla Khan," the *Edinburgh Review* found "not a ray of genius . . . a mixture of raving and drivelling." In a twenty-seven page review, *Biographia Literaria* was dismissed with "Till he can do something better we would rather hear no more of him." Mary Russell Mitford said *Biographia* "has more absurdities than were ever collected in a printed book before." Two years later, writing on Coleridge almost as if he were dead, Hazlitt said, "The present age is an age of talkers,

and not of doers; and the reason is, that the world is growing old. . . ."
Mr. Coleridge has a mind "reflecting ages past"; his voice is like the
roar of the "dark rearward abyss" of thought. Yet, when Coleridge
had lectured on the English poets, Hazlitt had said Coleridge was the
only person from whom he had learned anything.

Meanwhile, the Wordsworths in the Lake Country were busy,
indeed. The three-year tenancy of Allan Bank came to an end in May,
1813. Twelve months earlier, the Wordsworths had arranged to rent
the rectory. Allan Bank with its smoky chimneys, "half plastered walls,
half carpeted floors, and half furnished rooms" had never appealed to
Dorothy. The rectory, with its view of the wood behind it, the rocks,
the view of Easdale from them, the lake, and the church and village on
the other side—"is sweeter than Paradise itself," she wrote. The house
needed "much renovation to be habitable," and when they had to move
in at the end of May the workmen were still there, making a mess, and
seeming "to take delight in scattering lime about wherever they went."
By the end of June the house was more or less in order, though it had
its drawbacks. As it faced the East, the sitting rooms were dark early;
it was too near the road and lacked privacy; the field in which it sat
proved no fit playing place for children. Inside, however, it was comfortable.

While living there, the family began going to Grasmere parish
church. Dorothy and William stoutly defended the Established
Church; yet William could not remember when he had been to
church in England. "All our ministers," he said, "are so vile." The
rector at Grasmere had been feeble-minded; the curate, a drunkard.
At Grasmere now, the rector, a worthy man, was "very good as a
steward and a farmer, but totally unfit to preach or read prayers."
However, with the coming of Mr. William Johnson, amiable and inspiring, the Wordsworths found a man who would be good for the
children. Mary went with the children to church in the morning;
Dorothy in the afternoon. A short time later, Mr. Johnson persuaded
Dorothy and Mary to teach in the Sunday School. Dorothy said she
was not setting herself up as a regular teacher; "we have too much to
do all week to make us take on this voluntary labor as a regular duty,
but our curate is very earnest in his attention to Sunday schools, and
wished my sister and me to encourage them by our occasional presence, so as often as we may without inconvenience, we intend, one of
us to go in the mornings." This step was a decided change for Dorothy,
who abhorred books "full of breathings of godliness, explanations
without end, and 'God' in every fourth line of a page." She had even

been suspicious of a friend who savored religious contemplation. With the church assuming responsibility in facing current problems and with their brother Christopher finding in orthodox religion, spiritual inspiration, she and William were ready now to support the Established Church.

Later, after the deaths of Thomas and Catharine at the rectory, the Wordsworths longed to leave that house at Grasmere. When William was appointed Distributor of Stamps for Westmorland and his income increased, they were eager to move to Rydal Mount, close enough for them to go to the parish church, beside which their children were buried. The salary William received as Distributor of Stamps was from £400 to £600 a year; his task was supervisory, as most of the work was done by a clerk. In May, 1813, the Wordsworths moved to Rydal Mount, a beautiful house with an uninterrupted view of woods, the lake, and mountains. It was part of the estate of Sir Michel Fleming. There, the Wordsworths lived for thirty-seven years. Needing extra furniture, they all went shopping at the Westmorland sale. William was triumphant over six buff chairs with cane bottoms purchased for £9 and "drawing room curtains with a grand cornice the length of the room"; he thought them handsomer than those Dorothy and Mary had made with great labor. They thought otherwise and cut his purchase up for sofa covers. Beds and pillows, a sofa, chairs, knives, glasses, a decanter, a large looking glass, they purchased. They had smiled at a neighbor who was buying "bargains" recklessly; yet when their furniture arrived, the Wordsworths realized they, too, had been a little reckless. "We have far more chairs than we know what to do with, and the dining room will not be at all nice with the sofa," Dorothy lamented. Their only extravagances were carpets—"a Turkey!!! carpet in the dining room and a Brussels in William's study."

As William was in high favor with Lady Fleming from whom Rydal Mount was rented, the Wordsworths were regarded as members of county society. Now with three-year-old Willy in school during the day, Johnny and Sissy away at school, Mary and Dorothy had more time to themselves. Yet in 1814, Dorothy went to Keswick to help nurse Basil Montagu, who was quite ill. She was gone three months. She came home to find Mary far from well, thin, weak, and lonely without the children. Dorothy plotted with the cook to prepare "all sorts of nice things" for Mary, who "had had no appetite for weeks."

When, in August, 1814, Wordsworth's "The Excursion" appeared, Dorothy urged the Clarksons to help push the sale of the book. "There are few persons," she wrote them, "who can afford to buy a two-guinea book merely for admiration of the book. The book has no chance of being sold except to the wealthy and they buy books for fashion more than anything else, and alas! we are not yet in the fashion." Charles Lamb wrote the review of "The Excursion" for *The Quarterly Review*, but his work was so badly cut by the editor that it did not seem to praise the poem as Lamb had intended it should. By March, only three hundred copies had been sold; two hundred remained; a cheaper edition did not appear for seven years.

When Mr. and Mrs. Clarkson took advantage of the peace to visit Paris, Dorothy urged them to visit Annette and Caroline. The latter, she had been told, "resembles her Father most strikingly, and her letters give a picture of a feeling and ingenuous mind." She herself looked forward to going and wished to take them presents of English manufacture. "Can this be done without much risk or disagreeable trouble?" She would like also to bring back some things of French manufacture if this were practicable. "Of course, it would be easy enough to hide lace and such small articles, but can silks be brought unmade up—or if made up is there any danger of their being seized?" Dorothy queried. She had no conscience about deceiving the customs' officers. In November, 1814, she thought she would be able to go in April, 1815; by New Year's, she was more doubtful. When Napoleon landed at Elba, this plan had to be abandoned. Dorothy was especially sorry for Annette, who was still a strong Royalist.

In 1814 when news of Napoleon's abdication came, Dorothy wrote, "We have danced for joy. But how strange; it is like a dream—peace— peace, all in a moment—prisoners let loose—Englishmen and Frenchmen brothers at once. No treaties, no stipulations." She felt, however, that Napoleon should have been dealt with more severely. Among the prisoners freed, was Eustace Baudouin, a young French lieutenant who had been captured in Spain three years earlier. He had been asked by the Wordsworths to send news of Annette and Caroline when he got to France. The next they heard of him was that his older brother Jean Baptiste had sought Caroline's hand in marriage. Both Annette and Caroline urged Dorothy to come for the wedding. Their meeting in Calais in 1802 had strengthened Annette's affection for Dorothy. It was decided that Dorothy and Sara Hutchinson should go to the wedding. Young Baudouin, after Napoleon's return, had been working with Annette for the Royalist cause. Annette courageously posted proclamations for the legitimate dynasty at night, distributed them in the daytime, and aided brave men who wished to escape to aid the king; Baudouin was entrusted with exhibiting all posters designed to bring back the people to their king.

With the abdication of Napoleon, Caroline and Annette assured Dorothy all was safe and quiet, and urged her to come to France. Dorothy replied it was impossible for her to come then. Finally, in February, 1816, Caroline was married. There were thirty present at the dinner, ball, and supper; deputies and many notables were present. The bride was dressed in white sarsenet with a white veil. Four years passed before Dorothy went to France. In the meantime, on December 27, 1816, Caroline's daughter was born; she was named Louise Marie Caroline Dorothée.

The much-traveled Wordsworths continued to rove. The summer of 1814, William, Mary, and Sara Hutchinson went to Scotland; Dorothy and Sara later spent three months in Wales. In December, 1815, Dorothy and William, after a brief walking tour, visited Richard Wordsworth and his wife. They had been apprehensive, when some years before, to everyone's surprise, Richard suddenly married his servant, a young woman half his age. Dorothy was relieved to find "She is not vulgar, though there is nothing of the gentlewoman about her. Her face is very comely and her countenance excellent"; their son, "very pretty and most intelligent and engaging." Dorothy was planning "a little holiday" at Ullswater when news came of the complete mental breakdown of their neighbor, Charles Lloyd.

Mrs. Lloyd, William said, "has long been living in hourly apprehension that he will be obliged to be confined in a mad-house or he will destroy himself . . . the women of my family have in compassion given Mrs. Lloyd something of their company; she has no sympathy or advice from any other quarter. . . ." Dorothy could not "bear the thought of poor dear Mrs. Lloyd, with her family of eight children, worn out with sorrow and watching." She and Mary were the only persons, except his wife, whom Lloyd could bear to see or have near him. "To me," Dorothy says, "he has never objected—he liked me when he was well and the same liking has continued during his woeful depression." When Mrs. Lloyd decided to move her husband to his old home at Birmingham where she thought he would have better medical attention, William went with them as far as Manchester, while Dorothy looked after the children left at home. She found them "happy, cheerful, tractable children." While she was looking after the Lloyd children, her brother Christopher's wife, Priscilla, died. Dorothy offered to go to him as soon as Mrs. Lloyd returned, but he "did not seem to want anyone to lean upon, even for a time." After a short stay at Birmingham, Lloyd was sent to an asylum at York, from which he escaped. In 1819, he recovered his memory, lived for some time in London, then went abroad. His last years were marked by periodic mental breakdowns; he died at Versailles in 1839.

Mrs. Coleridge, in the meantime, managed to be happy at Greta Hall, "a kind of family paradise," where she was surrounded by Sara and, at times, by her sons; as well as her sister, Mrs. Lovell, whose husband, the pantisocrat, had died in 1796; his sister Edith and her very numerous children; her brother, Southey, Edith's husband—"no nonsense about 'in laws' for Mrs. Coleridge"—and a floating population of more distant friends, relatives, and friends of relatives. Visitors were also welcomed, provided they "kept clear of the business of the family, but to the family even Friendship, even Art, was subordinate. . . . One can understand the Fricker instinct to make a matriarchy out of Pantisocracy."

Her family problems, Mrs. Coleridge had always talked of and written freely about to Coleridge's and her friends. In February 1814, after Coleridge had left the Wordsworths, she wrote to Thomas Poole from Keswick, "Our intelligent neighbor Mr. de Quincey tells me, that you had been with Mr. C. in London during the last year; you would naturally imagine that he would mention this circumstance to me in his letters—but unhappily for me and the dear children and I may add, for himself, his aversion to writing of any kind seems to strengthen with every absence—we have not seen him for 2 years—and it will be 12 months in March since he wrote to Keswick—having sent me only one letter during 2 years. Mr. S., however, assured us that he would be here shortly, having gone to Bristol to deliver a course of Lectures, after which he would set off for Keswick to meet the Boys at the Christmas holidays—so I kept them at home in the hope of a letter giving some direction about Hartley's studies, but none coming, I sent the poor fellows back last Monday, with their Skaits across their shoulders; Derwent who is a very Keen Skaiter, casting many a ling'ring look behind upon our frozen Lake, and praying for a Snowstorm to drive him back again. His brother, on the contrary, marched back with cheerful feet, knowing he is only to stay at that School until his father comes—he wished to go back as soon as possible to be with Mr Dawes, whom he both loves & respects in very high degree. As H. is now turned of 17 I think I should not have sent (him) back to school at all, if it had not been for his very great desire to return—and among the many reasons he gave for it—one was, that he could not study Euclid so well without the assistance of his brother, who is much beyond him in this branch of science.

"You will be shocked to hear that I never hear from C. I dare not dwell upon the painful consequences of his desertion but if in the Spring he does not exert himself to pay some of my debts here— I really do not know what will be the result.—The poor children, are miserable if their father is mentioned for fear they should hear anything like blame attached to it, but I believe I mentioned to you before their great sensibility on this unhappy subject."

On March 28th, 1815, she wrote Poole: "We have just received a letter from Mr. C.'s friend Mr. Morgan of Calne in Wilts. He says he is not intirely without hope that C. will do something now for his family, as he is now in good health & spirits, & talks of beginning in good earnest a German translation which will be profitable and which will leave him at liberty to get his Poems ready for the press; he says he has been at Devises, Corsham, on visits, and Bath, & at each place got ill, and here he says, he is far too much in company, but nothing shall be wanting on his part to be of use, and to keep him in health. I am afraid, he has still his old habit of swallowing Opium, & if he continue in it, I fear no good will ever come from him."

On Saturday, May 24th, 1816, she told Tom Poole of the death of Mr. Richard Wordsworth, William's elder brother, at Lambeth at his brother Christopher's house. She then added, "You will be sorry to hear the bad account I send you of poor S.T.C. He went to Town with his Play—it would not do, was returned for alteration, which instead of instantly setting about he got in a fit of despondency and was confined 3 weeks to his bed, where his friend Mr. Morgan was obliged to attend him: they are now both in Town, and M. tells me he is fast recovering under a Physician at Highgate who undertakes to cure him of Opium: he will alter his play for next season.

"You will also be sorry for another thing respecting him—Oh! when will he ever give his friends anything but pain? he has been so unwise as to publish his fragments of 'Christabel' & 'Koula-Khan'. Murray is the publisher, & the price is 4s. 6d—we were all sadly vexed when we read the advertisement of these things."

Tremendously excited, in April, 1819, she wrote Poole: "My dear friend You will start at the sight of a folio sheet; but I have much to say, and some news to impart which Im sure will give you pleasure. To begin with the most recent, and consequently nearest my heart, i.e. Hartley Coleridge has had the singular good-fortune to be elected

Fellow of Oriel-College, Oxford! I can hardly believe it possible; for I expected he would be obliged to make many trials for a fellowship before he would obtain one; to be elected *at once*, and at *Oriel*, is so truly desirable for him that all our friends are more than I can express, satisfied with the event.—I wrote a note to my friends at Rydal-mount (by Coach) as soon as the news arrived, and in answer, my kind friend Dorothy, after saying all for herself and family that her good heart dictated, further says, 'We recd the Oxford paper soon after your letter; and an account from Mr. Wm. Jasckson (Fellow of Queen's) that H. C. had acquired great honour in his examination for Oriel.'—He told them that he was invited to dine with the Fellows the next day; a distinction of which I daresay he was not a little proud. H. had very little hope himself that he should succeed, for his competitors were most of them older than himself, and had been accustomed to similar Trials, had had more regular classical training, i.e. had been at the public Schools, (a great advantage we now find in gaining classic honours) 'and for all I know,' said he 'are my superiors in natural abilities.' He, therefore, went to bed on Thursday night with a full determination to sleep out the ringing of the Bells which would peal to the happiness of his rivals next day; when, sitting and yawning over a late breakfast, the welcome annunciation was brought in, which he thought must be only a deceitful dream, so much was he stunned by the tidings, until the succession of fees, with their 'impenarative faces' stamped the thing real.

"Little William Wordsworth on his return in the evening from School told his Mother, that he never saw *master* in such a good humour in his life: 'as soon as he got the letter about Hartley, he rose up, gave a shout, and proclaimed a *holiday*': 'the boys all huzza'd and there was *such an uproar*, Mother!!'

". . . The picture which I named to you last year, as painted by Collins, of Sara, was given by the artist to her father, and it seems, he is delighted at the possession.

"Miss Wordsworth is, in figure, activity and spirits much as when you knew her, with a much-altered face, and, I think, an improved character: she looks nearer 60 than 50 in her profile, owing to her extreme leanness, and the loss of teeth: at Xmas, when she joined the dances of the young people, Sara thought there was something unnatural, in the incongruity of her face and figure together with her extreme agility in the dance. While Sara was feeling thus; her good brother was pointing out to me, with expressions of delight, the thing which Sara was remarking; but with very different feelings: Wordsworth thought these lively movements were signs of strength, and deep enjoyment, which in a woman near fifty, and his beloved sister, (for this must be taken into the account) was worthy of admiration: good man, he forgot, in the contemplation of his own pleasure, that he was addressing one who, according to his notion, must be an object of commissiration; for I am so encreased in size, that I could no more go down a dance, or climb a mountain, than I could fly over the Derwent."

Fifty percent of Mrs. Coleridge's later letters to her son Hartley were confined to questions about the size of his shirts and whether his clothing was warm enough—and Hartley was in his thirties. Her earlier letters to Mr. Poole showed her pride in Hartley's happiness, his popularity, and his confidence, when he is in his teens; her excitement when he is elected Probationary Fellow of Oriole. They showed her grief when he is disappointed in winning the Newdigate Prize or in love, believing that women despise his short stature and awkward manners. Then came letters when she was grief-stricken by Hartley's going unshaven, and his being found drunk in the gutter by the Dean.

She was also absorbed by her daughter Sara, "the beauty of the family," whom kind Mr. De Quincey called "the most perfect of all pensive, nun-like, intellectual beauties that I have seen in real breathing life." Sir Walter Scott called her a "lovely vision of a creature . . . the very ideal of a novel heroine." Sara, a great reader, was also a writer of considerable merit; her first novel was written to help defray the expenses of her brother Derwent's education.

In her letters to Mr. Poole, Mrs. Coleridge showed her concern when Greta Hall was beginning to empty. The last of the Southey children had grown up. Mrs. Coleridge, almost lonely, worried at the persistence of Sara's lover, a Coleridge cousin, and at the fact that the two had "little means"; at length, she was relieved when the couple were finally married. As she wrote to Mr. Poole, "one is conscious that to her he stands for the time when she was really a wife, when the family was all her own, and her 'sweet Berkeley,' who died full thirty years ago, was still alive."

CHAPTER XI

Days "Worthy of the Elizabethan Age"

ON DECEMBER 28, 1817, THE ARTIST, BENJAMIN ROBERT HAYDON, GAVE A DINNER TO WHICH WILLIAM WORDSWORTH and John Keats were invited. Other guests included Charles Lamb and Thomas Monkhouse. "It was as gay an evening as Wordsworth ever spent," Haydon wrote. They had "a glorious set to,—on Homer, Shakespeare, Milton and Virgil. Lamb got exceedingly merry and exquisitely witty; and his fun in the midst of Wordsworth's solemn intonations of oratory was like the sarcasm of the fool in the midst of Lear's passion. . . . It was, indeed, an immortal evening. Wordsworth's fine intonation as he quoted Milton and Virgil, Keats' eager, inspired look, Lamb's quaint sparkle of lambent conversation, so speeded up the conversation, that in my life I never passed a more delightful time. All the fun was within bounds. Not a word passed that an apostle might not have listened to. It was a night worthy of the Elizabethan age. . . ." The dinner had been planned when Keats told Haydon of his desire to meet Wordsworth.

In 1817, when Wordsworth read Keats' "Hymn to Pan," he praised it as "a very pretty piece of paganism." In 1826, he spoke of Shelley and Keats as poets "who could endure criticism." In 1842, he said that the danger of both Keats and Tennyson was "over-lusciousness." Keats, Wordsworth had known better than the other younger poets.

John Keats was born October 31, 1795. His father, when a lad, handsome, energetic, and intelligent, had come from western England to make his way in London. There, he had found employment as an "ostler" at the Swan and Hoop, a livery stable owned by James Jennings. While there employed, he fell in love with and married the owner's daughter, Frances, an audacious nineteen-year-old-girl. Their first son, John, was followed by three more sons, George, Thomas, and Edward, and a daughter, Frances. This was an affectionate family, though John, with his intense feeling, vivid imagination, and energy, was his mother's favorite. After the early death of Edward, the members of the family were even closer bound to one another. When, in 1803, Mr. Jennings retired from active business because he was suffering from gout, Thomas Keats took charge of The Swan and Hoop; he had proved so diligent that even before this he had been affluent enough to move his family from its quarters above the livery stable to a brick dwelling in Craven Street, and to consider Harrow as the school for their son, John. He was sent, however, in 1803 to Mr. Clarke's Academy at Enfield, twelve miles north of London. Still "wearing the frilled dress of a little boy," he was remembered by Cowden Clarke, the headmaster, as the smallest of his seventy or eighty pupils. Young Keats was happy and popular at school; he saw much, too, of his grandparents, who lived only a few miles away at Ponders End; his parents often drove over on Sunday to visit him. Mr. Clarke's curriculum, much broader and more thorough than most in the day, included history, science, Greek, Latin, and modern languages. Though at first John Keats objected to having French "crammed" down his throat, he never regretted his ability to read Voltaire in the original. Mr. Clarke allowed his pupils to develop at their own pace; he encouraged such hobbies as gardening.

Suddenly, disaster struck the Keats family. Thomas Keats, riding home late the night of April 15, 1804, was thrown from his horse when it stumbled; his skull was fractured and he was speechless when he was found; two days later, he died and was buried in St. Stephen's Church in Coleman Street. Beside herself with grief, bewildered, trying to manage a thriving business and care for four children, with her parents a dozen miles away, Frances Keats did not realize how attractive a "catch" she was. A penniless young bank clerk, William Rawlings, did, with the result that he married the heiress two months after her husband's death. He soon proved so horrible that she left him, though, by the laws of the day, she thereby lost all claim to her children and her property. Three years later, he sold the stable and dropped out of her life; he had no interest in the Keats children. Frances Keats began drinking heavily and lived for a time with a Jew in Enfield; in 1808, she returned to her parents' home, broken in body and spirit, suffering from tuberculosis. Devoted to his mother, young

John Keats, during his holidays, took sole charge of nursing her, cooking her meals, giving her her medicine, reading to her, sitting up with her at nights when she was restless. Her death on March 10, 1810, was a staggering blow. He had realized the tragedy of death earlier, when, in 1805, his grandfather had died; but that experience had been lightened somewhat by the practical way his grandmother, Mrs. Jennings, had taken a house in Edmonton, which she made into a home for her grandchildren, thus giving the Keats children the stability they needed.

His father's and grandfather's deaths had matured John, who changed from a gentle child into a rebellious one, seeming to delight in fist-fights despite his small stature. The pluckiest fighter in school, "he would fight anyone, morning, noon, or night." Yet, he studied and did well in school. He seemed plagued by emotional conflict, evidenced by his quick changes in mood: at times in tears, again, "laughing outrageously." His mother's death wrought another dramatic change. Gone was the aggressive, fight-loving boy; in his place, was the silent lad, aloof, absorbed in reading. Retreating into books, he read everything from *Robinson Crusoe* to Shakespeare, from *The Arabian Nights* to Milton, from Kauffman's *Dictionary of Merchandise* to Beckford's *Vathek*. He became a close friend of Cowden Clarke, the headmaster's son, and soon an intimate friend of the headmaster, who encouraged Keats' love of poetry; a gifted pianist, Mr. Clarke played Mozart's and Handel's works, which Keats, too, grew to love; he discussed politics with the lad and gave him pertinent books in that field.

Realizing she must provide for her grandsons' futures, seventy-five-year-old Mrs. Jennings appointed two guardians for the boys, both London merchants, John Rowland Sandell and Richard Abbey. Though their grandfather had left an estate of £13,000, of which Mrs. Jennings was to receive an income of £200 and her grandchildren £250 each in trust, and more later, the estate was entangled in chancery proceedings. Hence, all thought of Harrow had to be abandoned; the Keats boys had to earn their livings. When Mr. Abbey discussed with the boys their careers, George decided at once to enter the counting house. Fourteen-year-old John finally decided he would become a doctor.

As an apprentice to Mr. Thomas Hammond, he was industrious, though he derived more pleasure from reading Bacon, Locke, Spenser, and Shakespeare than from his medical studies. William Wordsworth's poetry, he admired, though it was still unrecognized by many as being great. When Mr. Hammond found John Keats reading *The Examiner*, the liberal voice of that day, and learned he had begun reading it at Mr. Clarke's school, he swore, if he "had fifty children, he'd not send one of them to that school." But Keats was interested in Leigh Hunt's articles on the sale of army promotions by the Duke of York's mistress, the flogging of soldiers, the quality of George III's ministers, and finally the attack on the Regent as "a violator of his word, a libertine, over head and ears in disgrace, a despiser of domestic ties, and the companion of gamblers and demireps." When the Hunt brothers were sentenced, after a trial by a packed jury, to two-year terms in separate prisons, with fines of £500, and £500 as security for good behavior, they became martyrs; 10,000 copies of *The Examiner* were sold the day the verdict was passed. Mr. Clarke was among those who visited Leigh Hunt in prison; he regaled Keats with accounts of his visits and helped form the young man's political views. Keats's hero was a young man in prison discussing Spenser and writing editorials for *The Examiner*. Keats was a liberal. As Mr. Clarke and he read Spenser's poetry, Keats was inspired to write his first poem; political events of the day inspired others.

In 1814, his grandmother's death darkened his life and left him depressed. His meeting of two attractive girls, the Mathew sisters, lightened his mood and he was again inspired to write verse.

Eager to cut short his apprenticeship, he asked to take the Apothecaries' Examination in three years instead of the customary four. When Mr. Hammond consented, young Keats took the examination, passed it, and for his internship as a full-fledged medical student, entered the United Hospitals of Guy's and St. Thomas's in one of London's poorest districts. His skill and hard work so attracted his superiors that four weeks after he entered, he became an assistant to one of the surgeons. Yet, a typical student, he had time to play poker, whist, and billiards, to go to boxing matches, cockfights, and bear-baitings, to drink claret, smoke cigars, and take snuff. At the beginning of the second semester, his work became heavier and he suffered from his inability to develop a sense of detachment from the suffering he saw his patients undergoing. This troubled him increasingly as he assisted with operations. Again, he turned to writing poetry, and finally in the spring decided to submit one of his poems to *The Examiner*. The previous vacation he had purchased two volumes of poetry by Wordsworth, who, he decided, was one of the greatest poets living and had much to teach him. Here, he discovered "a man speaking to men," one who "rejoices more than other men in the spirit of life that is in him," who is also interested in "the goings-on of the universe around him," and who is willing to share also his own "passions and volitions." Keats was no Wordsworth, he knew, but now he had written and submitted his poetry. The twenty-year-old waited eagerly to see if his sonnet "To Solitude" would be accepted. On May 5, 1816, at the bottom of an inside page the sonnet appeared, signed with his initials. This was his first proof that he might one day be considered a poet.

When on July 25 he had passed his examinations, he had been found qualified to practice in the country, but not in London. In September, he entered Guy's Hospital for his final training. Shortly after he took up his internship, one night he and his friend Cowden Clarke read together parts of Chapman's translation of *The Iliad* and *The Odyssey*, an exhilarating experience; Clarke did most of the reading in his great, booming voice. Chapman's masculine translation with its virile, penetrating idiom, so different from that of Pope, was unlike anything Keats had read or heard. At daybreak, Keats set out for his lodgings, walking briskly for an hour-and-a-half. Reaching his home, he sat down and, in a couple of hours, wrote the sonnet, "On First Looking Into Chapman's Homer," later changing only a few words. He sent the sonnet to Clarke who found it when he came down for breakfast. Keats had written:

> Much have I travell'd in the Realms of Gold
> And many goodly States and Kingdoms seen;
> Round many western islands have I been.
> Which Bards in fealty to Apollo hold.
> Oft of one wide expanse had I been told,
> Which deep browed Homer ruled as his Desmesne:
> Yet could I never judge what men could mean
> Till I heard Chapman speak out loud and bold.
> Then felt I like some Watcher of the Skies
> When a new Planet swims into his ken,
> Or like stout Cortez when with wand'ring eyes
> He stared at the Pacific, and all his Men
> Looked at each other with a wild surmise
> Silent upon a Peak in Darien.

By February, he knew he could not and should not continue his medical training. One day, while he was operating, he thought of the disaster that would come if his lancet slipped; with great effort, he finished the operation successfully; but when he laid down his instruments, he knew he would never operate again. Moreover, his interest in writing poetry had become an overwhelming one. His guardians were amazed that he would, after all his training, give up the medical profession. Moreover, they had arranged for him to practice in Tottenham Court Road. Keats, however, was firm in his conviction that he could succeed as a poet and that through his writing he could earn a living. His guardians, powerless to change his decision, called him a "silly boy."

They did not know of the friends Keats was making in London. He had met and become friends with Benjamin Haydon, the broad-browed, long-haired painter with the loud voice and laugh, who said he had persuaded the government to purchase the Elgin Marbles, sculpture salvaged from the Parthenon. Impressed by him, Keats wrote a sonnet, praising Haydon, Wordsworth, and Hunt, "Great spirits now on earth sojourning" whose genius, he believed

> . . . . would never take
> A meaner sound than Raphael's whispering . . .

Leigh Hunt, now an intimate friend, had excited Keats by writing an article on "Young Poets," in which he listed three new recruits: Shelley, Reynolds, and Keats. Encouraged by this notice, Keats decided to bring out a book of poems. When he showed the poems to Shelley, who, following the drowning of his wife, was staying with Leigh Hunt, Shelley advised him not to publish them. This advice, Keats ignored, well aware that he was writing poetry quite different from that of Shelley, who was attempting just then to write poetry "with beautiful idealisms of moral excellence," whereas Keats had no desire "to move the globe with his own hands." His circle of friends was growing. John Hamilton Reynolds took him to Novello's rooms, where he heard the famous organist play Bach and Chopin; he met William Hazlitt, who kept a group enthralled until three o'clock one morning while he talked of "Monarchy and Republicanism"; he met Mary Shelley, who could out-argue the best of the group. All the while he was making these new friends, he was working hard at the hospital and writing poetry. Once he planned to publish a volume of poetry, he decided, too, that he would start work on a long poem, "Endymion." When he told his guardians of his decision to give up medicine, they had no idea of his other interests or of how far he had already progressed as a poet.

On March 3, 1817, his first book of poetry appeared. His publisher sent him the first copy with a sonnet of congratulations: "Keats, I admire thine upward, out-dating soul." The first review, by a fellow poet, Reynolds, in *The Champion*, praised the book, saying Keats would eclipse Byron, Thomas Campbell, and a number of other poets, and compared him with Shakespeare and Chaucer; Keats's sonnets, it said, were as good as those by Wordsworth and Milton. *Blackwood's Edinburgh Review*, on the other hand, castigated the book of poems:

> Our talk shall be (a theme we never tire on)
> Of Chaucer, Spenser, Shakespeare, Milton, Byron,
> (Our England's Dante)—Wordsworth, HUNT and KEATS
> The Muses' son of promise; and of what feats
> He yet may do . . . .

Thus, he suggested Keats would be dealt with later. Keats was shocked at the venomous attack on Leigh Hunt, saying, " I never read anything so virulent—accusing him of the greatest crimes—deprecating his Wife, his Poetry—his Habits—his company, his conversation— These Philipics are to come out in Numbers called 'The Cockney School of Poetry.' " Keats at first was incredulous, then bewildered and sad. *The Monthly Magazine* favorably reviewed the book of poems, and *The Examiner*, trying to arouse interest in the book, printed three of Keats's sonnets. Meanwhile, Keats continued to work on "Endymion."

In April 1817, John and Tom Keats decided to move to Hampstead where John could work more on "Endymion." Meanwhile, John took a brief vacation on the Isle of Wight, where he hoped to work again on the long poem. Though he attempted to write eight hours a day, he seemed to be accomplishing nothing. As the days dragged by and he became increasingly depressed, he decided to go to nearby Margate, where he hoped he would write. "One can write anyplace," he told himself as he found himself blaming "treeless Margate" for his failure to accomplish what he had set out to do. Reading Shakespeare, he despaired of ever writing well. Then Tom came to Margate and John again began writing eight hours a day. At length, the brothers went to Canterbury for two or three weeks and then returned to Hampstead on the outskirts of London. In late summer, Tom and George Keats sailed for France, while John stayed on at Hampstead until September, when he visited a "bookish friend," Benjamin Bailey, at Magdalen College, Oxford. Though the young men went boating in the late afternoons and spent profitable hours talking of books, Keats, by late September, had completed Book III of "Endymion." As the time drew near for Keats' departure, the two friends visited Stratford, going to Shakespeare's home and the church where the dramatist is buried. At the church, they signed the Visitors' Book. When Keats returned to Hampstead, he visited his friend Charles Brown. Settling down first at Burford Bridge then at Hampstead, he began writing Book IV of "Endymion." After a time, he moved to London to write reviews for *The Champion* and to work on "Endymion." In December, Tom, who was far from well, departed with his brother George to Devon.

With "Endymion" almost completed, in December 1818, Keats attended a dinner honoring William Wordsworth, who was visiting in London. The young poet was impressed with the "paronish-like," tall gentleman, about fifty, whose eyes seemed to smoulder, and whose deep, rough voice was like that of an Old Testament prophet. The other guests included Tom Monkhouse and Charles Lamb. They talked of Homer, Shakespeare, Virgil, and Milton, of Voltaire, and Newton, each of the men expressing his views incisively, while Lamb, who, as often happened, had become tipsy, finally toasted "the confusion of mathemics." Other distinguished guests dropped in during the evening.

Three days later, Wordsworth invited Keats to call. On the appointed day, when he arrived, it seemed that Wordsworth had forgotten his invitation. Dressed for the evening in knee britches, silk stockings, and a stiff collar, the older man told Keats he had a dinner engagement. Two days later, Keats accepted an invitation Wordsworth had not forgotten. In fact, Keats was invited to the Wordsworths' a number of times. He discovered that the older man insisted on dominating the conversation, sitting usually with his left hand stuck in his waistcoat; once, when Keats attempted to interrupt him, Mrs. Wordsworth put her hand on Keats's arm and said, "Mr. Wordsworth is never interrupted." Annoyed, Keats later told Haydon, "He cannot expect his fireside Divan to be infallible but that every Man of worth is as proud as himself." Keats was extremely critical of what he considered Wordsworth's "egotism, vanity, and bigotry." On another occasion, Keats was disturbed when a group talking of the fact that Walter Scott's *Rob Roy* was about to be published, was interrupted as Wordsworth solemnly read his own ballad by the same name and stated complacently, "I do not know what more Mr. Scott can have to say on the subject." Keats was beginning to re-evaluate Wordsworth, who, he decided now, was not a philosopher, though he admired increasingly his "intuitive awareness of life."

In March, 1818, John Keats went to Devon to be with his brother Tom, still ill. Their brother George, restless and depressed in London, and planning a new life, at length, in 1818 married Georgiana Wylie who had sympathized with both John and George when they, too, were depressed; he and his wife soon left for Philadelphia. He was certain that in America they would find a better life.

That same summer, John Keats and a friend, John Brown, had gone to the Lake Country where they found Wordsworth not at home, and then on to Scotland, where they visited Burns' birthplace. When Keats, suffering from a sore throat, returned home he was shocked to find Tom in the last stages of tuberculosis. John nursed Tom carefully through his chills, fever, and coughing spells; calmed him when his spirits were at low ebb, read to him often, and in his presence was cheerful. It was most difficult to seem gay before Tom, for in June *Blackwood's Magazine* had had an issue devoted to Keats' recently published *Endymion*, which it bitterly denounced, after first poking fun at the Cockney school of writers, whose members, it said, often were footmen and governesses who scribbled verses imitating those of Robert Burns and Joanna Baillie. The latest of these Cockney writers, the article sneered, was a young man destined to be an apothecary. But alas! he had fallen under the influence of Leigh Hunt, "the most worthless and affected of the versifiers of our time." Encouraged by him, "Johnny Keats" had "deserted his gallipots" and written a long poem "Endymion," which was "calm, settled, imperturbable idiocy." After bitterly attacking passages of the poem, the review concluded, "It is a better and wiser thing to be a starved apothecary than a starved poet; so back to the shop, Mr. John, back to the 'plasters, pills, ointment boxes et cetera.' But, for Heaven's sake, young Sangrado, be a little more sparing of extenuatives and soporifics in your practice than you have been in your poetry." Discouraged, in September while dining with friends in Fleet Street, Keats said he would write no more verse.

While in this mood, he met one day in a friend's drawing room, a beautiful, blue-eyed, high-spirited eighteen-year-old girl, Fanny Brawne, whose image haunted him for days. The fact that he was told she was a flirt mattered not at all; he could not forget her. "I was never in love—Yet the voice and shape of a woman has haunted me these two days—at such a time when the relief, the feverous relief of Poetry seems much less a crime—This morning poetry has conquered —and I feel escaped from a new strange and threatening sorrow," he wrote his friend John Hamilton Reynolds. Now, he began writing "Hyperion," an account of the struggle of the Olympian gods and their predecessors, the Titans. Having resolved to forget Fanny Brawne, he was delighted to meet another attractive girl, Jane Cox, an Anglo-Indian, "with the grace of a leopardess."

On November 18, 1818, Tom, just nineteen, died. John had nursed him through crisis after crisis, watching him grow "pale and spectre thin," more helpless, watching his features become more shrunken; dreading the fearful coughing that wracked the boy's feeble body. John Keats, too, was looking haggard now. Writing to George of Tom's death, John said, "I have scarce a doubt of immortality of some nature or other—neither had Tom." On St. Stephen's Day, Tom was buried beside his father, mother, and grandparents. John realized he had lost the one person who, George said, understood him "better than any other human being." As an antidote to grief, he went everywhere, calling on friends, attending prizefights, hunting, attending lectures and the theatre.

When he met Fanny Brawne again at Christmas time, he told her he loved her. The early days of their courtship were far from tranquil; yet they were productive of poetry. After a walking trip, on a cold winding morning while visiting friends, Keats had a sore throat and was confined to the house for a week. His thoughts kept turning to Fanny Brawne whom he loved passionately. He thought, too, of a friend of Tom's, Charles Wells, who had sent Tom fictitious love letters from a fictitious girl, Amena—a cruel deception. Despondent, Keats began writing "La Belle Dame Sans Merci," which owes much to a medieval French poem, to Spenser's *Faerie Queen*, and to Burton's *Anatomy of Melancholy*. Keats' poem is set in the Middle Ages and tells of the beautiful lady,

> . . . . a faery's child:
> Her hair was long, her foot was light,
>   And her eyes were wild.

A knight had met her one day, had set her on his pacing steed

> And nothing else saw all day long;
> For sideways would she lean, and sing
>   A faery's song.

She looked at him as if she loved him and finally said "I love thee true." But once under her power, as she kissed him, he fell asleep. On awaking, he found himself with pale kings, princes, too, and warriors, who told him mournfully, that the beautiful lady without mercy had him "in thrall." He concludes:

> And that is why I sojourn here,
>   Alone and palely loitering,
> Though the sedge is withered from the Lake
>   And no birds sing.

With his poem completed, and feeling better, Keats returned to London. Realizing that Fanny was not ready for his possessiveness, he found some consolation in another attractive girl, Isabella Jones. Encouraged by her, trying to keep his mind off Fanny Brawne, he started "The Eve of St. Agnes," also set in the Middle Ages, yet with echoes of Shakespeare's *Romeo and Juliet* and of Shakespeare's *Sonnets*. In Keats's poem, a young lad, Porphyro, in love with a beautiful girl, Madeline, and deprived of seeing her because of a family feud, manages to steal into her father's castle on St. Agnes Eve, when, according to legend, a young girl will dream of the man she is to wed. As an aged retainer saw him, she was relieved that there was a gay ball on the floor below, full of revelry

> With plume, tiara, and all rich array.

Yet, grasping his fingers in her palsied hand, she warned,

> . . . Mercy, Porphyro! hie thee from this place;
> They are all here tonight, the whole blood-thirsty race!

> "Get hence! Get hence! there's dwarfish Hildebrand;
> He had a fever late, and in the fit
> He cursed thee and thine, both house and land:
> And there's that old Lord Maurice, not a whit
> More tame for his gray hairs—Alas me! flit!
> Flit like a ghost away."—"Ah, Gossip dear,
> We're safe enough; here in this arm-chair sit,
> And tell me how"—"Good Saints! not here, not here!
> Follow me, child, or else these stones will be thy bier."

The young man followed her to Madeline's room, where he promised,

> "I will not harm her, by all the saints, I swear."

Hiding in a closet in her room, he waited until Madeline, "so pure a thing, so free from mortal taint," had gone to sleep. Then, he brought forth many delicacies which he heaped with glowing hand on golden dishes and in baskets bright; finally, taking her hollow lute, he played softly "an ancient ditty," "La Belle Dame sans Merci," close to her ear. Suddenly, Madeline awoke, and he told her of his love, beseeching her to leave with him.

> "Let us away, my love, with happy speed;
> There are no ears to hear, or eyes to see,—
> Drowned all in Rhenish and the sleepy mead:
> Awake! arise! my love, and fearless be,
> For o'er the southern moors I have a home for thee."

Beset with fears, she hurried at his words, for there were "sleeping dragons all around, some with ready spears." Down the wide stairs, they stole; in all the house "was heard no human sound"; a chain-dropped lamp flickered by each door; the tapestries fluttered in the night breeze and long carpets rose along gusty floors.

> They glide like phantoms, into the wide hall;
> Like phantoms, to the iron porch they glide,
> Where lay the Porter, in an uneasy sprawl,
> With a huge empty flagon by his side . . .

The poem, a gem, begins and ends with the picture of a Beadsman, sitting that cold night, among cold ashes, first saying his beads, and in the last stanza, having told his "thousand aves," sleeping "among his ashes cold." The poem is full of contrasts: between advanced age and frailty and youth and the eagerness of young love; the religious and the erotic; "the inner warmth and the all-enveloping cold"; "music and silence"; Porphyro's tenderness at thought of Madeline's innocent belief in the old legend and his ruse to take advantage of it.

Keats' sore, ulcerated throat lingered on for twelve months, during which time he felt fatigued, unable to sleep, and was easily irritated; at times, he was feverish. These early signs of tuberculosis and the accompanying depression, easily recognized today, were not so easily discerned in Keats' time. It is not strange that he contracted the disease, as he had been so close to his mother and Tom whom he had nursed through their last months of the disease. The fact that he avoided the night air, rested a great deal, and considered a trip south in 1818, probably is evidence that he realized he had contracted the "family disease." He was suffering too, a pressure on his chest, almost like suffocation. Anxious about himself, he kept a watchful eye on his sister Fanny, regularly questioning her about her health. She was thin and listless. In April, 1818, he spent much time with the Brawnes who had moved to London.

Back at Hampstead, in late April, he wrote "On a Grecian Urn," in which he first shows the contrasts between the visual arts and poetry: the urn is an "unravished bride of quietness"; in its silence, it can tell a tale "more sweetly than our rhyme." On the urn is depicted a bold, passionate lover, *almost* achieving his desire; yet, Keats consoles him:

> . . . . do not grieve;
> She cannot fade, though thou hast not thy bliss,
>   Forever wilt thou love, and she be fair!

As he tells of the pipes and timbrels playing, he adds,

> Heard melodies are sweet, but those unheard
> Are sweeter; therefore, ye soft pipes play on
> Not to the sensual ear, but, more endeared,
> Pipe to the spirit ditties of no tone.

The timeless perfection of art he sees, as he writes of one scene on the urn

> Ah happy, happy boughs! that cannot shed
> Your leaves, nor ever bid the Spring adieu;
> And happy melodist, unwearied,
> Forever piping songs forever new;
> More happy love! more happy, happy love!
> For ever warm and still to be enjoyed,
> For ever panting, and for ever young . . .

He realizes, however, that "the imaginary world of art and the real world of experience must complement one another." He concludes by saying that when old age shall waste this generation, the urn will remain, a friend to man, for,

> "Beauty is truth,—truth, beauty,"—that is all
> Ye know on earth, and all ye need to know.

On April 30, going out into the garden, he heard a nightingale sing. In *Ode to a Nightingale*, before he hears the bird sing, he says,

> My heart aches, and a drowsy numbness pains
> My sense, as though of hemlock I had drunk,
> Or emptied some dull opiate to the drains
> One minute past, and Lethe wards had sunk.

As the nightingale sang happily "of summer in full throated ease," its song lifted him out of the "drowsy numbness" and heart-ache he had felt since Tom's death and yet made him wish that he might drink from

> . . . a beaker full of the warm South,
> Full of the true, the blushful Hippocrene,
> With beaded bubbles winking at the brim,
> And purple-stained mouth;
> That I might drink, and leave the world unseen,
> And with thee fade away into the forest dim:
>
> Fade far away, dissolve, and quite forget
> What thou among the leaves hast never known,
> The weariness, the fever, and the fret

> Here where men sit and hear each other groan;
> Where palsy shakes a few, sad, last gray hairs,
> Where youth grows pale, and spectre-thin, and dies,
> Where but to think is to be full of sorrow
> And leaden-eyed despairs;
> Where beauty cannot keep her lustrous eyes,
> Or new love pine at them beyond tomorrow.

Yet, aroused from the magic of the nightingale's song, he knows he will not seek release through wine but through poetry. He realizes that at times he has been "half in love with easeful Death"; yet, he realizes he must face whatever life has to offer, for

> . . . the fancy cannot cheat so well
> As she is famed to do, deceiving elf.

Then, as the nightingale's singing ceases, he asks,

> Was it a vision, or a waking dream?
> Fled is that music:—do I wake or sleep?

Keats and Fanny Brawne were on closer terms when Mrs. Midgley Jennings filed suit for a larger share of the Keats children's grandfather's estate, thus tying up John's share for a time and raising the prospect of heavy lawyers' fees. He had finally decided to become an Apothecary, when his friend Brown persuaded him not to do so, but to write a play with him in the hope of having it produced at Drury Lane. Keats agreed; he decided, moreover, to stop work on "Hyperion" and put out a new volume of the shorter poems he had been writing. Dim as his financial prospects were, he discussed marriage with Fanny, giving her "the unpromising warning" of his life; yet telling her "I would never see anything but Pleasure in your eyes, love on your lips, and Happiness in your steps." He wished their love to be "a delight in the midst of Pleasures agreeable enough, rather than a resource from vexations and cares. . . . We might spend a pleasant year at Berne or Zurich—if it should please Venus to hear my 'Beseach thee to hear us O Goddess'." Otherwise, she must stay on at home, and he, at Hampstead, living upon "hope and chance." In June, Keats left for a holiday on the Isle of Wight, which he found not so pleasant as he had remembered it. As the summer passed and he was at home again, Fanny seemed so indifferent that he again decided to stifle his love for her. Writing constantly, he told a friend, "I feel it in my power to become a popular writer." When George, having financial troubles in America, wrote John for aid, the latter was able to assist him, though he himself could not obtain money due him.

As fall came, he walked every day past the fields that had been heavy with wheat. As he looked at the harvest landscape, he reflected how lush a season fall was. "How fine the air," he wrote. "A temperate sharpness about it. Really without joking, chaste weather—Dian skies—I never lik'd stubble fields so much as now—Aye better than the chilly green of spring. Somehow a stubble plain looks warm—in the same way that some pictures look warm—this struck me so much in my Sunday's walk that I composed upon it." In his poem "To Autumn," he portrayed that season as one of abundance, of vigorous life:

> Season of mists and mellow fruitfulness,
> Close bosom-friend of the maturing sun;
> Conspiring with him how to load and bless
> With fruit the vines that round the thatch-eaves run;
> To bend with apples the moss'd cottaged trees
> To swell the gourd, and plump the hazel shells
> With a sweet kernel; to set budding more,
> And still more, later flowers for the bees,
> Until they think warm days will never cease;
> For Summer has o'erbrimm'd their clammy cells.

Then, in a series of gorgeous metaphors, he personified autumn as a maiden sitting "careless on a granary floor," her hair "soft-lifted by the winnowing wind," or sound asleep on a half-reaped furrow, while her "hook spared the next swath and all its twined flowers," or as a gleaner, crossing a brook, or by a "cyder-press," patiently watching "the last oozings hour by hour." The songs of spring, he said, are fine, but autumn has its music too and its color. He pointed out the "barred clouds" as the day dies softly, touching

> . . . . the stubble plain with rosy hue;
> Then in a wailful choir the small gnats mourn
> Among the river shallows, borne aloft
> Or sinking as the light wind lives or dies;
> And full-grown lambs loud bleat from hilly bourn;
> Hedge-crickets sing; and now with treble soft
> The red-breast whistles from a garden-croft;
> And gathering swallows twitter in the skies.

The day he completed the poem, he decided he must earn a living, not through medicine but by writing for periodicals. This would mean giving up writing poetry, but his finances dictated that he do so. In April, 1819, John Keats attracted Coleridge who was talking to a friend in a lane near Highgate. Keats, whom Coleridge described as a "loose, slack, not well dressed youth," came over and walked with him nearly two miles. Many of Coleridge's thoughts on philosophy had been those on which Keats had long speculated.

Coleridge said that after Keats left him, the young man came back and said, "Let me carry away the memory, Coleridge, of having pressed your hand." When Keats left him, Coleridge said to his companion, "There is death in that hand."

On October 8, 1819, Keats again met Fanny Brawne, now more tender and certain about her love for him. Keats was too dazed to believe his good fortune real. It seems Mrs. Brawne had consented to the engagement, but that no date was set for the wedding, nor did Fanny openly wear the engagement ring for a year and a half. It probably was a garnet ring that had been Keats' mother's. Keats decided the engagement should be kept secret.

At the moment of his greatest happiness, he became ill again and took laudanum for a time until a friend persuaded him to stop. Realizing now he was in the first stages of tuberculosis, he felt himself drifting, despite all his efforts, toward a critical illness. He was elated when his play "Otho" was accepted to be presented at Drury Lane, though later he was told it would not be put on until the following season; Keats, eager for an immediate production, decided to offer it to Covent Garden. In the meantime, the publisher, Taylor, impressed by the recognition of Drury Lane, agreed to bring out his new book of poems. Suddenly, a letter from George Keats arrived in London, saying he wished to borrow a sizable sum from John.

With his health poor and his marriage pending, John never should have done what he did; but George was so persistent that John lent him £700. Now £20 in debt, John had financial problems that were augmented by Covent Garden's rejection of his play and by his catching cold one blustery February day when the weather suddenly changed and he was in town without his great coat. Badly chilled, he became quite ill and was bedfast; Fanny and other friends cared for him. Three days later, sitting up in bed, he had a hemorrhage. The doctor insisted it was caused by the crisis of his anger at his brother George; the physician insisted he found no traces of tuberculosis. In March, when he became worse, another doctor was summoned; he too, insisted John Keats was not tubercular. In June, again, he suffered from the rusty taste of blood, but there was no hemorrhage. That afternoon, he went to Leigh Hunt's for tea; in the evening, he had a severe hemorrhage. The physician summoned found Keats' condition so serious that he placed him in Leigh Hunt's house in Mortimer Terrace where someone would always be present to care for him. For seven weeks, he lay ill; then, Charles Lamb called another physician, under whose treatment Keats became somewhat better. It was decided he should go to Italy, an idea repugnant to the poet, who wrote Fanny Brawne, " 'Tis certain I shall never recover if I am to be so long separate from you." Friends who came to see him now were shocked at the change in his appearance. His color was faded; his hands swollen; his body emaciated. Finally, he went to the Brawnes' where Fanny and her mother nursed him carefully. Shelley, when he learned of his friend's illness, invited him to be his guest at Pisa. Fanny now was truly his young love; her mother, too, became deeply attached to him. Yet, all his friends knew, as did Mrs. Brawne and Fanny, that Keats must go to a warmer, gentler climate than that of England. Reluctant at first to sail to Italy, Keats finally agreed to go. Convinced that his death was inevitable, he decided to go; it would be better for Fanny, for she would be spared the sight of his death. When, in August, he had another hemorrhage, he decided his departure must not be postponed. Joseph Severn, a cheerful young man of limited experience, a painter struggling for recognition, agreed to accompany Keats.

After innumerable delays, they arrived in Italy on October 31, Keats' twenty-fifth birthday, determined to go to Rome to see Dr. Clark, a well-known physician. He gave Keats tender and devoted care; there were traces of tuberculosis, he said, in Keats' stomach. Interested in the young man's poetry, Dr. Clark encouraged him to write again, and Keats talked of doing so. But in December, he had more hemorrhages. Leigh Hunt wrote him his recovery was possible if only he'd hope for it. Keats' friends, when news that he was worse reached them, were agitated but did little to help him. Fanny Brawne, however, annoyed that some of Keats' friends dodged their responsibilities in really aiding him, was convinced he was being killed not only by indifference but also by "want of feeling in those who ought above all to have felt for him." Griefstricken, she wrote his sister, Fanny, addressing her as "My dear Sister, for so I feel you to be, forgive me if I have not sufficiently softened this wretched news. Indeed I am not now able to contrive words that would appear less harsh—if I am to lose him, I lose everything, and then you, after my mother, will be the only person I shall feel interest or attachment for—I feel that I love his sister as my own."

By the middle of February, thoroughly exhausted, as his body was relaxing its hold on life, Keats seemed at peace. Since December, when the mere sight of Fanny Brawne's handwriting unnerved him, making him far more ill, he had opened none of her letters nor any of those from England; yet he held almost constantly a small oval white cornelian that Fanny Brawne had given him. Hoping to stop the flow of blood, Dr. Clark put him on a starvation diet—a little bread and milk and occasionally a mouthful of fish. Yet the bleeding persisted; he is in "a deplorable state," Dr. Clark said. "His stomach is ruined and the state of his mind is the worst possible for one in his condition." Keats was convinced his English friends had sent him to Italy to die alone. His knowledge of anatomy made his illness "ten times worse at every change—every way he is unfortunate," said Dr. Clark. As Keats lay critically ill, listening to the constant play of water in the fountain outside his window, he thought of Beaumont's words: "All your better deeds shall be writ in water." He began to tell Severn of his last wishes: Severn was to have his set of Shakespeare plays and poems; the purse Fanny had made for him, her unopened letters, and a lock of her hair were to be placed in his casket. On his tomb, were to be placed only the words, "Here Lies One Whose Name Was Writ in Water"; above it, was to be carved a Greek lyre with four of its eight strings broken— "to show his Classical Genius cut off by death before its maturity," Severn said later, not knowing it was the device of the Tassie gem Fannie Brawne had given him on Christmas, 1818. Her seal, then, not his name, he had decided was to mark his final resting place. His death was painful: for three horrible days, he struggled against suffocation, coughing until he was weak. Finally on February 23, as he was dying, he told Severn, "Don't be frightened—I shall die easy— be firm, and thank God it has come." But he did not die easily; for seven hours, he struggled with the mucus in his throat until he lost the strength to cough. As Keats lay back at length exhausted, Severn thought he had fallen asleep, but slowly realized John Keats was dead. An autopsy showed his lungs were entirely destroyed; it was amazing that he had lived so long. On Monday, February 26, he was buried near the grave of Shelley's third child in the Protestant Cemetery. The English chaplain and eight mourners followed his body to the burial place; at the conclusion of the service, Dr. Clark and his friends heaped turfs of daisies on the grave.

When Fanny Brawne and her mother heard the news, they went into mourning; later, Fanny fell ill, and after her recovery, wore widow's clothing. Thin and disconsolate, she read and re-read Keats' letters. Often, she walked on the heath Keats so loved, by day and by night, at times so late the night watchman had to be sent for her. A year and a half after Keats' death, the gravestone was erected over the poet's grave at Severn's expense. His friends wished the inscription to be as Keats directed; but Brown insisted a preface should precede the inscription Keats desired. Accordingly, the gravestone read:

> This Grave
> contains all that Was Mortal
> of a
> YOUNG ENGLISH POET
> Who
> on his Death Bed,
> In the Bitterness of his Heart
> At the Malicious Power of His Enemies,
> Desired
> these Words to be engraven on his Tomb Stone
> "Here Lies One
> Whose Name was writ in Water."

The first real tribute to him came from Shelley who in "Adonais" eulogized him as one who

> . . . has outsoared the shadow of our night;
> Envy and calumny and hate and pain,
> And that unrest which men miscall delight,
> Can touch him not and torture not again;
> From the contagion of the world's slow stain
> He is secure . . . .

While Keats died feeling rejected, the Wordsworths were gaining popularity. In October 1819, Mrs. Coleridge wrote that "The Wordsworths are quite in request. You have no notion how much respectability attaches to them. Their society is much courted." They had, indeed, been royally entertained and they had entertained some distinguished visitors. Among them, were the Wilberforces and their party. Samuel Wilberforce, the great anti-slavery leader, whom Dorothy had known well in her girlhood, was now a famous man, an eminent statesman and a man of wealth. He had written Dorothy that his party would include nineteen people. Dorothy, eager to please the man she had not seen since her girlhood, secured two houses for him, his wife, and their servants at Rydal. Mr. Wilberforce had warned Dorothy that they were accustomed to conveniences and would send by wagon the greater part of their luggage. The mountain of luggage, seven servants, and five horses arrived first, on a wet, rainy day. When the cook heard she had to go to Ambleside for some items they required, she muttered, "Our men don't like doing errands. They're not used to it." The Wilberforces' arrogant servants commented, "What an inconvenient place," when they heard they could not procure beer except at Ambleside. The housemaid and the kitchen-maid didn't like the mattresses. But when the Wilberforces arrived, how different were the conversations and the comments. "The rooms were larger than they expected—and so *many* sitting rooms, it was quite delightful, and as to the garden, the situation, everything was to their minds," Dorothy wrote Mrs. Clarkson. On first meeting Mrs. Wilberforce, Dorothy thought she appeared to be good, patient, and meek; later, however, she disliked her "slowness and whininess of manner, tending to self righteousness." When Mr. Wilberforce arrived, all ran to meet him; his body was feeble and he seemed worn out, but his mind was "as lively as ever. . . . There never lived a man of sweeter temper. He is made up of benevolence and loving kindness. . . . His children very much resemble him in ardour and liveliness of mind," Dorothy said.

In 1819, Dorothy went on the first of a number of visits, beginning in London for dental work. Her three months there were gay, despite her dental surgery. She visited with Willy, who was there in school, with the Lambs, Tom Monkhouse, and Mrs. Clarkson. "Mary Lamb," Dorothy wrote, "is sadly fat and she dresses so loose she looks the worse for it. Yet she is still a good walker." She realized she herself was growing older; she commented on the fact she had worn glasses for three years and now was having her remaining teeth removed. She enjoyed her quarters at Lambeth, where her drawing room overlooked "the Archbishop's garden grounds, a beautiful green field with very fine trees and not a building to be seen except one rustic cattle shed." Often, Dorothy walked across Waterloo Bridge; she found the river beautiful, some days as clear and bright as if it were among the Lakes. Sometimes, she heard the notes of a thrush or a blackbird from the trees in the Archbishop's garden.

In June, Mary, William, and the newly wed Monkhouses joined her for a tour of the continent. They sailed from Calais; then they went to Dunkirk, to Bruges, Ghent, Brussels, Aix-la-Chapelle, Cologne, Frankfurt, and Heidelberg. They went to Zurich, Berne, and Interlaken, crossing the western Alps, and thence to Lucerne, Locarno, Milan, Como, Lausanne, and Geneva. Returning, they spent some time at Dijon and Fontainebleau, and were in Paris a month. Excited over the trip, attracted by mountains, lakes, and the landscapes so new to her, Dorothy arose at five each morning, and at midnight was again at her window enjoying the moonlight. She loved the Alps, at times "burnished by the sun," and at sunset with their "wintry marble coldness"; even as the evening gloom descended over the city, "the snowy laps of the Alps were still visible." She was delighted by the roaring of a stream, as she saw it "issuing from its icy cavern beneath the snow-like roof of the large glacier. A cold blast following the river blew upon us as we passed over the bridge. I shall never forget the sensation. The blast seemed as if its birthplace were in the icy cavern and thence issuing it would be fed with indestructible power." People, too, interested her, among them the good-natured, jolly landlord at Maypence who reminded her of Chaucer's Host of the Tabard Inn, arguing so hotly with the guests that she expected a serious quarrel, but who ended laughing; the landlady at Hamburg, "fat, merry, and Dutch-built; when she laughed (which she did almost constantly . . .) the thick, warm covering of her cheeks, throat, body, and arms shook in a manner that was perfectly ludicrous." She enjoyed the fat old gentleman and his wife who "passed from dish to dish, as if appetite grew with what it fed on"; the elderly woman with a blond wig who "was very fair and withered; she must formerly have been handsome, and seemed unwilling to think she had parted from her youth." Dorothy was sympathetic toward the doleful-looking ragged old beggar woman who sat on the steps at Calais Cathedral with her dog beside her, and, when given a penny, "brightened with a light and gracious smile," an effect almost "supernatural." Mary was amazed at the way Dorothy talked to everybody, made friends, and gained information, though her French and German were not good. She spoke to all she met in lonely places and treasured the stories they confided to her. In Paris, the party called on Annette and Caroline and visited with Miss Williams, a minor poet. Dorothy visited the Louvre six times. The party sailed from Boulogne to Dover, and soon were crossing Westminster Bridge, "the point whence our sixteen weeks pleasant rambling had begun."

In London, they spent their first night at a dreary hotel, then called on Crabb Robinson, the Lambs, and Coleridge. They toured the Royal Academy where recently effigies of Walter Scott and William Wordsworth had been placed as an honor. Willy joined them on Sundays and half-holidays. In Cambridge, the Wordsworths visited William's brother, Christopher, now Master of Trinity College and Vice-Chancellor of Cambridge University.

Back at home, Dorothy was pleased when her niece Dora came

from Ambleside to see her. She was impressed by the change a year had made in Dora. "She is grown thoughtful, steady, and womanly, but is more lively than she used to be since her first going to school. She is as lively as when she was ten years old and has nothing left of her boisterousness or want of gracefulness either in manner or deportment. . . . What a delight do I feel in seeing that dear girl." A new intimacy sprang up between them, one precious to both of them.

By Wordsworth's fiftieth birthday, his place as a great English poet was well established. In 1821, after his tour of the continent, where with Mary and Dorothy he had enjoyed places he had visited as a youth, Wordsworth published *Memorials of a Tour On The Continent* and *Ecclesiastical Sonnets;* some were narrow in their point of view; some mechanical; yet others, like "Mutability," "King's College, Cambridge," and "Old Abbeys," were exquisite. Though Wordsworth's friends realized these were not his best poems, Coleridge was the only one with courage to tell him so. Crabb Robinson had once tried to talk with him, and Lamb had long ago ceased to point out any deficiencies in his poetry.

Though he could not judge the value of his own verses, Wordsworth had distinct ideas about the work of his fellow authors. He contended that a poet must have not only great mental powers, but also "knowledge of the heart, and this can only be gained by time and tranquil leisure. No *great* poem was ever written by a young man or an unhappy one. It was clear Coleridge's constant infelicity had prevented him from being the poet that Nature intended him to be. He had always too much personal and domestic discontent to paint the sorrows of mankind. Not being able to dwell on natural woes, he took to the supernatural." Wordsworth told Sir Henry Taylor that Coleridge "had been 'in blossom' only four years—from 1796 to 1800. The plant was perennial, but the flowers were few." He admired much of Burns's poetry and at times quoted him; he liked Longfellow's poetry, but "regretted his name." William Blake, he thought wrote poetry greater than Byron or Scott. Though in 1796 Wordsworth had written that Southey was "certainly a coxcomb" and *Joan of Arc* "certainly proves it," in 1805, when Southey's *Madoc* appeared, Wordsworth said it abounded in "beautiful pictures and descriptions, happily introduced," yet it failed "in the highest gifts of the poet's mind, imagination in the true sense of the word." In 1812, he called the poet "one of the cleverest men that is now living," admired the research he did, and his industry, but contended "he does not give anything which impresses the mind strongly and is recollected in solitude." In 1829, he praised Southey's style as a prose writer, adding "His style is eminently clear, lively, and unemcumbered, and his information unbounded." In 1839, he regretted Southey was "completely dead" to all but books. Wordsworth then wondered if he himself would ever lose his "interest in things, and retain an interest only in books. . . . If I must lose my interest in one of them, I would rather give up books than men."

In 1816, when the Byron divorce scandal was at its height, Wordsworth said, "The man is insane, and will probably end his career in a madhouse. . . . The verses on his private affairs excite in me less indignation than pity." *Don Juan*, he criticized on moral grounds, calling it "an infamous publication which those who attacked Shelley were too cowardly to condemn." In 1827, he wrote that "Byron seems to me deficient in *feeling*"; his "critical prognostications have, for the most part, proved erroneous. . . ." Wordsworth believed some of Byron's lines, like

> I stood at Venice on the Bridge of Sighs,
> A palace and a prison on each hand

were "faulty." In fact, some "person ought to write a critical review, analyzing Lord Byron's language in order to guard others against imitating him in these respects." In 1836, he told how he abhorred Byron's morality, though he admired his genius and power. Wordsworth added he was forty-five when he first read Byron; his taste was already formed and "we cannot after that age love new things. New impressions are difficult to make. Had I been young, I should have enjoyed much of them, I have no doubt."

In 1826, he called Shelley "the greatest of modern geniuses . . . Shelley is one of the best artists of us all; I mean in workmanship of style," a greater poet than Byron. Wordsworth objected, however, to Shelley's losing his temper at the mere mention of kings and priests, without "reflecting that they could not have endured so long if there had not been some value in them." Shelley and Byron, he said, "would ever be favorites with the young, but would not satisfy men of all ages." In 1836, he told Gladstone that he thought Shelley had "the greatest native powers in poetry of all men of this age." Later, he said that Shelley's "To a Skylark" was full of imagination but that it did not show the same observation of nature as his (Wordsworth's) poem did.

Among prose writers, Wordsworth favored Walter Savage Landor, who, he thought, wrote "powerfully"; Hazlitt, he considered "a writer of extraordinary acuteness, but perverse." In 1831, he wrote that in Scott's novel, *Guy Mannering*, there was "considerable talent displayed," but believed the adventures were "not well chosen or invented, and they are still worse put together; and the characters, with the exception of Meg Merrilies, excite little interest. . . . *Waverley* heightened my opinion of Scott's talents considerably and if *Guy Mannering* has not added much, neither, it has not taken much away." In 1834, Jane Austen's novels he found were "an admirable copy of life," but lacked imagination. In 1839, he said he liked Carlyle "in small doses"; but bewailed Carlyle's lack of "sympathy with mankind."

When William was spending a great deal of time writing sonnets on the Church of England, Dorothy said, "This disturbs us. After fifty years of age there is no time to spare, and unfinished works should not, if possible, be left behind. This, he feels, but he will never govern his labours. How different from Southey who can go as regularly as clockwork, from history to poetry, from poetry to criticism, and so on to biography, or anything else. If their minds could each spare a little to the other, how much better for both!"

An addition to the Wordsworth circle, in 1821, was Edward Quillinan, a lieutenant in the third Dragoon Guards quartered in Edinburgh. More interested in literature than military affairs, Quillinan had long been fascinated with Wordsworth's poetry. Eager to make Wordsworth's acquaintance, he was taking a holiday at Penrith. His first call started out badly, as Wordsworth, who seemed annoyed at this intrusion, "twirled a chair about," was stiff, and angry. When seventeen-year-old Dora entered the room, William's mood changed; but once she departed, again he twirled the chair and resumed his frigidity until Sara Hutchinson entered, teased him for twirling the chair, laughed him into a good humor, and sent him out to show Quillinan the garden. There, they walked while Wordsworth talked of poetry in a good-natured mood. After that, Quillinan came frequently and soon settled nearby with his wife and child. Such a great friendship had developed between the Quillinans and the Wordsworths, that when the Quillinans' daughter Rotha was born, Dora was the baby's godmother. After little Rotha's birth, Mrs. Quillinan's mind became temporarily deranged; Mary and Dorothy helped nurse her until she could be taken to Lancaster for special treatment. Then Dorothy and Mary looked after the children, while William, to comfort the harassed father, took him on a walking tour in Yorkshire. By the following April, Mrs. Quillinan was restored to health and the family moved into Ivy Cottage at the foot of Rydal Mount. All the Wordsworths and Quillinans were happy that Mrs. Quillinan was so well; then, one summer day her clothing caught fire, and before the flames could be extinguished, she was frightfully burned. Two nurses cared for her; Dorothy and Mary at times relieved them. Mrs. Quillinan seemed to be doing well; her children caused little disturbance. Then came a sudden relapse while Dorothy was attending her. She died an agonizing death, leaving Dorothy harassed and exhausted, but relieved that Mary was spared "the last awful scene" as Mrs. Quillinan died. Dorothy had admired the deceased young woman's patience and disposition during her suffering. "We have every arrangement to make in his melancholy house," she wrote a friend. Most of the summer Dorothy spent helping Mr. Quillinan and the children, though she did visit the Clarksons briefly. Then Willy Wordsworth became seriously ill and Dorothy and Mary nursed him. After his recovery, there was a rush of visitors.

The next two years, Dorothy traveled again: in September, 1822, with Joanna Hutchinson to Scotland; in 1824, to London, where she heard Edward Irving, the eloquent Scotch divine, a figure noted in literary circles, who attacked Southey and "the Blasphemer Lord Byron for the impiety of their visions and judgments." She also visited with the Lambs and saw Tom Monkhouse, who was quite ill, and his brother John, now almost blind.

The summer of 1825 was marked by the visit of Walter Scott and his party, who passed through the Lake Country en route from Ireland where they had visited Sir Walter's son, who was quartered there with his regiment, and from Wales where they had visited the now old ladies of Llangollen. In Dublin, while Sir Walter was attending the theatre, as news spread that he was present, the whole audience arose to cheer him. John Wilson, now a Professor at Edinburgh, had come to Elleray to welcome Sir Walter; he, the Wordsworths, and a large party assembled to do honor to Scott, and to William Canning, whom the Wordsworths had visited in Paris. "The weather," wrote Sir Walter's son-in-law, Lockhart, "was as Elysian as the scenery. There were brilliant cavalcades through the woods in the mornings, and delicious boatings on the lake by moonlight; and the last day 'the Admiral of the Lake' presided over one of the most splendid regattas that ever enlivened Windermere. Perhaps there were not fewer than fifty barges following in the Professor's radiant procession, when it paused at the point of Storrs to admit into the place of honour the vessel that carried kind and happy Mr. Bolton and his guests. The bards of the Lakes led the cheers that hailed Scott and Canning; and music and sunshine, flags, streamers and gay dresses, the merry hum of voices, the rapid splashing of innumerable oars, made up a dazzling mixture of sensations as the flotilla wound its way among the richly foliaged islands, and along bays and promontories peopled with enthusiastic spectators." From Windermere, the party came to Rydal Mount; one day, William and Dora took the guests over to see Southey; the following day, Dorothy joined the party in an expedition over the Kirkstone to Airey Force and Lyulph's Tower to visit other friends, and to see Lowther Castle.

Scott later wrote of the "ovation" he received in the Lake Country; his son-in-law, delighted to see honor paid Scott, was, however, contemptuous of those who honored him. Wordsworth, Lockhart considered "proud and pompous and absurdly arrogant"; he resented Wordsworth's "spouting" his own verses en route to Keswick; the breakfast party at Rydal Mount, he considered "vulgar"; Dorothy Wordsworth, he said was "as yellow as a duck's foot"; Quillinan he believed was the only "genteelish figure" among "a great party of abominables" who stared at Sir Walter. That Dorothy did not so impress others is evidenced by the fact that that same summer her friend Maria Jane Jewsbury had spoken of dreading to grow old and had said to Dora Wordsworth, "if I could age like your Aunt Wordsworth, and unite green vigour with grey maturity, it were well; but who is like her?" Sir Walter, fond of her, had asked her to come again to visit him at Abbotsford, and not to wait too long, as "the years are slipping by faster than they did."

Dorothy's visits the next few years were largely with her nephews. She frequently visited John who had taken his degree at Oxford and entered the ministry. He was assigned a curacy at Whitmilk, near Coleorton. Willy, still undecided about his vocation, Dorothy said, "has the Army so strongly in his head that I'm afraid there's no turning him away from it and his poor mother will be wretched when she finds this to be the case—for she has no idea that he will persist in opposition to his Father's and her wishes." By March, however, Willy had decided to go abroad and study languages. Dorothy joined him for a visit on the Isle of Man. In the fall of 1828, on her way to keep house for John, she stopped to visit Miss Jewsbury at Manchester, who reported Dorothy "in excellent health and high spirits, tireless in tramping, visiting churches, museums, factories, then shopping, leaving everyone panting behind her. She is the very genius of popularity, an embodied spell." She spent a winter helping John with his parish duties, reading, visiting at Coleorton, three miles away, and walking in Charnwood Forest. In March, Willy visited them, before he left for Germany.

Then suddenly, in April, Dorothy became seriously ill with a bowel infection; a raging fever developed, and her life was in danger for twenty-four hours. At the same time, Willy was having eye trouble; Mary came to nurse the two of them. In a few days, she reported Dorothy was well, though she would require watchfulness. This was Dorothy's first illness in fifty-six years. A month later, all were discouraged at the slowness with which she was regaining her strength. On her return home, she again became ill, this time with "cholera morbitis." From November 1830 until the following April, she was bedfast or confined to the house. By April, she wrote, "It is very pleasing to observe the joy of every face at the sight of me, looking, as they say, healthy and well. So, indeed I am, but I find I must not use my strength at all." William, she wrote Mary Lamb, "is having more trouble with his eyes, which disables him from reading much" and renders the use of his pen "irksome to him. . . . His muscular powers are in no degree diminished. Indeed, I think he walks regularly, more than ever, finding fresh air the best bracing to his weak eyes. He is still the crack skater on Rydal Lake, and, as to climbing of mountains, the hardiest and the youngest are yet hardly a match for him." He depended a great deal on his daughter, Dora. Sara and Joanna Hutchinson were with the Wordsworths; the latter was an invalid. "Coleridge is declining in body, but they tell us as vigorous as ever in mind. . . . Hartley goes on as usual," Dorothy wrote.

In July 1828, Dora and William had accompanied Coleridge on a trip to Flanders, the Rhine Valley, and Holland. An Irish traveler, Thomas Colley Grattan, who spent three days with the poets on this trip, described them. Coleridge, he said, "was about five feet five inches in height, of a full and lazy appearance, but not actually stout. He was dressed in black and wore short breeches, buttoned and tied at the knees, and black silk stockings. . . . His face was extremely handsome, its expression, placid and benevolent. His mouth was particularly pleasing, and his grey eyes, neither large nor prominent, were full of intelligent softness. His hair, of which he had plenty, was entirely white. His forehead and cheeks were unfurrowed, and the latter showed a healthy bloom. . . . Wordsworth was a complete antithesis to Coleridge—tall, wiry, harsh in features, coarse in figure, inelegant in looks. He was roughly dressed in long brown *surtout*, striped duck trousers, fustian gaiters, and thick shoes. He more resembled a mountain farmer than a 'Lake poet.' His whole air was unrefined and unprepossessing. . . . He seemed satisfied to let his friend and fellow-traveler take the lead, with a want of pretension rarely found in men of literary reputation far inferior to his; while there was something unobtrusively amiable in his bearing toward his daughter." Grattan was tremendously impressed by Coleridge's flow of talk, while Wordsworth's remarks, which at first seemed commonplace, upon reflection, seemed solid and sensible. Wordsworth was especially interested in inspecting the battle field at Waterloo. Wordsworth, Grattan noted, spoke French haltingly, adding that "five-and-twenty years previously he understood and spoke it well, but that his abhorance of the Revolutionary excesses made him resolve to forget the language altogether and that for a long time he had not read nor spoken a word of it."

Another traveler, young Julian Charles Young, told how Coleridge and Wordsworth "soon attracted to Mrs. Ader's house all the illuminate of Bonn—Niebuhr, Becker, Augustus Schlegel, and many others. . . . Schlegel praised Scott's poetry. Coleridge decried it, stating that no poet ever lived of equal eminence, whose writings furnished so few quotable passages. Schlegel then praised Byron; Coleridge immediately tried to depreciate him. 'Ah,' said he, 'Byron is a meteor which will blaze and rove and die; Wordsworth there (pointing to him) is a star luminous and fixed'. . . . I must say I never saw any manifestation of small jealousy between Coleridge and Wordsworth, which, considering the vanity possessed by each, I thought uncommonly to the credit of both." Schlegel, Coleridge considered "a consumate coxcomb," but was pleased to be told by Schlegel that his translation of *Wallenstein* was better than the original. "If so," Coleridge said, "it is because I struck out a word from almost every line. Wherever I could retrench a syllable, I did so, and I cleared away the greatest possible quantity of stuffing."

Dora Wordsworth wrote her mother that her father, Coleridge and she "got on famously, but that Mr. C. sometimes detains them with his fiddle faddling, and that he likes prosing to the folks better than exerting himself to see the face of the country, and that father, with his few half dozen words of German makes himself better understood than Mr. C. with all his weight of German literature." She underestimated Coleridge's knowledge of German, for while at Bonn, he had visited the new school of German philosophy and derived considerable information, part of which he incorporated later in a series of lectures.

The summer of 1831 was a happy one for the Wordsworths. Willy was home from Germany, and a flock of company brought much gaiety to Rydal Mount. Dr. Christopher Wordsworth's three clever sons, as usual, were enjoying themselves on a visit there. Dora Wordsworth, young Sara Coleridge, and young Edith Southey, great friends, always had plenty of boy friends. One evening, there was a dance for forty.

Dorothy now was able to walk in the terrace garden; she had a pony chaise in which she called on neighbors. In October, Robert Jones, the friend of William's youth, with whom he had climbed the Alps forty years ago, visited the Wordsworths. He was now "fat and rostabout and rosy and puffing while he climbed the hill to Rydal Mount."

The week before Christmas, Dorothy again became violently ill, with recurrence of internal inflammation, "acute pain and nausea"; for the most part, she was unable to walk. The next few years were a series of repeated illnesses, from which she recovered only to be ill again. When the first spring flowers were carried up to her room, in 1832, she wrote:

> I felt a power unfelt before
> Controlling weakness, languor, pain;
> It bore me to the terrace walk;
> I trod the hills again.
>
> No prisoner in this lonely room
> I *saw* the green banks of the Wye,
> Recalling my prophetic words,
> Bard! Brother! Friend from infancy.
>
> No need of motion or of strength
> Or even the breathing air;
> I thought of Nature's loveliest scenes
> And with memory I was there.

Loving friends were eager to aid her. In 1833, she was again seriously ill, but before long Dora wrote, "She can read, write, walk, talk, and walk about her room without a stick—dress herself—and drives herself out every day. She has been sitting for her portrait to a Mr. Crosthwaite (a self-educated artist from Cockermouth)." Two months later there was another relapse. Through 1834, she gradually became more feeble. At times, she seemed dying, growing weaker and weaker; "at one moment, you might think she had not ten minutes to live, at another, she is so bright and strong that you are almost cheated into a belief that she may be spared even for years." For sixty-four years, she had asked "more of her body than it could give"; finally, successive illnesses took from her the willpower to perform even the normal functions of living, saving the body at the expense of the mind.

For the next twenty years only at times did she seem herself; for the most part, however, she was "mentally vague and wandering." At times she wept at a beautiful scene, "then, tragically, like Ophelia, she began to sing. When she is not comfortable," wrote Quillinan, "you ought to stop your ears." Even Mary Wordsworth admitted "She is exactly like a very clever, tyrannical, spoiled child (for she is acute and discriminating to a marvelous degree) yet she has intervals of mildness and is overcome by her old affections, and sometimes she is very languid and weeps, which is very afflicting . . . at times if you can fix her attention, her intellect is bright, and she will express an opinion when asked, with as much judgment, as in her best days—but alas these gleams are short lived." She still drew pleasure from poetry. One day, when William was quoting from Dyer's verses, she finished a line for him, to his amazement and that of the household. Birds and flowers, mountains, and views of the lake still gave her pleasure. The garden gate to Rydal Mount was now locked so that on a fine day emaciated, little Dorothy could be wheeled into the garden, yet be protected from strangers. At times, however, she called out to them. Quillinan, his daughters, and Crabb Robinson were frequent visitors. Wordsworth was usually at her side restlessly watching her with the same tenderness that had moved her in her youth. When she had fits of wayward passion, William alone could calm her. "The only enjoyment he seems to feel is his attachment on her," wrote a friend.

Depressed by Dorothy's illness, William traveled a little in 1831; he hoped to see Charles and Mary Lamb in London, but did not. "I have no beds for them if they come down, and but a sort of a house to receive them in," Charles wrote, thinking someone would accompany Wordsworth; "yet I shall regret their departure unseen. I feel cramped and straiten'd every way. Where are they?" he asked Crabb Robinson. Living in the suburbs, but longing for the shopwindows of London, Lamb had earlier tried to coax Wordsworth to come to London; then he realized he could not entertain him as he had. He did not feel that he could leave Mary to visit the Wordsworths, for he was anxious about her health. While in London, Wordsworth did see Francis Jeffrey who had written about him so bitterly in *Blackwood's Magazine*. Behaving as a man of the world, Wordsworth did not appear to be conscious of anything unpleasant ever having passed between them. At Uckfield, he dined with several magistrates whom he heard complain about the agricultural workers who, protesting against reduced wages, and the use of farm machinery, were rioting, burning barns. The magistrates were objecting to juries that would not convict the laborers, about poor cash payments and interest rates, "and that general incubus of universal agricultural distress." "Five times," he said, "I have dined at the table of an earl, and twice in the company of a prince. Therefore let you and Mrs. Kenyon prepare yourselves for something stately and august in my deportment and manners! But king, queen, prince, princess, dukes etc., are common articles at Brighton, so that I must descend from my elevation, or pass for a downright Malvolio."

That same year, in September, he and his daughter Dora visited Sir Walter Scott. They found Sir Walter greatly changed physically and mentally from the man who had said to them a few years before that he meant to live until he was eighty and to write as long as he lived. Before coming into the breakfast room one morning, Sir Walter had written in Dora's album a few stanzas addressed to her. Coming into the room, he handed her the book, and said, "I should not have done anything like this but for your father's sake: they are probably the last verses I shall ever write." Wordsworth, on reading the verses, later noted "how much his (Scott's) mind was impaired, not by the strain of thought but by the execution, some of the lines being imperfect, and one stanza lacking corresponding rhymes: one letter, the initial S, had been omitted in the spelling of his own name." The Wordsworths enjoyed, however, Sir Walter's hospitality and meeting his guests: "Major Scott (his son), Ann Scott (his daughter), and Mr. and Mrs. Lockhart, Mr. Liddell, his Lady and Brother, and Mr. Allan, the painter, and Mr. Laidlaw, a very old friend of Sir Walter's. One of Burns' sons, an officer in the Indian service, had left the house a day or two before. . . ." One evening, "Mr. and Mrs. Liddell sang, and Mr. and Mrs. Lockhart chanted old ballads to her boys; and Mr. Allan, hanging over the back of a chair, told and acted old stories in a humorous way." Another evening, Lockhart read to them "an incident of the old age of Cervantes." Sir Walter, Wordsworth, and Dora walked and rode to many of Sir Walter's favorite places while their host told of the happy life he led. Later, after the Wordsworths had gone, when Sir Walter's son-in-law told him that Wordsworth intended to visit him again in the autumn, Sir Walter said, "Wordsworth must come soon or he will not find me here." He died the following September.

In August, 1833, Ralph Waldo Emerson visited Wordsworth, whom he found "a plain, elderly, white-haired man, not prepossessing, who laid down the law on the subject of America, of which he knew little, and talked instead of listening." He was interested that Wordsworth thought Lucretius a greater poet than Virgil and that he abhorred Goethe's *Wilhelm Meister*, having read only the first part, which so revolted him that "he threw the book across the room." Emerson was amazed, when, as he walked with Wordsworth, the latter began reciting his own poems. "This recitation was so unlooked for and surprising—he, the old Wordsworth, standing apart and reciting to me in a garden-walk, like a schoolboy declaiming—that I at first was near to laugh; but recollecting myself, that I had come so far to see a poet, and he was chanting poems to me, I saw that he was right and I was wrong and gladly gave myself up to hear." Wordsworth impressed Emerson as having "a narrow and very English mind."

CHAPTER XII

The Shadows Deepen

COLERIDGE'S DEATH ON JULY 25, 1834, LEFT THE WORDS-WORTHS STUNNED. WILLIAM, IT IS TRUE, HAD NOT SEEN Coleridge often after their return from the continent in 1828, as Dr. Gillman with whom Coleridge now lived had curtailed his activities considerably, with the result that the poet's health had improved greatly. His body, however, had long been abused by neglect; yet, it had held out for sixty-two years, despite acute suffering. At times, even at Highgate, beside himself with pain, he had paced the floor for eighteen hours at a time. When better, he had loved to walk in his garden, to sit at his window overlooking Highgate, a village in unspoiled country, or to lie at peace in his room, a white-haired man, with a clear, unwrinkled face, and the eyes of a child. The years at Highgate had been productive, too, for the terrors that had plagued him all his life seemed to be ebbing away, and for the most part, he had been calmer than ever before. In 1832, a visitor had asked him if his intense physical pain had affected him mentally. "Not at all," he replied. "My body and head appear to hold no connection; the pain of my body, blessed be God, never reaches my mind." An autopsy proved that his suffering had, indeed, been real and physical: a greatly enlarged heart and arthritis had made his "mental and spiritual victory" a miracle.

Dorothy Wordsworth's mind was so confused that at first she did not seem to comprehend the fact that the man for whom she had long cared and for whom she had been solicitous so many years, had died. She merely told William that Hartley would "suffer the longest." She had not seen Coleridge for fourteen years, not since she, William, and Coleridge had stood in the garden at Dr. Gillman's and she had thought to herself, "There are no birds in last year's nest."

Later, William was told that Coleridge's last thoughts seemed to have gone back to earlier and happy days, for in a volume of his poems, he had found the one he had written when Dorothy, William, and Charles Lamb had first visited him at Nether Stowey. Too lame to go with his guests to the top of Quantock ridge, he had sat at home with his foot propped upon a chair and had written "The Lime Tree Bower My Prison," dedicated to Charles Lamb. Now, in the margin of that poem he had written: "Ch. and Mary Lamb—dear to my heart, yea, as it were, my heart. S.T.C. Aet. 63, 1834. 1797–1834–37 years."

Coleridge had written his own epitaph:

> Stop Christian passerby; stop, child of God
> And read, with gentle breast, Beneath this sod
> A poet lies, or that which once seemed he—
> O lift a thought in prayer for S.T.C.
> That he who many a year with toil of health
> Found death in life, may here find life in death;
> Mercy for praise—to be forgiven for fame.
> He asked, and hoped through Christ, Do thou the same.

Dr. James and Ann Gillman erected a tablet in his memory in Highgate New Church, testifying to his disposition "unalterably sweet and angelic" calling him "The gentlest and kindest teacher, the most engaging home companion."

In 1832, Wordsworth had said that Coleridge "and my beloved sister are the two things to whom my intellect is most indebted and they are now proceeding towards . . . a blessed immortality." At the time of Coleridge's death, Wordsworth added, "It is now nearly forty years since I first became acquainted with him whom we have just lost; and though with the exception of six weeks when we were on the Continent together, with my daughter, I have seen little of him for the last twenty years, his mind has been habitually present with me, with an accompanying feeling that he was still in the flesh. The frail tie is broken, and most of those who are nearest and dearest to me must prepare and endeavour to follow him."

The Sunday after Coleridge's death, R. P. Graves and his brother visited Wordsworth, who talked with them of Coleridge, saying the latter was "the most *wonderful* man he had even known—wonderful for the originality of his mind and the power he possessed of throwing out in profusion grand central truths from which might be evolved the most comprehensive systems." Wordsworth thought Coleridge had done "more permanently to enrich the literature and to influence the thought of the nation than any man of the age." Coleridge's mind, he said, "had been a widely fertilizing one, and that the seed he had so lavishly sown in his conversational discourses and the Sibylline leaves (not the poems so called by him) which he had scattered abroad so extensively covered with his annotations, had done much to form the opinions of the most educated men of the day; although this might be an influence not likely to meet with adequate recognition." Wordsworth, disliking Dr. Gillman's book about Coleridge, said, "Coleridge is a subject which no biographer ought to touch beyond what he himself was eyewitness of." In 1838, he told Barron Field that "Coleridge's talk was that of a majestic river; the sound or sight of whose course you caught at intervals, which was sometimes concealed by forests, sometimes lost in sand, then came flashing out, broad and distinct, then took a turn which your eye could not follow; yet you knew and felt it was the same river: so . . . there was always a train, a stream, in Coleridge's discourse, always a connection between the parts in his own mind, though one not always perceptible to others."

Though in the last years of his life, Coleridge had not continued writing poetry, he had been productive as an essayist and lecturer. In 1818 and 1819, encouraged by Dr. and Mrs. Gillman, he made very careful notes for his lectures, but delivered them without a book. These notes "will, I trust," he said, "answer all purposes—that of order of manner, and animation in the manner." It was necessary that Coleridge lecture well, for a host of significant people were lecturing at the time. Even Godwin's little son was speaking before a miniature pulpit and attracting large audiences. Hazlitt was lecturing on Shakespeare at the Surrey Institution, in a dry, monotonous tone, with his eyes glued to a manuscript. Coleridge's series of lectures, entitled "The History of Philosophy," were taken down in shorthand by a star shorthand writer, engaged at great expense, and put in notebook form; thus, some of his friends had copies of them. The first lecture was delivered in December, 1818; the last, in March, 1819. They were well received. In his notebook, he listed the title of the final talk, his *Last Address As a Public Lecturer;* this one was delivered without the copyist present. Opposite it, Coleridge wrote in his notebook, "O pray Heaven it may, indeed, be the last." Concluding his lectures, he turned his thoughts to religion, which had interested him increasingly. He had published one book, *Aids to Reflection*, a set of aphorisms of Archbishop Leighton with philosophical comments, that "became a moral guide to the coming generation," but which Henry Crabb Robinson called "the religion of the vulgar" with Coleridge's "own philosophy." Now, he wished to work on what he hoped would be his greatest work, that of the final justification of the Christian faith. Joseph Henry Green came each week to take dictation for it, but the work remained unpublished. Finally, not writing but at peace in his cheerful room at the Gillman's, white-haired Coleridge was pleased when his wife sent him the painting of his daughter Sara, which he hung near his bed so that he could view it often.

His delight that Hartley had been awarded a fellowship at Oxford in 1813 was later followed by distress at the news that Hartley had been deprived of his fellowship after he had been placed on probation for drinking. Coleridge did all he could to get the decision reversed, for he blamed himself: "This was the sin of his nature and this has been fostered by the culpable indulgence, at least non-interference on my part. Can anything be more dreadful than the thought that an innocent child has inherited from you a disease or a weakness . . . ?" Hartley, indeed, seemed to be following his father's footsteps when the latter had left Cambridge and joined the Royal Dragoons. Coleridge wrote his son Derwent that if it had been Hartley's "object to make it known and felt, that he considered me as having forfeited the interest and authority of a father . . . and as a Defaulter in the Duties, which I owed his youth, he could not have chosen a more intelligible (God knows! on his account too afflictive to be mortifying) way of realizing it." Coleridge saw clearly, too clearly, Hartley's ability to shove aside disagreeable reflections or lose them in daydreaming. Concerned about his delinquent son, Coleridge again became ill, awoke at nights screaming in agony. For a time, Hartley got hold of himself, worked as a journalist in London and taught capably at Mr. Dawes' school at Ambleside in 1825. He wrote some poetry which brought him an income. Dorothy Wordsworth reported his being now "very steady: he is the oddest looking creature you ever saw—not taller than Mr. De Quincey—with a beard as black as a raven." By 1830, he had relapsed into "a helpless state." The Wordsworths had "provided good lodgings for him," Dorothy said. "He had no want, was liked by people of the house, and for seven weeks was steady and industrious. Money came to repay him for his work, and what does he do? Instead of discharging his just debts, he pays a score off at a public house, and with eight sovereigns in his pocket, takes off; he is now wandering somewhere and will go on wandering until some charitable person leads the vagrant home. We have only heard of his lodging first at different inns—this no doubt while the money lasted—and of his having been seen on the roads and having lodged in this Barn and that." He was a kindly man, humble, "full of strange lore, but eccentric and intemperate." He died in 1849, "pitied and loved" by everyone in the neighborhood. William Wordsworth and Derwent Coleridge chose the place where he was to be buried near the Wordsworth children, Thomas and Catharine, one cold, inclement day.

After Hartley's failure at Oxford, Coleridge turned his attentions to Derwent, a far stabler person. When Coleridge found him enjoying balls, concerts, and a literary club, of which he was Premier or Secretary, he criticized him severely. Such things if they "did not dissipate your time and thought," do "dissipate and perplex your *character*. They are well maybe for BAs and MAs." Derwent, not a genius like his brother, did win an exhibition at St. John's, Cambridge, got his degree, and then served as Headmaster at Helston Grammar School in Cornwall. He was a quiet, unobtrusive man.

When Coleridge's daughter Sara, a beautiful and talented girl, married her cousin Henry Nelson Coleridge, her father, who had long opposed the marriage, said his opposition came not because Sara was writing and setting out on what seemed to be a brilliant career, while Henry was only a struggling barrister who had written one good book on the West Indies, but because he was anxious about the closeness of the relationship. The marriage had been long delayed because of Coleridge's opposition; young Henry's patience had been strained almost to the breaking point. In 1822, Coleridge had written a letter to a young lady on her choice of a husband, saying, "The tree of *full* life . . . 'whose mortal taste brings death into the heart,' these, my dear—grow in the probationary Eden of courtship alone. To many of both sexes I am well aware this Eden of matrimony is but a kitchen garden, a thing of profit and convenience, in an even temperature between indifference and liking . . . if there be ought of richer fragrance and more delicate hues, it is put or suffered there, not for the blossom, but for the pod . . . in order not to be miserable you must have a *soul mate* as well as a house or a yoke-mate." Sara was twenty-seven when she finally was married, to her mother's delight. Following the birth of her child, the first Coleridge grandchild, she was ill with puerperal fever, and an invalid for a long time. She lived to become, however, a brilliant figure among the literary group of her day, to become also among her father's most conscientious apologists and editors.

Throughout his life, Samuel Taylor Coleridge refused to consider politics other than as a branch of ethics. Thomas Poole said that in religion Coleridge was a Unitarian, if not a deist; in politics, a Democrat, "to the utmost extent of the word." Among the circumstances that produce evil, must be numbered monarchy and "that leprous strain, nobility," Coleridge declared. Priests and judges serve only to bolster the frame of government. Looking at France, he said he knew that country would face better days when "The age of superstition will soon be no more—that of philosophers and Christians will succeed, and the torch of superstition be extinguished forever." In England, he believed the government was capable of steady improvement; "its whole endurableness consists in motion . . . a corrupt government . . . is doing its best to prevent the proper working of the constitution. It must come from private citizens inspired with a high sense of duty and a lofty benevolence; these leaders will guide the state towards its goal of government by the people, that is by the people *morally* present in a representative body whose members act according to instructions from their constituents." Without freedom of the press, England, with its unrepresentative government, Coleridge thought, would be a mere despotism. Through a free press, he believed England could achieve a democracy without a revolution. Though loving democracy, he never loved the crowd. In fact, in 1818, he said he distrusted the "oppositionists to things as they are." These consisted first of men of little education and little real thought who knew that something was wrong and who would vote for reform if they were not too frightened by news from France; second, those ignorant men who were bitter because they were denied the better things of life, the men who caused revolutions; third, those who sought freedom because of hope of personal profit; and fourth, a small group of calm, pure-minded men, not slaves of jealousy or lust, but seekers of a good life for all. Wisdom and the ability to govern, he believed to be possessed by only a few. When, during the French wars and the English industrial expansion, he saw the use the people made of their newly gained power, he became convinced that the major problem was not to free men but to discipline them. They needed to realize that in addition to rights granted there were also duties imposed. Thus, authority and law should be stressed. "The principle of all constitutional law is to make the claims of each as much as possible compatible with the claims of all." Reason, he said, should determine the duties of a good citizen.

Abandoning his belief in the Unitarian Church, he later insisted the Church of England should be given more power to support great universities and schools of liberal learning; to maintain a pastor in every parish; to maintain a schoolmaster in every parish, this man later to become the pastor. In 1830, he insisted this importance of the church and its new role were imperative, for education for the masses, then a private charity, was at a low ebb, and placed its sole emphasis on science; the great masses of people were being exploited. Desiring universal education, he saw it as a danger if it ceased, as it did for common people, with the ability only to read and write. He pointed out the fact that England had "game laws, corn laws, cotton factories, spital fields, the tillers paid by poor rates, and the remainder of the population mechanized into engines for the manufactury of new rich men; yes, the machinery of the wealth of the nation made up of wretchedness, disease, and depravity of those who should constitute the strength of the nation." The materialism of his age was a mechanism grown from the desire to sail ships faster, to make engines that would create money and human misery on a scale never before attempted. Coleridge saw no hope in mobs trying to secure their rights; working people in his age had not achieved trade unions to represent them. Man, he concluded, was selfish, rebellious, often self-destructive unless he surrendered to a corporate society which disciplined his animal instincts. Through union of Church and State this, he believed, could be achieved. He advocated Catholic Emancipation, free trade, repeal of game laws, universal education, and factory Acts. The great danger in his day, he felt, was excessive striving for material gratification, cloaked by a desire for freedom and individualism. He feared the power of the new, restless, predatory merchants and industrialists. Yet he believed in change and progress.

Coleridge left no literary descendants. Though his presence touched and influenced the younger poets of the romantic age, he had little in common with them. Though friendly with Lord Byron, who had been one of the few to admire "Kubla Khan," Coleridge was satirized by Byron in "English Bards and Scotch Reviewers" and in "Don Juan." Good naturedly, Byron had laughed:

> And Coleridge too has lately taken wing
> But like a hawk encumbered with his hood—
> Explaining metaphysics to the nation—
> I wish he would explain his explanation.

Later, Byron had written more sharply of

> . . . Coleridge, long before his mighty pen
> Let to the Morning Post its aristocracy,
> When he and Southey, following the same path,
> Espoused two partners (milliners of Bath)

Such names at present cut a convict figure,
The very Botany Bay in moral geography,
Their loyal treason, renegade vigour,
Are good natured for their more bare biography.

Though Coleridge never met Shelley, he found him possessing "great power as a poet." Had Shelley had "some plane on which to stand, and look down upon his own mind, he would have succeeded," Coleridge said. He regretted not meeting Shelley, who had come to Keswick to see him. Unable to see Coleridge, Shelley had fallen in with Southey instead. Coleridge believed he could have done Shelley good by laughing "at his atheism."

For some other poets, Coleridge had a closer affinity. Ludwig Tieck, the German Romantic poet, revived his interest in mystics. Inspired by him, Coleridge began to study Swedenborg. Charles Augustus Tulke, who had established the "New Church" in Great Britain, an admirer of Swedenborg, introduced him to the poetry of William Blake. In 1826, Coleridge called on Blake, then living in great poverty in England, visited by literary people as a kind of curiosity, a freak, who had visions, talked with angels, and saw his words, as he wrote them, fly about the room. Blake and Coleridge seemed like "congenial spirits, from another sphere, breathing for a while on our earth." Coleridge wrote the Rev. H. F. Carey, "You may perhaps smile at *my* calling another poet a *Mystic;* but verily I am in the very mire of commonplace compared with Mr. Blake, also rather an anacalyptic Poet and Painter!" Blake, however, was a happy man, a true though unorthodox Christian, who believed the Church had become false and failed the common man. Blake had used the language of the common man and physical images of nature in his poetry ten years before *Lyrical Ballads* appeared. Blake believed that man's redemption lay in man himself; for Coleridge, redemption was "a personal release from misery."

In May, 1825, Coleridge had delivered his paper on the *Prometheus* of Aeschylus to the Royal Society of Literature. Occupying his niche as a poet, he had begun his Thursday afternoon conversations at Highgate, where a group of literary men, artists, and philosophers gathered to hear him talk. The white-haired, benign man, who resembled a bishop, would enthrall his visitors while he talked on and on. Young Tom Hood, greatly impressed, was fascinated by the "full-bodied poet, with his waving white hair, and his face, round, ruddy, and unfurrowed as a holy friar's," who would talk, and, "if interrupted or questioned, would wave a hand, concede the point, and continue as if the interruption had never been made." Tennyson was fascinated by him. Though he did not influence the young poets, he did influence essayists and those in the Church. Dr. Arnold, Thomas Carlyle, Charles Kingsley, and John Henry Newman were all influenced by Coleridge's ideas. Some say the Church was "broadened and humanised by his influence."

Coleridge had always loved to talk. Lamb told of "going from my house at Enfield to the India-House one morning, and . . . hurrying, for I was rather late, when I met Coleridge on his way to pay me a visit; he was brimful of some new idea, and in spite of my assuring him that time was precious, he drew me within the door of an unoccupied garden by the roadside, and there, sheltered from observation by a hedge of evergreen, he took me by the coat, and closing his eyes, began an eloquent discourse, waving his right hand gently, as the musical words flowed in unbroken stream from his lips. I listened, entranced; but the striking of a church clock recalled me to my sense of duty. I saw it was no use to attempt to break away, so, taking advantage of his absorption in the subject, I, with my penknife quietly severed the button from my coat and decamped. Five hours afterwards, in passing the same garden, on my way home, I heard Coleridge's voice, and, on looking in, there he was, with closed eyes—the button in his fingers—and his right hand gracefully waving, just as when I left him. He had never missed me!" Carlyle attacked Coleridge again and again, saying "He cannot speak, he can only *tal—k* (so he names it). Hence, I found him unprofitable, even tedious . . . I reckon him a man of great and useless genius; a strange, not at all a great, man." He went yet further in attacking Coleridge as "a mass of richest spices putrefied to a dunghill. I never hear him *tawlk* without feeling ready to worship him, and toss him in a blanket. . . ." Yet, after Coleridge's death, Carlyle called him "A sublime man; who, alone in those dark days, had saved his crown of spiritual manhood, escaping from the black materialisms, and revolutionary deluges, with 'God, Freedom, Immortality' still his; a king of men." The children who rolled their hoops along the avenue at Highgate would quail as Coleridge approached. "The Kingdom of Heaven-ites," as Coleridge called the children, would run as he approached; but if he caught up with one, he would lay his hand on the child's shoulder, talking a lot of nonsense or using great, long words that seemed to have no meaning at all, while those children who had fled, or had hidden behind trees, would peer out grinning and hooting at him once he was a safe distance away. Wordsworth is said to have visited him at Highgate while Coleridge talked steadily for two hours. When asked if he had understood what Coleridge had said, Wordsworth answered, "Not a word." The American painter, Charles Robert Leslie, who often talked with Coleridge, said, "His eloquence threw a new and beautiful light on most subjects, and when he was beyond my comprehension, the melody of his voice, and the impressiveness of his manner held me a willing listener, and I was flattered at being supposed capable of understanding him." Always, Coleridge's first "commandment" was, "Thou shalt think." Far in advance of his age in his theological work and scientific speculations, he was battling some of the same forces thinkers are battling today.

The Wordsworths had hardly recovered from the shock and grief over Coleridge's death when in December, 1834, word came that Charles Lamb had died. Lamb's last letters had been written to Wordsworth, one ending with "prayers for dear Dorothy" and a later one saying that Mary Lamb "is ill again, after a short interval of four or five months. In short, I may call her half dead to me."

Charles Lamb had, indeed, been lonely since Coleridge's death, for Coleridge had always spent considerable time with the Lambs, occasionally, as a guest for an evening, often for longer periods, though after Coleridge moved to Dr. Gillman's his visits had, at his doctor's orders, been fewer. Lamb realized it was good for him to have Coleridge as a guest, as Mary's recurring spells of insanity forced Charles to realize he had to expect her illnesses the rest of his life. His tenseness was relieved by vacations to various parts of England, made possible by a fund his employers regularly withheld from employees' salaries to make vacations possible.

Griefstricken, Charles once wrote Dorothy Wordsworth blaming himself for Mary's illnesses. "She is older and wiser and better than me, and all my wretched imperfections I cover to myself by resolutely thinking on her goodness. She would share life and death, heaven and hell, with me. She lives but for me. And yet I know I have been wasting and teasing her life for five years past incessantly with my cursed drinking and ways of going on. But even in this upbraiding of myself I am thinking of her, for I know she has cleaved to me for better, for worse; and if the balance has been against her hitherto, it was a noble trade." He also sent Dorothy two scraps of verse Mary had written shortly before she went to the asylum: one of six lines about Leonardo da Vinci's "Virgin of the Rocks" that she had seen at an auction, and another of ten lines about a portrait of a Lady by Titian.

This attack of 1805 proved to be Mary's longest illness to date, as she had to spend ten weeks in the asylum. In August, when she emerged, she felt it best to refuse the invitation of the Wordsworths to visit them at Grasmere. She still suffered from severe headaches, and Charles was in poor health, too. The latter laughingly called the two Lambs Gumbail and Toothache. Yet, when John Stoddard found that his sister Sarah had had an illicit affair with a soldier and decided that the girl should thereafter spend half her time at home with her mother and the rest in London under Mary's supervision, Mary accepted the responsibility, though it meant that Charles had to rent a room nearby to complete a play he had begun. Once Sarah had departed at the end of March, Mary began work on *Tales From Shakespeare.*

In the fall of 1806, the Lambs began their Wednesday evening informal social evenings, at Coleridge's suggestion. These social events, where the men played whist, ate cold meat and hot potatoes, and where any gentleman who chose, smoked, developed into an institution in English letters. Here came young Hazlitt, snobbish young Thomas De Quincey, Wordsworth, Southey, and John Stoddard, who was one of the pantisocracy group. The Wednesday evenings "grew into literary symposia"; the quality of the company grew "to higher and higher levels of talent." William Hazlitt, one of the most frequent guests, Lamb always liked; however, it was difficult for him to be friendly with William Godwin, though he found Godwin's wife, Mary Wollstonecraft, "vibrant and passionate." When Lamb learned, six months after he met Godwin, that while the latter's young wife lay dying, Godwin sat meticulously observing and recording her death, Lamb said he simply could not understand such a man.

The Lambs were astonished at Godwin's second marriage to Mrs. Mary Jane Clairmont, whose daughter was Lord Byron's concubine, just as they had been amazed at his over-sentimental courtship. Godwin, the heir to Mary Wollstonecraft's apartment, books, portrait, and fortune, allowed his new wife to go over the previous wife's notes. Observing that the latter had been an authority on education and that Godwin had been consulted by parents and publishers about educating children, Mary Jane persuaded him to set up a publication business in Hanway Street. In order to augment his income, William Godwin established this publishing business. To escape the radical sound of his name that was repugnant to many, Godwin announced the name of the head of the firm as Thomas Hodgkins, and he himself wrote for it under the name of Edward Baldwin. Charles Lamb contributed to it anonymously, and Mary was also an early contributor. Among Mary Wollstonecraft's books was a volume by Perrin who, in 1783, had translated Shakespeare's plays into tales for children. Why not ask Charles and Mary Lamb to do this same thing, reasoned the second Mrs. Godwin, who had found Perrin's volume.

Lamb's *Tales From Shakespeare* resulted. Mary had agreed to write twenty tales based on the plays of Shakespeare. Her enthusiasm proved so contagious that Charles agreed to write the stories of the ten tragedies while Mary wrote as many tales based on the comedies. By the middle of May, Charles had completed tales on *Othello* and *Macbeth*, while Mary had written those on *The Tempest, The Winter's Tale, Midsummer Night's Dream, Much Ado About Nothing, Two Gentlemen of Verona*, and *Cymbeline;* she was at the time working on *The Merchant of Venice.* Godwin was printing the tales separately in twelve penny booklets almost as fast as the Lambs completed them. Interrupted at times, and eager to have the tales published in their entirety in book form, they spent their summer vacation at home writing the rest of them. In all, Charles wrote six of the tales; Mary, fourteen. To their amazement, the volume came out entitled *Lamb's Tales from Shakespeare, Designed for Young Persons. By Charles Lamb.* Charles was unhappy over the lack of recognition of his sister, but Godwin had felt the work would have a better reception if it seemed to be written by a man. As it was, the book enhanced Lamb's reputation. Mary, who had thought "I shall get fifty pounds a year at the latest calculations," had so written Sarah Stoddard. There is no evidence of her ever obtaining any money for her work. Yet the book was well received and, one of the most frequently published and translated works in literature, has never been out of print since its publication in 1807. Dissatisfied as the Lambs were with the statement that Lamb had written all the tales, they disliked even more the illustrations Mrs. Godwin had selected for the first edition. Yet, they sent copies to Wordsworth's son, John, and the Clarkson's son, Thomas.

In June, 1807, over-tired from her work on the book, Mary felt her madness recurring while she and Charles were visiting the Clarksons. Hurrying back to London, she went to the asylum where she remained until the end of the summer. For fifty years, Mary's life at times was normal; again at periods ranging from two to five months she was forced to be in a private asylum. When well, she led a useful, happy life. Twice, she even served as bridesmaid for devoted friends, one of them, Sarah Stoddard, who married William Hazlitt. Forty-four-year-old Mary had remarked, "Next to the pleasure of being married is the pleasure of working or helping marriages forward." When again herself in 1807, she contributed ten stories to a collection *Mrs. Leicester's School*, while Charles contributed three; she collaborated with Charles on the book *Poetry for Children*, which also contained some verses by John Lamb.

When Coleridge, returning from Malta, came to the Lambs, he caused some excitement by showing them the first "segar" they had seen, a new invention on the Continent. After the misunderstanding between Coleridge and Wordsworth, Coleridge, back in London, at once sought the Lambs. He was griefstricken as he wept, "Wordsworth has given me up." Mary comforted him, telling him not to take the break so seriously. She succeeded in helping him get hold of himself. While he stayed for a time with John Morgan, a retired merchant, he often visited with the Lambs; "God keep him away from the traps and pitfalls," wrote Lamb. Finally, Coleridge went to Dr. Joseph Adams, a frequent visitor at the Lambs' Wednesday evenings. It was he who proposed that Dr. James Gillman of Highgate, a practicing physician, treat Coleridge as a resident patient.

Lonely without Coleridge, whose visits were restricted by the doctor who kept close watch over him, the Lambs, now with improved financial status, moved from the Old Inner Temple to the theatre district, No. 20 in Russell Street, Covent Garden, with, Mary wrote Dorothy Wordsworth, "Drury Lane Theatre in sight from our front and Covent Garden from our back windows." Charles added, "We are in the individual spot I like best in all this great city; the theatres with all their noises." Shortly after the Lambs moved, Charles began to be interested in Fanny Kelly, an actress, now twenty-seven, who had been on the stage since she was seven. She was the one woman except Mary Lamb welcomed at his Wednesday evenings. Well-known and admired both for her personality and her ability as an actress, Frances Kelly had achieved success through a hard struggle. Suddenly, one rainy July morning in 1819, the forty-two-year-old man wrote her a letter, proposing marriage. He suggested that she "throw off forever the burden of your profession" and "cast your lot with us." He knew he was "a most unworthy match for such a one as you, but you have for years been a principal object in my mind." He urged her to "leave off harrassing yourself to please a thankless multitude who know

nothing of you, and begin, at last, to live to yourself and your friends."
Miss Kelly answered at once, declining the proposal and hoping "that
all thought upon this subject will end with this letter, and that you
will henceforth encourage no other sentiment towards me than esteem
of my private character and a continuance of that approbation of my
humble talents which you have already expressed so much and so
often to my advantage and gratification." Lamb replied, "*Your in-
junctions shall be obeyed to a tittle*," but added his hope that "you
will be good friends with us; will you not?" and added "Do not paste
that last letter of mine into your book." Not only did she remain
friends with him; she returned to him his letter of proposal, which he
kept. Many years later, when a biographer of Lamb's discovered the
letter and asked Miss Kelly why she refused Lamb's offer of marriage, she said it was because of "the constitutional malady in the
family." Did she also note that in the proposal Lamb was suggesting
that she cast her lot, not with him but with *us*? Moreover, she was devoted to the stage. She remained an actress for many years, then
became a producer of plays, and finally founded a school for training
young actresses. Obviously, Lamb had not realized that at heart she
was a career woman.

Three years later, when Lamb's *Complete Works* were published
through the influence of Leigh Hunt, Charles Lamb was a significant
English writer. In 1820, when his "Recollections of Christ's Hospital
Five and Thirty Years Ago" appeared in a new journal, *The London
Magazine*, he emerged as an essayist of note, despite the fact that
the *Edinburgh Review* attacked him savagely. Mary's understanding
comments on his detractors lessened for him the bitterness of their
reviews. He seems to have realized that he wrote best when she was
nearby. Had not she and Sarah Stoddard once sought out rooms that
rented for three shillings a week where he could write undisturbed by
callers? This experiment had not worked, yet five years later Mary
again found some unused rooms adjoining their apartment in the Inner
Temple where he could write. She says she "put in an old grate, and
made him a fire in the largest of the garretts and bid him write away,
and consider himself as much alone as if he were in a new lodging
in the midst of Salisbury Plain." Using the rooms, he did write well for
a while, but finally he said he wrote best with Mary by his side.

While Charles was prospering, his brother John, still employed at
the East India House, was also, though he wrote very little. In addition to the one poem in Mary's book of verses, John wrote one
pamphlet and several letters to editors, expressing his ideas on the

treatment of the poor and the cruel treatment of animals. He bitterly attacked politicians who protected social abuses. Seeing a group of Eton boys at play, he once remarked, "What a pity it is to think that these ingenious lads in a few years will all be changed into frivolous members of Parliament." Realizing that the Sunday School movement had many opportunists among its leaders, he scoffed at the distribution of Bibles to children who worked seven days a week and long hours for little pay. He concluded a letter to an editor by saying that it was "a mockery of God" to have "unkempt little wretches of children" say "Give us this day our daily Bread." "When they read the gospel for themselves, will not they read with emphasis the woe-denouncing judgments of Jesus Christ, hanging over the heads of the canting hypocrites who are starving them?"

Late in life, John's hope of a trip to Paris became a reality. He even managed to purchase a portrait of John Milton that today hangs in the New York Public Library. Finally, he married Mrs. Isaac Dowden, a wealthy widow. Happy, successful, on good terms with Mary and Charles, he died in 1821, when his sixtieth birthday was approaching. He left to Charles everything he owned and made him his executor.

Disturbed by his sister's frequent attacks of insanity, believing many of them came from worry over his drinking or from over-exertion, or after long visits of friends, Charles for a time stopped drinking, and, at the risk of losing some of his friends, wrote a number of them that they must not come to the Lamb home for prolonged visits or even to stay overnight; at times, he informed them it was not convenient for them to come at all. Yet, the attacks came, though at times brother and sister could point to a whole year without one. Charles then reasoned that the fatigue of too much writing also brought on the attacks. Nevertheless, the Lambs lived a fairly normal life, including visiting friends. Mary was quite well when Lamb's *Essays of Elia* appeared, and rejoiced in its success.

In 1821, Charles and Mary decided to go to Paris. They had traveled to many parts of the British Isles, but a trip to Paris was not one casually made. Charles felt that, in case of emergency, there should be a nurse for Mary and, since neither of them knew much French, a good courier, to handle their luggage and make their reservations. At length, tired and excited, they set out on the grand tour. At Amiens, "the unexpected happened" and Mary became ill. With her and her nurse established in a hotel, Charles set out with the courier for what turned out to be a disappointing trip. He did enjoy the French wine and he reveled in seeking prints and books in the bookstalls along the Seine. By the time Mary recovered, Charles had gone home, but friends he had met entertained Mary in Paris, finding her a charming and delightful guest. She had a far better trip than her brother had had.

Shortly after their return to England, they moved to the country, to Islington, where Lamb kept a garden, with pears, strawberries, carrots, and cabbages. Mary had questioned the wisdom of this move, but Charles felt he must have some rest. His hospitality and fame seldom left him alone with Mary. Moreover, he was contemplating retirement, and that meant a reduced income. In 1821, three days before his fiftieth birthday, Charles, increasingly conscious of a loss of vitality and a distaste for office work, resigned from his position. When his resignation was accepted and a sizable pension given him and provision made for Mary should she live the longer, Charles rejoiced. He had once remarked that he was always late for work but made up for it by leaving early. "Mary," he wrote friends after his retirement, "wakes every morning with an obscure feeling that some good has happened to us." It really did seem so, as she had no attacks for a two-year period.

Lamb was supporting three people—himself, Mary, and Emma Isola, a motherless girl who had come to visit the Lambs but had remained as a fixture. After her father's death in 1823, she had no other home. Her father had been a professor at Cambridge University; her aunt, Miss Humphreys, often played whist with the Lambs when they visited in Cambridge. Little eleven-year-old Emma, lingering near the whist tables, attracted the interest of the Lambs, who invited her to spend Christmas with them. This visit was prolonged until February. Afterwards, she came frequently. When the Lambs moved to Islington, Emma was given the guest room, and before long was called Charles' adopted daughter. He indulged her, permitting her to keep late hours and to have much company. He sent her to Dulwich Boarding School, where she was an average student, far from interested in books. Despite the failure of both Charles' and Mary's trying to interest her in things intellectual, Emma, now eighteen, agreed to accept a position they secured for her as governess. Though she resisted the education the Lambs wished to give her, Emma did enjoy the long, long walks she took with Charles. And Charles' walks were long, often twenty-four mile ones. Presently, he realized he had for years been in love with the girl. He wrote verses in which he stated his belief that love inevitably would come to all. While he agonized over a love he felt he should not acknowledge, Emma fell in love with a man nearer her age. Twenty-two-year-old Edward Moxon, a clerk in the firm of Longmans, Green, had called on Charles Lamb, bringing verses for him to criticize. He returned, bringing new novels for Mary and to drink with Charles. After three years, young Moxon gave up his ambition to write and became a publisher. Charles Lamb's *Album Verses and Other Poems* was the firm's first publication. Some hastened to criticize the verses, trumpeting that Lamb's gifts had fallen off; but Robert Southey came to his friend's rescue, lambasting "witling critics" who proclaimed to the world "In lead, their own dolt imbecility." The book did not harm Moxon's reputation either, for, through Lamb's influence, he published poets whose works were some of the finest contributions of the century: Coleridge, Shelley, Keats, Tennyson, Browning, and Mrs. Browning. Only Mary Lamb suffered from the criticism, which sent her again to the asylum.

With Mary away and Emma serving as a governess, Charles decided to sell his home and furniture and take up residence with old Mr. and Mrs. Thomas Westwood. Later, he planned that Mary and Emma should join him there. Mary returned to find their furniture, chairs, and rugs, being sold by an auctioneer. Carrying only books, pictures, snuff boxes, and silver, the Lambs moved into Thomas Westwood's home. Some believe Charles, having decided no good could come from loving Emma, had tried by the move to shut out all-too-painful memories of her. But Emma, becoming ill, returned home to the Lambs and never again resumed her position as governess. With her in such proximity, Lamb was almost frantic. He could not write, no matter how hard he tried. Concerned about his own feelings, Lamb seems not to have realized how frequently Edward Moxon visited his quarters at the Westwood's, until in March, 1833, the young man asked Emma's hand in marriage. Charles consented at once, and secretly transferred some stock to her. On July 30, 1833, Lamb "gave away the bride"; he had provided for Emma Isola wedding and trousseau gowns of real silk and, as a wedding gift, had given the couple the portrait of John Milton and a wedding trip to Paris. Despite the gaiety at the wedding, Charles remained cold sober. Mary, the day before the wedding, again lapsed into insanity. But, strangely, once her nurse brought her a glass of wine to drink the health of the now-married couple, "as if by an electrical strike," she regained possession of her senses.

Just as Charles had written his *Album Poems*, Mary wrote, as a Letter to the Editor, a brilliant essay for the *British Lady's Maga-*

zine "On Needle Work." Though men were discussing new principles of political economy, until Mary Lamb wrote her essay, no one had expressed the thought of applying these principles to the occupations of women. Clearly, emphatically, she stated that the work of women in the home was not adequately evaluated or paid for. She continued, "it would prove an incalculable addition to general happiness and the domestic comfort of both sexes, if needlework were never practiced but for remuneration." She stated that "Real business and real leisure make up the portions of men's time, whereas women in the home have little real leisure, which may be one reason some are so dull and unattractive to their husbands." Thus, she believed it wise that women have sufficient leisure to be the "helpmates of *man*, who, in return for all he does for us, expects, and justly expects, us to do all in our power to soften and sweeten life." Women, Mary contended, should have time to make men's homes such desirable places as to preclude their having a wish to spend their leisure hours at any fireside in preference to their own, time to develop intellects so that they could contribute to men's discussions.

Mary had no idea she had written anything of value; Charles made no reference to her article. Yet, in it she showed an awareness of the feminist movement of the time. About the time of Mary's birth, the Bluestocking Clubs had flourished in London. Women of social and economic position, the leaders of the Bluestockings, had rebelled against the idea that women did not have brains equal to men's. They wrote and published letters and books taking their rebellious stands; they entertained groups of women at drawing room discussions. Hundreds of women and girls throughout England, girls like Sarah Stoddard, Mary Wollstonecraft, the Fricker sisters, and Mary Lamb, heard of the movement and shared their sisters' views. Some went further than the Bluestockings and asserted women's rights to lead their own lives. Most spectacular were the Ladies of Llangollen, the two eccentric young women who "made a brilliant career" of their rebellion. Others of these women made names for themselves in the only fields of writing open to women: fiction, considered a lesser type of literature, and children's books. Came Maria Edgeworth with *Castle Rockrent*, Fanny Burney with *Evelina*, and Jane Austen with *Pride and Prejudice*. Some, like Hannah More and Mrs. Fricker, set up schools for girls and thus found expression. Mary Lamb's good friend Sara Hutchinson had gone to Wales and brought back exciting accounts of the Llangollen girls. On the surface, Mary Lamb showed little of the influence of these women. "I make it a point of conscience never to interfere or cross my brother in the mood he happens to be in," she once wrote. "Let men alone and at last we find them come around to the right way, which we, by a kind of intuition, perceive at once." Yes, Mary held a high opinion of her sex.

At a time when Charles Lamb was writing little and feeling discouraged, on September 18, 1830, Hazlitt, dying in his shabby quarters in Bohemian Soho, had his son bring Lamb to him. Knowing that the Lambs had kept in touch with his first wife, Sarah, he asked Lamb to summon her. It was too late for her to reach the dying man, who meanwhile told Charles, "Well, I've lived a happy life." Another friend of Hazlitt's, R. H. Harve, an English actor, cut off a lock of Hazlitt's hair and sent it to Sarah. She wrapped it carefully in a sheet of paper on which she wrote, "William Hazlitt's hair, cut off the day after his death. Born 10th April, 1778. Died 18th September 1830. Aged 52 years, 5 months, and 8 days." After her death, this paper, the letters of Mary Lamb reflecting Hazlitt's courtship and marriage to Sarah, and the diary in which Sarah told of the divorce, were found.

Lamb reflected that Hazlitt had died while his reputation as an essayist was transcendent. His, he knew, was declining. Once, years before, in 1823, self-confident Robert Southey, conscious that he was poet laureate of England, had criticized Lamb's *Essays of Elia* in his *Quarterly Magazine*, accusing the highly successful Lamb of lack of proper religious feeling; the attack was calculated to destroy the successful Lamb's reputation. Lamb, amazed, did not question whether the motive was jealousy. At first, when he heard of the criticism, he merely said he loved and respected Southey and would not reply. When finally he read the article, highly indignant, he wrote a bitter reply, defending the free spirit of man and attacking repression and superstition, scourging those who charged an admission to such churches as Westminster Abbey and St. Paul's Cathedral with the result that the poor could not attend them, lambasting those who refused to allow a worshiper to linger after services to reflect alone in the church to which he had gone. Brilliantly written, Lamb's letter in *The London Magazine* rallied support from all sides. *The London Times* strongly supported Lamb's point of view. Southey was silent. After this, Lamb, too, was silent; he seemed suddenly old and shrunken.

The Lambs now saw Coleridge infrequently. For a time he had lectured brilliantly in London, where he was being cared for by Dr. and Mrs. Gillman. He was in good health until after the receipt of a letter which, like any letter from the persistent Mrs. Coleridge who had moved to a new home at Hampstead Heath in London, upset him. After 1830, Coleridge was bedfast a great deal of the time. He died, as we have already noted, on July 25, 1834. Following her husband's death, Mrs. Coleridge visited the Gillmans and seemed to share their grief. Returning home, she wrote her thoughts as a widow on black-bordered paper.

Five months later, Charles Lamb died. Always a little lame, he had become increasingly so as he grew older. Strolling to a tavern the morning of December 22, he stumbled and fell, scratching his face against a stone. The cut, which seemed of little consequence, received no medical attention until Lamb developed a case of erysipelas; when Charles Ryle, a friend, came over to see Lamb the day after Christmas he found him very ill. He sent a message to Judge Talfourd, who came the next morning and found Lamb dying. That afternoon, December 27, 1834, Charles Lamb died as the result of what had seemed a slight accident. Mary, undergoing an attack of insanity at the time, seemed to recover her sanity at the news and was able to point out to her brother's friends the spot in Edmonton churchyard where he had said he wished to be buried. She appeared, in fact, amazingly able to cope with her brother's death. But four-and-a-half months later, when she seemed to realize the full impact of his death, she became violently insane and remained deranged for five months. Her friends saw that she was well cared for. To the surprise of everyone, her brother's estate was sizable. With his estate and the £120 given her as a pension by the India Company, Mary, so long as she lived, had an income amounting to four-fifths of that on which both brother and sister had lived.

When she was herself again, Mary surprised Wordsworth by objecting to some of the verses he had written as an epitaph for her brother at a friend's request. The lines,

> . . . . Here he lies apart
> From the great city where he first drew breath,
> Was reared and taught; and humbly earned his bread,
> To the strict labours of the merchants' desk
> By duty chained . . . .

Mary felt might make future generations think her brother a servile man.

She chose as her last home that of a Mrs. Parsons in St. Johns Wood. "I long to show you what a nice snug place I have," she wrote friends, "in the midst of a garden. I have a room for myself and my old books on the ground floor and a little bedroom up two flights of stairs." Miss James, a nurse, and her sister, Mrs. Parsons, looked after her. As usual, Mary alternated between periods of sanity and insanity; as she grew older, the latter spells lasted longer. During her "mental absences," at times she imagined herself living in the days of Queen Anne or George I; she would "describe the brocaded dames and courtly women as though she had been bred among them, in the best style of the old comedy," said John Hollingshead. "It was all broken and disjointed, so that the hearer could remember little of her discourse; but the fragments were like the jeweled speeches of Congreve, only shaken from their settings. There was sometimes even a vein of crazy logic running through them, associating things essentially most dissimilar, but connecting them, by a verbal association in a strange order. It was as if the finest elements of the mind had been shaken into fantastic combinations, like those of a kaleidoscope."

Many of Mary Lamb's ideas were too revolutionary and ahead of her time for her to have a large following; yet she did have influence upon people like Coleridge, Sarah Hazlitt, and Crabb Robinson. She had a tremendous influence on children, even in her old age. Mary Cowden Clark acquired her taste in Shakespeare from Mary Lamb; young William Hazlitt learned Latin from her; even young John Hollingshead received an exciting idea of drama from the eighty-year-old woman. Her influence is said to have made possible Hollingshead's later productions at the Gaiety Theatre and to have given him so fine an idea of what great actresses should be that later he brought Sarah Bernhardt to the English stage. "Sometimes," said young Hollingshead of Mary, "we played at cards, her favorite pastime, such games as I had any knowledge of; and sometimes when she was tired and liked to roam about the garden, I was allowed to browse among the books which walled in the apartment. Most of them were authors' copies, simply bound in rough paper or boards, with ragged-edged leaves and ample margins. Many of the folios were there that had been bought by Charles Lamb in his roamings, and brought home and carefully collated with his sister by the aid of a tallow candle. The old dramatists were, of course, well represented and the picaresque school of fiction, noticeably *The Rogue* and *The Adventures of Don Guzman etc.* Visitors sometimes came in and I was allowed to watch them from a corner. William Godwin . . . Tom Hood . . . little Miss Kelly, the actress . . . and Crabb Robinson, who had a trustee air.

"In my wanderings, especially in the autumn, I found my way to this orchard . . . I spent the rest of the afternoon with the dreamy old lady, who looked over me rather than at me and seemed to see many visions that were beyond my limited intelligence."

What her skill as a teacher did for young Hazlitt and young Hollingshead was just what it had done when, at the age of ten, she taught her brother to distinguish the letters on the tombstones among which the two loitered, and culminated in her gift of herself to help him become an ornament of English letters.

Growing feeble, handicapped by deafness and the loss of most of her teeth, fluctuating between sanity and insanity, Mary Lamb still had good eyesight and enjoyed her old books and new ones, too. Gradually, though tenderly cared for first by Charles and after his death by her friends, she slipped into invalidism. The last four months of her life she was bedridden, and kindly taken care of by Mrs. Parsons and Miss James. She died on May 20, 1847, eighty-two years of age, having outlived all of her family and most of her friends.

Because Charles Lamb was ill, the Wordsworths found the Christmas season of 1834 a melancholy one. They were deeply concerned about Lamb. Moreover, Dora Wordsworth was lonely without Edward Quillinan, who, discouraged because William did not now favor his marriage to Dora, had gone to Portugal for the winter. Dora grew pale and thin; she did not complain but was busy caring for Sara Hutchinson who was ailing and who suddenly seemed to age ten years; William at times seemed almost blind, and Dorothy was in bed most of time, lying quietly, saying nothing, smiling at those who approached her. When the fiddlers came to celebrate Christmas Eve, they were sent away, for the family was now grieving over Charles Lamb's death.

Eighteen-thirty-five, too, was a difficult year for those at Rydal Mount. The Wordsworths had been concerned about young Sara Coleridge who had seemed to brood intensely and to become despondent. After her father's death, she appeared to be loosed from the melancholy that had engulfed her and "determined to get well." Dora Wordsworth, however, became seriously ill with inflammation of the spine and spent most of her time resting in bed or on the sofa. Dorothy Wordsworth was growing "weaker and weaker." Sara Hutchinson also became seriously ill with an attack of lumbago that developed into rheumatic fever. William, wrote his daughter Dora, greatly concerned about Dorothy who, she thought, was near death, "keeps up his spirits most patiently though I see his heart is well-nigh breaking, and when the blow comes, I am sure he will meet it with resignation." As days lengthened into months, Sara seemed to be better, but Dorothy was kept alive only by stimulants. On June 27, suddenly Sara Hutchinson died—Sara, who had so aided Coleridge, Wordsworth and her sister Mary—Sara, who had never rested, who had never thought of herself. She had kept house for her brothers, then after coming to live with Mary and William had been content to serve them in any way they wished. When Coleridge's love turned from Dorothy to Sara, the latter had blossomed, but she seemed destined to serve only as a copyist for him, to endeavor to keep him writing, until she broke under the strain. After the Coleridge and William misunderstanding, she never heard from Coleridge again; she had grown sharp and censorious.

Dorothy slowly regained her physical strength, but her mind remained cloudy; at times she regained it for short intervals. When wheeled out into the garden, she would still call out to passersby, seeming, childlike, to crave attention. Indoors, she appeared delighted to hear the cuckoo-clock; as she listened to its notes she would lift a finger to show her pleasure. William, grieving to see her so changed, spent much time with her, often emerging from her room with tears in his eyes. On her better days, she could write letters interestingly, telling the news of the neighbors, "News! News!" she wrote Dora in 1838, "Poor Peggy Benson lies in Grasmere Church-yard beside her once beautiful Mother. Fanny Haigh is gone to a better world. My friend Mrs. Rawson has ended her ninety and two year pilgrimage— and I have fought and fretted and striven and am here beside the fire. The Doves behind me at the small window—and the laburnum with its naked seedpods shivers before my window and the pine-trees rock from their base. More I cannot write, so farewell! and may God bless you and your kind Friend, Miss Fenwick to whom I send love and all the best of wishes. Yours evermore, Dorothy Wordsworth."

When Julia Wedgwood, the great-niece of Tom Wedgwood, came in 1849 to call at Rydal Mount, she tells of looking into Dorothy Wordsworth's "wild eyes" which "kept all their life and light, though the mind had grown dim. There was no dimness in her interest when she heard my name. 'From whom are you sprung?' she inquired eagerly. My father's name meant nothing to her, and his uncle's alas! meant nothing to me, but her allusion to the latter clothes him with a halo perhaps more vivid to my eyes because the vision is absolutely untransferable." Dorothy loved to watch the robin who was a daily visitor at her bedroom window; she enjoyed writing little verses and copying them for her friends. Though her mind was dimmed, she had an extraordinary power to recall earlier days; William and she frequently relived days long past when they had roamed the hills together, met the radiant Coleridge and visited with him, the days at Dove Cottage, Racedown, and Alfoxden.

At times, the urge to travel again came to William, and in March, 1835, he and Mary went to London and Cambridge; in 1836, again, he went to London; in 1837, prodded by Dora and Mary, he went abroad with friends to France, Italy, Austria, and Southern Germany. He left as eagerly as the boy, who a half-century before, had gone to France and Switzerland. These trips, he really needed, for the strain of the illnesses and deaths of those he loved had been great; moreover he had worked hard on his volume of poetry, *Yarrow Revisited and Other Poems* which had appeared in 1835. It contained poems written during a tour of Scotland and on the English border in 1831, *Evening Voluntaries*, and *Sonnets Composed or Suggested During a Tour in Scotland in the Summer of 1831*. Appended to the volume was a discussion of the Poor Laws, the conditions under which laborers were expected to work in factories, and the question of Church disestablishment. In 1836, the first two volumes of the fifth collected edition of his poems began to appear; in 1837, came the other four volumes. Getting these editions ready by himself was a tremendous strain for Wordsworth, as, in preparing previous editions, he had had the expert assistance of Dorothy and Sara Hutchinson, as well as some aid from his wife. These last volumes proved he still had the hand of an artist and the mind of a thinker. The two subjects closest to his heart now were the status quo of the Church of England and life after death. His visit to Italy had inspired him again to write poetry; the tone of these poems showed his despondency; the times, he was finding "mixed and disordered"; he pled for "mystical faith." He still found delight, however, in rustic scenes. After he had visited Justice Coleridge in 1836, the latter had commented, "I never knew a man who seemed to know a country and the people so well, to love them better, nor one who had such exquisite taste for rural scenery; he had evidently cultivated it with great care; he not only admired the beauties, but he could tell you what were the peculiar features in each scene, or what the incidents to which it owed its peculiar charm. . . . In examining the parts of a landscape he would be minute; and he dealt with shrubs, flower-beds, and lawns with the readiness of a practised landscape gardener."

Honors to Wordsworth now were numerous. He refused in 1838

to accede to the proposal made by a committee at the University of Glasgow to become a candidate for the Lord Rectorship; but he went to Durham to receive the degree of D.C.L., the first time the honor had been conferred upon anyone in person. In 1839, his appearance at Oxford where he received the D.C.L. degree was enthusiastic. The degree, according to the Rev. John Keble who conferred it, was given because Wordsworth was an excellent religious poet. Dr. Thomas Arnold, who went to Oxford to see the degree conferred, said there were "thunders of applause, repeated over and over again . . . by the undergraduates and the Masters of Arts alike." In 1840, when the Queen Dowager and her sister came to Rydal, Wordsworth accompanied them through the park and his own grounds. In 1842, when he resigned his position as stamp collector, a post he had held thirty years, in favor of his son William, thus depriving himself of £400 a year, or more than half his income, W. E. Gladstone and Lord Montagle secured a pension for him of £300. Robert Peel, in offering him the pension, said "It is some compensation for the severe toil and anxiety of public life to have, occasionally, the opportunity of serving or gratifying those who are an honour to their country."

In 1843, ten days after Southey's death, Wordsworth received a letter from the Lord Chamberlain offering him the poet laureatship, formerly held by Southey. Wordsworth replied that he was honored by the offer, but stated: "The appointment I feel, however, imposes duties which, far advanced in life as I am, I cannot venture to undertake and therefore must beg leave to decline the acceptance of an offer that I shall always remember with no unbecoming pride." At once, the Lord Chamberlain and Sir Robert Peel assured him the offer was made, "not for the purpose of imposing on you any onerous or disagreeable duties, but to pay you that tribute of respect which is justly due to the first of living poets. The Queen entirely approved of the nomination, and there is one unanimous feeling on the part of all who heard of the proposal (and it is pretty generally known) that there could not be a question about the succession." Wordsworth then accepted the honor. Accordingly, when Prince Albert was installed as Chancellor at Cambridge, Wordsworth wrote no poem for the occasion; nor did he attend the Queen's ball for which he had received a formal invitation; he pled the lateness of arrival of the invitation as his excuse for not going, but the fact that it seemed foolish for a man of seventy-five to travel three hundred miles for a dance probably was his real reason for declining. On his seventy-fourth birthday, three hundred children and adults gathered by Rydal Mount to do him honor.

Tables were set in the grounds; "music, dancing, feasting" entertained the guests. On April 25, 1845, he went, by invitation, to attend a Queen's Fancy Ball. He smiled at his attire, saying he had borrowed "sword, bay-wig, and court dress." He added that the Queen had been most gracious, but he observed that Mrs. Everett, the wife of the American Minister to Great Britain, was moved "to the shedding of tears. . . . To see a grey-haired man of seventy-five years of age kneeling down in a large assembly to kiss the hand of a young woman is a sight for which Institutions especially democratic do not prepare a spectator of either sex. . . ."

Lonely without Dorothy and Sara, he found stimulation in Miss Isabella Fenwick, an enthusiastic, exalted woman, a good conversationalist, about ten years younger than Mary Wordsworth, related to Sir Henry Taylor, the poet, and the friend of many literary men. She had taken a small house near Rydal Mount, and soon was a friend of all the Wordsworths. She had long admired William's poetry. Her influence over Wordsworth, her cousin said, "was invaluable to the family."

His love for his own daughter was passionately jealous, and the marriage "which was indispensable to her peace and happiness, was intolerable to his feelings." Moreover, Quillinan, in financial difficulties, through no fault of his own, seemed hardly able to support a wife without a large dowry. The fact that Quillinan was a Roman Catholic, Wordsworth did not find objectionable, though he was aware of the difficulties a mixed marriage might present. Miss Fenwick was well aware that Dora's health suffered as the result of her father's continued resistance. Hence, she set out to break the poet's opposition to the marriage; finally, her persistent pressure, aided by her companionship with the family, broke his stubborn resistance and "at length, though far too tardily," he consented to the union. Strangely, Wordsworth had always liked Edward Quillinan; but Dora, he felt, belonged to him alone. On May 11, 1841, the couple were married. Dora was in ill health at the time of her marriage, and as she did not improve, Quillinan, who was interested in Portugal, took her to that warmer country for a time in 1845. They returned in 1846, but Dora's health was no better; gradually, it declined until, in 1847, she died, leaving her husband and father disconsolate. Her gaiety, happiness, and joy in living had for years enlivened the Wordsworth household.

Wordsworth had also suffered when his five-year-old grandson had died in 1845 in Spain, where the child's mother was on holiday with her six children; he had grieved over the death in 1846 of his brother Christopher; but Dora—Dora was somehow part of him, as his sister Dorothy had been. She had known how to make him feel cheerful; at times, it seemed, almost against his will. Miss Fenwick consoled him as no one else could.

For several years, he had gone over to her house on dark or rainy afternoons to escape the crowd of visitors, sometimes twenty or thirty a day, at his home. He recited to her some of his poems—a performance his grandson called "Grandpapa reading without a book"—talked with her about revision of other poems, on which he was spending seven or eight hours a day. Admiring him, convinced of his greatness, she saw that he needed sympathy and praise. One day, he told her how Mary to whom he was dictating had remarked, "William, I declare you are cleverer than ever." The tears had come into his eyes as he said, "It is not often I have had such praise; she has always been sparing of it." In June, 1839, he had taken Miss Fenwick to St. John's College, Cambridge, and showed her the room he occupied as a student. Here, he told her, he had been "joyous as a lark." In 1840, she accepted the Wordsworths' invitation to come and live with them at Rydal Mount. After Dora's death, she was there to render any assistance needed. Among her and Mary Wordsworth's tasks was that of protecting William from too great distraction, as relatives, friends, and others admiring his poetry came to Rydal Mount in large numbers. The Coleridge children, too, made the Wordsworth's their second home. William remained vigorous and strong despite the fact that he almost lost his life when his gig and a four-in-hand coach collided three miles south of Keswick in 1840. Dr. Thomas Arnold, writing of Robert Southey's tragic mental failure, said, "Wordsworth is in body and mind still sound and vigorous; it is beautiful to see and hear him." Southey died in 1843; Thomas Poole had died in 1839; Mrs. Southey's mind had given way that same year. Mrs. Coleridge died in 1845.

In the summer of 1849, Mary and William visited Mary's brother Thomas at West Malvern. That year and in 1850 appeared the six volume edition of William's poems embodying his revisions over which he had worked so hard.

On March 12, 1850, William took a cold which developed into pneumonia. By the twentieth, his illness was recognized as serious; on his birthday, Sunday, April the seventh, his eightieth birthday, prayers were offered for him at Rydal Chapel. On Saturday, April the twentieth, he received communion from his son, John. Realizing that her husband was dying, Mary Wordsworth said gently to him, "William, you are going to Dora." At the time, he made no reply and Mary was uncertain that he had heard what she said. The following Tuesday, April 23, 1850, as one of his nieces came into his room and was opening the draperies at the windows, William seemed to awake as if from a quiet sleep. "Is that Dora?" he asked. As the clock was striking noon, he died quietly, calmly as he had lived. A large assemblage attended his funeral on April twenty-seventh at Grasmere Churchyard. *The London Times*, in its obituary notice, dwelt on the example of Wordsworth's "spotless life, as pure and spotless as his song." Poets, *The Times* said, spread moral infection wider than other men; Wordsworth, it was comforting to note, unlike Shelley and Byron, had not "corrupted or enervated our youth."

In 1880, the Wordsworth Society was organized at Grasmere, where a distinguished group, including James Bryce, Lord Shelbourne, and Lord Houghton, came from various parts of England to honor the Lake poet. They issued an accurate bibliography of the many editions of his poems and gathered pertinent facts concerning him from people still living who had known him.

While William lay dying, as though by a miracle, Dorothy Wordsworth's mind was restored to her. Quillinan wrote: "Dorothy Wordsworth is as much herself as she ever was in her life, and has an absolute command of her own will! does not make noises; is not all self; thinks of the feelings of others (Mrs. Wordsworth's for example); is tenderly anxious about her brother; and, in short, but for age and infirmity, is almost *the* Miss Wordsworth we knew in past days. Whether this will last, or be the sign that she will not long survive her brother is beyond us." At his death, she again sank into insensibility; at mention of his name, however, she aroused from lethargy; "her love for her brother was as great as ever."

When Wordsworth died he was still a man of strong passions and feelings, his intellect, clear. His thoughts on life, literature, and politics, were as independent in the last as in the first half of his life. True, he had mellowed, but he had not weakened nor become rigid in his thinking. John Stuart Mill and Sir Henry Taylor told in 1831 of his holding forth "on poetry, painting, politics, and metaphysics, and with a good deal of eloquence." Impressed by Wordsworth's freedom from prejudice and willingness to argue and understand the other side of issues, Mill was especially impressed by "the extensive range of his thoughts and the largeness and expansiveness of his feelings. This does not appear in his writings, especially his poetry, where the contemplative part of his mind is the only part of it that appears." About 1840, Thomas Carlyle, after talking with Wordsworth, wrote that "Never, never but once had I seen a stronger intellect, a man of luminous and veracious power of insight, directed upon such a survey of fellow-men and their contemporary journey through the world." He said that Wordsworth "took his bit of lionism very quietly, with a smile sardonic rather than triumphant, and certainly got no harm by it, if he got or expected very little good." In 1849, R. P. Graves and William Johnson found the aged man still as interested in literature and in political as well as economic questions as he had been twenty years earlier. Now, however, he was more hopeful than he had been a quarter of a century before. "Though his vitality was not so great as it had been, his energy was as great as ever."

Wordsworth called himself a liberal-conservative. Some have noted that he said that "Perilous sweeping change" was "unsound" and have used this statement and his objection to the railroad's coming to Grasmere as evidence that he was far from liberal. An examination of his views may prove fruitful.

He had emerged from the Revolutionary Wars and the Napoleonic Wars with the firm conviction that men could not be freed at a stroke without preparation, and that too hastily bestowing freedom upon the uneducated would lead to one form or another of despotism. His close friends, Crabb Robinson and the Clarksons, were liberals. One friend, Aubrey de Vere, averred that Wordsworth always supported the weaker side. Knowing that Wordsworth's sympathies were always with "the cottage hearth rather than with the palace," he said that if the poet "became a strong supporter of what has been called 'the hierarcy of the society,' it was chiefly because he believed the principle of 'equality' to be fatal to the well-being and true dignity of the poor. Moreover, in siding politically with the Crown and the coronet, he considered himself to be siding with the weaker party in our democratic days."

In February, 1826, Crabb Robinson protested to Dorothy that some future biographer might say that Wordsworth, the "great poet, appeared to have died in 1814," as he now seemed unconcerned with the welfare of his fellow creatures. He said Wordsworth had written heroically and divinely against the tyranny of Napoleon, but was quite "indifferent to all the successive tyrannies which disgraced succeeding times." Wordsworth, however, as a matter of fact, had had much to say on foreign policy after 1814, and his ideas are clear. He rebuked emperors and kings, but, unlike Shelley and Keats, he did not see

Europe falling back under their oppression into a worse slavery than before. Wordsworth stated that "a nation has a right to chose its own government, but it has no right to force its ideas of government on other nations, even though these ideas may be better than those that are held by other nations." In 1821, he said he sympathized immensely with France in her early Revolutionary wars, but abandoned her, "and her rulers when they abandoned the struggle for liberty, gave themselves up to tyranny and endeavored to enslave the world." After the war, he sympathized with the Liberal or National Party in countries on the Continent; but his sympathy did not mean that he believed anyone should interfere with the domestic concerns of these countries. When a thoroughly bad government was overthrown by its own subjects he rejoiced, but he did not, like many Liberals, continually demand British intervention for oppressed minorities or majorities.

The French Revolution of 1830 delighted him; yet he feared that too rapid democratization would lead to the return of despotism. His fears proved justified. He lamented the extinction of the Venetian Republic, but, unlike many of his contemporaries, he was not heartened to see the Austrian soldiers who had overthrown the tyrannical government exercising authority in Venice; he was convinced there would be, through Italy herself, a revival of Italian independence and unity. He did not like the Holy Alliance, but he looked on it as a transitory thing. He spoke with strong feeling in 1839 on the present state of Italy and the crushing despotism of Austria "supported, as it is in secret by Russia and Prussia." He had not talked so heatedly about Spain, Austria, and Prussia, for he believed they would ultimately find their own salvation because they were suffering under native, not foreign, tyranny as most of Italy was. Yet he did not favor an armed uprising in Italy—partly because the lovers of freedom were so badly organized that their struggle, he feared, would be in vain, partly because he favored peaceful methods. He was not a pacifist, but he was most uncertain of the wisdom of using violence even to secure freedom; it should be used only as a last resort, he contended. As he grew older, he was increasingly convinced that good, in the long run, might come out of violence, but he reiterated it was "the last, most desperate weapon to be used." He grew firmer in his belief in "the gradual influence of increasing knowledge and the justice of the cause," whether to defeat Napoleon, to free Italy, or to spread political freedom in England. This process necessarily, he realized, was a slow one, distasteful to the undisciplined, but he believed the results once achieved would be more permanent than those more hastily and hostilely achieved.

Wordsworth was firmly convinced that there should be a strong union of church and state; in England, there should be but *one* recognized religion, that of the Church of England. Catholic emancipation, and concessions to Nonconformists he opposed, believing that they tended to weaken the temporal power of the Church, causing a confusion of authorities and interests both in Parliament and in the nation at large. Yet he was no bigot, for in 1837 while in Italy, he procured for his daughter Caroline and her child rosaries blessed by the Pope; he respected Catholicism, though he did not believe "their profession of faith is in itself as good as ours, as consistent with Civil Liberty."

He spoke firmly on many social issues. In 1809, he advocated universal and equal suffrage. In 1817, as he saw rural England changing, he said, "I see clearly that the principal ties which held the different classes of society in a vital and harmonious dependence upon each other have, within these thirty years, either been greatly impaired or wholly dissolved. Everything has been put up to market, and sold for the highest price it would buy. Farmers used formerly to be attached to their landlords, and labourers to the farmers who employed them. All that kind of feeling is vanished . . . All this moral cement is dissolved; habits and prejudices are broken and rooted up, nothing being substituted in their place but a quickened self-interest. . . . The ministry will do well if they keep things quiet for the present, but if our present constitution in church and state is to last, it must rest as heretofore upon a moral basis. And they who govern the country must be something superior to mere financiers and political economists." In 1833, he wrote that "an unbridled Democracy is the worst of all Tyrannies," and, in 1834, stated, "Now that the mob are become Reformers, I am alarmed. . . . it seems to me to be the great problem of all institutions to put shackles as well on the people as on the Government . . . and my fear is, that under the new House of Commons, there will be no check on popular passions."

Concerned about the lack of education of lower classes, Wordsworth said in 1831 it would be very well if that zeal to educate this group "did not blind us to what we stand more in need of, an improved education of the middle and upper classes; which ought to begin in our great Public Schools, thence ascend to the Universities (from which first suggestions should come) and then go to the very nursery." By the time of the Reform Bill, he said "everyone should be able to read, and perhaps (for that is far from being equally apparent) to write." Education must be a slow and natural development. The trend in English politics, he believed, was toward the rule of an ignorant and lawless proletariat. "The Predominance in Parliament to the dissenting interest and to towns which have grown up recently, without a possibility of being trained in habits of attachment either to the Constitution in Church or State . . . will inevitably bring on a political or a social revolution," he stated.

In 1836, Gladstone said Wordsworth believed the Reform Act had brought out too prominently the strength of the towns; the cure, the poet had contended, would be in a large further enfranchisement of the country, thus extending "the base of the pyramid" for added strength. Wordsworth wished the old institutions of the country preserved, and thought this was the best way to preserve them. Thus, he said that the townsmen, many of them corrupt, whose views were filtering down through all ranks of society, would be counteracted by enfranchizing the more honest rural laborers. In 1876 when Wordsworth's prose writings were collected, his *Letter to the Bishop* of Llandaff was published. Here, he stated that government is a creature of the General Will of society; it is best when its acts are those agreed to by most people. This implies universal suffrage. Yet, once elected, a government may go against the will of the majority of the electorate; hence, elections must be held at regular intervals and elected representatives rotated in office. A democratic, elective government is the goal, to be achieved slowly by legislative reform.

Deeply conscious of the warfare of classes, after 1832 Wordsworth showed he was deeply sympathetic with the victims of industrial tyranny; he proposed extending the Poor Laws, permitting free combinations of workmen, governmental regulation, and inspection of industrial undertakings. He was convinced that the landed aristocracy had assumed its place as the result of men's passions. He did not see that the aristocratic system was fundamentally weak and had outlived the loyalty that produced it.

In 1836, his objection to the proposed extension of the railroad from Kendal to Low Wood, near the head of Lake Windermere, with the possibility that it might be afterwards carried on to Grasmere, was on aesthetic grounds. Access to the Lakes, he contended, was already easy; to carry the railroad further would spoil the very seclusion which was one of the charms of the district. Here, he anticipated by over one hundred years the views of the Council for the Preservation of Rural England. When some proponents of the railroad extension said it would enable manufacturers to send "large bodies of their workmen by rail to Windermere," Wordsworth objected, saying it would be far better for employers to pay their men decent wages, give them a decent work day (ten hours was proposed) and let the laborer choose "excursions in any directions that would be most inviting to him." There would then be no need for masters to send their workmen in droves to places the latter did not choose.

Wordsworth expressed himself forcefully on other social problems. In 1839, he opposed the complete abolition of the death penalty; it should be received, he said, by traitors. He abhorred slavery; he said the slave owner should be prepared to make financial sacrifices to give his slave freedom; on the other hand, a slave might be willing "to make a recompense for the sacrifice, should the master, from the state of affairs, feel himself justified in accepting a recompense." Certainly, Wordsworth was actively interested in the social and economic issues of his day.

A few weeks after William's death, Mary read again an unpublished poem her husband had completed eleven years before which had never been published. A title page which Wordsworth had in a copy for Coleridge read:

Poem
Title not yet fixed upon
by
William Wordsworth
addressed to
S. T. Coleridge

Mary now named it "The Prelude or the Growth of a Poet's Mind, an Autobiographical Poem." She sent this most famous of her husband's poems to Moxon for publication; the first edition appeared in 1850. She also carried out a request her husband had made three years before his death, that his nephew, Dr. Christopher Wordsworth, should prepare for publication "any notices that may be necessary to illustrate my writings." Mary knew her husband wished no formal biography since he had said, "a poet's works were the only biography the world has any right to call for." Dr. Christopher Wordsworth disagreed and contended that a full biography must be written to discourage any unauthorized biographies. Although Mary did not share this point of view, rather than quarrel with her nephew, she yielded and permitted him to write the full biography he wished. When it appeared in 1851, it made no mention of Annette Vallon or Caroline.

Mary, devoted to Dorothy, still cared for her tenderly as ever. She noted that as the years passed, Dorothy was less excitable, less interested in reminiscing about the past. Five years after William's death, Mary was told that Dorothy, nearing her eighty-fourth birthday, would not live long. At Christmas time, as Dorothy lay dying, when she heard the Christmas fiddlers going down the road, playing and singing, she wished to have the window open so that she might hear them better. After they had passed and the window of her room was closed lest she take cold, she insisted she still heard them playing somewhere far off, their music going right up to the stars. On January 25, 1855, Dorothy died and was buried "under the Thorn in the South East corner of the Churchyard" by the side of the grave of her friend, Sara Hutchinson, and near the graves of William, Dora Quillinan, Hartley Coleridge, and the two Wordsworth children, Thomas and Catharine, whom she had so loved and cared for. Nearby, was a memorial to her brother, John. The remaining Wordsworth children came for the funeral, and some of them remained with their mother for a short time at Rydal Mount. Dorothy's friends, the Cooksons, Mary said, were "kindness itself."

Mary, almost the last of her generation, continued to live at Rydal Mount. Lady Beaumont, Christopher Wordsworth, Jane Marshall, Mary's brother Thomas Hutchinson, Dorothy's friend Mrs. Clarkson, and Miss Fenwick, all preceded her in death. Mary, deaf and almost totally blind, died in 1859 in her ninetieth year. As serene, placid, courageous, and cheerful as she had been in her youth, she was, in her declining years, "the most lovely image of old age I have ever seen," one of her friends, Miss Bronson, said. Mary was buried beside her husband in Grasmere Churchyard.

A SELECTED BIBLIOGRAPHY

I BOOKS

Lascelles Abercrombie: *The Art of Wordsworth*, 1952
Meyer H. Abrams: *The Milk of Paradise: The Effects of Opium Vision on the Works of De Quincey, Crabbe, Thompson, and Coleridge*, 1934
————: *The Mirror and the Lamp: Romantic Theory and the Critical Tradition*, 1958
Harold Acton: *The Bourbons of Naples*, 1956
Marie Adami: *Fanny Keats*, 1937
Alfred Ainger: *Charles Lamb, a Biography*, 1882
Thomas Allsop: *Letters, Conversations, and Recollections of Samuel Taylor Coleridge*, 2 vols., 1836
Richard Altick: *The Cowden Clarkes*, 1948
Annals of a Publishing House, William Blackwood and His Sons, ed. M.O.W. Oliphant, 3 vols., 1897–1898
Katherine Anthony: *The Lambs*, 1945
Mary L. Armitt: *The Church at Grasmere*, 1912
————: *Rydal*, 1916
D. Aspinall: *The Early English Trade Unions*, 1949
Walter Bagehot: *Biographical Studies*, 1879
Carlos Baker: *Shelley's Major Poetry*, 1948
Herschel Baker: *William Hazlitt*, 1962
James V. Baker: *The Sacred River: Coleridge's Theory of the Imagination*, 1957
Roy P. Basler: *Sex, Symbolism and Psychology in Literature*, 1948
Walter Jackson Bate: *From Classic to Romantic: Premises of Taste in Eighteenth Century England*, 1946
————: *John Keats*, 1963
————: *The Stylistic Development of Keats*, 1945
F. W. Bateson: *Wordsworth: A Reinterpretation*, 1954
Edith C. Batho: *The Later Wordsworth*, 1963
Rosamond Bayne-Powell: *Eighteenth Century London Life*, 1938
Mary A. Beard: *Woman as a Force in History*, 1946
Arthur Beatty: *William Wordsworth: His Doctrine and Art*, 1922
Frederika Beatty: *William Wordsworth and Rydal Mount: An Account of the Poet and His Friends in the Last Decade*, 1939
J. B. Beer: *Coleridge, the Visionary*, 1959

Ernest Bernbaum: *A Guide Through the Romantic Movement*, 1931
Werner W. Beyer: *The Enchanted Forest*, 1963
————: *Keats and the Daemon King*, 1947
Bernard Blackstone: *The Consecrated Urn, An Interpretation of Keats in Terms of Growth and Form*, 1959
Frances Blanchard: *Portraits of Wordsworth*, 1959
Harold Bloom: *Shelley's Mythmaking*, 1959
Edmund Blunden: *Charles Lamb and His Contemporaries*, 1934
————: *Leigh Hunt and His Circle*, 1930
————: *John Keats*, 1950
————: *Shelley*, 1947
————: *Shelley and Keats As They Struck Their Contemporaries*, 1925
————, and Earl Leslie Griggs: *Coleridge: Studies by Several Hands*, 1934
James Boaden: *Memoirs of Mrs. Inchbald*, 2 vols., 1833
Willard H. Bonner: *De Quincey at Work*, 1936
Edward E. Bostetter: *The Romantic Ventriloquists*, 1962
Elizabeth Boyd: *Byron's Don Juan*, 1945
Gamaliel Bradford: *Bare Souls*, 1929
Fanny Brawne: *Letters of Fanny Brawne to Fanny Keats, 1820–1824*, ed. Fred Edgcumbe, 1937
Celia L. Brightwell: *Memorials of the Life of Amelia Opie*, 1854
Crane Brinton: *The Political Ideas of the English Romantics*, 1926
Cleanth Brooks: *The Well Wrought Urn*, 1947
Charles Armitage Brown: *The Life of John Keats*, ed. Dorothy Bodurtha and Willard B. Pope, 1937
Ford K. Brown: *The Life of William Godwin*, 1926
P. A. Brown: *The French Revolution in English History*, 1918
Eliza Southgate Browne: *A Girl's Life Eighty Years Ago*, ed. Clarence Cook, 1888
Arthur Bryant: *The Age of Elegance—1812–1822*, 1950
John Buchan: *Sir Walter Scott*, 1932
E. L. Bulwer and Sargeant Talfourd: *Literary Remains of William Hazlitt With a Notice of His Life by His Son, and Thoughts on His Genius and His Writings*, 2 vols., 1836
Edmund Burke: *The Works of the Right Honourable Edmund Burke*, 9th ed., 12 vols., 1889
Kenneth Burke: *The Philosophy of Literary Form*, 1941
Aaron Burr: *The Private Journal of Aaron Burr, During His Residence of Four Years in Europe, With Selections from His Correspondence*, ed. M. L. Davis, 2 vols., 1838
Peter Burra: *Wordsworth*, 1950
Douglas Bush: *Mythology and the Romantic Tradition in English Poetry*, 1937
Peter Butter: *Shelley's Idols of the Cave*, 1954
George Gordon, Lord Byron: *Byron, A Self Portrait: Letters and Diaries*, ed. Peter Quennell, 2 vols., 1950
————: *Don Juan*, ed. Truman Guy Steffan and Willis W. Pratt, 2 vols., 1950; 4 vols., 1957

————: *Letters and Journals of Lord Byron*, ed. R. E. Prothero, 6 vols., 1898–1901

————: *Lord Byron's Correspondence*, ed. John Murray, 2 vols., 1922

————: *Poetical Works of Lord Byron*, ed. E. H. Coleridge, 7 vols., 1898–1904

Hall Caine: *The Life of Samuel Taylor Coleridge*, 1887

James Caldwell: *John Keats' Fancy*, 1945

Kenneth N. Cameron: *The Young Shelley*, 1951

James Dykes Campbell: *Samuel Taylor Coleridge*, 1894

Thomas Carlyle: *Letters, 1826–1836*, 1889

————: *Reminiscences*, ed. J. A. Froude, 2 vols., 1881

G. Carnall: *Robert Southey and His Age: The Development of a Conservative Mind*, 1960

Maurice Carpenter: *The Indifferent Horseman: The Divine Comedy of Samuel Taylor Coleridge*, 1962

Mary Carr: *Thomas Wilkinson, A Friend of Wordsworth*, 1905

Donald Carswell: *Sir Walter Scott: A Four Part Study in Biography*, 1930

Sir Edmund K. Chambers: *Samuel Taylor Coleridge: A Biographical Study*, 1938

Robert Chambers: *The Life of Walter Scott*, 1871

John Charpentier: *Coleridge, the Sublime Somnambulist*, 1929

John Chisholm, K. C.: *Sir Walter Scott as a Judge*, 1918

David Lee Clark: *Shelley's Prose or The Trumpet of a Prophecy*, 1954

Charles and Mary Cowden Clarke: *Recollections of Writers*, 1878

P. W. Clayden: *The Early Life of Samuel Rogers*, 1888

Alfred Cobban: *Edmund Burke and the Revolt Against the Eighteenth Century*, 1929

Kathleen Coburn: *The Inquiring Spirit, a New Presentation of Coleridge, from His Published and Unpublished Writings*, 1951

William Cole: *The Blecheley Diary*, 1932

Hartley Coleridge: *Letters*, ed. G. E. and E. L. Griggs, 1936

Samuel Taylor Coleridge: *Animae Poetae*, ed. E. H. Coleridge, 1895

————: *Biographia Literaria*, ed. John Shawcross, 2 vols., 1907

————: *Coleridge's Shakespearean Criticism*, ed. T. M. Raysor, 2 vols., 1930

————: *Complete Poetical Works of Samuel Taylor Coleridge*, ed. Ernest Hartley Coleridge, 2 vols., 1912

————: *Essays on His Own Times*, ed. by his Daughter, 3 vols., 1850

————: *The Friend: A Series of Essays to Aid in the Formation of Fixed Principle, in Politics, Morals, and Religion, with Literary Amusements Interspersed*, 1899

————: *The Letters of Samuel Taylor Coleridge*, ed. Earl Leslie Griggs, 4 vols., 1956–1959

————: *Miscellaneous Criticism of Samuel Taylor Coleridge*, ed. T. M. Raysor, 1936

————: *A Moral and Political Lecture Delivered at Bristol*, 1795

————: *The Notebooks of Samuel Taylor Coleridge (1794–1801)*, 2 vols., ed. Kathleen Coburn, 1957–1962

————: *On the Constitution of the Church and the State*, 1830

————: *Philosophical Lectures*, ed. Kathleen Coburn, 1949

————: *The Poems of Samuel Taylor Coleridge*, ed. Ernest Hartley Coleridge, 1940

————: *Rime of the Ancient Mariner with an Essay by Robert Penn Warren*, 1946

————: *Two Addresses on Sir R. Peel's Bill*, privately printed by T. J. Wise, 1919

Sara Coleridge: *Memoirs and Letters of Sara Coleridge*, ed. by her Daughter, Edith Coleridge, 2 vols., 1873

————: *Minnow Among Tritons: Mrs. Samuel Taylor Coleridge's Letters to Thomas Poole*, ed. Stephen Potter, 1934

John Colmer: *Coleridge, Critic of Society*, 1959

Sir Sidney Colvin: *John Keats: His Life and Poetry, Friends, Critics, and After-Fame*, 2nd ed., 1920

Clarence Cook: *A Girl's Life Eighty Years Ago*, 1888

G. A. Cooke: *Excursions to the Lakes of Cumberland*, 1840

Barry Cornwall: *Charles Lamb, A Memoir*, 1866

Joseph Cottle: *Early Recollections Chiefly Relating to the late Samuel Taylor Coleridge*, 2 vols., 1837; revised as *Reminiscences of Samuel Taylor Coleridge and Robert Southey*, 1847

George G. Cunningham: *Lives of Eminent and Illustrious Englishmen*, 6 vols., 1835–1837

John F. Danby: *The Simple Wordsworth*, 1960

H. Darbishire: *Wordsworth*, 1950

Angus Davidson: *Miss Douglas of New York*, 1952

Hugh Sykes Davies: *Thomas De Quincey*, 1964

Matthew L. Davis: *Memoirs of Aaron Burr*, 1836

Thomas De Quincey: *Collected Writing of Thomas De Quincey*, ed. David Masson, 14 vols., 1889–1890

————: *Confessions of an English Opium-Eater*, ed. Richard Garnett, 1885

————: *A Diary of De Quincey*, ed. Horace A. Eaton, 1927

————: *Literary Criticism*, with an Introduction by H. Darbishire, 1909

————: *Posthumous Works*, with Introduction and Notes by A. H. Japp, 2 vols., 1891–1893

————: *Reminiscences of the English Lakes and the Lake Poets*, 1834

————: *Selections, Grave and Gay*, 16 vols., 1860

Ernest de Selincourt: *Dorothy Wordsworth: A Biography*, 1933

Aubrey De Vere: *Essays, Chiefly on Poetry*, 1887

————: *A Memoir*, 1905

Albert Venn Dicey: *The Statesmanship of Wordsworth*, 1917

Sir Charles W. Dilke: *The Papers of a Critic*, 2 vols., 1875

Bertram Dobell: *Sidelights on Charles Lamb*, 1903

Janet Marcy Douglas: *Life and Selections from the Correspondence of William Whewell, D.D.*, 1881

Edward Dowden: *The French Revolution and English Literature*, 1897

————: *Letters About Shelley*, ed. R. S. Garnett, 1917

————: *The Life of Percy Bysshe Shelley*, 2 vols., 1886

————: *Robert Southey*, 1880

Gilbert T. Dunklin: *Wordsworth: Centenary Studies*, 1951
James Campbell Dykes: *Samuel Taylor Coleridge: A Narrative of His Friends and the Events of His Life*, 1894
Horace A. Eaton: *A Biography*, 1936
T. S. Eliot: *Selected Essays*, 1950
Amanda M. Ellis: *The Literature of England*, 1937
Grace A. Ellis: *A Memoir of Mrs. Anna Laetitia Barbauld*, 1874
Barnard Ellsworth: *Shelley's Religion*, 1937
Mrs. Anne Ellwood: *Memoirs of the Literary Ladies of London*, 1843
Malcolm Elwin: *Autobiography and Journals of B. R. Haydon*, 1950
————: *De Quincey*, 1935
————: *The First Romantics*, 1947
————: *Lord Byron's Wife*, 1962
Ralph Waldo Emerson: *Journals*, 10 vols., 1912
Friedrich Engels: *Life of the Working Class in England in 1844*, 1892
Marynia F. Farnham: *Modern Woman: The Lost Sex*, 1947
Hugh l'Anson Fausset: *Coleridge*, 1926
————: *The Lost Leader*, 1933
David Ferry: *The Limits of Mortality: An Essay on Wordsworth's Major Poems*, 1959
J. R. Findlay: *Personal Recollections of Thomas De Quincey*, 1886
Claude Lee Finney: *The Evolution of Keats's Poetry*, 2 vols., 1936
Percy Fitz-Gerald: *Charles Lamb, His Friends, His Haunts, and His Books*, 1866
Mrs. Eliza Fletcher of Edinburgh: *Autobiography*, Privately Printed, 1875
R. A. Foakes: *The Romantic Assertion*, 1958
James Fordyce: *Sermons for Young Women*, 1792
H. B. Forman: *Percy B. Shelley*, 1913
Richard Foster: *The New Romantics: A Reappraisal of the New Criticism*, 1962
William Foster: *The East India House*, 1924
Caroline Fox: *Memories of Old Friends*, 1883
Sigmund Freud: *A General Introduction to Psychoanalysis*, tr. Joan Riviere, 1953
J. A. Froude: *Thomas Carlyle*, 2 vols., 1884
Marguerite Gardiner, Countess of Blessington: *A Journal of Conversations with Lord Byron*, 1859
Richard Garnett: *Coleridge*, 1904
H. W. Garrod: *William Wordsworth: Lectures and Essays*, 1949
John Gibson, N. S.: *Reminiscences of Sir Walter Scott*, 1871
Ann Gilchrist: *Mary Lamb*, 1909
R. P. Gillies: *Memoirs of a Literary Veteran*, 1851
————: *Recollections of Sir Walter Scott*, 1837
James Gillman: *The Life of Samuel Taylor Coleridge*, 1838
Robert Gittings: *John Keats: The Living Year*, 1954
William Godwin: *An Enquiry Concerning The Principles of Political Justice and Its Influence on General Virtue and Happiness*, 2 vols., 1798
————: *Essays*, 1873
————: *The Memoirs of Mary Wollstonecraft Godwin*, 1799

————: *On Population: An Enquiry on the Power of Increase in the Numbers of Mankind, being an Answer to Mr. Malthus' Essay*, 1820

————: *Things as They Are: or, The Adventures of Caleb Williams*, 1904

Mary Gordon: *The Chase of the Wild Goose, The Story of Lady Eleanor Butler and Miss Sarah Ponsonby, Known as the Ladies of Llangollen*, 1936

Mary H. Gordon: *Christopher North: A Memoir of John Wilson*, 1862

Robert Graves: *The Meaning of Dreams*, 1924

James A. Greig: *Francis Jeffrey of the Edinburgh Review*, 1948

Sir Herbert Grierson: *Sir Walter Scott, Bart.*, 1938

R. Glynn Grylls: *Claire Clairmont*, 1939

————: *Mary Shelley*, 1938

Countess Teresa Guiccioli: *My Recollections of Lord Byron*, tr. H. E. H. Jenningham, 1869

Charles W. Hagelman, Jr.: *John Keats and the Medical Profession*, an unpublished dissertation, University of Texas, 1956

Sir William Hale-White: *Keats as Doctor and Patient*, 1938

W. P. Hall: *British Radicalism*, 5th ed., 1837

William Haller: *The Early Life of Robert Southey, 1774–1803*, 1917

J. L. and Barbara Hammond: *The Village Laborer*, 1911

Lawrence Hanson: *The Life of Samuel Taylor Coleridge: The Early Years*, 1938

George McLean Harper: *William Wordsworth, His Life, Works, and Influence*, 2 vols., 1916; 1929

————: *Wordsworth's French Daughter*, 1921

————: *Spirit of Delight*, 1928

F. Harrison: *Lamb and Keats*, 1899

Raymond Dexter Havens: *The Mind of a Poet: A Study of Wordsworth's Thought With Particular Reference to the Prelude*, 1941

Benjamin Robert Haydon: *Autobiography and Journals*, ed. Malcolm Elwin, 1950

————: *Autobiography and Memoirs*, 1927

————: *Correspondence and Table Talk*, with a Memoir by his son, F. W. Haydon, 2 vols., 1876

————: *Diary*, ed. Willard Bissell Pope, 5 vols., 1960–1963

William Hazlitt: *Complete Works*, ed. P. P. Howe, 21 vols., 1931–1934

————: *Lectures on the English Poets*, 1818; 1910

————: *My First Acquaintance with Poets*, 1798

W. Carew Hazlitt: *Four Generations of a Literary Family*, 2 vols., 1897

————: *The Hazlitts: An Account of Their Origin and Descent*, 1911

————: *Lamb and Hazlitt*, 1899

————: *The Lambs, Their Lives, Their Friends, and Their Correspondence*, 1897

————: *Mary and Charles Lamb*, 1874

C. H. Herford: *The Age of Wordsworth*, 1905

————: *Wordsworth*, 1930

Dorothy Hewlitt: *A Life of John Keats*, 2nd ed., revised, 1949

R. H. Hill: *Toryism and The People, 1832–1846*, 1929

Thomas Hill Burton: *The Book Hunter*, 1862

F. Hodgson: *Childe Harold's Monitor*, 1818

James Hogg: *De Quincey and His Friends*, 1895

————: *Domestic Manners of Sir Walter Scott*, 1909

————: *Poetical Works*, 1855

Thomas Jefferson Hogg and Edward Trelawney: *The Life of Percy Bysshe Shelley*, ed. Humbert Wolfe, 1913

Elizabeth, Lady Holland: *Journal*, 2 vol., 1908

John Hollingshead: *My Lifetime*, 1895

Thomas Hood: *Literary Reminiscences*, 1839

Humphrey House: *Coleridge: The Clark Lectures, 1951–1952*, 1953

C. W. Houtchens and L. H. Houtchens: *The English Romantic Poets and Essayists*, 1957

P. P. Howe: *The Life of William Hazlitt*, new ed., with an Introduction by Frank Swinnerton, 2 vols., 1947

Will D. Howe: *Charles Lamb and His Friends*, 1944

Leigh Hunt: *Autobiography*, ed. J. E. Morpurgo, 1949

————: *Autobiography*, with an Introduction by Edmund Blunden, 1928

————: *The Correspondence of Leigh Hunt*, edited by his eldest son, 1862

————: *The Feast of the Poets*, 1815

————: *Lord Byron and Some of His Contemporaries*, 1828

Sara Hutchinson: *The Letters of Sara Hutchinson from 1800 to 1835*, ed. Kathleen Coburn, 1954

Laurence Hutton: *Literary Landmarks of London*, 1885

Aldous Huxley: *Life and Letters*, 1929

W. R. Inge: *Studies of English Mystics*, 1906

Robert Ingpen: *Shelley in England*, 1917

Washington Irving: *Abbotsford and Newstead Abbey*, 1850

H. R. James: *Mary Wollstonecraft: A Sketch*, 1932

Alexander H. Japp: *Thomas De Quincey: His Life and Writings*, 2 vols., 1877, 1890

Walter Jerrold: *Charles Lamb*, 1905

————: *Thomas Hood and Charles Lamb*, 1930

Edith C. Johnson: *Lamb Always Elia*, 1935

Bernard Jones: *The Consecrated Urn: An Interpretation of Keats in Terms of Growth and Form*, 1959

Edmund D. Jones: *English Critical Essays, Nineteenth Century*, 1940

John Jones: *The Egotistical Sublime: A History of Wordsworth's Imagination*, 1954

John E. Jordan: *De Quincey to Wordsworth: A Biography of a Relationship*, 1954

John Keats: *Anatomical and Physiological Note Book*, ed. Maurice Buxton Forman, 1934

————: *Complete Poems and Selected Letters*, ed. Clarence D. Thorpe, 1935

————: *Letters of John Keats*, ed. Maurice Buxton Forman, 2nd ed., revised, 1935

————: *The Letters of John Keats*, ed. Hyder Edward Rollins, 2 vols., 1958

————: *Letters of John Keats to Fanny Brawne*, ed. Harry Buxton Forman, 1878; revised, 1935

————: *Keats' Letters, Papers and Other Relics Forming the Dilke Bequest in the Hampstead Public Library*, ed. George C. Williamson, 1914

————: *Poetical Works and Other Writings*, ed. Harry Buxton Forman; Revised, Maurice Buxton Forman, 8 vols., 1938–1939

The John Keats Memorial Volume, ed. G. C. Williamson, 1921

The Keats Circle: Letters and Papers, 1816–1878, ed. Hyder Edward Rollins, 3 vols., 1948

More Letters and Papers of the Keats Circle, ed. Hyder Edward Rollins, 1955

R. Y. Keers and B. G. Rigdon: *Pulmonary Tuberculosis*, 1955

Frances Ann Kembell: *Recollections of a Girlhood*, 1879

Frank Kermode: *The Romantic Image*, 1957

Charles Knight: *De Quincey Memorials*, 2 vols., 1891

————: *Passages of a Working Life*, 4 vols., 1865

G. Wilson Knight: *Lord Byron: Christian Virtues*, 1952

————: *Lord Byron's Marriage, The Evidence of Asterisks*, 1957

————: *The Starlit Dome*, 1941

William Angus Knight: *Coleridge and Wordsworth in the West Country*, 1913

————: *Life of William Wordsworth*, 3 vols., 1889

————: *Memorials of Coleorton*, 2 vols., 1887

————: *William Wordsworth*, 3 vols., 1889

————: *Wordsworthiana*, 1889

John Knowles: *The Life and Writing of Henry Fuseli*, 2 vols., 1831

Lawrence Kolb: *Pleasures and Deterioration from Drug Addiction*, 1925

B. P. Kurtz: *The Pursuit of Death*, 1933

Charles Lamb: *The Complete Correspondence and Works*, ed. Edward Moxon, 4 vols., 1870

————: *Essays*, 1935

————: *Letters*, ed. E. V. Lucas, 3 vols., 1935

————: *Letters, to Which Are Added Those of His Sister, Mary Lamb*, ed. E. V. Lucas, 3 vols., 1935

————: *Works*, ed. William Macdonald, 1903

The Works of Charles and Mary Lamb, ed. E. V. Lucas, 7 vols., 1903–1905

Andrew Lang: *The Life and Letters of John Gibson Lockhart*, 2 vols., 1897

F. R. Leavis: *Revaluations*, 1947

Emile Legouis: *The Early Life of Wordsworth*, tr. J. W. Matthews, 2nd ed., 1921

————: *William Wordsworth and Annette Vallon*, 1922

Letters from the Lake Poets to Daniel Stuart, 1889

Stephen Liberty: *Religion in Wordsworth*, 1923

Alfred R. Lindesmith: *Opiate Addiction*, 1947
R. B. Litchfield: *Tom Wedgwood: The First Photographer*, 1903
Charles Lloyd: *Edmund Oliver*, 1798
C. S. M. Lockhart: *The Centenary Memorial of Sir Walter Scott, Bart.*, 1871
John Gibson Lockhart: *The Life of Sir Walter Scott, Bart.*, 5 vols., 1905
——: *Memoirs of the Life of Sir Walter Scott*, 10 vols., 1839
J. V. Logan: *Wordsworthian Criticism: A Guide and Bibliography*, 1947
Arthur O. Lovejoy: *The Great Chain of Being*, 1936
Ernest J. Lovell, Jr.: *Byron: The Record of a Quest*, 1949
Amy Lowell: *John Keats*, 2 vols., 1925
John Livingston Lowes: *The Road to Xanadu*, 1930
E. V. Lucas: *Charles Lamb and the Lloyds*, 1898
——: *The Life of Charles Lamb*, 2 vols., 1905; revised, 1921
Harvey T. Lyon: *Keats' Well-Read Urn*, 1958
Thomas B. Macaulay: *Critical and Historical Essays Contributed to the Edinburgh Review*, ed. F. C. Montagu, 3 vols., 1903
Mrs. Desmond MacCarthy: *Handicaps, Six Studies*, 1936
Simon Maccoby: *English Radicalism, 1776–1882*, 1955
Florence MacCunn: *Sir Walter Scott's Friends*, 1909
Catherine M. Maclean: *Born Under Saturn, A Biography of William Hazlitt*, 1934
——: *Dorothy and William Wordsworth*, 1927
——: *Dorothy Wordsworth: The Early Years*, 1927
T. R. Malthus: *An Essay on the Principles of Population*, 1803
Leslie A. Marchand: *Byron: A Biography*, 3 vols., 1957
H. M. Margoliouth: *Wordsworth and Coleridge*, 1953
Florence Marsh: *Wordsworth's Imagery: A Study in Poetic Vision*, 1966
Mrs. Julian Marshall: *Life and Letters of Mary Wollstonecraft Shelley* 2 vols., 1889
William Marshall: *Byron, Shelley, Hunt and the Liberal*, 1960
E. Bernard Martin: *In the Footsteps of Lamb*, 1891
Harriet Martineau, *Autobiography*, ed. M. D. Chapman, 1877
Frank E. Marvel: *The Eighteenth Century Confronts the Gods*, 1959
F. S. Marvin: *The Century of Hope*, 1919
André Maurois: *Ariel, The Life of Shelley*, 1931
——: *Byron*, 1930
David Masson: *Thomas De Quincey*, 1899
Flora Masson: *Charles Lamb*, n.d.
Major General Sir Walter Maxwell-Scott: *Abbotsford*, n.d.
James Lewis May: *Charles Lamb: A Study*, 1934
Ethel Colburn Mayne: *The Life and Letters of Anne Isabella, Lady Noel Byron*, 1929
——: *Byron*, 2 vols., 1912
Thomas Medwin: *Conversations of Lord Byron at Pisa*, Printed for Henry Colburn, 1824
——: *The Life of Percy Bysshe Shelley*, ed. H. B. Forman, 1913
G. W. Meyer: *Wordsworth's Formative Years*, 1943

F. W. H. Meyers: *Wordsworth*, 1881

Richard Monckton Milnes: *Life, Letters, and Literary Remains of John Keats*, 2 vols., 1848

Mary Jane Mitford: *Correspondence with Charles Boner and John Ruskin*, ed. Elizabeth Lee, 1914

Mary Russell Mitford: *Life, Related in a Selection from Her Letters*, ed. A. G. L'Estrange and H. Chorley, 1869–1872

Doris L. Moore: *The Late Lord Byron*, 1961

Thomas Moore: *Life of Lord Byron*, 1830

————: *Memoir, Journal, and Correspondence*, ed. Lord John Russell, 1853–1856

Mary Moorman: *William Wordsworth: 1770–1803*, 1957

————: *William Wordsworth: Later Years, 1803–1850*, 1965

Edith J. Morley: *Blake, Coleridge, and Wordsworth*, 1922

————: *Life and Times of Henry Crabb Robinson*, 1935

Frank V. Morley: *Dora Wordsworth: Her Book*, 1924

————: *Lamb Before Elia*, 1932

Lord John Morley: *The Life of Gladstone*, 1903

James and Lucretia Mott: *Life and Letters*, ed. A. D. Hallowell, 1884

J. H. Muirhead: *Coleridge As Philosopher*, 1930

John Middleton Murry: *Keats*, 1955

————: *Keats and Shakespeare*, 1925

Alfred de Musset: *L'Anglais, Mangeur d'Opium*, 1828

Jacques Necker: *Of The Importance of Religious Opinions*, tr. Mary Wollstonecraft, 1788

Harold Nicolson: *Byron: The Last Journey*, 1924

Mrs. M. O. W. Oliphant: *Annals of a Publishing House: William Blackwood and Sons*, 3 vols., 1897–1898

Margaret Fuller Ossoli: *Woman in the Nineteenth Century*, 1855

Thomas Paine: *Representative Selections*, ed. Harry Hayden Clark, 1944

William Parry: *The Last Days of Lord Byron*, ed. Knight and Lacey, 1825

H. T. Parker: *The Cult of Antiquity and the French Revolutionaries*, 1937

Wilfred Partington: *Sir Walter's Post Bag*, 1932

Peter George Patmore: *My Friends and Acquaintance*, 3 vols., 1854

Charles Kegan Paul: *William Godwin: His Friends and Contemporaries*, 2 vols., 1876

James Payn: *Some Literary Recollections*, 1884

Hesketh Pearson: *Sir Walter Scott, His Life and Personality*, 1954

Elizabeth Robbins Pennell: *The Life of Mary Wollstonecraft*, 1884

Charles Pollitt: *De Quincey's Editorship of the Westmorland Gazette*, 1890

Richard Polwhele: *The Unsex'd Females*, 1798

Willard B. Pope: *Studies in the Keats Circle*, an unpublished dissertation, Harvard, 1932

J. Pope-Hennessy: *Monckton Milnes, The Years of Promise*, 1950

Una Pope-Hennessy: *The Laird of Abbotsford: An Informal Account of Sir Walter Scott*, 1932

Stephen Potter: *Coleridge and S. T. C.*, 1935
Abbie F. Potts: *Wordsworth's Prelude: A Study of its Literary Form*, 1953
Richard Price: *A Discourse on the Love of Our Country*, 1790
Bryan Waller Proctor: *An Autobiographical Fragment*, ed. Coventry Patmore, 1877
————: *Charles Lamb: A Memoir*, 1866
C. E. Pulos: *The Deep Truth, A Study of Shelley's Skepticism*, 1954
Walter Raleigh: *William Wordsworth*, 1903
Dora N. Raymond: *The Political Career of Lord Byron*, 1925
Thomas Raysor et al.: *The English Romantic Poets*, 2nd ed. rev., 1956
Herbert Read: *Wordsworth*, 1930
I. A. Richards: *Coleridge on the Imagination*, 1934
Sir Benjamin Ward Richardson: *The Asclepiad*, 1884
Joanna Richardson: *Fanny Brawne*, 1952
Maurice R. Ridley: *Keats's Craftsmanship*, 1933
Henry Crabb Robinson: *The Correspondence of Henry Crabb Robinson with the Wordsworth Circle, 1808–1866*, ed. Edith J. Morley, 2 vols., 1927
————: *Diary, Reminiscences, and Correspondence*, ed. Thomas Sadler, 2 vols., 1869
————: *On Books and Their Writers*, 2 vols., ed. Edith J. Morley, 1938
Ernest C. Ross: *The Ordeal of Bridget Elia: A Chronicle of the Lambs*, 1940
Andrew Rutherford: *Byron: A Critical Study*, 1961
Edward Sackville-West: *A Flame in Sunlight: The Life and Works of Thomas De Quincey*, 1936
————: *Thomas De Quincey, His Life and Work*, 1936
H. S. Salt: *Shelley's Principles: Has Time Refuted or Condemned Them?*, 1892
Mrs. Henry Sandford: *Thomas Poole and His Friends*, 2 vols., 1888
Elisabeth Schneider, *Coleridge, Opium, and Kubla Khan*, 1953
Mark Schorer: *William Blake: The Politics of Vision*, 1946
Adam Scott: *The Story of Sir Walter Scott's First Love*, 1896
John Scott: *Journal of a Tour to Waterloo and Paris in Company with Sir Walter Scott in 1812*, 1842
Sir Walter Scott: *Familiar Letters*, ed. David Douglas, 1894
————: *The Journal of Sir Walter Scott*, ed. David Douglas, 1891; revised and ed. J. G. Tait, 1950
————: *The Letters of Sir Walter Scott, 1787–1807*, Centenary ed., ed. H. J. C. Grierson, assisted by Davidson Scott and Others, 12 vols., 1932–1937
————: *Miscellaneous Prose Works*, 1827
————: *Novels, The Border Edition of the Waverly*, ed. Andrew Lang, 1892–1894
————: *Poetical Works*, ed. J. Logie Robertson, 1921
————: *The Private Letter-Books*, ed. Wilfred Partington, 1930
E. M. Sellar: *Recollections and Impressions*, 1907
Joseph Severn: *Letters of James Severn to H. B. Forman*, 1933
Elizabeth Sewell: *Autobiography*, 1907

William Sharp: *The Life and Letters of Joseph Severn*, 1892
Lady Jane Shelley: *Shelley Memorials*, 1859
Mary Shelley: *Journal*, ed. Frederick L. Jones, 1947
———: *The Letters of Mary W. Shelley*, ed. Frederick L. Jones, 2 vols., 1944
Percy B. Shelley: *Complete Poetical Works*, ed. George E. Woodberry, 1901
———: *The Complete Works of Percy Bysshe Shelley*, ed. Roger Ingpen and W. E. Peck, 10 vols., 1926–1930
———: *New Shelley Letters*, ed. W. S. Scott, 1949
Jack Simmons: *Southey*, 1945
James Skeave: *Memoirs of Sir Walter Scott*, 1909
Bernice Slote: *Keats and The Dramatic Principle*, 1958
Samuel Smiles: *Josiah Wedgwood*, 1895
Elsie Smith: *An Estimate of William Wordsworth by His Contemporaries*, (*1793–1822*), 1932
C. Southern: *Shelley as a Philosopher and Reformer*, 1876
Robert Southey: *Essays Moral and Political*, 2 vols., 1832
———: *The Life and Correspondence of Robert Southey*, ed. by his son, Charles Cuthbert Southey, 6 vols., 1849–1850
———: *Poems*, ed. Maurice H. Fitzgerald, 1909
———: *Poems*, ed. W. Haller, 1917
———: *The Poetical Works of Robert Southey*, Collected by Himself, 10 vols., 1837–1838
———: *Selections from the Letters of Robert Southey*, ed. John Wood Warter, 4 vols., 1856
———: *Sir Thomas More or Colloquies on the Progress and Prospects of Society*, 1824
———: *The Correspondence of Robert Southey with Caroline Bowles*, ed. Edward Dowden, 1881
———: *Robert Southey's Common-place Book*, ed. J. W. Warter, 4 vols., 1850–1851
Willard L. Sperry: *Wordsworth's Anticlimax*, 1935
Archibald Stalker: *The Intimate Life of Sir Walter Scott*, 1921
Leslie Stephen: *History of English Thought in the Eighteenth Century*, 1876
———: *Hours in a Library*, Vol. I, 1874
———: *Wordsworth's Ethics*, 1876
Richard Henry Stoddard: *Personal Recollections of Lamb, Hazlitt, and Others*, 1875
Marshall Suther: *The Dark Night of Samuel Taylor Coleridge*, 1960
Algernon C. Swinburne: *Miscellanies*, 1886
Thomas Noon Talfourd: *Final Memorials of Charles Lamb*, 2 vols., 1848
———: *Memoirs of Charles Lamb*, ed. Percy Fitzgerald, 1896
G. R. Stirling Taylor: *Mary Wollstonecraft: A Study in Economics and Romance*, 1911
Sir Henry Taylor: *Autobiography*, 1885
———: *Correspondence of Sir Henry Taylor*, ed. E. Dowden, 1888
Charles E. Terry and Mildred Pellens: *The Opium Problem*, 1928

J. Thelwell: *The Peripatetics,* 1793

Henry Thomas, Lord Cockburn: *The Life of Lord Jeffrey,* 2 vols., 1852

————: *Memorials of His Time,* 1856

Clarence D. Thorpe: *The Mind of John Keats,* 1926

Alexis de Tocqueville: *The State of Society in France before the Revolution of 1789,* tr. H. Reeves, 1882

H. D. Traill: *Coleridge,* 1884

Edward John Trelawney: *Letters,* ed. H. Buxton Forman, 1910

————: *Recollections of the Last Days of Shelley and Byron,* ed. Edward Dowden, 1923

Lionel Trilling: *The Liberal Imagination,* 1950

Paul Trueblood: *The Flowering of Byron's Genius: Studies in Don Juan,* 1945

A. S. Turberville: *English Men and Manners in the Eighteenth Century,* 1932

George Walker: *The Vagabond,* 1800

A. R. Wallace: *The Progress of the Century,* 1902

Aileen Ward: *John Keats, The Making of a Poet,* 1963

Wilfrid Ward: *Aubrey De Vere, A Memoir,* 1904

Ralph M. Wardle: *Godwin and Mary: Letters of William Godwin and Mary Wollstonecraft,* 1966

————: *Mary Wollstonecraft,* 1951, 1966

Earl R. Wasserman: *The Finer Tone: Keats' Major Poems,* 1953

————: *The Subtler Language,* 1959

Lucy E. Watson: *Coleridge at Highgate,* 1925

A. A. Watts: *Alaric Watts, A Narrative of His Life,* 1884

Clement C. J. Webb: *Religious Thought in the Oxford Movement,* 1928

Thomas Wedgwood: *The Value of a Maimed Life,* 1912

George Whalley: *Coleridge and Sara Hutchinson and the 'Asra' Poems,* 1950

Newman Ivey White: *Shelley,* 2 vols., 1940

William A. White, M. D.: *Outlines of Psychiatry,* 1926

W. Hale White: *An Examination of the Charges of Apostasy Against Wordsworth,* 1898

W. H. Wickwar: *The Struggle for Freedom of the Press, 1819–1832,* 1928

R. I. and S. Wilberforce: *The Life of William Wilberforce,* 1838

William Wilberforce: *Correspondence,* 1840

Orlo Williams: *Charles Lamb,* 1934

John Wilson (Christopher North): *Noctes Ambrosianae,* 1855

Humbert Wolfe: *The Life of Percy B. Shelley,* 2 vols., 1933

Mary Wollstonecraft: *Four New Letters of Mary Wollstonecraft and Helen M. Williams,* ed. B. P. Kurtz and Carrie C. Autrey, 1937

————: *An Historical and Moral View of the Origin and Progress of the French Revolution,* 2 vols., 1794

————: *Letters to Imlay,* 1879

————: *Letters Written During a Short Residence in Sweden, Norway, and Denmark,* 1796

————: *Mary, A Fiction,* 1788

————: *Memoirs*, ed. W. Clark Durant, 1927

————: *Posthumous Works of the Author of "Vindication of the Rights of Woman,"* 4 vols., 1798

————: *A Sketch on the Rights of Boys and Girls*, 1792

————: *Thoughts on the Education of Daughters: With Reflections on Female Conduct in the More Important Duties of Life*, 1787

————: *A Vindication of the Rights of Men, in a Letter to the Right Honourable William Burke*, 1790

————: *A Vindication of the Rights of Woman*, 1792; 1908

————: *The Wrongs of Woman or Maria*, 1798; 1908

Carl Woodring: *Politics in the Poetry of Coleridge*, 1961

Virginia Woolf: *The Second Common Reader*, 1932

Christopher Wordsworth: *Letters of De Quincey to Dorothy and William Wordsworth*, 1851

————: *Memoirs of William Wordsworth*, 1851

————: *Social Life in English Universities in the Eighteenth Century*, 1874

Dora Wordsworth: *Letters*, ed. Howard P. Vincent, 1944

Dorothy Wordsworth: *George and Sarah Green, A Narrative*, ed. E. de Selincourt, 1936

————: *Journals*, ed. Ernest de Selincourt, 2 vols., 1941

————: *Journals*, ed. William Knight, 1925

Mary Wordsworth: *Letters*, ed. Mary E. Burton, 1958

Wordsworth and Coleridge: Studies in Honor of George McLean Harper, ed. E. L. Griggs, 1939

William Wordsworth: *Pocket Note Book*, ed. G. Healey, 1942

————: *Poetical Works*, ed. William Knight, 1896

————: *Poetical Works of William Wordsworth*, ed. Ernest de Selincourt and Helen Darbishire, 5 vols., 1940–1949

————: *Poems*, 3 vols., ed. Nowell C. Smith, 1908

————: *The Prelude*, ed. E. de Selincourt, 1926; revised by Helen Darbishire, 1959

————: *Prose Works of William Wordsworth*, ed. Alexander B. Groshart, 3 vols., 1876

————: *Prose Works of William Wordsworth*, ed. William Knight, Eversley ed., 2 vols., 1896

William and Dorothy Wordsworth: *The Early Letters of William and Dorothy Wordsworth*, ed. E. de Selincourt, 1935

————: *The Letters of William and Dorothy Wordsworth: The Middle Years*, ed. E. de Selincourt, 2 vols., 1937

————: *The Letters of William and Dorothy Wordsworth: The Later Years*, ed. E. de Selincourt, 3 vols., 1939

Wordsworth and Reed: The Poet's Correspondence with his American Editor, ed. Leslie N. Broughton, 1933

Letters of the Wordsworth Family, 3 vols., ed. William Knight, 1907

Some Letters of the Wordsworth Family, ed. L. N. Broughton, 1942

Ellis Yarnall: *Wordsworth and the Coleridges*, 1899

Arthur Young: *Autobiography*, ed. M. Betham Edwards, 1898

————: *A Tour Through the Kingdom of Ireland*, 2 vols., 1780

II   MANUSCRIPTS, MONOGRAPHS, TRACTS, MAGAZINES,
NEWSPAPERS, ARTICLES, UNPUBLISHED LETTERS, AND NOTES

The Analytical Review, December, 1789; April, 1790

The Arrangement of British Plants, According to the Latest Improvements of the Linnaean System, 4 vols., 1793 (Filled with Wordsworth's marginal notes about flowers and plants he and Dorothy found), Dove Cottage Papers

J. B. Beres: "A Dream, a Vision and a Poem: A Psycho-analytic Study of the 'Rime of the Ancient Mariner,' " *International Journal of Psychoanalysis,* Part I (1951)

Blackwood's Magazine, Vol. II (1817) pp. 6; 40 ff.; Vol. III (1818) pp. 50, 53, 55, 200, 300, 453, 476, 524, 587, 599; Vol. IV (1819) pp. 12 ff.; 540–548; Vol. XI (1822) p. 91; Vol. XIII (1833) pp. 640–646; Vol. XIV (1823) pp. 219–221; Vol. XVI (1824) p. 179; Vol. XXVII (1830) p. 862

Bodleian MS. Don.d. 86, *The Chronicle,* December 3, 1792

H. L. Briggs: "Birth and Death of John Keats," *Publications, Modern Language Association,* Vol. LVI (June, 1941) pp. 592–6

————: "Keats' Conscious and Unconscious Reactions to Criticisms of Endymion," *PMLA,* Vol. LX (1945) pp. 106–29

British Museum Add. MSS. 27,925; 30,046; 30,927; 30,928; 31037; 34225; 35344; 36997; 38109; 43257; 46136; 47496–47545

Georges Bussière and Emile Legouis: *Le Général Michel Beaupuy, 1755–1796,* 1891

James R. Caldwell: "Woodehouse's Annotations in Keats's First Volume of Poems," *PMLA,* LXIII (1948) p. 759 ff.

O. J. Campbell: "Sentimental Morality in Wordsworth's Narrative Poetry," *University of Wisconsin Studies in Language and Literature,* 1920, no. 11

Sir Edmund K. Chambers: "The Date of Kubla Khan," *Review of English Studies,* Vol. XI (1935), pp. 78–80

Kathleen Coburn: "Coleridge and Wordsworth and the Supernatural," *University of Toronto Quarterly,* Vol. XXV (1956) pp. 121–30

Samuel Taylor Coleridge: *Notebooks,* Nos. 16, 19, 60–63 and 65, Victoria College Library, Toronto

————: *Unpublished Letters, Miscellanies of the Philobiblion Society,* Vol. XV, 1877–1884

"Letter from Coleridge to Poole," *The Illustrated London News,* April 22, 1893

Lane Cooper: "Wordsworth's Reading," *Modern Language Notes,* Vol. XXII, (March, 1907) pp. 83–92; (April, 1907) pp. 110–117

K. Curry: "Southey's Visit to Caroline Wordsworth Baudouin," *PMLA,* Vol. LIX (June, 1944), pp. 599–602

————: "Uncollected Translations of Michelangelo by Wordsworth and Shelley," *Review of English Studies,* Vol. XIV, April, 1938

Angus Douglas: "The Theme of Love and Guilt in Coleridge's Three Major Poems," *Journal of English and Germanic Philology*, Vol. LIX (1960) pp. 655–68

W. W. Douglas: "Wordsworth in Politics: The Westmorland Election of 1818," *Modern Language Notes*, Vol. XLIII (November, 1948)

The Eclectic Review, 1808; 1809; 1815

The Edinburgh Review, January, 1807; January, 1809; August, 1811; January, September, 1816; October, 1817; March and June, 1818; June and November, 1819; August, 1822; August and October, 1824; 1830

Sister Eugenia: "Coleridge's Scheme of Pantisocracy and American Travel," *PMLA*, Vol. XLV (December, 1930) pp. 1069–1084

The Examiner, December 25, August 2, 4, 7, 26, 1814; January 1, 8, 16, April 16, June 11, 1815; December 1, February 4, 9, 1816; April 12, 1818; September 26, 1819; June 9, 1820

Richard H. Fogle: "The Romantic Unity of 'Kubla Khan,'" *College English*, Vol. XXII (1960) pp. 112–116

The Gentleman's Magazine, September 26, 1796; May, June, July, August, 1838

Robert Gittings: "Keats Sailor Relation," *London Times Literary Supplement*, April 15, 1960

William Godwin: *Diary*, MS. in Abbinger Collection, Duke University

W. Graham: "Politics of the Greater Romantics," *PMLA*, Vol. XXXVI (January, 1921) pp. 60–78

Albert Guérard: "Prometheus and the Aeolian Lyre," *Yale Review*, XXXIII (1944) pp. 482–97

R. D. Havens: "A Project of Wordsworth's," *Review of English Studies*, Vol. IV (July, 1929)

James Hogg: "Nights and Days with De Quincey," *Harpers Magazine*, Vol. LXXX (February, 1890) pp. 446–456

Hogg's Weekly Instructor and Titan, 1850–1858

Leigh Hunt: "Letter to Wordsworth," May, 1815, Dove Cottage Papers

Alexander H. Japp: "Early Intercourse of the Wordsworths and De Quincey," *Century Magazine*, Vol. 19 (April, 1891) pp. 853–864

John E. Jordan: "De Quincey on Wordsworth's Theory of Diction," *PMLA*, Vol. LXVIII (September, 1953) pp. 764–768

"Keats' Roman Landlady," from a correspondent, *The London Times*, February 2, 1953

John Kebels' Letter to Robert Southey, 1933, National Library of Scotland, MS. 25292

Lawrence Kolb: "Types and Characteristics of Drug Addicts," *Mental Hygiene*, Vol. IX (1915) pp. 312–13

The Lake Poets, Forster Collection, Victoria and Albert Museum

"Charles Lloyd's Letter to Mary Wordsworth" and "Mr. Lloyd's Letter to William Wordsworth," Dove Cottage Papers

John Livingston Lowes: "Hyperion and Purgatorio," *Times Literary Supplement*, June 11, 1936

The London Courier, May 4, 10, 1809; April 12, 1810; September 26, 1810; January 25, 1811

The London Morning Chronicle, December 3, 1792; September 26, 1796
The London Morning Post, July 11, 1797; February 12, April 2, July 13, 1798; February 7, 12, April 2, July 13, 1798; February 9, August 2, 1799
The London Times, September 19, 1819
T. N. Longman, "A Letter to William Wordsworth," October 10, 1825, Dove Cottage Papers
Judson Lyon: "The Excursion," Yale Studies in English, 1950
E. L. McAdam, Jr.: "Wordsworth's Shipwreck," *PMLA*, Vol. LXXVII (June, 1962) pp. 240–247
Leslie A. Marchand: "Trelawny on the Death of Shelley," *Keats-Shelley Memorial Bulletin*, 1952
G. I. Marsh: "The Peter Bell Parodies of 1819," *Modern Philology*, Vol. XL (February, 1943) pp. 267–274
"Medicine," *Encyclopaedia Britannica*, XIII, 6th ed. (1893) pp. 225; 349 ff.
Thomas Medwin: "Hazlitt in Switzerland, A Conversation," *Fraser's Magazine*, 1939
Charles Moorman: "Wordsworth's Prelude: I, 1–269," *Modern Language Notes*, Vol. LXXII (1957) pp. 416–427
Mary Moorman: "An Eighteenth Century Account Book"—*Transactions of the Cumberland and Westmorland Antiquarian and Archeological Society*, 1952
Edith Morley: "Coleridge in Germany," *London Mercury*, April, 1931
The National Library of Scotland MS, 1817; MS. 3884; MS. 2529
New Monthly Magazine, May, June, July, 1799; October, 1830
The New Times, July 19, 1820
Elizabeth Nietzsche: "An Early Suitor of Mary Wollstonecraft," *PMLA*, Vol. LVIII (March, 1943) pp. 163–169
Russell Noyes: "Wordsworth and Burns," *PMLA*, Vol. LIX (1944) pp. 813–832
Papers, The Dove Cottage Library, Grasmere
The Pinney Papers, a Letter from Azariah Pinney to William Wordsworth, November 26, 1795, at Racedown
John Paul Pritchard: "On the Making of Wordsworth's *Dion*," *Studies in Philology*, Vol. XLIX (January, 1952) pp. 66–74
The Quarterly Review, April, October, 1814; October, 1815; October, 1821
T. H. Raysor: "Coleridge and Asra," *Studies in Philology*, Vol. XXVI (July, 1929) pp. 305–324
"Reminiscences of Wordsworth Among the Peasantry of Westmorland," *"Transactions of the Wordsworth Society*, 1884
Ralph L. Rusk: *The Adventures of Gilbert Imlay*, Indiana University Studies, No. 57, 1923
Bertrand Russell: "The Harm That Good Men Do," *Harper's Magazine*, Vol. 153 (1926) pp. 529–534
H. S. Salt: "De Quincey and Wordsworth," *Manchester Guardian*, August 20, 1904
The Scotsman, Edinburgh, editorial, December 9, 1859

Jane Worthington Smyser: "Wordsworth's Dream of Poetry and Science," *PMLA*, Vol. LXXI (March, 1956) pp. 269–275

F. B. Snyder: "Burns and His Biographers," *Studies in Philology*, Vol. XXV (1928) pp. 401–404

L. S. Swindall: "Thomas De Quincey and Wordsworth," *Manchester Guardian*, September 4, 1899

The Stafford Advertiser, June 29, 1895

Tait's Magazine, 1833–1851

"The New Poet Laureate," *Illustrated London News*, April 15, 1843

Times Literary Supplement, September 5, 1929; June 12, 1930

Tracts for the London Times, 1833–1841

Transactions of the Wordsworth Society, No. 8 (Meeting of 1886)

Ralph Thomas: *Manuscript Notes*, The Keats Museum, Hampstead

Clarence Thorpe: "Keats and Hazlitt," *PMLA*, Vol. LXXII (1947) pp. 487–502

Mary Tyson's Account Book, Trustees, The Hawkshead School

Alvin Waggoner: "The Lawyer Friends of Charles Lamb," *American Law Review*, 1916

Aileen Ward: "Keats and Burton, a Reappraisal," *Philological Quarterly*, Vol. XL (October, 1961) pp. 535–552

Ralph M. Wardle: "Mary Wollstonecraft, Analytical Reviewer," *PMLA*, Vol. LXII (December, 1947) pp. 1000–1009

J. E. Wells: "Wordsworth and De Quincey in Westmorland Politics," *PMLA*, Vol. LV (December, 1940) pp. 1080–1128

Mary Wollstonecraft: "Problems Exemplified and Illustrated by Pictures from Real Life," *Analytical Review*, 1790

G. Gordon Wordsworth: "Wordsworth's French Daughter," *London Times Literary Supplement*, April 17, 1930

Mary Wordsworth: *Journal*, 1820, Dove Cottage Papers

"William Wordsworth to Longman," the Henry W. and Albert A. Berg Collection, the New York Public Library

"A Letter of William Wordsworth to Sir Walter Scott," n.d., about June, 1806, Hugh Walpole Collection, National Library of Scotland

INDEX